UNDERSTANDING SPORT PSYCHOLOGY

Sara Miller McCune founded SAGE Publishing in 1965 to support the dissemination of usable knowledge and educate a global community. SAGE publishes more than 1000 journals and over 800 new books each year, spanning a wide range of subject areas. Our growing selection of library products includes archives, data, case studies and video. SAGE remains majority owned by our founder and after her lifetime will become owned by a charitable trust that secures the company's continued independence.

Los Angeles | London | New Delhi | Singapore | Washington DC | Melbourne

UNDERSTANDING SPORT PSYCHOLOGY

GAVIN BRESLIN
JOHN KREMER
AIDAN MORAN
CATHY CRAIG
STEPHEN SHANNON

Los Angeles | London | New Delhi
Singapore | Washington DC | Melbourne

SAGE Publications Ltd
1 Oliver's Yard
55 City Road
London EC1Y 1SP

SAGE Publications Inc.
2455 Teller Road
Thousand Oaks, California 91320

SAGE Publications India Pvt Ltd
B 1/I 1 Mohan Cooperative Industrial Area
Mathura Road
New Delhi 110 044

SAGE Publications Asia-Pacific Pte Ltd
3 Church Street
#10-04 Samsung Hub
Singapore 049483

Editor: Donna Goddard
Editorial assistant: Esmé Carter
Production editor: Rachel Burrows
Copyeditor: Jane Robson
Proofreader: Brian McDowell
Indexer: Silvia Benvenuto
Marketing manager: Camille Richmond
Cover design: Wendy Scott
Typeset by: KnowledgeWorks Global Ltd
Printed in the UK

Library of Congress Control Number: 2021933932

British Library Cataloguing in Publication data

A catalogue record for this book is available from the British Library

ISBN 978-1-5297-4464-4
ISBN 978-1-5297-4463-7 (pbk)

Understanding Sport Psychology is dedicated to the memory of our co-author, colleague and friend, Professor Aidan Moran. Over his long and distinguished career, Aidan's work served to inspire and inform countless people from within the worlds of both sport and psychology. We hope that this book will continue to meet his goal of making sport psychology understandable and accessible to all.

Contents

About the Authors ix
Preface xi

1 INTRODUCING SPORT PSYCHOLOGY 1
1.1 The History of Sport Psychology 2
1.2 Practising Sport Psychology 7
1.3 Ethical Issues in Sport Psychology 14
1.4 Sport Psychology Organisations, Sources and Resources 21

2 ANXIETY AND STRESS IN SPORT 29
2.5 Stress, Anxiety and Arousal 30
2.6 Measuring Stress and Anxiety 37
2.7 Pre-performance Routines 43
2.8 Choking Under Pressure 49
2.9 Coping Strategies 54

3 MOTIVATION 61
3.10 Sport Participation: Motives and Correlates 62
3.11 Burnout and Drop-out 70
3.12 Goal Setting 76
3.13 Fear of Failure and Need to Achieve 82
3.14 Self-Determination Theory 87
3.15 Achievement Goal Theory 92
3.16 Self-Efficacy and Perceived Competence 98

4 COGNITIVE PROCESSES IN SPORT 105
4.17 Mental Imagery 106
4.18 Mental Practice 111
4.19 Attention and Concentration 117

4.20 Positive Self-Talk and Thought Control 122
4.21 Mental Toughness 127

5 SOCIAL PSYCHOLOGY OF SPORT 135
5.22 Team Cohesion 136
5.23 Team Building 142
5.24 Causal Attribution 148
5.25 Social Facilitation and Social Loafing 154
5.26 Leadership and Management 159
5.27 Effective Coaching Styles 165
5.28 Home Advantage 171
5.29 Aggression 177
5.30 Fans and Spectators 182
5.31 Social Identity Theory 190

6 MOTOR SKILLS 195
6.32 Motor Development 196
6.33 Expertise 201
6.34 Decision-Making 206
6.35 Practising Motor Skills 212
6.36 Analysis and Measurement of Motor Performance 219

7 SPORT, MENTAL HEALTH AND WELLBEING 225
7.37 Gender, Diversity and Inclusion 226
7.38 Overtraining and Exercise Addiction 234
7.39 Injury and Retirement 243
7.40 Mental Health Awareness in Sport 251
7.41 Mental Health Disorder in Sport 256
7.42 Resilience 260
7.43 Mindfulness and Wellbeing in Sport 264

Index 271

About the Authors

Gavin Breslin is a Senior Lecturer in the Bamford Centre for Mental Health and Wellbeing, School of Psychology, Ulster University, Coleraine. He has applied sport psychology to national and international athletes across a range of sports. He is the Chief Assessor for the British Psychological Society's Qualification in Sport and Exercise Psychology. His book publications include *Sport and Exercise Psychology Practitioner Case Studies* (2016), and *Mental Health and Wellbeing Interventions in Sport: Research, Theory and Practice* (2019).

John Kremer is a former Reader in Psychology at Queen's University Belfast, where he lectured from 1980. He combines his academic interest in sport and exercise psychology with practical work with numerous sports, including several national and international teams and individual athletes. His list of book publications includes *Pure Sport: Sport Psychology in Action* (2019), *Key Concepts in Sport Psychology* (2012), *Sport Psychology: Contemporary Themes* (2012), *Psychology in Sport* (1994) and *Young People's Involvement in Sport* (1997).

Aidan Moran was Professor of Cognitive Psychology and Director of the Psychology Research Laboratory in University College, Dublin. A Fulbright Scholar and former Editor-in-Chief of the *International Review of Sport and Exercise Psychology*, he has published extensively on mental imagery and attentional processes in athletes. A former psychologist to the Irish Olympic squad, Aidan advised many of Ireland's leading athletes and teams and is rightly credited as the founding father of sport psychology in Ireland.

Cathy Craig is a Professor in Perception and Action Psychology at the School of Psychology, Ulster University, and CEO/Co-Founder of INCISIV, a neuro-technology company based in Belfast, Northern Ireland. She publishes extensively on motor timing, perception/action and decision-making in sport. Much of her work involves working closely with elite sporting organisations to develop innovative solutions, using technologies such as immersive, interactive virtual reality, to better understand how perception influences decisions about action.

Stephen Shannon is a Lecturer and Researcher in the School of Sport, Ulster University Magee, Derry. He has published extensively in the area of physical activity, motivation and wellbeing, and in the field of mental health in sport through the Bamford Centre for Mental Health and Wellbeing.

Preface

Being successful and staying well in competitive sport requires athletes to develop and harness their physical and mental skills. Sport psychology has a long history that demonstrates how research and theory can be applied to support athletes in the development of mental skills. This collection has been brought together to further promote an understanding of sport psychology. Divided into seven chapters that reflect recognisable fields within sport psychology, the 43 sections, when read either separately or collectively, should provide the reader with a thorough overview of key issues that currently engage those who work in the field. Furthermore, for those who work with teams and athletes directly, it is hoped that the contributions will help give you a grasp of what sport psychology can contribute to your sport organisation, your team, your athletes.

Our aim was to give an insight into both practical and theoretical considerations but to present the material in a style that is accessible to those new to sport psychology and the seasoned psychologist alike. Each chapter gives insight into how the field has developed, what are the major priority areas today and what are key findings that can help inform both theory and practice. We have endeavoured to bring together contemporary international literature under titles that are each discrete, easily recognisable and, in combination, we hope provide coverage of the many fields and perspectives that define modern-day sport psychology. We hope you enjoy this collection; we have certainly enjoyed putting it together.

The book was written before and during the COVID-19 global pandemic that changed many of our working and family lives. We would like to acknowledge the unending support of all our families during this time. We would also like to thank Dr Graham Walker for his contributions.

Gavin, John, Aidan, Cathy and Stephen.

Introducing Sport Psychology

Chapter Summary: Achieving peak performance requires a combination of both physical and mental strength. This chapter introduces the history of how and where sport psychology first emerged, and when sport psychologists pioneered support to athletes. Various models as to how sport psychology can be applied are described, as are the accredited training routes that can be completed to become a sport psychologist. Key ethical considerations that govern sport psychology practice and research are outlined, as are the significant sport psychology organisations that are available to support sport psychologists from training through to practice.

1.1 The History of Sport Psychology 2
1.2 Practising Sport Psychology 7
1.3 Ethical Issues in Sport Psychology 14
1.4 Sport Psychology: Organisations, Sources and Resources 21

1.1 THE HISTORY OF SPORT PSYCHOLOGY

Definition: The chronology of key events in the development of sport psychology from its earliest roots through to the present day.

Sport psychology is not a new phenomenon (Lavallee et al., 2012). From the time of the ancient Greeks there is strong evidence that preparation for sporting competition has acknowledged the importance of the mental alongside the physical. Indeed, the standard four-day procedure followed by Greek athletes in the build-up to their games (known as the tetrad) seamlessly blended both the physical and psychological in each of the four stages. These were characterised as preparation (Day 1), concentration (Day 2), moderation (Day 3) and relaxation (Day 4). In other words, even in these early years, nothing was left to chance in terms of 'total preparation', and sport psychology featured prominently.

Given the importance that commentators routinely attach to 'the mind' in athletic performance, it should come as no surprise to learn that the world of sport has long recognised that success will depend on 'total preparation' involving the mind as well as the body. However, despite this tacit acceptance, sport psychology had to wait several centuries before finally being afforded due recognition as an academic discipline in its own right (Green and Benjamin, 2009), and even today there remains some resistance from traditionalists who resent the interference of 'shrinks' in what they see as their unsullied world of sport.

From ancient roots it took until the early 20th century to see the coming-together of the subdiscipline from diverse sources – but not before a number of false trails had been laid. While there had been some interest in topics including sporting personalities, play, motor learning and development, reaction times and transfer of training around the turn of the 19th century, the individual who is now generally credited with carrying out the earliest systematic sport psychology research was Dr Norman Triplett.

Born in Illinois in 1861, Triplett was awarded his baccalaureate degree by Illinois College (Jacksonville) at the age of 28, followed by his Master's degree two years later in 1898 and finally his PhD from Clark University in 1900. Although his interests were wide-ranging (his PhD was on the topic of conjuring deceptions), it is his Master's thesis that has become his lasting legacy not only to sport psychology but the subdiscipline of social psychology. His dissertation was based on archival and experimental investigations of what he coined 'dynamogism' (now known as social facilitation, increased effort as a result of the real, imagined, or implied presence of others – see **5.25**).

The archival research considered recorded cycling times either alone, paced or in competition, while his experimental work involved children winding silk line onto a fishing reel so as to pull a flag around a track. A keen sportsperson (he was one of the first US athletes to run 100 yards in under 10 seconds) and an active supporter of all forms of sport, in 1901 he became Head of the Department of Child Study at Kansas State Normal School (KSNS) where he continued to work until his retirement in 1931, all the while extending his fulsome support to all forms of sporting activity within the college (Davis et al., 1995).

While Triplett had made several important observations, evidence of sustained sport psychology activity in the western world remained sparse until the 1930s. In contrast, from the late 19th century onwards in eastern European universities there had been concerted efforts to establish sport psychology as a scientific discipline. The world's first dedicated sport psychology laboratory opened in 1920 at the Deutsche Sporthochschule (German Sport University) in Berlin under Dr Carl Diem, a person who played a positive and significant role in the development of European sport, including being the instigator of the Olympic torch relay during his time as chief organiser of the infamous 1936 Berlin Olympics (later referred to as Hitler's Games).

In the former USSR, from the 1920s onwards both Avksenty Cezarevich (A.C.) Puni (1898–1986) and Piotr (Peter) Roudik played key roles in the establishment of sport psychology (see Ryba et al., 2005). Professor Puni opened a sport psychology laboratory at the Institute of Physical Culture in Leningrad in the 1920s and had a wide-ranging interest in both pure and applied sport psychology. At around the same time, Roudik established the first Soviet sport psychology laboratory in Moscow (1925), where he focused his attention not on competitive sport but on the psychophysiology of motor behaviour. These endeavours were reflected in longstanding interests in the psychology of sport that stretched throughout the 20th century in eastern Europe.

Back in the western world, it was in the 1920s that the person now generally regarded as the founding father of contemporary western sport psychology began to carve out his career at the University of Illinois. Born in 1893, Coleman Griffith was a lecturer in educational psychology at the University of Illinois when, with the help of his Dean and mentor, Professor George Huff, he turned his sights towards sport psychology. Following his introduction of taught courses in sport psychology from 1923, in 1925 he set up the Athletic Research Laboratory and worked frenetically, writing more than 20 sport psychology articles and two books up until 1931. Sadly, the entire enterprise within the university then came apart for reasons now obscure but perhaps related to the Great Depression, or perhaps because the college's head football coach, the legendary and highly influential Robert Zuppke, failed to see any benefit accruing to his team from these academic endeavours (Green, 2003).

Disillusioned, Griffith then turned his attention back towards educational psychology, only once returning to sport psychology in 1937 when he was asked to work with the Chicago Cubs Baseball Club by the club's owner, Philip Wrigley. Griffith worked more or less closely with management for three years but the relationship eventually petered out. The Cubs' manager, Charlie Grimm, referred to Griffith as the 'headshrinker', and would have nothing to do with his work (Gould and Pick, 1995) despite the considerable investment that the club had made in recording equipment and the huge commitment that Griffith himself made in time, effort and report writing, including detailed analyses of every player's performances, a very early forerunner of what is now so influential in most professional sports, notational analysis or the systematic recording and analysis of performance.

The years following Griffith were fallow for most of sport psychology in the West, apart from a continuation of the longstanding interest in motor learning and motor control on both sides of the Atlantic. Nevertheless, many physical educationalists touched on themes that are still relevant to sport psychology today. Records of early meetings, conferences and organisation attendance reveal sport psychology was heavily male dominated, yet a small number of influential women were able to play a leading role in shaping the subdiscipline. According to Diane Gill (1995), the role that women have played in shaping the profession should now be afforded due acknowledgement (Gill, 1995). *The Sportswoman*, a magazine that began publication in 1924, included articles on sports skills and organisational information, but also included an article written by Agnes Lamme (1935) on 'Attitudes in match play', describing the self-discipline required to control nerves during competition. In other examples, Vera Skubic in the late 1940s and 1950s studied emotional responses in little league baseball. In the late 1960s, Dorothy Harris adopted a research approach highlighting the importance of women's issues in sport and physical activity, and published widely, including on topics such as stress, gender roles and imagery. Harris actually produced one of the first applied sport psychology guides (Harris and Harris, 1984), and is today still associated most closely with Pennsylvania State University where she started the first graduate sport psychology programme in the US. She was the first woman President of NASPSPA (1974–5) and the first to receive a Fulbright Research Scholarship in sport psychology. In the 1960s, Eleanor Methany (1965) is recognised for her classical work on gender, stereotypes and sociocultural factors in sport, later linked to developmental psychology, and Ema Geron (from Israel), the only woman to attend the inaugural 1968 International Society of Sport Psychology (ISSP) meeting, went on to receive the society's highest honour at the 1993 ISSP congress in recognition of her distinguished career. These female scholars, and many since, through their work have enhanced and diversified the subdiscipline, important work that continues to the present day and at long last is receiving due recognition (see **7.37**).

During the mid part of the 20th century, in eastern Europe the early work involving competitive sport continued in European universities such as Leipzig, often in conjunction with applied research, for example involving the mental preparation of Soviet cosmonauts. By 1960, sport psychologists were routinely working with elite Eastern Bloc athletes and from the 1970s onwards Olympic competitors from countries including the USSR, East Germany, Hungary and Czechoslovakia used sport psychologists to help with self-regulation, mental practice and imagery (Roberts and Kimiecik, 1989).

It was around this time that sport science began to truly emerge as a discipline in its own right (Massengale and Swanson, 1997), as coaches considered how various disciplines, including psychology, could help improve performance. Ahead of its time, the Brazilian soccer team that won the World Cup in Sweden in 1958 had brought along not only a nutritionist and a dentist but also a psychologist, Prof. Joao Carvalhaes. Carvalhaes conducted various tests on the players to determine their mental toughness, including asking them to sketch pictures of men. From such tests he concluded that the 17-year-old Pelé was, 'obviously infantile. He lacks fighting spirit. He is too young to feel aggression and react in an adequate fashion.' Fortunately, the team coach Feola ignored Carvalhaes and instead trusted his own instincts. According to Pelé's autobiography, 'He just nodded gravely at the psychologist, saying: "You may be right. The thing is, you don't know anything about football. If Pelé's knee is ready, he plays." Which he did' (Pelé, 1977).

Prominent among European practitioners at this time was Dr Miroslav Vanek (Vanek and Cratty, 1970). As well as working directly with athletes, and including the Czechoslovakian team that travelled to the Olympic Games in Mexico in 1968, along with Ferrucio Antonelli he was instrumental in helping found the ISSP in 1965 (see above), a pioneering body specifically constituted to further the advancement of sport psychology. ISSP held its first congress in Rome in 1965, while five years later the ISSP founded the *International Journal of Sport Psychology*, the first dedicated journal to sport psychology. In 1983 the United States Olympic Committee (USOC) hired a full-time sport psychologist with a target of improving performance and winning medals, a goal the Soviet Union had achieved helped by psychologist A.Z. Puni at the Mexico Olympics in 1968.

Over the next ten years numerous other organisations were established on either side of the Atlantic including the North American Society for the Psychology of Sport and Activity (NASPSPA, 1969), the Fédération Européenne de Psychologie de Sport et des Activités Corporelles (FEPSAC, 1969) and the Association for the Advancement of Applied Sport Psychology (AAASP, 1986) (see **1.4**). However, the driving force behind these initiatives came not from within psychology but from physical education and sport science where the major 'players' within sport psychology were to be found at that time. Indeed, the first body to regulate the practice of sport psychologists in the United Kingdom was not the British Psychological Society but the British Association of Sport and Exercise Sciences (BASES, first founded in 1984), and it was not until the late 1980s that the parent discipline of psychology slowly began to take greater interest in sport psychology. For example, the American Psychological Association (APA) formed a separate division in 1987 (Division 47: Exercise and Sport Psychology), and it was not until 1993 that the British Psychological Society (BPS) first set in motion the long procedure that eventually led to the creation of a separate BPS division, 'Sport and Exercise Psychology', in 2004, a division which now has over 850 members (see **1.4**).

Nowadays the subdiscipline's governing bodies are increasingly concerned with regulating the use of the term 'Sport and Exercise Psychologist'. Rigorous accreditation procedures and *bona fide* professional qualifications have been established to help candidates navigate the protected route to becoming a registered sport psychology practitioner, while, as importantly, ensuring that those who choose to work with a registered or chartered sport and exercise psychologist can rest assured that the person they are working with actually knows what they are talking about, and will do more good than harm (see **1.2** and **1.3**)!

KEY READINGS

Gill, D.L. (1995) 'Women's place in the history of sport psychology', *The Sport Psychologist*, 9 (4), 418–33.

Lavallee, D., Kremer, J., Moran, A. and Williams, M. (2012) *Sport Psychology: Contemporary Themes*. Houndmills, Basingstoke: Palgrave Macmillan.

Moran, A. and Toner, J. (2017) *Sport and Exercise Psychology: A Critical Introduction*. London: Taylor & Francis.

Weinberg, R.S. and Gould, D. (2018) *Foundations of Sport and Exercise Psychology* (7th ed.). Chicago, IL: Human Kinetics.

PRACTICAL QUESTIONS

- Describe the history and key periods in the development of sport psychology, highlighting differences between East and West.
- Who were the pioneers of sport psychology, what were their primary interests and in what way did they help to promote the development of the subdiscipline?

REFERENCES

Davis, S.F., Becker, A.H. and Huss, M.T. (1995) 'Norman Triplett and the dawning of sport psychology', *The Sport Psychologist*, 9 (4), 366–75.

Gill, D.L. (1995) 'Women's place in the history of sport psychology', *The Sport Psychologist*, 9 (4), 418–33.

Gould, D. and Pick, S. (1995) 'Sport psychology: The Griffith era, 1920–1940', *The Sport Psychologist*, 9 (4), 391–405.

Green, C.D. (2003) 'Psychology strikes out: Coleman R. Griffith and the Chicago Cubs', *History of Psychology*, 6, 267–83.

Green, C.D. and Benjamin, L.T. (eds) (2009) *Psychology Gets in the Game: Sport, Mind, and Behavior, 1880–1960*. Lincoln, NE: University of Nebraska Press

Harris, D.V. and Harris, B.L. (1984) *The Athlete's Guide to Sport Psychology: Mental Skills for Physical People*. New York: Leisure Press.

Lamme, A., (1935) 'Attitudes in match play', *The Sportswoman*, 11 (9), 7, 18–19.

Lavallee, D., Kremer, J., Moran, A., and Williams, M. (2012) *Sport Psychology: Contemporary Themes*. Houndmills, Basingstoke: Palgrave Macmillan.

Massengale, J.D. and Swanson, R.A. (eds) (1997) *The History of Exercise and Sport Sciences*. Champaign, IL: Human Kinetics.

Metheny, E. (1965) 'Symbolic forms of movement: The feminine image in sports', in E. Metheny, *Connotations of Movement in Sport and Dance*. Dubuque, IA: Brown. pp. 43–56.

Pelé, with Fish, R.L. (1977) *My Life and the Beautiful Game: The Autobiography of Pelé*. New York: Doubleday.

Roberts, G.C. and Kimiecik, J.C. (1989) 'Sport psychology in the German Democratic Republic: An interview with Dr Gerard Konzag', *The Sport Psychologist*, 3, 72–7.

Ryba, T., Stambulova, N. and Wrisberg, C. (2005) 'The Russian origins of sport psychology: A translation of an early work of A.C. Puni', *Journal of Applied Sport Psychology*, 17, 157–69.

Vanek, M. and Cratty, B.J. (1970) *Psychology and the Superior Athlete*. New York: Macmillan.

1.2 PRACTISING SPORT PSYCHOLOGY

Definition: The translation of sport psychology theory into practice through appropriate professional interventions with athletes, teams and sport organisations.

Following on from the previous section, how do you actually become a practising sport psychologist? On the one hand, the trite answer would be, 'It isn't hard as anyone who voices an opinion on sport performance by definition *is* a naïve sport psychologist.' These views may not be informed, solicited or even welcomed, but if they have an effect on an athlete's thoughts, feelings or behaviours that subsequently link to performance, either positively or negatively, then unwittingly that person will already have practised as a sport psychologist. However, that type of spontaneous intervention is quite different from one that has been grounded in the necessary psychological skills, experience and knowledge to make a positive and long-lasting impact for the good of the athlete, team or organisation. Good sport psychologists try to sort the wheat from the chaff in terms of helping the psychological work in harmony with the physical in improving sport performance and athlete wellness (Andersen, 2000, 2005; Cotterill et al., 2016).

To ensure that the goods on offer are genuine and are not damaged, psychology's governing bodies have worked hard to establish strict criteria and regulations governing the use of the title 'sport and exercise psychologist'. For example, to become accredited as a sport and exercise psychologist in the UK, at the time of writing, you can follow one of three routes. The body that oversees the governance of professional psychology across the UK, the British Psychological Society (BPS), normally requires a first degree in psychology (or a closely related discipline) which qualifies the person for Graduate Basis for Chartered Member (GBC), followed by a BPS accredited and approved Master of Science (MSc) degree in Sport and Exercise Psychology, followed in turn by a two-year period of supervised experience. In contrast, the British Association of Sport and Exercise Sciences (BASES) requires a first degree in either psychology or sport and exercise science, followed by a higher degree in the other discipline, together with a period of supervised experience.

To aid good practice in supervisory experience, in 2008 the BPS put in place the Qualification in Sport and Exercise Psychology (QSEP) where a candidate is required to complete a portfolio and viva examination that evidences competency in: applied consultancy, research, communication and professional and ethical practice. In January 2020, BASES designed the Sport and Exercise Psychology Accreditation Route (SEPAR), through which a candidate receives supervision, produces a portfolio of work to meet 65 competencies across four categories: Knowledge, Skills, Self-Development and Management, and Experience. Both qualifications lead to 'Practitioner Psychologist' status on application to the Health and Care Professions Council (HCPC) which oversees the practice register in the UK, and has done since 2009. The third option available in the UK is where the HCPC has accredited professional doctorate courses in Sport and Exercise Psychology that lead to the register through the amalgamation of the MSc, supervised practice and research training. There are approximately 250 individuals registered with the HCPC, 102 candidates undertaking the BPS qualification and 40 the BASES qualification. The number of candidates completing the professional doctorate is in the region of 40–50. Collectively, these figures reflect positively on substantial and continual growth across the sub-discipline in the UK.

Today there is a considerable and growing number of accredited sport and exercise psychologists working across the globe, and the number seems set to continue to rise for the foreseeable future (Morris et al., 2003; Morris and Terry 2011). Across countries various terminology is used to reflect accreditation, including certification, licensing and registration, with some countries having more robust routes to accreditation than others (Morris et al., 2003). Operating outside the bounds of these professional bodies, are a great many self-styled 'sport consultants' who often have no formal training in psychology but who adopt the role of sport psychologist, mental or performance skills coach. When choosing a sport psychologist, the watch-words for any athlete must be *caveat emptor* (buyer beware) for, as with any profession, the potential to harm as well as help is ever present. Many sportspeople have had difficult experiences with non-qualified sport consultants whose advice may have been given with the best of intentions but which lacked the psychological know-how to ensure good quality control. When searching for a sport psychologist, depending on the country and the association, a list of qualified practitioners should be available and should be accessed.

Having first established the credentials to be able to work with teams, athletes and sport organisations, a great many ways to practise then present themselves. Typically sport psychologists operate in at least three ways: as basic researchers (investigating the science of sport psychology but not necessarily working with athletes or teams); as educational sport psychologists (teaching and educating athletes and coaches); and as clinical sport psychologists (counselling or supporting individual athletes with problems). In reality, many sport psychologists will fulfil all three roles at some stage in their careers, but the primary focus of this chapter will be on those who work directly with sportspeople and teams, in either educational or clinical roles, or a combination of the two.

The distinction between the educational and clinical role can be blurred but was neatly characterised by Rainer Martens (1987) as the difference in the direction of travel of the intervention: either from abnormal to normal (clinical), or from normal to 'supernormal' (educational). That is, clinical sport psychologists will tend to use their clinical training to help address psychopathologies, including emotional, behavioural and personality disorders (see **7.40** and **7.41**), while educational sport psychologists will aspire to enhance 'normal' sports' performance through appropriate interventions with both athletes and their coaches. When these two worlds come together, ethical problems can arise. In particular, an intervention may reveal an underlying clinical condition that would go beyond the professional competence of the practitioner, raising serious ethical and professional considerations (Schinke et al., 2018) (see **1.3**).

The work of a clinical sport psychologist is likely to vary depending on the 'practice philosophy' that he or she brings to the intervention (Stainback et al., 2007; Moore and Bonagura, 2017). This is likely to incorporate personal beliefs and values along with a theoretical paradigm that has been acquired through appropriate training. This then is reflected in a model of practice and ultimately in the particular types of intervention that are employed. Given the wide range of perspectives that can underpin clinical psychology, it is not surprising that the types of intervention can vary considerably, including psychodynamic (Freudian), humanist (Rogerian), rational emotive behavioural therapy (REBT) and systems, or family therapy. While very different in approach, all rely on establishing a good relationship between client and therapist, and are underpinned by a medical model of intervention.

Alongside clinical sport psychologists, recent years have witnessed a growth in the number of psychiatrists operating in the field of sport (see **7.41**). The key difference between a clinical sport psychologist and a sport psychiatrist lies in their training. While a psychiatrist will have had training as a medical doctor, accompanied by a later specialism in psychiatry, a clinical psychologist will have a first degree in psychology followed by postgraduate training in clinical psychology. In relation to practice, while interventions may often overlap, qualified psychiatrists have the authority to prescribe psychotropic drugs while clinical psychologists do not.

Educational sport psychologists are often first confronted with 'problems' (e.g. confidence, concentration, commitment, stress), but these issues are not typically pathological but instead are obstacles that stand in the way of optimal performance. Furthermore, while one specific concern may trigger the engagement with a sport psychologist, it rarely remains the dominant issue over time as performance enhancement in more general terms is addressed through a wider array of interventions.

The practice model underpinning a clinical intervention is probably best characterised as medical, aimed at 'curing', healing or 'fixing' the athlete, but over recent years it has become apparent that this model is less effective in helping athletes to truly grow and mature. Instead, it is argued that the goal of the sport psychologist may be different, to carefully nurture autonomy and self-reliance to a point where the athlete is equipped with the right psychological skills and techniques to be able to self-regulate behaviour, and hence performance, as and when required. That is not to say that there may not still be the need to seek out occasional advice and support but this need is likely to diminish, not grow, over time if the intervention has been successful and the athlete is not experiencing poor mental health.

In addition, according to Kremer and Scully (1998), the best person to help this process may not be the sport psychologist but rather the person who on a daily basis works most closely with the team or athlete, in other words, the coach or manager. This opens the possibility of an alternative model where the coach or manager becomes the primary point of contact but is supported in this role by the sport psychologist. This has advantages in many ways, not least because it avoids the player or team potentially being caught in the crossfire between different messages. At the same time, this approach ensures that the 'naïve psychology' that may have informed the coach's previous interactions has now been cross-referenced and balanced by input from sport psychology. In this way the sport psychologist becomes an integral part of the support team used by the coach or manager but is not centre-stage. Indeed, most coach development programmes now include significant elements devoted to sport psychology, and this model then becomes the natural progression.

Robin Vealey (2007) has suggested that, apart from distinguishing between educational and clinical approaches, it is also useful to categorise interventions as being either programme-centred (i.e. a pre-planned sequence of activities) or athlete-centred (i.e. an interactive, needs-based approach), and also whether the intervention is concerned primarily with performance enhancement or with personal development. The suggestion is that the most successful interventions are not narrowly confined but succeed in addressing not only immediate performance concerns but also broader lifestyle issues, and are tailored to the needs of individual athletes. Indeed, many of the recent views on supporting athlete performance and wellbeing recommend taking a holistic perspective to include lifestyle behaviours, dual career progression (see **7.39**) and encouraging the broadening of psychosocial support networks (Debois et al., 2015). Beyond this point the model of intervention will vary depending on the perspective of the sport psychologist and the context. According to Vealey (2007), these include the following models:

- systems for individual, team, organisational and family interventions;
- self-regulatory or cognitive-behavioural models;
- behavioural management models;
- educational mental skills models;
- developmental models;
- sport-specific mental skills models;
- clinical intervention models;
- perceptual training models.

Whichever model is adopted it is likely to follow a particular strategy. Over the years a number of staged practice strategies have been suggested, but all are broadly similar in approach. Among the most popular is Morris and Thomas's (2003) seven-phase model or strategy.

SEVEN PHASE MODEL (MORRIS AND THOMAS, 2003)

1. Orientation
2. Sport analysis
3. Assessment
4. Conceptualisation
5. Psychological skills training
6. Implementation
7. Evaluation

The first stage is *orientation*, where the purpose of the intervention is clarified, objectives identified and commitment determined in relation to performance enhancement. Once the task is identified, the sport psychologist then conducts an *analysis* of the particular sport, followed by an individual/team *assessment* that is completed to develop a profile of strengths and weaknesses. This profile can be based on a number of quantitative and qualitative techniques including psychological tests and inventories, interviews, observations of the athlete performing (via videos, diaries and/or performance statistics) and talking to coaches and significant others about the athlete. The fourth stage is *conceptualisation* through a profile analysis, where the personal characteristics of the athlete are placed in the context of his or her sport. The fifth stage is *psychological skills training*, involving practical skills relating to e.g. imagery, goal setting, cognitive techniques, stress management, attention/concentration skills, thought stopping and building self-confidence. These skills are then *practised* in the sixth stage before being implemented within competition. The seventh and final stage in this process is *evaluation*, and this considers evidence of performance enhancement, improved personal adjustment and adherence to the psychological skills training programme.

In essence, the seven phases describe the process of action research and, while it may appear overly prescriptive, the detail comprising a systematic intervention is valuable. For more information, an example of a detailed sport psychology intervention using each of the seven phases is available in a case study involving an ultra endurance athlete before, during and after the event (Breslin et al., 2014).

Beyond this, however, there is a widespread agreement that the cornerstone of a successful intervention must be based on establishing and developing a trusting relationship with the athlete. This is not to imply that the relationship is equivalent to that between a counsellor and client. Instead, counselling skills may be brought to bear at certain occasions during the intervention but at other times the relationship may be fundamentally different, for example when testing an athlete or instructing in the use of mental skills. To aid an initial consultation, recommendations from a performance interview guide are available (Aoyagi, 2017). The components include: (a) identifying relevant information; (b) establishing the reason for seeking consultation; (c) conducting a background search of areas for improvement, growth or concern with the athlete; (d) exploring details of the sport; (e) understanding life and identity outside of sport; (f) identifying which significant relationships and support the athlete has around him/her; and (g) discussing self-care. The philosophy underpinning the support lies in holistic consulting, thereby attending to the person's entire identity, including the role of performer.

To many athletes and coaches, professional sport psychologists are still viewed with a degree of suspicion, perhaps because of previous negative experiences or stereotypical images of 'Mr Motivator' type characters, as often graphically portrayed in the media. For most practising sport psychologists nothing could be further from the truth, but these stereotypes can be difficult to dispel. However, as the sub-discipline continues to mature and the profession regulates the work of those who describe themselves as sport psychologists, so it is to be hoped that the image will change and will come to reflect reality more closely and accurately.

KEY READINGS

Cotterill, S., Weston, N., and Breslin, G. (eds) (2016) *Sport and Exercise Psychology: Practitioner Case Studies*. London: John Wiley & Sons.

Eubank, M. and Tod, D. (2017) *How to Become a Sport and Exercise Psychologist*. London: Routledge.

Morris, T., Alfermann, D., Lintunen, T. and Hall, H. (2003) 'Training and selection of sport psychologists: An international review', *International Journal of Sport and Exercise Psychology*, 1 (2), 139–54. DOI: 10.1080/1612197X.2003.9671708.

Tod, D., Hutter, R.V. and Eubank, M. (2017) 'Professional development for sport psychology practice', *Current Opinion in Psychology*, 16, 134–7.

PRACTICAL QUESTIONS

- What are the three routes to becoming a registered Sport and Exercise Psychology Practitioner in the United Kingdom?
- Describe how you would approach a sport psychology consultation with an athlete using one of the models above?

REFERENCES

Andersen, M.B. (ed.) (2000) *Doing Sport Psychology*. Champaign, IL: Human Kinetics.

Andersen, M.B. (ed.) (2005) *Sport Psychology in Practice*. Champaign, IL: Human Kinetics.

Aoyagi, M.W., Poczwardowski, A., Statler, T., Shapiro, J.L. and Cohen, A.B. (2017) 'The performance interview guide: Recommendations for initial consultations in sport and performance psychology', *Professional Psychology: Research and Practice*, 48 (5), 352–60.

Breslin, G., Murphy, M.H., Kremer, J., McClean, C. and Davison, G. (2014) 'Providing sport psychology support to an athlete in a unique, ultra-endurance event', *Journal of Sport Psychology in Action*, 5 (2), 59–72.

Cotterill, S., Weston, N. and Breslin, G. (eds) (2016) *Sport and Exercise Psychology: Practitioner Case Studies*. London: John Wiley & Sons.

Debois, N., Ledon, A. and Wylleman, P. (2015) 'A lifespan perspective on the dual career of elite male athletes', *Psychology of Sport and Exercise*, 21, 15–26.

Kremer, J. and Scully, D. (1998) 'What sport psychologists often don't do: On empowerment and independence', in H. Steinberg, I. Cockerill and A. Dewey (eds), *What Sport Psychologists Do*. Leicester: BPS Books. pp. 75–88.

Martens, R. (1987) *Coaches Guide to Sport Psychology*. Champaign, IL: Human Kinetics.

Moore, Z.E., and Bonagura, K. (2017) 'Current opinion in clinical sport psychology: From athletic performance to psychological well-being', *Current Opinion in Psychology*, 16, 176–9.

Morris, T. and Terry, P.C. (eds.) (2011) *The New Sport and Exercise Psychology Companion*. West Virginia University, WV: Fitness Information Technology.

Morris, T. and Thomas, P. (2003) 'Approaches to applied sport psychology', in T. Morris and J. Summers (eds), *Sport Psychology: Theory, Applications and Issues* (2nd ed.). Brisbane: Jacaranda Wiley. pp. 215–52.

Morris, T., Alfermann, D., Lintunen, T. and Hall, H. (2003) 'Training and selection of sport psychologists: An international review', *International Journal of Sport and Exercise Psychology*, 1 (2), 139–54, DOI: 10.1080/1612197X.2003.9671708.

Schinke, R.J., Stambulova, N.B., Si, G. and Moore, Z. (2018) 'International society of sport psychology position stand: Athletes' mental health, performance, and development', *International Journal of Sport and Exercise Psychology*, 16 (6), 622–39.

Stainback, R.D., Moncier, J.C. III and Taylor, R.E. (2007) 'Sport psychology: A clinician's perspective', in G. Tenenbaum and R.C. Eklund (eds), *Handbook of Sport Psychology* (3rd ed.). Hoboken, NJ: Wiley. pp. 310–31.

Vealey, R. (2007) 'Mental skills training in sport', *Handbook of Sport Psychology* (3rd ed.). Hoboken, NJ: Wiley. pp. 287–309.

1.3 ETHICAL ISSUES IN SPORT PSYCHOLOGY

Definition: A code of ethical principles and standards with associated procedures and rules to ensure that practising sport psychologists act responsibly at all times and in accordance with the profession's primary values.

In keeping with other branches of applied psychology and the helping professions, sport psychologists are obliged to adhere to strict professional principles and codes of conduct in relation to their work and engagement with clients. Ethics codes help identify, promote and differentiate appropriate versus unacceptable professional behaviour (Koocher and Keith-Spiegel, 2008) and are primarily designed to help protect both the public (Schultze, 2007) and the profession (Zeigler, 1987). The codes attached to each international psychology professional body may vary but all are governed by similar general principles worldwide (Watson et al., 2020). These include the Code of Ethics (2007) for the Australian Psychologcal Society, the British Psychological Society's (BPS, 2018) Code of Ethics and Conduct, and the American Psychological Association's (2002, 2017) Ethical Priniciples and Code of Conduct.

As one example, the American Psychological Association (APA) (2002, 2017) revised their ethical principles and code of conduct in 2017. The revised guide includes five general principles, along with ten standards (see Figure 1.1). The general principles are designed to be aspirational in nature with the intention of guiding and inspiring psychologists to uphold the highest ethical ideals of the profession. The ten standards, in contrast, represent obligations and can form the basis for imposing sanctions on the psychologist. The five general principles are described below, followed by the standards:

- *Principle 1: Beneficence and Nonmaleficence* – Psychologists strive to benefit those with whom they work and take care to do no harm. Psychologists should seek to safeguard the welfare and rights of those they interact professionally with and other affected persons. They should also strive to be aware of their own physical and mental health, and implications of this on their ability to help those with whom they work.
- *Principle 2: Fidelity and Responsibility* – Psychologists establish relationships of trust with those with whom they work and are aware of their professional and scientific responsibility to society. Psychologists clarify their professional roles, obligations standards of conduct and seek to manage conflicts of interest avoiding exploitation or harm.
- *Principle 3: Integrity* – Psychologists seek to promote accuracy, honesty and truthfulness in the science, teaching and practice of psychology.
- *Principle 4: Justice* – Psychologists recognise that fairness and justice entitle all persons to access to and benefit from the contributions of psychology and to equal

quality in the processes, procedures and services being conducted by psychologists. Psychologists recognise their potential biases, limitations of their expertise and competence and ensure their expertise does not lead to unjust practices.

- *Principle 5: Respect for People's Rights and Dignity* – Psychologists respect the dignity and worth of all people, and the rights of individuals to privacy, confidentiality and self-determination. Psychologists are aware of and respect difference, whether in age, gender, cultural, ethnic religious, sexual orientation, disability, language, and socioeconomic status. Psychologists attempt to eliminate or avoid condoning biases or prejudices.

American Psychological Association (APA) (2017) Ethical Principle and Code of Conduct: 10 Standards

Standard 1: Resolving Ethical Issues

Standard 2: Competence

Standard 3: Human Relations

Standard 4: Privacy and Confidentiality

Standard 5: Advertising and Other Public Statements

Standard 6: Record Keeping and Fees

Standard 7: Education and Training

Standard 8: Research and Publication

Standard 9: Assessment

Standard 10: Therapy

This Ethics Code and information regarding the Code can be found on the APA website: www.apa.org/ethics.

Figure 1.1 American Psychological Association's Ten Ethical Standards
Source: © 2017 American Psychological Association

While it would be expected that any professional sport psychologist would have little difficulty in adhering to these principles, the special nature of sport psychology interventions often presents real and significant challenges that must be addressed in order to balance effective practice with ethical good practice (Sachs, 1993; Moore, 2003; Andersen, 2005). Unfortunately, history would suggest that, in the past, not all interventions may have achieved this balance. Some argue that sport psychology is unique and varies so much from traditional counselling or clinical types of practice that it should adopt its own ethics code (Zeigler, 1987). This view enjoys support to the extent that multiple practices that appear routinely in applied sport psychology do not align with traditional therapy models, for example, those based on weekly individual one-to-one office-based counselling sessions (Aoyagi and Portenga, 2010).

In a survey of 508 professional and student members of the Association for the Advancement of Applied Sport Psychology (AAASP), Petitpas et al. (1994) asked respondents to indicate their engagement with, or awareness of, the existence of 47 different behaviours, 24 of which were deemed to be ethically controversial (e.g. 'Including athlete testimonials in advertising'; 'Using profanity in your professional work'; 'Serving concurrently as coach and sport psychologist for a team'; 'Being sexually attracted to a client'). In a further open-ended question, participants were asked to describe ethically challenging or troubling incidents that they or a colleague had faced in the last two years. Of the 89 incidents mentioned, 78 referred either to General Standards (e.g. providing services without training; engaging in dual role relationships; failing to make referrals), or to Confidentiality (e.g. coaches who want information on athletes; responding to coaches who abuse their athletes). While acknowledging the real difficulties faced by practitioners out in the field, the authors nevertheless concluded that many reported practices could correspond to violations of APA Ethical Standards, and hence they recommended that all applied sport psychologists should routinely be trained in ethical considerations and how to deal with ethical dilemmas.

A follow-up, online survey of AAASP members was issued subsequent to the publication of the AAASP ethics code in 1992 (Etzel et al., 2004). This survey found fewer examples of controversial behaviour but more differences within the sample (e.g. men v. women; professionals v. students; certified v. non-certified consultants; PE v. psychology background), suggesting on the one hand that awareness of ethical issues had been raised since the earlier survey, but on the other hand flagging that there were now worrying inconsistencies in knowledge/awareness/practice across the membership.

As to what makes sport psychology so unique within the discipline, there are a number of issues that warrant close attention relating to the consultant/athlete relationship (Kremer, 2003; Watson et al., 2020): these will be discussed later. While unique in certain ways, applied sport psychology is not exceptional in others, including the need to base the intervention on a good and honest personal relationship with the athlete or team. At the same time, in common with other client/consultant relationships, by its nature, it will inevitably be characterised by a power imbalance and hence carries the potential to become abusive.

In order to begin to operate according to clear ethical standards there is a need to identify a sovereign regulating body, and this can present immediate problems given the fractured history of sport psychology (see **1.1, 1.2** and **1.4**). Within the UK, some practising sport psychologists would regard themselves primarily as sport scientists but with a specialism in psychology and so align themselves with the British Association of Sport and Exercise Sciences (BASES). Others would see themselves as psychologists but with a specialism in sport and/or exercise, and be chartered as sport and exercise psychologists under the aegis of the British Psychological Society (BPS) and hence are bound professionally by its ethical code.

This can obviously lead to confusion and divided loyalties as to which professional standards apply. In the US this issue has been avoided as all those who work as sport psychologists, including the broad church of sport counsellors, therapists and consultants, have agreed to adopt the American Psychological Association's (2017) revised Ethical

Standards. This includes those members of the North American Society for the Psychology of Sport and Physical Activity (NASPSPA) and AAASP who may not belong to the APA, nor are necessarily trained or qualified as psychologists.

Within the UK and Ireland, the picture is rather murkier as potentially three separate bodies (BASES, BPS, and the Psychological Society of Ireland (PSI)) can claim to govern the work of sport psychologists and each currently operates according to separate codes of conduct. The BPS updated its code in August 2009 to coincide with the date from which the regulation of activities of UK applied psychologists fell under the governance of the Health Care Professions Council (HCPC).

All practising sport psychologists should be guided by the code of ethical conduct as agreed by the professional body or bodies to which they belong, and should regularly keep up to date through a working model of reflexive practice (Moore, 2003; Anderson et al., 2004). While it is unlikely that the guidance offered from each body will be contradictory, from a practical, ethical and legal standpoint, where there are differences, common sense would dictate that the more rigorous code should be adhered to.

Having established a set of guiding principles for practice, a number of authors have gone on to describe the special ethical characteristics attaching to a sport psychology intervention (Biddle et al., 1992; Sachs, 1993; Moore, 2003; Andersen, 2005; Pope and Vasquez, 2011), and these are summarised below.

CONFIDENTIALITY AND ALLEGIANCE

In the first place many interventions are set up not by the client (the athlete) but by a third party (e.g. the coach, manager or parent), immediately creating the possibility of divided loyalties with regard to confidentiality. This dilemma is familiar to many applied sport psychologists and can undermine the personal relationship with the athlete unless handled carefully. The 2009 BPS Code states that psychologists should 'Restrict the scope of disclosure to that which is consistent with professional purposes, the specifics of the initiating request or event, and (so far as required by the law) the specifics of the client's authorisation' (p. 11). From the first meeting it is important to establish ground rules with the athlete, followed by an open and honest discussion of the nature of the relationship, and including the rules of confidentiality, with all those involved (see Andersen et al., 2001).

COMPETENCY

This can become problematic where an intervention opens up issues which are beyond the professional expertise of the sport psychologist. This could include the need for: (a) other sport science specialisms (e.g. biomechanics, physiology); (b) knowledge of the sport; or (c) psychological competence. In relation to the first two areas then common sense must prevail in establishing the extent of 'knowledge and expertise boundaries', and being disciplined not to move beyond that point. In relation to the third area, Heyman and Andersen (1998) suggest the following three criteria should be used to establish when the issues are of a clinical nature and deserving of a referral: (a) how long a problem has existed, its severity and its relationship with other life events; (b) unusual emotional reactions (e.g. depression and anger); and (c) lack of efficacy of traditional performance enhancement interventions.

While the list of issues which have the potential to become problematic is considerable, any of the following may warrant a specialist intervention: an eating disorder; drug and alcohol abuse; psychopathology/personality disorders; anger and aggression control; identity conflict issues and including sense of self; gender dysphoria; relationship issues.

To help deal with such situations quickly and effectively it is useful to have an established network of contacts, although recent research would suggest that many sport psychologists are disturbingly reluctant to pass clients on (Gayman and Crossman, 2006). For those applied sport psychologists who are trained in counselling and/or clinical psychology the boundaries of competence will be broader but, even here, there may be particular issues which arise which are beyond their experience and once more a referral network that is readily to hand is likely to be useful.

DEPENDENCY, ATTACHMENT AND ABUSE

Any one-to-one counselling relationship has the potential to be problematic, especially when the athlete comes to depend overly on the person providing him or her with specialist or expert knowledge. To counter this danger, the fundamental goal of the intervention should be clear from the start. The sport psychologist is not setting out to foster long-term dependency but rather to empower and equip the athlete with a set of skills and knowledge so that he or she can become independent and in control of future life events (Kremer and Scully, 1998). These matters aside, where a relationship begins to become unprofessional or dysfunctional then the onus falls on the sport psychologist to take whatever steps are necessary to remedy the situation, including terminating the relationship if necessary.

USE OF PSYCHOMETRIC TESTS

The use of psychometric tests in applied sport psychology has attracted some attention, and controversy, over the years. Lay people can often place uncritical faith in results obtained from such tests, reinforcing the need to use tests sensibly and ethically. Where tests are employed, it is important that the measures are appropriate, that their psychometric properties are robust, that they are used for the purpose and population for which they were designed and that they are not used to inform selection procedures. Interpretation of the results and subsequent feedback must be appropriate and written consent should be obtained for the release of any data.

DRUGS, CHEATING AND ILLEGALITY

When a sport psychologist becomes aware that a client is using drugs or any illegal means to enhance performance, does this create an ethical dilemma? The answer should be 'no', because it would be difficult to imagine how any meaningful intervention could ever continue in such circumstances.

VIRTUAL ENGAGEMENT

Further to these longstanding concerns, over recent years, accompanied by the recent surge in sport psychology provision online or via telephone, care has to be given to risks associated with assessing security, confidentiality and between-country law violation. The APA have established Telepsychology Guidelines for Psychologists (2013) to ensure professional practice and stimulate research and debate around consulting from a distance (Watson et al., 2020).

KEY READINGS

American Psychological Association (2017) 'Revision of ethical standard 3.04 of the "Ethical Principles of Psychologists and Code of Conduct" (2002, as amended 2010)', *American Psychologist*, 71, 900.

Kerr, G. and Stirling, A. (2019) 'Where is safeguarding in sport psychology research and practice?', *Journal of Applied Sport Psychology*, 31 (4), 367–84.

Tenenbaum, G. and Eklund, R.C. (eds) (2020) *Handbook of Sport Psychology*. Hoboken, NJ: John Wiley & Sons.

Watson, J.C., Harris, B.S. and Baillie, P. (2020) 'Ethical issues impacting the profession of sport psychology', in G. Tenenbaum and R.C. Eklund (eds), *Handbook of Sport Psychology*. London: John Wiley & Sons. pp. 751–72.

PRACTICAL QUESTIONS

- Describe the key ethical principles outlined by the American Psychological Association, and, using practical examples, identify how these are important in sport psychology practice.
- Sport psychology practice requires the practitioner to work in various environments such as pitch/court side, travelling with athletes, staying in the same accommodation, etc. What are the ethical considerations for a sport psychologist when compared to a clinical or counselling psychologist and how can these issues be addressed practically?

REFERENCES

Anderson, A.G., Knowles, Z. and Gilbourne, D. (2004) 'Reflective practice for applied sport psychologists: A review of concepts, models, practical implications and thoughts on dissemination', *The Sport Psychologist*, 18, 188–201.

Andersen, M.B. (2005) '"Yeah I work with Beckham": Issues of confidentiality, privacy and privilege in sport psychology service delivery', *Sport and Exercise Psychology Review*, 1, 5–13.

Andersen, M.B., Van Raalte, J.L. and Brewer, B.W. (2001) 'Sport psychology service delivery: Staying ethical while keeping loose', *Professional Psychology: Research and Practice*, 32 (1), 12–18.

American Psychological Association (2002) 'Ethical principles of psychologists and code of conduct', *American Psychologist*, 57, 1060–73.

American Psychological Association (2017) 'Revision of ethical standard 3.04 of the "Ethical Principles of Psychologists and Code of Conduct" (2002, as amended 2010)', *American Psychologist*, 71, 900.

Aoyagi, M.W. and Portenga, S.T. (2010) 'The role of positive ethics and virtues in the context of sport and performance psychology service delivery', *Professional Psychology: Research and Practice*, 41 (3), 253.

Australian Psychological Society (2007) *Code of Ethics*. Melbourne: Australian Psychological Society.

Biddle, S., Bull, S. and Seheult, C. (1992) 'Ethical and professional issues in contemporary British sport psychology', *The Sport Psychologist*, 6, 66–76.

British Psychological Society (BPS) (2009) 'Code of ethics and conduct'. Leicester: BPS.

British Psychological Society (2018) 'Code of ethics and conduct', retrieved from www.bps.org.uk/sites/www.bps.org.uk/files/Policy/Policy%20-%20Files/BPS%20Code%20of%20Ethics%20and%20Conduct%20%28Updated%20July%202018%29.pdf.

Etzel, E., Watson, J. and Zizzi, S. (2004) 'A web-based survey of AAASP members' ethical beliefs and behaviors in the new millennium', *Journal of Applied Sport Psychology*, 16 (3), 236–50.

Gayman, A.M. and Crossman, J. (2006) 'Referral practices: Are sport psychology consultants out of their league?', *Athletic Insight: The Online Journal of Sport Psychology*, 8 (1), 47–59.

Heyman, S.R. and Andersen, M.B. (1998) 'When to offer athletes for counseling or psychotherapy', in J.M. Williams (ed.), *Applied Sport Psychology*. Mountain View, CA: Mayfield Publishing. pp. 359–71.

Koocher, G.P. and Keith-Spiegel, P. (2008) *Ethics in Psychology and the Mental Health Professions: Standards and Cases*. Oxford: Oxford University Press.

Kremer, J. (2003) 'Ethical considerations in sport psychology', in D. Lavallee and I. Cockerill (eds), *Counselling in Sport and Exercise Contexts*. Leicester: BPS Books. pp. 18–26.

Kremer, J. and Scully, D. (1998) 'What sport psychologists often don't do: On empowerment and independence', in H. Steinberg, I. Cockerill and A. Dewey (eds), *What Sport Psychologists Do*. Leicester: BPS Books. pp. 75–88.

Moore, Z.E. (2003) 'Ethical dilemmas in sport psychology: Discussion and recommendations for practice', *Professional Psychology: Research and Practice*, 34, 601–10.

Petitpas, A.J., Brewer, B.W., Rivera, P.M. and Van Raalte, J.L. (1994) 'Ethical beliefs and behaviors in applied sport psychology: The AAASP Ethics Survey', *Journal of Applied Sport Psychology*, 6, 135–51.

Pope, K.S. and Vasquez, M.J.T. (2011) *Ethics in Psychotherapy and Counseling: A Practical Guide* (4th ed.). Hoboken, NJ: Wiley.

Schultze, R. (2007) 'What does it mena to be a self-governing regulated profession?', *Journal of Property Tax Assessment and Administration*, 4, 41–53.

Sachs, M. (1993) 'Professional ethics in sport psychology', in R. Singer, M. Murphey and L.K. Tennant (eds), *Handbook of Research on Sport Psychology*. New York: Macmillan. Pp. 921–32.

Watson, J.C., Harris, B.S., and Baillie, P. (2020) 'Ethical issues impacting the profession of sport psychology', in G. Tenenbaum and R.C. Eklund (eds), *Handbook of Sport Psychology*. Hoboken, NJ: John Wiley & Sons. pp. 751–72.

Zeigler, E.F. (1987) 'Rationale and suggested dimensions for a code of ethics for sport psychologists', *The Sport Psychologist*, 1 (2), 138–50.

1.4 SPORT PSYCHOLOGY ORGANISATIONS, SOURCES AND RESOURCES

Definition: Organisations, sources and resources devoted to the science, practice and promotion of sport and exercise psychology.

Sport psychology can be defined as the application of psychological theory and methods to the understanding and enhancement of athletic performance (Kremer et al., 2019). As the history of this discipline is well documented (see **1.1**), it is sufficient merely to note that empirical research on mental aspects of athletic performance is at least as old as psychology itself. Unfortunately, despite this research tradition spanning over a century (Green and Benjamin, 2009; Tenenbaum and Eklund, 2020), the field of sport psychology is difficult to define precisely. This imprecision is due, in part, to the nature of the discipline. To explain: sport psychology is not only a growing field of mainstream psychology but is also a key component of the sport sciences. In particular, the areas of motor learning, motor development, skill acquisition, motivation, social processes, personality, psychological skills, emotion, anxiety, psychophysiology, mental health and wellbeing all feature as topics of relevance to supporting athlete performance in sport science. Not surprisingly, therefore, sport psychology organisations may be found both in psychology and in sport science and, more recently, psychiatry. Against this background, here is an alphabetical list of the main contemporary sport psychology organisations and their respective mission statements, along with key publication resources for members (where such information is available at the time of writing).

AMERICAN PSYCHOLOGICAL ASSOCIATION (APA)

APA Division 47 (Society for Sport, Exercise and Performance Psychology) was founded in 1986 and brings together psychologists as well as sport scientists to further the clinical, educational, biobehavioural and scientific foundations of exercise and sport psychology. Applied service interests include: promoting best practices in mental training techniques; ethical considerations in sport psychology service provision; practitioner self-care; clinical issues and diversity issues. Areas of scientific inquiry include: motivation to persist and achieve; psychological considerations in sport injury and rehabilitation; counselling techniques with athletes; assessing talent; exercise adherence and wellbeing; self-perceptions related to achieving; expertise in sport; youth sport; and performance enhancement and self-regulation techniques. Among its resources are an official newsletter (*Div47 SportPsych Works* – www.apadivisions.org/division-47/publications/sportpsych-works), which is published three times a year (spring, autumn and summer), a list of books, a quarterly peer-reviewed journal (*Sport, Exercise and Performance Psychology*), along with toolkits for practitioners; training materials and opportunities; and a convention.

ASSOCIATION FOR APPLIED SPORT PSYCHOLOGY (AASP)

AASP (founded in 1986) aims to promote the science and practice of sport and exercise psychology. It advocates the application of psychological principles that have been supported by research in sport and exercise. It is an interdisciplinary organisation, drawing from the fields of exercise and sport sciences as well as psychology. AASP provides opportunities to share information-related theory development, research and the provision of psychological services to consumers. Among its resources are:

- *Journal of Applied Sport Psychology* and *Journal of Sport Psychology in Action*
- AASP Newsletter
- Member Directory
- Position Statements

- Career Centre
- Webinars

AUSTRALIAN PSYCHOLOGICAL SOCIETY (APS)

The APS advances psychology for members and their communities via advocacy, education and evidence-based practice. Sport and Exercise Psychology is one of nine APS Colleges representing a range of different areas in psychology. The College of Sport and Exercise Psychologists:

- Works to develop and safeguard the standards of practice and supervised experience;
- Sets the quality of service in sport and exercise psychology;
- Advises and makes recommendations regarding education and training of sport and exercise psychologists;
- Acts as a focal point for consumer and other general inquiries relating to sport and exercise.

The society provides a register of members, regular newsletters, webinars and hosts a national conference.

BRITISH ASSOCIATION OF SPORT AND EXERCISE SCIENCES (BASES)

The British Association of Sport and Exercise Sciences (BASES), formerly the British Association of Sports Science (BASS), is the professional body for sport and exercise sciences in the UK. Its vision is to raise standards and lead excellence through evidence-based practice. BASES have a number of Divisions, one of which is the Psychology Division whose objective is to promote the progression of evidence-based practice, support innovative research and establish stronger communication links between sport scientists with an interest in the field of sport psychology. In particular, the Division promotes the engagement and knowledge-development of its members through three core strands: Performance Excellence; Engagement and Development; and Mental Health. BASES provides support to become a practitioner through the recent introduction of their Sport and Exercise Psychology Accreditation Route (SEPAR) qualification, and also hosts regular workshops, an annual conference and publishes expert position statements.

BRITISH PSYCHOLOGICAL SOCIETY (BPS)

The BPS Division of Sport and Exercise Psychology (DSEP, established in 2004) represents the interests of psychologists working in sport and exercise settings and aims to further the development of sport and exercise psychology. It draws its membership from a broad range of psychologists, including those working in academic settings and professional practice. The Division was formed in 2004 in response to the increase in academic status and public recognition of sport and exercise psychology and ensures that members who practise and offer services within sport and exercise psychology are qualified and trained according to the Charter, Statutes and Rules of the British Psychological Society. Among its resources are:

- Applied regional hubs
- DSEP annual conference
- DSEP Division days
- E-newsletters
- Research working groups
- *Sport and Exercise Psychology Review* (*SEPR*) – peer-reviewed journal
- Accreditation of Stage 1 MSc Sport and Exercise Psychology Programmes
- BPS Stage 2 Qualification in Sport and Exercise Psychology
- Workshops

EUROPEAN NETWORK OF YOUNG SPECIALISTS IN SPORT PSYCHOLOGY (ENYSSP)

ENYSSP is an international organisation concerned with the promotion and dissemination of knowledge in the field of sport and exercise psychology in the areas of research, education and applied work. The network provides annual conferences, and has a representative for each country. The website hosts practical tools for applied work, useful web links, general and new books/journals, a list of European universities and higher education institutes offering sport and exercise psychology degrees, as well as other contacts to start a sport psychology network.

FÉDÉRATION EUROPÉENNE DE PSYCHOLOGIE DES SPORTS ET DES ACTIVITÉS CORPORELLES (FEPSAC; EUROPEAN FEDERATION OF SPORT PSYCHOLOGY)

FEPSAC consists of 24 group members (associations of sport psychology) and a small number of individual members. It aims to promote scientific, educational and professional work in sport psychology across Europe. FEPSAC organises congresses, courses, publishes position statements, organises the publication of books and supports students and young specialists in sport psychology.

INTERNATIONAL SOCIETY FOR SPORTS PSYCHIATRY (ISSP)

The ISSP was founded in 1994 to advance the medical speciality of sports psychiatry. It aims to treat and prevent mental disorders in athletes and employs different techniques in order to enhance performance. First mentioned in the literature in 1967, it is a developing area that draws on other fields, including sport psychology. In response to growing interest, the World Psychiatric Association created a section on Exercise and Sports Psychiatry. Both sport psychologists and psychiatrists aim to enhance athletes' performance but psychiatry also focuses on disorders and psychopathology and, additionally, psychiatrists are able to prescribe psychotropic medication.

INTERNATIONAL SOCIETY OF SPORT PSYCHOLOGY (ISSP)

ISSP (founded in 1965) is a worldwide organisation devoted to promoting research, practice and development in the discipline of sport psychology. Its members are those whose research interests focus on some aspects of sport psychology. The Society aims to:

- encourage and promote the study of human behaviour within sport, physical activity and health settings;
- facilitate the sharing of knowledge through a newsletter, meetings and a quadrennial World Congress;
- improve the quality of research and professional practice in sport psychology.

ISSP hosts conferences, produces the *International Journal of Sport and Exercise Psychology* (*IJSEP*) and has a Consultant Register for practitioners.

NORTH AMERICAN SOCIETY FOR PSYCHOLOGY OF SPORT AND PHYSICAL ACTIVITY (NASPSPA)

NASPSPA is a multidisciplinary association of scholars from the behavioural sciences and related professions. The purpose of NASPSPA is to develop and advance the study of motor behaviour (development, learning, and control) and sport and exercise psychology. The Society aims to:

- develop and advance the scientific study of human behaviour when individuals are engaged in sport and physical activity;

- facilitate the dissemination of information;
- improve the quality of research and teaching in the psychology of sport, motor development, and motor learning and control.

NASPSPA hosts an annual conference. The *Journal of Sport and Exercise Psychology* (*JSEP*) and the *Journal of Motor Learning and Development* (*JMLD*) are NASPSPA's official journals. It hosts workshops and seminars and provides employment postings and teaching resources.

LISTSERV INFORMATION (A BULLETIN BOARD ON SPORT PSYCHOLOGY)

If you would like to learn more about sport and exercise psychology, you can subscribe to an electronic bulletin board called SPORTPSY that is devoted to sport and exercise psychology. SPORTPSY can be found at: http://listserv.temple.edu/.

The purpose of this list is to post issues, questions and findings concerning research in sport and exercise psychology as well as related professional practice issues in this field.

To join SPORTPSY, go to http://listserv.temple.edu/archives/sportpsy.html and select, 'Join or leave the list', which will take you to a secure page, or send a message to listserv@listserv.temple.edu with nothing in the subject heading and only the following in the text: SUB SPORTPSY [your name].

KEY READINGS

Useful sport and exercise psychology association websites:

www.psychology.org.au/

www.apa.org/about/division/div47

www.bps.org.uk/

https://appliedsportpsych.org/

PRACTICAL QUESTIONS

- Name the professional associations for the promotion of sport and exercise psychology nationally and internationally. Determine what associations would be useful for you in advancing your professional development.
- What are the main benefits to you from being a member of the association in your country?

REFERENCES

Green, C.D. and Benjamin, L.T., Jr. (2009) *Psychology Gets in the Game: Sport, Mind and Behaviour, 1880–1960*. Lincoln, NE: University of Nebraska Press.

Kremer, J., Moran, A.P. and Kearney, C.J. (2019) *Pure Sport: Sport Psychology in Action*. London: Routledge.

Tenenbaum, G. and Eklund, R.C. (eds) (2020) *Handbook of Sport Psychology*. London: John Wiley & Sons.

Anxiety and Stress in Sport

Chapter Summary: Over several decades, one of the 'hottest' topics in both pure and applied sport psychology has been the relationship between anxiety, stress and performance. This chapter begins by defining key terms, including anxiety, arousal and stress, and looking at theoretical perspectives that incorporate distinctions between somatic/physiological and psychological responses, along with trait and state anxiety, before reviewing quantitative and qualitative techniques for measuring stress and anxiety in sport. The chapter then turns to more practical concerns, beginning with an overview of pre-performance routines that are used to control and manage 'nerves' prior to performance, before highlighting the phenomenon of choking under pressure, and finally techniques and strategies that can be employed to cope with stress attached to competitive sport, in both the short and longer term.

2.5 Stress, Anxiety and Arousal 30

2.6 Measuring Stress and Anxiety 37

2.7 Pre-performance Routines 43

2.8 Choking Under Pressure 49

2.9 Coping Strategies 54

2.5 STRESS, ANXIETY AND AROUSAL

Definitions: Arousal is a form of diffuse or undifferentiated bodily energy which primes us for action. Anxiety can be defined as negatively interpreted arousal or an emotional state characterised by worry, feelings of apprehension and bodily tension that tends to occur in response to real, imagined or obvious danger.

Most athletes know from personal experience that, in order to perform consistently well in competition, they have to manage their stress, anxiety or arousal levels effectively. According to the 2020 world number one ranked tennis player, Rafael Nadal, 'The important thing is for me to have the calm. It is what is needed to play my best' (cited in Flatman, 2010: 14). However, what works for one person may not for another. World Formula One champion Lewis Hamilton insists that he always has, and needs, big-race nerves before every race as they help him to focus on the task in hand. 'With the nerves it's about how I control them, control that energy and try and maintain it through the race, and that's always a key' (Skysports, 2008).

In different ways, both these quotations serve to highlight vital issues for both the theory and the practice of sport psychology, complex issues that have been wrestled with for decades, and show no signs of fading from view. For example, a recent systematic review and meta-analysis of determinants of anxiety in sport (Rice et al., 2019) noted that 75 per cent of the included articles had been published not decades ago but in the last five years. Increasingly, the focus on anxiety and/or stress in sport psychology can be categorised within two fields: mental health and performance. A mental health focus on anxiety and stress is relevant to the measurement, diagnosis and treatment of clinical symptoms, as outlined by the Diagnostic and Statistical Manual of Mental Disorders, for example. Chapter 7 (see **7.40** and **7.41**) offers a more thorough discussion of anxiety and mental health disorders generally in sport, while in this chapter the focus falls instead on anxiety and stress as related to sporting performance. Before exploring such literature further, three questions immediately spring to mind – first, what exactly is arousal; second, how does it differ from anxiety; and crucially, third, what is the relationship between arousal, anxiety and actual performance?

While stress is defined very broadly to encompass both physiological and psychological dimensions (see **2.6**), in the discipline of psychology the term arousal is typically used to refer specifically to a form of diffuse or undifferentiated bodily or somatic energy which primes us for action. According to Gould et al. (2002: 227), it is the 'General physiological and psychological activation of the organism which varies on a continuum from deep sleep to intense excitement'. Physiologically, feelings of arousal are mediated by the sympathetic nervous system. In particular, when we become aroused, our brain's reticular activating system triggers the release of biochemical substances such as epinephrine and norepinephrine into the bloodstream so that our body is energised for action.

While arousal involves *undifferentiated* bodily energy, anxiety is an emotional label for a particular type of arousal experience. In short, anxiety may be defined as a response to *negatively interpreted* arousal – an emotional state characterised by worry, feelings of apprehension and bodily tension that tends to occur in the absence of real or obvious danger. This proposition immediately raises the question of individual differences in arousal interpretation.

It has long been known that athletes differ from each other in how they perceive and interpret their arousal states, and that different sports and tasks have unique arousal demands. For example, a low level of arousal may be experienced either as a relaxed state of readiness or as an undesirable 'flat' or sluggish feeling. Conversely, symptoms of high arousal, such as a rapid heartbeat and a feeling of 'butterflies' in one's stomach may be perceived as welcome excitement by one athlete but as uncomfortable anxiety by another. To illustrate the former interpretation, consider Tiger Woods's view that, 'The challenge is hitting good golf shots when you have to … to do it when the nerves are fluttering, the heart pounding, the palms sweating … that's the *thrill*' (cited in Davies, 2001: 26). Taken together, these observations suggest that it is not the *amount* of arousal that affects performance but the way in which such arousal is *interpreted.*

Exploring this idea empirically, Jones and Swain (1992) found that somatic symptoms of anxiety can have either a *facilitative* or a *debilitative* effect on sport performance depending on how the athlete perceives them. Interestingly, Thomas et al. (2009) claimed that athletes who perceive arousal symptoms as facilitative tend to perform better, have higher levels of self-confidence, use more effective coping strategies and display more resilience than do those who perceive such symptoms as debilitative of performance. Unfortunately, there is a semantic problem at the heart of research on 'directional' anxiety effects (Wagstaff et al., 2011). Specifically, as 'anxiety' is usually defined as negatively interpreted arousal, it makes little sense to talk of facilitative *anxiety*. Instead, it is more accurate to refer to facilitative *arousal*.

Not unsurprisingly, various theories and models have been advanced to consider the relationship between arousal, anxiety and athletic performance (Ford et al., 2017; Mellalieu et al., 2006) (see Table 2.1). While there is overlap between many of these approaches, each offers a unique perspective, with a different narrative and different priorities, and there is little sign that a truly integrative approach is yet on the horizon.

Earlier approaches did not tend to make a clear distinction between arousal and anxiety, while most later perspectives not only distinguish between cognitive anxiety and somatic/physiological arousal but also between trait anxiety, described as a longstanding disposition, and state anxiety, defined as the immediate response to the perception of a forthcoming challenge. The cornerstone of contemporary approaches is the assumption that individual differences are key and that physiological arousal may have different effects on athletic performance depending on the interplay between trait and state anxiety. In the case of Catastrophe Theory (Hardy et al., 2007), it is argued that, when an athlete experiences high cognitive anxiety, the arousal-performance curve should follow a

Table 2.1 Anxiety and Performance in Sport: Summary of Models, Theories and Hypotheses (adapted from Ford et al., 2017).

Drive Theory (Hull, 1943)	A positive linear relationship between arousal/anxiety and performance.
Inverted-U Hypothesis (Yerkes and Dodson, 1908)	Low levels of arousal are associated with poorer performance; higher levels facilitate performance but only to an optimal level, beyond which performance is impaired.
Catastrophe Theory (Hardy, 1990)	Somatic anxiety and performance are related in an inverted-U fashion when the individual has low cognitive state anxiety. However, those with higher state anxiety may suffer rapid decline in performance when anxiety levels are beyond the optimum.
Conscious Processing Hypothesis (Masters and Maxwell, 2008)	Skilled performance tends to deteriorate whenever an athlete tries to exert conscious control over actions that had previously been under automatic control.
Processing Efficiency Theory/Attentional Control Theory (Eysenck and Calvo, 1992; Eysenck et al. 2007)	Cognitive anxiety (or worry) depletes the resources of working memory and diverts the performer's attention from task-relevant to task-irrelevant information. Anxious individuals are also motivated to increase effort in order to avoid peceived threat.
The Conceptual Model of Athletic Performance Anxiety (Smith and Smoll, 1990)	Arousal/anxiety influence an athlete's stress response to a competitive situation, which then influences performance through a range of physiological, behavioural and/or cognitive responses.
Multidimensional Anxiety Theory (Martens et al., 1990)	Cognitive state anxiety is negatively related to performance while somatic state anxiety is related to performance in an inverted-U manner.
Reversal Theory (Apter, 1982; Kerr, 1999)	The relationship between arousal/anxiety and performance will depend on the individual's interpretation of their arousal/anxiety levels. Performers with either low or high arousal may perceive this with either negative or positive feelings (boredom or relaxation; excitement or anxiety).
Individual Zone of Optimal Functioning (IZOF) Hypothesis (Hanin, 1997)	Each individual has an idiosyncratic zone of optimal arousal/anxiety which is associated with his/her peak performance level. If their arousal/anxiety is outside the zone (too low or too high), performance will decline.

different path under conditions of *increasing* versus *decreasing* arousal. This hypothesis was supported, in part, by Vickers and Williams (2007), who discovered that when a high level of cognitive anxiety was combined with a high level of physiological arousal, this could lead to 'choking under pressure' (see **2.8**) among biathletes – but not when these athletes were able to pay attention to task-relevant information. Unfortunately, the complex three-dimensional nature of Catastrophe Theory has made it difficult to test in its entirety, as is also true of approaches that share related constructs, including Multi-Dimensional Anxiety Theory (Martens et al., 1990) and the Conceptual Model of Athletic Performance Anxiety (Smith and Smoll, 1990).

An alternative and more focused approach, the Conscious Processing Hypothesis, continues to generate a considerable amount of research and practical interest (Masters and Maxwell, 2008). It looks specifically at the relationship between conscious attention and skilled performance under anxiety-provoking conditions and was spawned in part by an attempt to explain the well-known 'paralysis-by-analysis' phenomenon (see **2.8**), along with related 'clinical' conditions across a range of sports including the yips and jitters in golf, and dartitis in darts. This is where skilled performance tends to deteriorate whenever people try to exert conscious control over movements that had previously been under automatic control. Hence, one marker of expertise in athletes is the ability to divert attention away from ruminating and towards kinaesthetic bodily sensations that allow for fluent and efficient movements (Moran et al., 2019).

According to Masters (1992), when athletes experience increases in anxiety levels, they attempt to ensure task success by reverting to a mode of conscious control that is associated mainly with an *early* stage of motor learning (i.e. one that relies on explicit rules and that typically results in slow and effortful movements). This temporary regression is held to involve a reinvestment of cognitive processes in perceptual-motor control. In this way, the Conscious Processing Hypothesis postulates that anxiety exerts a debilitating influence on performance by increasing a participant's self-consciousness of his or her movements. If this hypothesis is correct then anxiety should have *differential* effects on skilled performance depending on how the skill had been acquired originally (i.e. whether it had been learned explicitly or implicitly). In an effort to test this prediction, Masters devised an ingenious experimental paradigm in which participants who acquired the skill of golf putting using *explicit* knowledge subsequently experienced impaired performance when tested under conditions of high anxiety. Two conditions were crucial to the experiment. In the explicit condition, participants were instructed to read coaching manuals on putting. Conversely, in the implicit condition, participants were given no instructions but had to putt golf balls while performing a secondary task which had been designed to prevent them from thinking about the instructions on putting. Results suggested that the implicit learning group showed no deterioration in performance under stress, in contrast to the golfers in the explicit learning condition. Masters interpreted this result as indicating that the skills of athletes with a small pool of explicit knowledge were *less* likely to fail than were those of performers with relatively larger amounts of explicit knowledge.

To summarise, the Conscious Processing Hypothesis predicts that athletes whose cognitive anxiety increases will tend to revert to conscious control of normally automatic skills. This prediction has been corroborated reliably. For example, Wilson et al. (2007) found that people's performance deteriorates when pressure manipulations require them to consciously attend to their movements. Furthermore, Gröpel and Mesagno (2019), in a systematic review, highlighted several studies which contended that athletes' performance tends to be impaired when they begin to focus on step-by-step execution and monitoring of an already well-learned motor skill.

In a similar vein, Attentional Control Theory (ACT), and its predecessor, Processing Efficiency Theory (PET) (Wilson, 2008), both consider the impact of anxiety on processing capacity. In this case, it is postulated that cognitive anxiety (or worrying) depletes the resources of working memory and diverts the performer's attention from task-relevant to task-irrelevant information. According to Wood and Wilson (2010), ACT proposes that attentional control depends on the interaction between two systems – a top-down, goal-driven system that is influenced by the performer's current goals, and a bottom-up, stimulus-driven system that is influenced by salient information such as noises, temperature and bodily tension.

ACT also suggests that anxiety increases the influence of a stimulus-driven attentional system at the expense of a goal-driven system. In a test of this latter prediction, Wilson et al. (2009) analysed the visual search behaviour of five-a-side soccer players taking penalties under various conditions of anxiety. Results confirmed that, when anxious, the penalty takers displayed an attentional bias towards a salient and threatening stimulus (the goalkeeper) rather than to the ideal target for their kick (just inside the goal-post).

More recent approaches tend to share one theme if nothing else and that is the need to acknowledge not nomothetic rules but the idiosyncracies of the relationship between anxiety, arousal and performance. Nowhere is this made more explicit than in the work of Yuri Hanin (1997), who argues that, with regard to arousal/anxiety, each athlete has a unique or individual zone of optimum functioning (IZOF), shaped by their perceptions, their personality and their experience. Implicitly, this work therefore acknowledges that no two athletes can ever be considered alike in their response to the stresses of sport, and that idiographic research techniques must therefore be employed to identify what works best for each (Wagstaff et al., 2011).

Across the board, a plethora of research continues to explore the ways in which performance is impacted by anxiety and arousal (Gröpel and Mesagno, 2019). This work shows the range of personal and situation variables that may be relevant, including trait anxiety, cognitive bias, positive and negative affect, self-confidence, flow, mindfulness, neuroticism and extraversion, hardiness, coping strategies, psychological skills, achievement motivation, competitiveness, gender, skill level, competitive experience sport type, cohesion, control, performance level and temporal patterning (Mellalieu et al., 2006; Moran et al., 2019).

Adding yet further to this complex picture, recent research is calling for the term 'performance' itself to be broadened beyond practice and competition to include performance activities associated with sport injury prevention, rehabilitation and return/retirement (see **7.39**). In this way, athlete-specific factors such as musculoskeletal injury and sporting career dissatisfaction can be considered along with typical anxiety symptoms (Rice et al., 2019).

Standing back from this wealth of research data on anxiety and arousal, two general conclusions become apparent (Moran and Toner, 2017). First, anxiety and arousal should be regarded as multidimensional constructs which do not have simple linear relationships with athletic performance. Second, increases in physiological arousal and cognitive state anxiety do not inevitably lead to a deterioration in athletic performance. More precisely, the effects of arousal and anxiety on sport performance depend crucially on the way in which the athlete appraises them cognitively, and idiosyncratically (see **4.19** and **4.20**).

KEY READINGS

Ford, J.L., Ildefonso, K., Jones, M.L. and Arvinen-Barrow, M. (2017) 'Sport-related anxiety: Current insights', *Open Access Journal of Sports Medicine*, 8, 205–12. https://doi.org/10.2147/OAJSM.S125845.

Hanin, Y.L. (1997) 'Emotions and athletic performance: Individual Zones of Optimal Functioning Model', *European Yearbook of Sport Psychology*, 1, 29–72.

Rice, S.M., Gwyther, K., Santesteban-Echarri, O. et al. (2019) 'Determinants of anxiety in elite athletes: A systematic review and meta-analysis', *British Journal of Sports Medicine*, 53, 722–30.

Mellalieu, S.D., Hanton, S. and Fletcher, D. (2006) 'A competitive anxiety review: Recent directions in sport psychology research', in S. Hanton and S.D. Mellalieu (eds), *Literature Reviews in Sport Psychology*. New York: Nova Science. pp. 1–45.

PRACTICAL QUESTIONS

- An athlete contacts you with concerns about pre-match nerves. Outline how you would initially deal with this enquiry, and which model/theories would be relevant to shaping your intervention.
- What are the 'yips' in golf, and suggest ways in which cognitive restructuring can be employed to help alleviate the problem?

REFERENCES

Apter, M.J. (1982) *The Experience of Motivation: The Theory of Psychological Reversals*. London: Academic Press.

Davies, D. (2001) 'Relaxed Woods identifies the major pressure points', *The Guardian*, 6 April, p. 26.

Eysenck, M.W. and Calvo, M.G. (1992) 'Anxiety and performance: The processing efficiency theory', *Cognition and Emotion*, 6, 409–34.

Eysenck, M.W., Derakshan, N., Santos, R. and Calvo, M.G. (2007) 'Anxiety and cognitive performance: Attentional control theory', *Emotion*, 7, 336–53.

Flatman, B. (2010) 'Holding court', *The Sunday Times*, 4 July, p. 14 (Sport).

Ford, J.L., Ildefonso, K., Jones, M.L. and Arvinen-Barrow, M. (2017) 'Sport-related anxiety: current insights', *Open Access Journal of Sports Medicine*, 8, 205–12. https://doi.org/10.2147/OAJSM.S125845.

Gould, D., Greenleaf, C. and Krane, V. (2002) 'Arousal-anxiety and sport', in T.S. Horn (ed.), *Advances in Sport Psychology* (2nd ed.). Champaign, IL: Human Kinetics. pp. 207–41.

Gröpel, P. and Mesagno, C. (2019) 'Choking interventions in sports: A systematic review', *International Review of Sport and Exercise Psychology*, 12 (1), 176–201.

Hanin, Y.L. (1989) 'Interpersonal and intragroup anxiety in sports', in D. Hackfort and C.D. Spielberger (eds), *Anxiety in Sports: An International Perspective*. Washington, DC: Hemisphere. pp. 19–28.

Hanin, Y.L. (1997) 'Emotions and athletic performance: Individual zones of optimal functioning model', *European Yearbook of Sport Psychology*, 1, 29–72.

Hardy, L. (1990) 'A catastrophe model of anxiety and performance', in G. Jones and L. Hardy (eds), *Stress and Performance in Sport*. Chichester: John Wiley. pp. 81–106.

Hardy, L., Beattie, S. and Woodman, T. (2007) 'Anxiety-induced performance catastrophes: Investigating effort required as an asymmetry factor', *British Journal of Psychology*, 98, 15–31.

Hull, C.L. (1943) *Principles of Behavior*. New York: Appleton-Century-Crofts.

Jones, G. and Swain, A.B.J. (1992) 'Intensity and direction as dimensions of competitive state anxiety and relationships with competitiveness', *Perceptual and Motor Skills*, 74, 467–72.

Kerr, J.H. (1999) *Motivation and Emotion in Sport: Reversal Theory*. Oxford: Psychology Press.

Martens, R., Vealey, R.S. and Burton, D. (1990) *Competitive Anxiety in Sport*. Champaign, IL: Human Kinetics.

Masters, R.S.W. (1992) 'Knowledge, "knerves", and know-how: The role of explicit versus implicit knowledge in the breakdown of a complex motor skill under pressure', *British Journal of Psychology*, 83, 343–58.

Masters, R.S.W. and Maxwell, J.P. (2008) 'The theory of reinvestment', *International Review of Sport and Exercise Psychology*, 2, 160–83.

Mellalieu, S.D., Hanton, S. and Fletcher, D. (2006) 'A competitive anxiety review: Recent directions in sport psychology research', in S. Hanton and S.D. Mellalieu (eds), *Literature Reviews in Sport Psychology*. New York: Nova Science. pp. 1–45.

Mellalieu, S.D., Hanton, S. and Shearer, D.A. (2008) 'Hearts in the fire, heads in the fridge: A qualitative investigation into the temporal patterning of the precompetitive psychological response in elite performers', *Journal of Sports Sciences*, 26 (8), 811–24.

Moran, A. and Toner, J. (2017) *Sport and Exercise Psychology* (3rd ed.). London: Routledge.

Moran, A., Campbell, M. and Toner, J. (2019) 'Exploring the cognitive mechanisms of expertise in sport: Progress and prospects', *Psychology of Sport and Exercise*, 42, 8–15.

Rice, S.M., Gwyther, K., Santesteban-Echarri, O., et al. (2019) 'Determinants of anxiety in elite athletes: A systematic review and meta-analysis', *British Journal of Sports Medicine*, 53, 722–30.

Skysports (2008) www.skysports.com/f1/news/12433/3833056/nerves-no-problem-for-lewis.

Smith, R.E. and Smoll, F.L. (1990) 'Sport performance anxiety', in H. Leitenberg (ed.), *Handbook of Social and Evaluation Anxiety*. New York: Plenum Press. pp. 417–54.

The Guardian (2009) '*The Guardian and Observer guides to keeping fit with Britain's medal winners*', January, p. 35.

Thomas, O., Mellalieu, S.D. and Hanton, S. (2009) 'Stress management in applied sport psychology', in S.D. Mellalieu and S. Hanton (eds), *Advances in Applied Sport Psychology*. London: Routledge. pp. 124–61.

Vickers, J.N. and Williams, A.M. (2007) 'Performing under pressure: The effects of physiological arousal, cognitive anxiety and gaze control in biathlon', *Journal of Motor Behaviour*, 39, 381–94.

Wagstaff, C.R.D., Neil, R., Mellalieu, S.D. and Hanton, S. (2011) 'Key movements in directional research in competitive anxiety', in R. Neil, S. Mellalieu and S. Hanton (eds), *Coping and Emotion in Sport*. London: Taylor & Francis, pp. 143–66.

Wilson, M. (2008) 'From processing efficiency to attentional control: A mechanistic account of the anxiety-performance relationship', *International Review of Sport and Exercise Psychology*, 1 (2), 184–201.

Wilson, M., Smith, N.C. and Holmes, P.S. (2007) 'The role of effort in influencing the effect of anxiety on performance: Testing the conflicting predictions of processing efficiency theory and the conscious processing hypothesis', *British Journal of Psychology*, 98, 411–28.

Wilson, M.R., Wood, G. and Vine, S.J. (2009) 'Anxiety, attentional control, and performance impairment in penalty kicks', *Journal of Sport and Exercise Psychology*, 31, 761–75.

Wood, G. and Wilson, M.R. (2010) 'A moving goalkeeper distracts penalty takers and impairs shooting accuracy', *Journal of Sports Sciences*, 28, 937–46.

Yerkes, R.M.D. and Dodson, J.D. (1908) 'The relation of strength of stimulus to rapidity of habit formation', *Journal of Comparative Neurology and Psychology*, 18 (5), 459–82.

2.6 MEASURING STRESS AND ANXIETY

Definitions: Stress is a pattern of physiological, behavioural, emotional and cognitive responses to real or imagined stimuli that are perceived as a challenge to our personal resources and capacity to cope. Anxiety may be defined as negatively interpreted arousal – an emotional state characterised by worry, feelings of apprehension and bodily tension that tend to occur in the absence of real or obvious danger.

Without doubt, competitive sport, and especially at the highest level, has the potential to be extremely stressful. Take Rebecca Adlington, the first British woman to win two Olympic gold medals for swimming. Rebecca later admitted that she had to lie down on the floor before her races in the 2008 Games in Beijing in order to avoid 'standing up and being sick, because I was more nervous than I've ever been in my life' (cited in Moss et al., 2008). In view of such experiences, terms such as stress and anxiety have attracted considerable research interest in sport psychology (see reviews by Hanton et al., 2008; Thomas et al., 2009; Ford et al., 2017). In keeping with the previous section (see **2.5**), we will define key terms before considering measurement issues.

Although terms such as 'stress', 'arousal' and 'anxiety' are used interchangeably in everyday life, psychologists do not regard them as synonymous. To explain: psychologists (e.g. Lazarus, 1966) believe that stress is a broader construct than either anxiety or arousal alone. Specifically, stress refers to a pattern of physiological, behavioural, emotional and cognitive responses to real or imagined demands that threaten to tax or exceed our coping resources (Martin et al., 2009). The key proposition here is that cognitive appraisal (or how a person interprets a situation) is central to the experience of stress. 'Stressors' are normal, and a central part of the demands that people face in pressure situations such as competitive sport (e.g. competing for one's country). In sport, these demands include competitive (e.g. the pressure of performance expectations), organisational (e.g. logistical), social (e.g. family issues) and personal (e.g. emotional) stressors (Fletcher et al., 2006). Finally, as explained above (see **2.5**) 'anxiety' is typically described as a negative emotional response to perceived stressors – an emotional state characterised by worry, feelings of apprehension and bodily tension that tends to occur in the absence of real or obvious danger.

Since the seminal research of Spielberger (1966), psychologists have distinguished between anxiety as a mood state ('state' anxiety) and anxiety as a disposition or personality characteristic ('trait' anxiety). For example, a basketball player may feel anxious in the dressing-room before an important match but may become calmer once the game begins. On the other hand, a player who scores highly on trait anxiety may ruminate and feel apprehension both before and during the match.

As we explained in section **2.5**, anxiety is often regarded as a tri-dimensional construct comprising cognitive, somatic and behavioural components. *Cognitive* anxiety involves worrying or having negative expectations about oneself or about an impending situation or performance. For example, Martinent and Ferrand (2007) found that competitive athletes worried a lot about poor performances, especially the possibility of making mistakes. Such levels of reflection and fear of failure are then often accompanied by burnout and exhaustion (Gustafsson et al., 2017). *Somatic* anxiety refers to the physical manifestations of the stress response which include neuroendocrine secretions (e.g. the production of cortisol – the 'stress hormone'), increased perspiration, a pounding heart, rapid shallow breathing, clammy hands and a feeling of 'butterflies' in one's stomach. Through chronic stress, maladaptive levels of cortisol production can lead to impaired health, raising the question about the potential role of intense, competitive, sporting endeavours for athletes' long-term wellbeing. Strahler et al. (2010) used the 'cortisol awakening response' (CAR) to investigate anticipatory anxiety among athletes one week before an important competition.

Surprisingly, their results indicated that, although these athletes reported experiencing a significant rise in somatic anxiety as the day of a competition loomed, there was no significant increase in CAR activity. This finding suggests that neuroendocrine indices of athletes' somatic anxiety do not always correspond with these performers' subjective experience. Finally, *behavioural* anxiety refers to the way in which nervousness affects people's posture, movement and actions. For example, Pijpers et al. (2003) found that, as predicted, the bodily movements of highly anxious climbers were jerkier and displaced more from their centre of gravity than were those of less anxious counterparts.

Historically, sport psychology researchers have used psychometric scales rather than psychophysiological instruments or behavioural indices to measure anxiety processes in athletes, atributable mainly to the simplicity, brevity and administrative convenience of such measures. However, there is a growing trend towards using non-intrusive, wearable monitors to track psychophysiological indices related to stress (e.g. heart rate variability) in recent sport psychology research (e.g. Tanguy et al., 2018). Among the most popular psychometric measures of anxiety are the Sport Competition Anxiety Test (SCAT; Martens, 1977), the Sport Anxiety Scale (SAS; Smith et al., 1990), its successor the Sport Anxiety Scale-2 (SAS-2; Smith et al., 2006) and the Competitive State Anxiety Inventory-2 (CSAI-2; Martens et al., 1990). These scales, which are concerned more with the measurement of anxiety *intensity* in athletes rather than how anxiety is interpreted by them, are summarised below.

First, the SCAT is a ten-item unidimensional trait anxiety inventory (i.e. it assumes that trait anxiety has only a single dimension). Parallel versions of the test are available for children (aged 10–14 years) and for adults (of 15 years and above). Typical items include 'When I compete I worry about making mistakes' and 'Before I compete I get a queasy feeling in my stomach'. Respondents are required to indicate their agreement with each item by selecting their preferred answer from the three categories of 'hardly ever', 'sometimes' and 'often'. Reverse scoring is used on certain items (e.g. 'Before I compete I feel calm') and overall test scores can range from 10 to 30. Unfortunately, although the SCAT appears to be quite reliable, it has limited utility because it does not distinguish between, or measure adequately, individual differences in cognitive and somatic anxiety.

Next, the SAS-2, which is a revised (15-item) version of the Sport Anxiety Scale (SAS), is a multidimensional instrument that purports to measure individual differences in somatic anxiety, worry and concentration disruption in children and adults. It contains 15 items that load onto *three subscales*, each comprising five items: somatic anxiety (e.g. 'my body feels tense'), worry (e.g. 'I worry that I will not play well') and concentration disruption (e.g. 'It is hard to concentrate on the game'). According to Smith et al. (2006), the SAS-2 not only correlates highly (r = 0.90) with its predecessor, the SAS – a sign of convergent validity – but also has strong reliability. For example, subscale reliabilities were estimated at 0.84 (for somatic anxiety), 0.89 (for worry) and 0.84 (for concentration disruption). In summary, the SAS-2 appears to be a reliable and valid measure of multidimensional anxiety in children and adults.

Third, the CSAI-2 is a popular test of cognitive and somatic anxiety in athletes. It comprises 27 items which are divided into *three subscales*, each containing nine items: cognitive anxiety (e.g. 'I am concerned about losing'), somatic anxiety (e.g. 'I feel nervous') and self-confidence (e.g. 'I am confident I can meet the challenge'). Respondents are required to rate the intensity of their anxiety experiences prior to competition on a four-point Likert scale (with 1 = 'not at all' and 4 = 'very much so').

Doubts about the psychometric adequacy of the CSAI-2 were first raised by Lane et al. (1999). For example, these authors pointed out that being 'concerned' about an impending athletic event does not necessarily mean that the performer is actually worrying about it. Thus, items such as, 'I am concerned about this competition' may not be valid indices of cognitive anxiety but may instead reflect the importance that the performer attaches to the event. Based on such arguments, and on a confirmatory factor analysis of the test, Lane et al. (1999) urged researchers to be cautious when interpreting data obtained from the CSAI-2. In response to some of these issues, the Revised Competitive State Anxiety Inventory (CSAI-2R) was developed by Cox et al. (2003). This 17-item scale purports to measure the intensity components of cognitive anxiety (five items), somatic anxiety (seven items) and self-confidence (five items). Unfortunately, according to Uphill (2008), the construct validity of this revised measure is also questionable.

Earlier, we mentioned the importance of cognitive appraisal processes in anxiety. Taking account of such individual differences in athletes' perception of the personal meaning of anxiety symptoms, Jones and Swain (1992) recommended that a 'directional' measure of anxiety should be appended to scales such as the CSAI-2. Using this new measure of anxiety (which these authors called the CSAI-2D), respondents are required first to complete the CSAI-2 in order to elicit the *intensity* with which they experience the 27 symptoms listed in this test. Next, they are asked to rate anxiety *direction* by evaluating the degree to which the experienced intensity of each symptom is either *facilitative* or *debilitative* of their athletic performance. A seven-item Likert response scale is used, with values ranging from –3 (indicating 'very negative') to +3 (indicating 'very positive'). To illustrate, an athlete might respond with a maximum '4' to the statement 'I am concerned about losing' but might then rate this concern with a +3 on the interpretation scale. Through these scores, the performer is indicating that he or she feels that this concern about losing is likely to have a facilitative effect on his or her forthcoming performance. With this modification, CSAI-2D scores can vary between –27 and +27. The discriminative value of the CSAI-2D was supported in a study by Jones et al. (1993) which showed that high-performance gymnasts reported their cognitive anxiety symptoms as being more facilitative of, and less debilitating to, their performance than did low-performance counterparts – even though there were no significant differences between these groups in CSAI-2 anxiety subscale intensity scores.

While psychometric instruments such as the CSAI-2 continue to dominate the literature in this field, it is also true that, at a practical applied level, given the direction of travel of recent research towards understanding idiosyncractic experiences of stress and anxiety, qualitative approaches are now growing in popularity, and look likely to continue to do so for the foreseeable future (Wagstaff et al., 2011). In one example, Mellalieu et al. (2008) used structured interviews to consider how elite rugby players responded to the impending prospect of important matches. They found that, while match-related cognitions remained stable, perceptions of physical symptoms peaked at the onset of performance. Affective responses were linked to feelings of anxiety and tension early on but this was replaced with excitement, confidence and efficacy in team performance just before kick off.

KEY READINGS

Hanton, S., Neil, R. and Mellalieu, S.D. (2008) 'Recent developments in competitive anxiety direction and competition stress research', *International Review of Sport and Exercise Psychology*, 1, 45–57.

Mellalieu, S.D., Hanton, S. and Shearer, D.A. (2008) 'Hearts in the fire, heads in the fridge: A qualitative investigation into the temporal patterning of the precompetitive psychological response in elite performers', *Journal of Sports Sciences*, 26 (8), 811–24.

Uphill, M. (2008) 'Anxiety in sport: Should we be worried or excited?', in A. Lane (ed.), *Sport and Exercise Psychology*. London: Hodder Education. pp. 35–51.

Wagstaff, C.R.D., Neil, R., Mellalieu, S.D. and Hanton, S. (2011) 'Key movements in directional research in competitive anxiety', in R. Neil, S. Mellalieu and S. Hanton (eds), *Coping and Emotion in Sport*. London: Taylor & Francis. pp. 143–66.

PRACTICAL QUESTIONS

- Compare and contrast two psychometric instruments used to measure and profile anxiety in athletes. Which has greater practical utility for a practising sport psychologist?
- When working with an athlete, would you prefer to use quantitative or qualitative techniques to help understand your client, and why?

REFERENCES

Cox, R.H., Martens, M.P. and Russell, W.D. (2003) 'Measuring anxiety in athletes: The revised Competitive State Anxiety Inventory-2', *Journal of Sport and Exercise Psychology*, 25, 519–33.

Fletcher, D., Hanton, S. and Mellalieu, S.D. (2006) 'An organizational stress review: Conceptual and theoretical issues in competitive sport', in S. Hanton and S.D. Mellalieu (eds), *Literature Reviews in Sport Psychology*. New York: Nova Science. pp. 321–73.

Ford, J.L., Ildefonso, K., Jones, M.L. and Arvinen-Barrow, M. (2017) 'Sport-related anxiety: Current insights', *Open Access Journal of Sports Medicine*, 8, 205–12. https://doi.org/10.2147/OAJSM.S125845.

Gustafsson, H., Sagar, S.S. and Stenling, A. (2017) 'Fear of failure, psychological stress, and burnout among adolescent athletes competing in high level sport', *Scandinavian Journal of Medicine and Science in Sports*, 27 (12), 2091–2102.

Hanton, S., Neil, R. and Mellalieu, S.D. (2008) 'Recent developments in competitive anxiety direction and competition stress research', *International Review of Sport and Exercise Psychology*, 1, 45–57.

Jones, J.G. and Swain, A.B.J. (1992) 'Intensity and direction as dimensions of competitive state anxiety and relationships with competitiveness', *Perceptual and Motor Skills*, 74, 467–72.

Jones, J.G., Swain, A. and Hardy, L. (1993) 'Intensity and direction dimensions of competitive state anxiety and relationships with performance', *Journal of Sports Sciences*, 11, 525–32.

Lane, A.M., Sewell, D.F., Terry, P.C., Bartram, D. and Nesti, M.S. (1999) 'Confirmatory factor analysis of the Competitive State Anxiety Inventory-2', *Journal of Sports Sciences*, 17, 505–12.

Lazarus, R.S. (1966) *Psychological Stress and the Coping Process*. New York: McGraw-Hill.

Martens, R. (1977) *Sport Competition Anxiety Test*. Champaign, IL: Human Kinetics.

Martens, R., Burton, D., Vealey, R.S., Bump, L.A. and Smith, D.E. (1990) 'Development and validation of the Competitive State Anxiety Inventory-2 (CSAI-2)', in R. Martens, R.S. Vealey and D. Burton (eds), *Competitive Anxiety in Sport*. Champaign, IL: Human Kinetics. pp. 117–90.

Martin, G.N., Carlson, N.R. and Buskist, W. (2009) *Psychology* (4th ed.). Harlow: Pearson Education.

Martinent, G. and Ferrand, C. (2007) 'A cluster analysis of precompetitive anxiety: Relationship with perfectionism and trait anxiety', *Personality and Individual Differences*, 43, 1676–86.

Mellalieu, S.D., Hanton, S. and Shearer, D.A. (2008) 'Hearts in the fire, heads in the fridge: A qualitative investigation into the temporal patterning of the precompetitive psychological response in elite performers', *Journal of Sports Sciences*, 26 (8), 811–24.

Moss, S., Cochrane, K. and Burnton, S. (2008) 'Baffled by Beijing', *The Guardian* (g2 magazine), 19 August. (Retrieved from www.guardian.co.uk/sport/2008/aug/19/britisholympicteam.olympics2008 on 25 October 2010.)

Pijpers, J.R., Oudejans, R.R.D., Holsheimer, F. and Bakker, F.C. (2003) 'Anxiety-performance relationships in climbing: A process-oriented approach', *Psychology of Sport and Exercise*, 4, 283–304.

Smith, R.E., Smoll, F.L. and Schutz, R.W. (1990) 'Measurement and correlates of sport-specific cognitive and somatic trait anxiety: The Sport Anxiety Scale', *Anxiety Research*, 2, 263–80.

Smith, R.E., Smoll, F.L., Cumming, S.P. and Grossbard, J.R. (2006) 'Measurement of multidimensional sport performance anxiety in children and adults: The Sport Anxiety Scale-2', *Journal of Sport and Exercise Psychology*, 28, 479–501.

Spielberger, C.S. (1966) 'Theory and research on anxiety', in C.S. Spielberger (ed.) *Anxiety and Behaviour*. New York: Academic Press. pp. 3–20.

Strahler, K., Ehrlenspiel, F., Heene, M. and Brand, R. (2010) 'Competitive anxiety and cortisol awakening response in the week leading up to a competition', *Psychology of Sport and Exercise*, 11, 148–54.

Tanguy, G., Sagui, E., Fabien, Z., Martin-Krumm, C., Canini, F. and Trousselard, M. (2018) 'Anxiety and psycho-physiological stress response to competitive sport exercise', *Frontiers in Psychology*, 9, 1469.

Thomas, O., Mellalieu, S.D. and Hanton, S. (2009) 'Stress management in applied sport psychology', in S.D. Mellalieu and S. Hanton (eds), *Advances in Applied Sport Psychology*. London: Routledge. pp. 124–61.

Uphill, M. (2008) 'Anxiety in sport: Should we be worried or excited?', in A. Lane (ed.), *Sport and Exercise Psychology*. London: Hodder Education. pp. 35–51.

Wagstaff, C.R.D., Neil, R., Mellalieu, S.D. and Hanton, S. (2011) 'Key movements in directional research in competitive anxiety', in R. Neil, S. Mellalieu and S. Hanton (eds), *Coping and Emotion in Sport*. London: Taylor & Francis. pp. 143–66.

2.7 PRE-PERFORMANCE ROUTINES

Definition: A pre-performance routine is a preferred sequence of task-relevant thoughts and actions which athletes engage in systematically prior to the performance of specific sport skills.

Competitive sport is often a highly ritualised activity. For example, golfers tend to 'waggle' their clubs a consistent number of times before striking the ball, while tennis players like to bounce the ball a set number of times before serving. These preferred action sequences are called 'pre-performance routines' (PPRs) and involve task-relevant thoughts and actions which athletes engage in systematically prior to the performance of specific sport skills (Moran, 1996). Usually, PPRs are evident prior to the execution of closed skills and self-paced actions (i.e. those that are carried out largely at one's own speed and without interference from other people) such as taking a shot in snooker, free-throwing in basketball, putting in golf or place-kicking in American football or rugby. Such routines are used extensively by athletes, and recommended by coaches and psychologists, as a form of mental preparation both to improve focusing skills (see **4.19**) and to enhance competitive performance. In short, according to Singer (2002: 6), the purpose of a PPR is to 'put oneself in an optimal state immediately prior to execution, and to remain that way during the act'. Over many years, PPRs have attracted considerable interest across a wide range of sports, and continue to demonstrate their practical value for controlling anxiety, regulating stress, focusing attention and enhancing performance (e.g. Hazell et al., 2014; Lautenbach et al., 2015; Gretton et al., 2020).

Three main types of routines tend to be found. First, *pre-event* routines are preferred sequences of actions that athletes habitually engage in prior to a competitive event. Included here are preferences for what to do on the night before (e.g. watching a film, to 'switch off'), and on the morning of, the competition itself. Second, as mentioned above, *pre-performance routines* are characteristic sequences of thoughts and actions which athletes adhere to immediately preceding skill execution (e.g. imagery of a successful throw/kick). Third, *post-mistake routines* are action sequences which athletes use in an effort to forget about setbacks, mistakes or missed opportunities so that they can refocus on the task at hand. For example, a golfer may 'shadow' the correct swing of a shot that had led to an error. Of these three types of routines, PPRs have attracted the greatest amount of research attention in sport psychology (see Cotterill, 2010, for a comprehensive review of studies on this topic).

Typically, the efficacy of PPRs has been investigated using a research design in which the performance of a control group is compared with that of an experimental group that has been taught and has practised a designated pre-performance routine. Cotterill (2010) has summarised the results of 27 studies on PPRs using this experimental method. Although the findings from these studies are far from consistent, there is evidence to suggest that systematic routines do facilitate performance. For example, Crews and Boutcher (1986) compared the performances of two groups of golfers – those who had been given an eight-week training programme of swing practice only and those who had participated in a 'practice-plus-routine' programme for the same duration. Results revealed that the more proficient golfers benefited more from using routines than did the less skilled players. However, a more recent study by Mesagno et al. (2019) concluded that both inexperienced and experienced athletes benefited equally when compared to control groups, on task performance using a pre-performance routine intervention.

Research on the efficacy of pre-performance routines raises at least three key practical and theoretical questions. First, are athletes consistent in their implementation of a given PPR in different competitive situations? Second, can athletes' PPRs be distinguished from superstitious rituals? Third, what theoretical mechanisms underlie the effects of PPRs? Let us now consider each of these questions in turn.

To begin with, some studies have challenged the assumption that routines are always unwavering when executed by top-class athletes. For example, Jackson and Baker (2001) analysed the pre-kick routine of the prolific former British and Irish Lions rugby kicker, Neil Jenkins, who is Wales's highest-ever points scorer and who was the first player to score over 1,000 points in international matches. As expected, Jenkins reported using a variety of concentration techniques (see **4.17**) as part of his pre-kick routine. However, what surprised Jackson and Baker was the discovery that Jenkins *varied* the timing of his pre-strike behaviour depending on the difficulty of the kick that he faced. This finding shows that routines are fluid and not as rigid or stereotyped as was originally believed. In a further investigation of this phenomenon, Jackson (2003) analysed over 500 goal-kicking attempts in the 1999 rugby World Cup. He found that players spent on average about ten seconds in quiet contemplation before a typical kick, but they took several seconds longer when there was a narrow angle between the ball and the posts. In other words, they varied the duration of their pre-kick routine in accordance with the perceived difficulty of the task. Lonsdale and Tam (2008) examined the consistency of the pre-performance routines of a sample of elite National Basketball Association (NBA) players by analysing their 'free throw' shooting behaviour from televised match footage. Results showed that, contrary to expectations, the *temporal* consistency of the basketball players' pre-performance routines was not associated with accurate skill execution. However, there was evidence that the *behavioural* consistency of these routines *was* related to proficient performance. Specifically, Lonsdale and Tam found that the basketball players were more successful when they adhered to their dominant behavioural sequence prior to their free throws.

Turning to a second key issue in relevant scientific literature, are pre-performance routines merely superstitious rituals in disguise? It is well known that athletes are notoriously superstitious – perhaps because of the capricious nature of sport itself (Dömötör et al., 2016). For example, Rafael Nadal apparently must have two water bottles beside the court, perfectly aligned and with the labels facing the baseline, and Tiger Woods usually wears a 'lucky' red shirt on the last day of a golf tournament. At first glance, such superstitions (i.e. beliefs that, despite scientific evidence to the contrary, certain actions are causally related to certain outcomes; see Vyse, 1997) may be distinguished from PPR on the basis of two criteria: control and purpose. First, the essence of superstitious behaviour is the belief that one's fate is governed by factors that lie *outside* one's control. But the value of a routine is that it allows the player to exert complete control over his or her preparation. Thus, athletes can shorten their pre-performance routines in adverse circumstances (e.g. if the time of a competition is brought forward unexpectedly). Unfortunately, the converse is true for superstitions. They tend to grow longer over time as performers 'chain together' more and more illogical links between their behaviour and the desired outcome. The second criterion which helps us to distinguish between routines and rituals concerns the technical role of each behavioural step followed. Specifically, whereas each part of a PPR usually has a rational basis, the components of a superstitious ritual are invariably spurious in nature and randomly associated.

Despite these neat conceptual distinctions, however, the boundaries between PPRs and superstitions in sport are often rather fuzzy. For example, consider how Serena Williams explained her defeat at the 2007 French Open tennis championship: 'I didn't tie my laces right and I didn't bounce the ball five times and I didn't bring my shower sandals to the court with me … I just knew fate, it wasn't going to happen' (cited in Hyde, 2009: 3). Notably, although many see an overlap with superstitious practices and religious beliefs, Maranise (2013) points to the importance of meaning and purpose to life for religious beliefs, whereas superstitious beliefs tend to be more mercurial.

Interestingly, several studies have explored the impact of ritualised behaviour, including religious prayer (see Noh and Shahdan, 2020), on athletic performance. For example, using a sample of basketball players, Foster et al. (2006) evaluated the effect of removing superstitious behaviour (e.g. kissing the tape covering a wedding ring on the shooter's hand) and introducing a pre-performance routine (of bouncing the ball, taking a deep breath, visualising the perfect shot and then using a cue word before executing the skill) before free-throw skill execution. Contrary to expectation, there was very little difference between the players' performance following either superstitious behaviour or a pre-performance routine – perhaps because many of the basketballers had been using superstitious behaviour for years prior to the study whereas the routine was only a recent addition to their mental preparation repertoire. Similarly, Schippers and Van Lange (2006) analysed the psychological benefits of superstitious rituals among elite athletes. Based on an examination of the circumstances in which such rituals are displayed before games, these investigators concluded that superstitious behaviour was most likely to occur when games were perceived as especially important. In addition, these researchers reported that players with an *external* locus of control tended to display *more* superstitious rituals than those with an internal locus of control (see **4.19**).

More recently, evidence has emerged to suggest that, despite their irrational origins, superstitions can sometimes be helpful to performers. Thus Damisch et al. (2010) conducted a series of experiments which appear to highlight some benefits of superstitions to motor and cognitive task performance. Specifically, they showed that playing with a ball described as 'lucky' seemed to improve participants' putting accuracy and that the presence of a personal charm enhances participants' performance on memory and anagram tests. In an effort to explain these results, Damisch et al. postulated that good-luck superstitions may have increased participants' self-efficacy (or belief in their own ability to succeed on the tasks in question) which, in turn, may have improved their performance.

Finally, what theoretical mechanisms underlie the effects of pre-performance routines in enhancing performance? Although few studies have addressed this question empirically, it is plausible that they work because they consume working memory resources and hence prevent athletes from engaging in 'reinvestment' (Masters and Maxwell, 2008) – or devoting too much attention to the mechanics of automatic skills (see **2.8**). In other words, pre-performance routines may help to suppress the type of inappropriate conscious control that athletes may regress to when in pressure situations (see **6.33**).

In this regard, an important challenge for applied sport psychologists is to help athletes to attain an appropriate level of conscious control over their actions before skill execution. Another reason why routines may enhance performance is that they encourage athletes to focus only on task-relevant information (Moran, 1996). Augmenting such arguments, empirical evidence to support the value of routines comes from case studies. For example, Cotterill et al. (2010) conducted in-depth interviews with a sample of amateur international golfers in an effort to understand the nature and perceived benefits of their use of PPRs. Results showed that these golfers used routines for attentional purposes such as attempting to 'switch on and off' (p. 55) and 'staying in the present and not dwelling on the past or engaging in fortune telling' (p. 55). This finding perhaps highlights the overlapping roles played by religious practices and PPRs in sport, with both activating belief systems that help alleviate performance-related anxieties (Noh and Shahdan, 2020).

KEY READINGS

Cotterill, S. (2010) 'Pre-performance routines in sport: Current understanding and future directions', *International Review of Sport and Exercise Psychology*, 3, 132–53.

Damisch, L., Stoberock, B. and Musseweiler, T. (2010) 'Keep your fingers crossed! How superstition improves performance', *Psychological Science*, 21, 1014–20.

Dömötör, Z., Ruíz-Barquín, R. and Szabo, A. (2016) 'Superstitious behavior in sport: A literature review', *Scandinavian Journal of Psychology*, 57 (4), 368–82.

Noh, Y.E. and Shahdan, S. (2020) 'A systematic review of religion/spirituality and sport: A psychological perspective', *Psychology of Sport and Exercise*, 46, 101603.

PRACTICAL QUESTIONS

- A player has contacted you with problems of 'focusing' before big matches. What advice would you offer on appropriate pre-performance routines to address this issue?
- What are the key differences between a pre-performance routine and a superstition, and what are the likely effects of both on performance?

REFERENCES

Cotterill, S. (2010) 'Pre-performance routines in sport: Current understanding and future directions', *International Review of Sport and Exercise Psychology*, 3, 132–53.

Cotterill, S., Sanders, R. and Collins, D. (2010) 'Developing effective pre-performance routines in golf: Why don't we ask the golfer?', *Journal of Applied Sport Psychology*, 22 (1), 51–64.

Crews, D.J. and Boutcher, S.H. (1986) 'Effects of structured preshot behaviours on beginning golf performance', *Perceptual and Motor Skills*, 62, 291–4.

Damisch, L., Stoberock, B. and Musseweiler, T. (2010) 'Keep your fingers crossed! How superstition improves performance', *Psychological Science*, 21, 1014–20.

Dömötör, Z., Ruíz-Barquín, R., and Szabo, A. (2016) 'Superstitious behavior in sport: A literature review', *Scandinavian Journal of Psychology*, 57 (4), 368–82.

Foster, D.J., Weigand, D.A. and Baines, D. (2006) 'The effect of removing superstitious behaviour and introducing a pre-performance routine on basketball free-throw performance', *Journal of Applied Sport Psychology*, 18, 167–71.

Gretton, T., Blom, L., Hankemeier, D. and Judge, L. (2020) 'The cognitive component of elite high jumpers' pre-performance routines', *The Sport Psychologist* 34 (2), 99–110.

Hazell, J., Cotterill, S. and Hill, J.M. (2014) 'An exploration of pre-performance routines, self-efficacy, anxiety and performance in semi-professional soccer', *European Journal of Sport Science*, 14 (6), 603–10.

Hyde, M. (2009) 'Obsessive? Compulsive? Order of the day at SW19', *The Guardian (Sport)*, 1 July, pp. 2–3.

Jackson, R.C. (2003) 'Pre-performance routine consistency: Temporal analysis of goal kicking in the Rugby Union World Cup', *Journal of Sports Sciences*, 21, 803–14.

Jackson, R.C. and Baker, J.S. (2001) 'Routines, rituals, and rugby: Case study of a world class goal kicker', *The Sport Psychologist*, 15, 48–65.

Lautenbach, F., Laborde, S., Mesagno, C., Lobinger, B.H., Achtzehn, S. and Arimond, F. (2015) 'Nonautomated pre-performance routine in tennis: An intervention study', *Journal of Applied Sport Psychology*, 27 (2), 123–31.

Lonsdale, C. and Tam, J.T.M. (2008) 'On the temporal and behavioural consistency of pre-performance routines: An intra-individual analysis of elite basketball players' free throw shooting accuracy', *Journal of Sports Sciences*, 26, 259–66.

Masters, R.S.W. and Maxwell, J.P. (2008) 'The theory of reinvestment', *International Review of Sport and Exercise Psychology*, 2, 160–83.

Maranise, A. M. (2013) 'Superstition and religious ritual: An examination of their effects and utilization in sport', *The Sport Psychologist*, 27 (1), 83–91.

Mesagno, C., Beckmann, J., Wergin, V.V. and Gröpel, P. (2019) 'Primed to perform: Comparing different pre-performance routine interventions to improve accuracy in closed, self-paced motor tasks', *Psychology of Sport and Exercise*, 43, 73–81.

Moran, A.P. (1996) *The Psychology of Concentration in Sport Performers: A Cognitive Analysis*. Hove: Psychology Press.

Noh, Y.E. and Shahdan, S. (2020) 'A systematic review of religion/spirituality and sport: A psychological perspective'. *Psychology of Sport and Exercise*, 46, 101603.

Schippers, M.C. and Van Lange, P.A. (2006) 'The psychological benefits of superstitious rituals in top sport: A study among top sportspersons', *Journal of Applied Social Psychology*, 36, 2532–53.

Singer, R.N. (2002) 'Pre-performance state, routines, and automaticity: What does it take to realize expertise in self-paced tasks?', *Journal of Sport and Exercise Psychology*, 24, 359–75.

Vyse, S. (1997) *Believing in Magic: The Psychology of Superstition*. New York: Oxford University Press.

2.8 CHOKING UNDER PRESSURE

Definition: Choking under pressure is a phenomenon in which an athlete's normally expert level of performance deteriorates suddenly and significantly under conditions of perceived pressure.

At the time of writing, Rory McIlroy is still pursuing that elusive Masters title to complete a career 'grand slam' of golf's 'Majors'. In 2011, McIlroy famously led going into the last round of the Masters at Augusta, before carding a series of bogeys and driving his shot into the trees on the 13th hole, finishing on an eight-over-par score of 80. Reflecting on this episode, McIlroy later reported 'I hate using the word choke but that's exactly what happened at the Masters'.

At first glance, the term 'choking under pressure' is easy to define. Specifically, it refers to a phenomenon in which athletic performance deteriorates suddenly as a result of anxiety (Mesagno and Hill, 2013). On closer inspection, however, this definition has two main problems. To begin with, as Hill et al. (2009; 2010) have pointed out, we must be sure, for any suboptimal performance to be regarded as an example of 'choking' in sport, and not just a random lapse, that the athlete in question was *capable* of performing better than he or she did, was *motivated* sufficiently to succeed and he or she perceived the sport situation as being *important*. Second, Gucciardi and Dimmock (2008) have argued that the deterioration in performance that characterises choking should be *significant* – not trivial. As a consequence, choking is probably best defined as a phenomenon in which an athlete's normally expert level of performance deteriorates suddenly and significantly under conditions of perceived pressure. Two other features of choking are notable. First, as the term 'anxiety' is derived from the Latin word *angere* which means 'to choke', there are clear links between choking and anxiety in sport. In addition, choking is an intriguing mental state because it reflects a motivational paradox. Specifically, the more effort the 'choker' exerts on his or her performance, the more it appears to deteriorate. In short, choking is paradoxical because it occurs when anxious people try *too* hard to perform well. Not surprisingly, this phenomenon has attracted considerable attention from psychologists – ranging from coverage in popular science (e.g. Beilock, 2010) to systematic reviews of relevant research (e.g. Gröpel and Mesagno, 2019; Hill et al., 2010).

Choking is ubiquitous among competitive athletes. As Tom Watson (the former world number one golfer) remarked, 'We all choke. You just try to choke last!' (cited in MacRury, 1997: 99). It is known as the 'yips' in golf, 'icing' or 'bricking' in basketball, 'dartitis' in darts and 'bottling' in a range of sports, including soccer. Within such sports, choking is especially prevalent and visible among performers of closed, self-paced skills (i.e. actions that are executed largely at one's own speed and without interference from other performers). To illustrate, leading golfers such as Greg Norman, Stewart Cink, Scott Hoch, and perhaps most famously, Jean van de Velde (who led by three strokes at the final hole of the 1999 Open Championship at Carnoustie but who triple-bogied the hole before losing to Paul Lawrie in a play-off) have all admitted publicly that they have choked in major competitions (Dixon and Kidd, 2006). Choking has also precipitated dramatic collapses in tennis. To illustrate, consider what happened in the 1993 Wimbledon Ladies' Singles final between Jana Novotna (the Czech Republic) and Steffi Graf (Germany). Serving at 4–1 in the third set, with a point for 5–1, Novotna became anxious. She produced a double-fault and some wild shots to lose that game. Later, she served three consecutive double-faults in an attempt to increase her 4–3 lead over Graf. Interestingly, Novotna choked in a similar fashion in the third round of the 1995 French Open championship in Paris when she lost a match to the American player Chanda Rubin, despite having nine match points when leading 5–0, 40–0 in the third set.

But choking is not confined solely to athletes engaged in individual sports. It is also evident in team games (e.g. football) when precise execution of a technical skill is crucial to the outcome of the match. To illustrate, many of the world's best footballers have crumbled under the pressure of penalty-taking. For example, Roberto Baggio (Italy) blazed his kick over the bar in a penalty shootout in the 1994 soccer World Cup final – a mistake that allowed Brazil to win the trophy. In attempting to explain the phenomenon of penalty misses by highly skilled players, Jordet (2009) discovered from analysis of video footage taken at major international soccer tournaments that publicly esteemed 'superstar' players (i.e. those who had received prestigious awards for their skills) tended to perform *worse* than less renowned players in penalty shootouts – presumably because of the additional pressure of expectation that they bore in such situations.

What causes choking? Although most researchers agree that it is best regarded as an anxiety-based attentional difficulty, there is little consensus on the precise theoretical mechanisms underlying it (see **4.19**). At present, two main attentional theories of choking are especially prominent in the research literature: *distraction* theories (e.g. processing efficiency theory or PET; Eysenck and Calvo, 1992) and *self-focus* theories (e.g. Beilock and Carr, 2001; Masters, 1992). In general, distraction theories postulate that perceived pressure induces anxiety which consumes working memory resources and causes inefficient processing of task-relevant information – thereby shifting attention away from task execution. By contrast, self-focus models of choking typically propose that anxiety increases athletes' levels of self-consciousness and causes them to focus their attention inwards. This shift to self-focused attention encourages athletes to attempt to consciously monitor and/or control their skill execution which may subsequently induce choking through a form of 'paralysis by analysis' (Gröpel and Mesagno, 2019). This term refers to skill failure that can occur when people think too much about actions that are usually executed automatically. As Beilock (2010) explained, just as thinking about where to place our feet as we rush downstairs may cause us to trip, focusing deliberately on activities that normally operate outside our conscious awareness can lead to choking (see **2.5**).

One of the most influential distraction theories of choking is processing efficiency theory (PET) (Eysenck and Calvo, 1992). Briefly, PET distinguishes between processing *effectiveness* (the quality of task performance) and processing *efficiency* (the relationship between the effectiveness of performance and the effort or resources that have been invested in task performance). It predicts that the adverse effects of anxiety on performance effectiveness are often *less* than those on processing efficiency. This prediction stems from the assumption that increased effort by the performer can compensate for the reduction in attentional resources that are typically caused by anxiety. According to PET, anxious athletes may try to maintain their level of performance by investing extra effort in it. Although this increased effort investment may appear to generate immediate benefits, it soon reaches a point of diminishing returns. At this stage, the athlete may conclude that too much effort is required, and so he or she gives up. Then, his or her performance deteriorates rapidly.

Turning to self-focus accounts of choking, two theoretical approaches are especially prominent: the 'conscious processing' or reinvestment hypothesis (CPH) (Masters, 1992; Masters and Maxwell, 2008) (see **2.5**) and the 'explicit monitoring' hypothesis (EMH) (Beilock and Carr, 2001). Although these two approaches share many ideas, they differ in at least one important regard (Hill et al., 2010): whereas the EMH suggests that athletic performance is disrupted by performers *monitoring* their step-by-step execution of the skill, the CPH postulates that the disruption is caused by athletes consciously *controlling* the skill involved. Either way, self-focus models explain choking by postulating that, when people experience a great deal of pressure to perform well, they tend to think more about themselves and the importance of the event in which they are competing than they would normally. This excessive self-consciousness causes people to attempt to gain conscious control over previously automatic and well-learned skills – just as a novice would do. As a result of this attempt to invest automatic processes with conscious control, skilled performance tends to unravel. Interestingly, according to some athletes, this unravelling of skill, which is caused by thinking too much about automatic movements, may happen more frequently as one gets older. For example, consider the golfer Ian Woosnam's experience of trying to correct his putting stroke. Specifically, he said that 'putting shouldn't be hard … but that's where the mind comes in. So much is running through your mind – hold it this way, keep the blade square – whereas when you're young, you just get hold of it and hit it. When you get old too much goes through your mind' (cited in White, 2002: 22). As yet, however, this hypothesis that ageing increases the proclivity to think too much about one's sport skills remains speculative. But one individual difference variable that *has* been shown to be a reliable moderator of choking in sport is 'dispositional reinvestment' or a person's tendency to attempt to consciously control a well-learned skill under pressure (Masters et al., 1993). In an effort to measure this personality dimension, Masters et al. developed the 20-item Reinvestment Scale and found that athletes who scored lower on this test tended to perform better under pressure than counterparts who scored relatively higher. Similar results were reported by Jackson et al. (2006).

Overall, according to Gucciardi and Dimmock (2008), empirical support for distraction models of choking is strongest for tasks (e.g. mathematical computation) that depend heavily on working memory resources. By contrast, self-focus models of choking appear to be supported best by studies involving tasks that make few demands on working memory (e.g. golf putting). A good explanation for this finding comes from Beilock (2010). If we are performing a complex thinking task that drains our working memory resources, then anxiety alone can induce choking. But if we are performing a highly automatic motor skill, then worrying in itself will not lead to choking, but attempting to exert conscious control over one's automatic skills (which is a consequence of anxiety) *will* do so.

More recently, in a systematic review of distraction and self-focus models (along with interventions based on acclimatising the athlete to pressure situations; Mesagno et al., 2015), Gröpel and Mesagno (2019) found that all types of interventions aided performance under pressure, with the most effective interventions including quiet eye training, left-hand contractions and acclimatisation training, while the use of dual task helped performance under pressure in competition but not training. Mixed evidence was found for analogy learning, and no effects were reported for goal setting, neurofeedback training and reappraisal cues.

In summary, although choking under pressure is a pervasive problem in sport, as yet no consensus has been reached regarding the precise theoretical mechanisms that cause it. Nevertheless, most theories of this phenomenon agree that anxiety impairs performance by inducing the athlete to think too much, causing him or her to regress to an earlier stage of learning – effectively making him or her a beginner again.

How can we counteract choking under pressure? Until recently, little or no research had been conducted on theoretically based interventions designed to alleviate this problem. However, systematic reviews suggest that this gap in the literature is gradually being addressed (Gröpel and Mesagno, 2019). For example, Oudejans and Pijpers (2010) investigated whether exposing athletes to mild levels of anxiety (a form of simulation training) can help them to perform better under conditions that could give rise to choking. In this study, a sample of novices was assigned to one of two groups. In the experimental group, participants practised darts throwing under experimentally induced levels of mild anxiety – achieved by requiring participants to hang high rather than low on an indoor climbing wall. In the control group, participants practised without any additional anxiety. Manipulation checks using heart-rate (an index of arousal/anxiety) were conducted to ensure that the anxiety manipulation had been effective. After training, participants were tested under conditions of low, mild and high anxiety. Results showed that, despite systematic increases in anxiety, heart rate and effort from low to mid to high anxiety, the experimental group (i.e. the one that had trained under mild anxiety) performed equally well on all three tests, whereas the performance of the control group deteriorated in the high anxiety condition.

In summary, Oudejans and Pijper (2010) interpreted their results as indicating that training with mild anxiety may help to prevent performers from 'choking' under conditions of high anxiety. In a similar manner, Mesagno and Mullane-Grant (2010) examined which aspects of a pre-performance routine (PPR) (see also **2.7** and **4.19**) were most beneficial in alleviating choking among a sample of Australian football players. In this study, the footballers attempted kicks at scoring zones under conditions of low and high pressure. They were assigned to one of four different intervention groups which varied in the component of PPR used (e.g. diaphragmatic breathing, use of a 'trigger word', temporal consistency and an extensive PPR) for 15-minute sessions. Results showed that the most effective pre-performance routine in alleviating choking was one that included psychological and behavioural components and that occupied the footballers' attention prior to kick-execution.

KEY READINGS

Gröpel, P. and Mesagno, C. (2019) 'Choking interventions in sports: A systematic review', *International Review of Sport and Exercise Psychology*, 12 (1), 176–201.

Mesagno, C. and Mullane-Grant, T. (2010) 'A comparison of different pre-performance routines as possible choking interventions', *Journal of Applied Sport Psychology*, 22, 343–60.

Mesagno, C., Geukes, K. and Larkin, P. (2015) 'Choking under pressure: A review of current debates, literature, and interventions', in S. Mellalieu and S. Hanton (eds), *Contemporary Advances in Sport Psychology: A Review*. London: Routledge. pp. 148–74.

Oudejans, R.R.D. and Pijpers, J.R. (2010) 'Training with mild anxiety may prevent choking under higher levels of anxiety', *Psychology of Sport and Exercise*, 11, 44–50.

PRACTICAL QUESTIONS

- What causes choking in sport?
- A football manager has been in contact seeking advice on how to protect players from choking during penalty shootouts. What advice would you offer?

REFERENCES

Beilock, S.L. (2010) *Choke*. New York: Free Press.

Beilock, S.L. and Carr, T.H. (2001) 'On the fragility of skilled performance: What governs choking under pressure?', *Journal of Experimental Psychology: General*, 130, 701–25.

Dixon, P. and Kidd, P. (2006) 'The golf pro who missed from 3ft and lost £230,000', *The Times*, 21 March. p. 5.

Eysenck, M.W. and Calvo, M. (1992) 'Anxiety and performance: The processing efficiency theory', *Cognition and Emotion*, 6, 409–34.

Gröpel, P. and Mesagno, C. (2019)' Choking interventions in sports: A systematic review', *International Review of Sport and Exercise Psychology*, 12 (1), 176–201.

Gucciardi, D.F. and Dimmock, J.A. (2008) 'Choking under pressure in sensorimotor skills: Conscious processing or depleted attentional resources?', *Psychology of Sport and Exercise*, 9, 45–59.

Hill, D.M., Hanton, S., Fleming, S. and Matthews, N. (2009) 'A re-examination of choking in sport', *European Journal of Sport Science*, 9 (4), 203–12. DOI: 10.1080/17461390902818278.

Hill, D., Hanton, S.M., Matthews, N. and Fleming, S. (2010) 'Choking in sport: A review', *International Review of Sport and Exercise Psychology*, 3, 24–39.

Jackson, R.C., Ashford, K.J. and Norsworthy, G. (2006) 'Attentional focus, dispositional reinvestment, and skilled motor performance under pressure', *Journal of Sport and Exercise Psychology*, 28, 49–68.

Jordet, G. (2009) 'When superstars flop: Public status and choking under pressure in international soccer penalty shootouts', *Journal of Applied Sport Psychology*, 21, 125–30.

MacRury, D. (1997) *Golfers on Golf*. London: Virgin Books.

Masters, R.S.W. (1992) 'Knowledge, "knerves" and know-how: The role of explicit versus implicit knowledge in the breakdown of a complex motor skill under pressure', *British Journal of Psychology*, 83, 343–58.

Masters, R.S.W. and Maxwell, J.P. (2008) 'The theory of reinvestment', *International Review of Sport and Exercise Psychology*, 2, 160–83.

Masters, R.S.W., Polman, R.C.J. and Hammond, C.V. (1993) '"Reinvestment": A dimension of personality implicated in skill breakdown under pressure', *Personality and Individual Differences*, 14, 655–66.

Mesagno, C. and Hill, D.M. (2013) 'Definition of choking in sport: Re-conceptualization and debate', *International Journal of Sport Psychology*, 44, 267–77.

Mesagno, C. and Mullane-Grant, T. (2010) 'A comparison of different pre-performance routines as possible choking interventions', *Journal of Applied Sport Psychology*, 22, 343–60.

Mesagno, C., Geukes, K. and Larkin, P. (2015) 'Choking under pressure: A review of current debates, literature, and interventions', in S. Mellalieu and S. Hanton (eds), *Contemporary Advances in Sport Psychology: A Review*. London: Routledge. pp. 148–74.

Oudejans, R.R.D. and Pijpers, J.R. (2010) 'Training with mild anxiety may prevent choking under higher levels of anxiety', *Psychology of Sport and Exercise*, 11, 44–50.

White, J. (2002) 'Interview: Ian Woosnam', *The Guardian*, 15 July, pp. 22–3.

2.9 COPING STRATEGIES

Definition: Coping strategies are plans of actions that people follow, either in anticipation of encountering a stressor or as a direct response to stress as it occurs, in order to alleviate or manage that condition.

As earlier sections in this chapter make abundantly clear, competitive sport is a stressful experience for many athletes, regardless of ability or experience. Reflecting on her early career, Dina Asher-Smith, the fastest ever recorded British woman track athlete and current world champion at 200 metres, spoke about the challenges of managing her emotions in competition: 'I used to get nervous, [have] butterflies in my stomach and my heart rate would speed up … I used to sometimes think, "Oh, what if this doesn't go well, I'm really nervous.".' However, when considering her state of mind at present, Asher-Smith indicates that nervousness is no longer perceived as a problem, and that the pre-race adrenaline is, 'Good (and) means it's all within my control … I wasn't nervous because I knew that I had it within me'. This anectodal account indicates a successful transition from a somewhat negative relationship with her emotional state towards a more focused, approach-oriented coping style. Yet, many coping strategies, either devised by athletes themselves, and/or with coaches, can be counterproductive to performance, and even destructive to athletes' mental health. Given the ubiquity of the experience of competitive anxiety in sport (see **2.5** and **2.6**), it is vital for researchers and practitioners in the psychological community to understand the nature and efficacy of the coping strategies used by athletes to alleviate stress (Brown and Fletcher, 2017; Ford et al., 2017).

According to Lazarus and Folkman (1984: 141), coping involves 'constantly changing cognitive and behavioural efforts to manage specific external and/or internal demands that are appraised as taxing or exceeding the resources of the person'. Coping is a dynamic ongoing process that can change from situation to situation and involves any methods that a person uses in an effort to master, reduce or otherwise tolerate stress. This emphasis on the ever-changing nature of sporting demands and associated coping mechanisms raises an interesting methodological issue for research in this field. Specifically, Nicholls (2008) has pointed out that, in order to study coping as a dynamic process, researchers should collect data from repeated measures of the same person over time. However, most research on coping in sport uses static 'snapshot' designs in which participants are required to provide a single retrospective report on their coping experiences. Clearly, in order to rectify this methodological problem, researchers should prioritise the use of longitudinal designs in future studies of coping strategies, and indeed the study of competitive anxiety in sport more generally (Wagstaff et al., 2011).

In psychology, a *coping strategy* is 'a plan of action that we follow, either in anticipation of encountering a stressor or as a direct response to stress as it occurs' (Martin et al., 2009: 765) in an effort to reduce the level of stress that we experience. In their seminal work, Lazarus and Folkman (1984) postulated two main types of coping responses, 'problem-focused' and 'emotion-focused' strategies. Whereas *problem-focused* coping strategies attempt to reduce stress by tackling the stressful event or situation directly, *emotion-focused* coping strategies attempt to regulate the emotional distress that is normally elicited by a given stressor. Typical problem-focused coping strategies include obtaining as much information as possible about the stressful situation to be faced, making a plan of action by setting specific and relevant goals, increasing effort in the situation, and trying to block out the source of stress. For instance, some boxers on the way to the ring listen to music on headphones in order to drown out crowd noise, while others may play pre-recorded crowd noises during sparring and during their walk to the practice ring. By contrast, emotion-focused coping includes such strategies as seeking emotional support from others, engaging in physical relaxation exercises (e.g. deep breathing) (Hanton et al., 2020) and/or trying to change one's perception of the stressful event or situation (also called 'cognitive reappraisal').

To illustrate cognitive reappraisal in action, consider how Jack Nicklaus, who has won more golf major championships than any other player in history, changed the way he labelled the anxiety that he felt before competitions, 'Sure, you're nervous, but that's the difference between being able to win and not being able to win. And that's the fun of it, to put yourself in the position of being nervous, being excited. I never look on it as pressure. *I look on it as fun and excitement*' (cited in Gilleece, 1996: 7).

A third general coping strategy proposed by Endler and Parker (1990) is *avoidance* or removing oneself from the stressful situation. Negative effects have been shown for avoidance coping, including increased burnout across a competitive season (e.g., Madigan et al., 2020). Despite the maladaptive connotations of its name, on occasion avoidance coping may actually be helpful in competitive sport. For example, a badminton player who is worried about an impending match may seek to avoid meeting officials and other players (including his or her opponent) before the game itself by warming up alone in an effort to avoid being distracted (see Chapter 4).

Although problem-focused, emotion-focused and avoidance-coping strategies are distinguishable from each other on theoretical grounds, they may overlap considerably when practised in everyday life. To illustrate, using an example from Richards (2004), imagine an athlete who has just received bad news about an injury, and decides to go out for a drink with a friend. If this friend happens to be a physiotherapist, then the athlete may be regarded as using a combination of problem-focused coping (seeking advice on the injury from an expert), emotion-focused coping (seeking social support from a friend) and/or perhaps even avoidance (using alcohol as a temporary distraction from the stressful news).

Over the past two decades, a considerable amount of research has been conducted on coping processes among sportspeople, revealing a diversity of strategies and techniques. For example, Pété et al. (2021) conducted a survey of 526 French athletes during cessation of sporting activity due to the COVID-19 lockdown, and profiled them according to their coping strategies. A variety of coping methods were apparent, ranging from seeking social support, to denial and substance misuse. Four distinct coping profiles emerged, with those characterised by more avoidance-coping strategies being more likely to experience anxiety and stress.

To date, the literature has been characterised by a lack of consensus as to how to measure coping. For instance, the 64 studies that were included in a meta-analysis by Nicholls and Polman (2007) revealed that investigators varied considerably with respect to their choice of coping measures. As one example, Anshel et al. (2001) used the Coping Strategies Inventory; Pensgaard and Roberts (2003) employed a version of the COPE inventory (Carver et al., 1989); while Johnson (1997) used the General Coping Questionnaire. Nevertheless, based on this review and on subsequent studies (Brown and Fletcher, 2017), the following insights have emerged into the nature and efficacy of coping strategies in sport.

To begin with, research suggests that athletes turn to a wide variety of idiosyncratic problem-focused coping strategies when responding to stressful situations (Hanin, 2011).

These strategies include concentrating on goals, learning time management skills, learning about opponents, and practising. In a similar vein, commonly reported emotion-focused coping strategies include seeking social support, using mental imagery (see **4.17**), using positive self talk (see **4.20**), relying on humour, and attempting to remain confident in the face of stressful situations. Sometimes, age-related changes are evident in strategy use. For example, Reeves et al. (2009) investigated stress and coping in adolescent academy soccer players. They found that, although problem-focused coping strategies were common among all ages of players, the mid-adolescent footballers used more social support coping strategies than their early-adolescent counterparts.

Second, another issue addressed in the literature concerns the attempt to identify functional relationships between specific stressors and particular coping strategies. In this regard, Weston et al. (2009) used in-depth interviews to explore the stressors faced, and coping strategies employed, by five, single-handed, round-the-world sailors. Among the stressors experienced by these mariners were environmental hazards (e.g. isolation and sleep deprivation), competitive stressors (e.g. yacht-related difficulties) and personal issues (e.g. family problems). In response to these stressors, the sailors reported using a combination of problem-focused coping strategies (e.g. making detailed plans for what to do in various hypothetical scenarios) and emotion-focused coping strategies (e.g. relying on social support from family and supporters to counteract the isolation of single-handed sailing). Interestingly, Weston et al. acknowledged that their research did not establish specific causal or temporal links between the stressors experienced by these sailors and the resulting coping strategies adopted. However, they suggested that future research in this field could benefit from equipping participants with electronic diaries to log the time-course of their stressor-coping strategy interactions.

Third, there has been an upsurge of research interest in the coping strategies of elite coaches. For example, Olusoga et al. (2010) used in-depth interviews to investigate the responses to stress of, and coping techniques used by, a sample of world-class UK coaches from a range of sports (e.g. swimming, field hockey). Thematic analysis showed that the most frequently reported coping strategy was 'structuring and planning' – a problem-focused approach that involved using past experience to anticipate and circumvent likely stressors. Attending coaching courses and seeking continuous professional development were also widely cited as preferred coping strategies.

As a final and highly significant theme characterising research in this field, some investigators have addressed the crucial issue of the *efficacy* of coping strategies in sport. According to Nicholls and Polman (2007), coping effectiveness refers to 'the extent to which a coping strategy, or combination of strategies, is successful in alleviating the negative emotions caused by stress' (p. 15). Unfortunately, there has been a dearth of theoretically driven attempts to evaluate the efficacy of coping strategies in athletes. Nevertheless, some sport psychology researchers have tested Folkman's (1991) 'goodness of fit' proposal that problem-focused coping techniques should be used when people face personally *controllable* stressors (e.g. those arising from their own behaviour), whereas emotion-focused strategies may be more appropriate when the stressful situations are *uncontrollable* (e.g. those arising from an opponent's performance). This hypothesis was corroborated by Anshel (1996) who reported that high perceived controllability was linked to problem-focused coping strategies, whereas low perceived controllability was associated with emotion-focused coping strategies in competitive athletes. Similarly, Kim and Duda (2003) discovered that when stressors were perceived to be controllable, athletes tended to use problem-based coping strategies.

As cited previously, the study by Pété et al. (2021) has highlighted how one contemporary and insightful methodology may have the potential to advance the coping literature. The use of person-centred profiling allows each athlete to be considered as an individual rather than one member of a homogeneous group, and so distinct 'at-risk' athletes (e.g. avoidance-oriented) can thereby be targeted for specific coping interventions. Despite such encouraging findings, person-centred research on coping is in its infancy and, overall, little progress has been made in understanding the theoretical mechanisms underlying the apparent efficacy of problem-focused and emotion-focused coping strategies (Brown and Fletcher, 2017). Clearly, additional studies are required in which theoretically derived hypotheses concerning coping strategies are tested using longitudinal research designs.

KEY READINGS

Brown, D.J. and Fletcher, D. (2017) 'Effects of psychological and psychosocial interventions on sport performance: A meta-analysis', *Sports Medicine*, 47 (1), 77–99.

Nicholls, A.R. and Polman, R.C. (2007) 'Coping in sport: A systematic review', *Journal of Sports Sciences*, 25, 11–31.

Hanton, S., Mellalieu, S. and Williams, J.M. (2020) 'Understanding and managing stress in sport', in J.M. Williams and V. Crane (eds), *Applied Sport Psychology: Personal Growth to Peak Performance* (8th ed.). New York: McGraw-Hill. pp. 210–43.

Pété, E., Leprince, C., Lienhart, N. and Doron, J. (2021) 'Dealing with the impact of the COVID-19 outbreak: Are some athletes' coping profiles more adaptive than others?', *European Journal of Sport Science*, 1–27. DOI: 10.1080/17461391.2021.1873422.

PRACTICAL QUESTIONS

- Are problem-focused or emotion-focused coping strategies in sport likely to be generally more effective, and why?
- Which techniques attached to coping strategies tend to be most successful in open or closed skill sports?

REFERENCES

Anshel, M.H. (1996) 'Coping styles among adolescent competitive athletes', *Journal of Social Psychology*, 136, 311–24.

Anshel, M.H., Jamieson, J. and Raviv, S. (2001) 'Cognitive appraisals and coping strategies following acute stress among skilled competitive male and female athletes', *Journal of Sport Behavior*, 24, 128–43.

Brown, D.J. and Fletcher, D. (2017) 'Effects of psychological and psychosocial interventions on sport performance: A meta-analysis', *Sports Medicine*, 47(1), 77–99.

Carver, C.S., Scheier, M.F. and Weintraub, J.K. (1989) 'Assessing coping strategies: A theoretically based approach', *Journal of Personality and Social Psychology*, 56, 267–83.

Endler, N. and Parker, J. (1990) 'Multi-dimensional assessment of coping: A critical review', *Journal of Personality and Social Psychology*, 58, 844–54.

Folkman, S. (1991) 'Coping across the life span: Theoretical issues', in E.H. Cummings and K.H. Karraker (eds), *Life-span Developmental Psychology: Perspectives on Stress and Coping*. Hillsdale, NJ: Erlbaum. pp. 3–19.

Ford, J.L., Ildefonso, K., Jones, M.L. and Arvinen-Barrow, M. (2017) 'Sport-related anxiety: current insights', *Open Access Journal of Sports Medicine*, 8, 205–12. https://doi.org/10.2147/OAJSM.S125845

Gilleece, D. (1996) 'Breathe deeply and be happy with second', *The Irish Times*, 27 September. p. 7.

Hanin, Y.L. (2011) 'Coping with anxiety in sport', in A.R. Nicholls (ed.). *Coping in Sport: Concepts, Issues, and Related Constructs*. Hauppauge, NY: Nova Science Publishers Inc. pp. 159–75.

Hanton, S., Mellalieu, S. and Williams, J.M. (2020) 'Understanding and managing stress in sport', in J.M. Williams and V. Crane (eds), *Applied Sport Psychology: Personal Growth to Peak Performance* (8th ed.). New York: McGraw-Hill. pp. 210–43.

Johnson, U. (1997) 'Coping strategies among long-term injured competitive athletes: A study of 81 men and women in team and individual sports', *Scandinavian Journal of Medicine and Science in Sports*, 7, 367–72.

Kim, K.A. and Duda, J.L. (2003) 'The coping process: Cognitive appraisals of stress, coping strategies, and coping effectiveness', *The Sport Psychologist*, 17, 406–25.

Lazarus, R.S. and Folkman, S. (1984) *Stress, Appraisal, and Coping*. New York: Springer.

Madigan, D.J., Rumbold, J.L., Gerber, M. and Nicholls, A.R. (2020) 'Coping tendencies and changes in athlete burnout over time', *Psychology of Sport and Exercise*, 48, 101666.

Martin, G.N., Carlson, N.R. and Buskist, W. (2009) *Psychology* (4th ed.). Harlow: Pearson Education.

Nicholls, A.R. (2008) 'Coping in sport', in D. Kirk, C. Cooke, A. Flintoff and J. McKenna (eds), *Key Concepts in Sport and Exercise Sciences*. London: SAGE. pp. 109–11.

Nicholls, A.R. and Polman, R.C. (2007) 'Coping in sport: A systematic review', *Journal of Sports Sciences*, 25, 11–31.

Olusoga, P., Butt, J., Maynard, I. and Hays, K. (2010) 'Stress and coping: A study of world-class coaches', *Journal of Applied Sport Psychology*, 22, 274–93.

Pensgaard, A.M. and Roberts, G.C. (2003) 'Achievement goal orientation and the use of coping strategies among Winter Olympians', *Psychology of Sport and Exercise*, 4, 101–16.

Pété, E., Leprince, C., Lienhart, N. and Doron, J. (2021) 'Dealing with the impact of the COVID-19 outbreak: Are some athletes' coping profiles more adaptive than others?',

European Journal of Sport Science, 1–27. DOI: 10.1080/17461391.2021.1873422

Reeves, C.W., Nicholls, A.R. and Polman, J. (2009) 'Stressors and coping strategies among early and middle adolescent Premier League academy soccer players: Differences according to age', *Journal of Applied Sport Psychology*, 21, 31–48.

Richards, H. (2004) 'Coping in sport', in D. Lavallee, J. Thatcher and M.V. Jones (eds) *Coping and Emotion in Sport*. New York: Nova Science. pp. 29–51.

Wagstaff, C.R.D., Neil, R., Mellalieu, S.D. and Hanton, S. (2011) 'Key movements in directional research in competitive anxiety', in R. Neil, S. Mellalieu and S. Hanton (eds), *Coping and Emotion in Sport*. London: Taylor & Francis. pp. 143–66.

Weston, N.J.V., Thelwell, R.C., Bond, S. and Hutchings, N.V. (2009) 'Stress and coping in single-handed round-the-world ocean sailing', *Journal of Applied Sport Psychology*, 21, 468–74.

Motivation

Chapter Summary: The sport psychology literature bears witness to the many reasons why individuals take up, sustain, succeed (or fail) or finally withdraw from sport. This chapter on motivation begins with a discussion of motivational correlates for sports participation, and then introduces the construct of burnout and its mitigating impact on athletes' engagement. The use of short-, medium- and long-term goal setting as a motivational tool is described, as are some of the key theories underpinning goal-setting effectiveness. Fear of failure and the need to achieve are next described, followed by an exploration of self-determination theory, the most cited theory and explanation of motivation in sport and exercise psychology to date. Achievement goal theory is also outlined and evaluated, and the chapter then ends with a description of the origins and similarities between self-efficacy and perceived competence. In combination, these various theories have substantially progressed our understanding of motivation, including the distinction between autonomous (both intrinsic and extrinsic) and controlled motives, an appreciation of how multiple motives can relate to the same behaviour; and a recognition that the social environment, including significant others (e.g. coaches), can have a causal influence on how athletes will orient towards goal strivings in their sport, along with their sense of wellbeing.

3.10 Sport Participation: Motives and Correlates 62
3.11 Burnout and Drop-out 70
3.12 Goal Setting 76
3.13 Fear of Failure and Need to Achieve 82
3.14 Self-Determination Theory 87
3.15 Achievement Goal Theory 92
3.16 Self-Efficacy and Perceived Competence 98

3.10 SPORT PARTICIPATION: MOTIVES AND CORRELATES

Definitions: Motivation is the process that initiates, guides, and maintains behaviours, from the most basic and instinctive to the most complex and social. It involves the combination of biological, emotional, social and cognitive forces that activate, moderate and sustain behaviour. A motive is something (such as a need, want or desire) that causes a person to act.

In many ways, the Irish boxer Katie Taylor exemplifies an athlete who has reached the pinnacle of sporting success. A former international footballer, Katie went on to become an Olympic gold medallist in amateur boxing and then one of only eight professional boxers to simultaneously hold four major world titles, in the process becoming the highest paid female combat sports' athlete in history. In a 2020 interview, she reported, 'I just want to be the best I can be in every single fight', suggesting her motive to self-actualise remains undiminished. Katie maintains that the fuel for her continued motivation derives from a variety of sources, not least her love of boxing, coupled with her strong religious faith, her fervent national support, her need to achieve extrinsic and personal goals, and her desire to secure an enduring global legacy for women in sport. The interplay of such diverse motives represents a picture that is of immediate scientific and practical interest to scholars, practitioners and athletes alike.

Katie Taylor represents one of that elite group of athletes who have climbed to the summit of their chosen sport. Beneath this peak, it is estimated that 20 per cent of the global population of adults, and 40 per cent of young people, are now engaged in some form of sport participation (Hulteen et al., 2017). The vast majority of these participants are classified as no more than 'recreational', with sport now firmly embedded into cultural traditions, education and socio-political life across the globe. Yet, despite these healthy levels of engagement, between 20 and 50 per cent of adolescents drop out of sport on a yearly basis, and many elite athletes' biographies are characterised by tales of disenchantment, burnout and unmet goals, often preceding retirement. Against this backcloth, it is little wonder that the reasons for initiating and sustaining motivation for sport participation, and giving it up, have long preoccupied sport psychologists.

As should already be apparent, motivation is a complex, latent (i.e. unobservable) construct. Over time, its role in theoretical models has taken many forms, from an antecedent (i.e. an underlying cause of sports' participation), to a mediator (i.e. exerting a role in between other variables such as competence and sports' behaviour), to an outcome (i.e. a consequence of engagement). Based on a combination of one or more of these three roles, Figure 3.1 illustrates some of the diverse ways in which motivation has been modelled in contemporary sport research.

According to earlier writers in the 18th and 19th centuries, the primary motive for taking part in sport was to satisfy base instincts, with descriptions often characterised by evolutionary or psychoanalytic constructs including catharsis (see **5.29**). It was only in the 1960s that more systematic attention came to bear directly on the issue through work on intrinsic motivation (see **3.14**), albeit that these approaches were linked to earlier drive theories of motivation, such as those advanced by Hull and Spence in the 1950s.

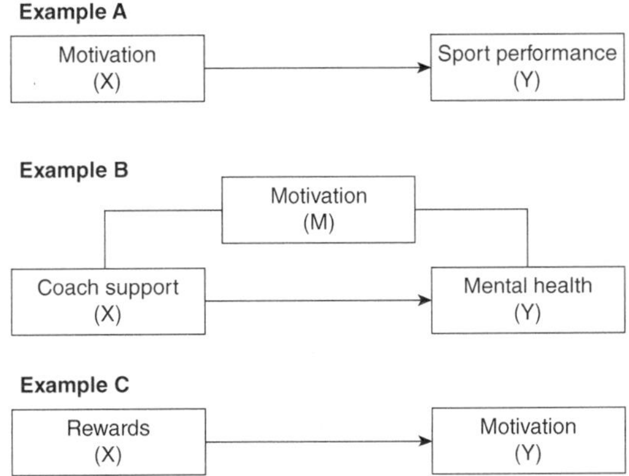

Figure 3.1 The Diverse Modelling of Sport Motivation in Contemporary Theoretical Research

Note: X = antecedent variable, M = mediator, and Y = outcome variable.

The most important pioneering model adopted by sport psychology derived from McClelland and Atkinson's research on achievement motivation (see **3.13** and **3.15**). The McClelland-Atkinson model in turn was based on a concept described in the approach–avoidance or the fight–flight response. This work reflected a wider trend in psychology during the 1970s, a time when social cognitive paradigms first rose to prominence. One of the most important was causal attribution theory (see **5.24**), although research interest in this field waned during the early 1990s, with criticisms that the theory was too general and unable to account for either the role played by emotion or large individual differences. This fuelled a call for ever-more sophisticated models which could accommodate attribution processes alongside a wider range of psychological and contextual constructs, including factors such as perceived competence.

Since that time sport psychologists have been interested both in developing theoretical frameworks for understanding sport motivation (see **3.14**, **3.15** and **3.16**), as well as describing the motives that influence why people take up and sustain sport participation, through to more recent approaches describing the mental health benefits of specific sport motivational orientations (Sheehan et al., 2018). While these perspectives vary widely in content and focus (see Figure 3.2), a commonality shared by many is the conscious deliberation of thoughts, feelings and/or values that may directly or indirectly impact on sport behaviour.

A recent review of contemporary sports motivation research by Clancy et al. (2016) cited Self-Determination Theory (SDT) as the dominant motivational theory currently adopted, although it is noteworthy that close to one-fifth of studies chose not to explicitly apply any one particular theory.

The available research is based on samples ranging from older elite athletes to young children, and has revealed diverse and changing motives across the life cycle. For example, the reasons that children typically cite for playing sport usually relate to fun and/or interest, whereas adults typically espouse the salience of social connection, perceived value and identity. It is interesting that while intrinsic motives have attracted considerable

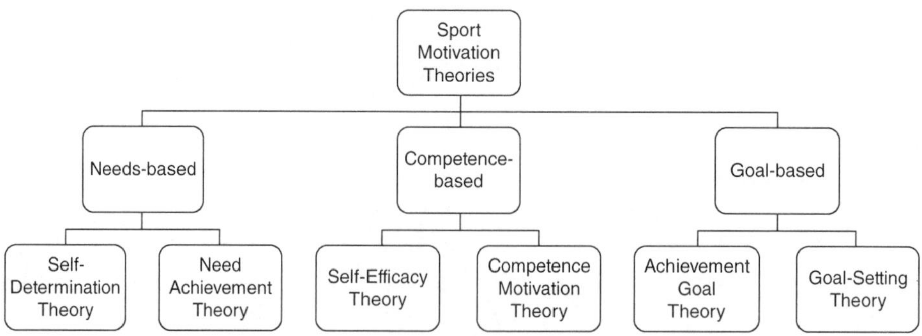

Figure 3.2 Examples of Widely Used Motivation Theories in Sport Psychology

research interest, the motive of what is actually *meant* by fun or enjoyment has been largely ignored. Reasons for withdrawal from sport have also been identified, including a lack of improvement, interest in/conflict with other activities, lack of fun, boredom, lack of playing time, excessive pressure from significant others (including parents, teachers and coaches), and competing pressures on time (e.g. school work and exams).

In the literature, increasingly the construct 'amotivation' has been used to capture the state of lacking an intention to continue with sport, or in other words, 'going through the motions'. Around adolescence in particular, subsequent withdrawal from sport can then be temporary or permanent being either specific to a particular activity or a total rejection of sport in all its forms. Estimates of withdrawal rates from sport vary depending on the sport in question and the populations under scrutiny. For example, Fraser-Thomas et al. (2018) reported a yearly withdrawal rate of 20–50 per cent in young people, with particular sports (e.g. swimming), gender (i.e. girls) and age groupings (i.e. pre-adulthood) revealing drop-out rates that are far higher.

As will be already apparent, the literature on sport motivation is vast and continues to expand. In subsequent sections we will delve further into the 'what', 'why' and 'how' of engagement in sport but, to set the scene, a brief summary of the most significant sport motivation correlates is presented below.

MOOD STATE

Not surprisingly, the literature confirms a positive relationship between sport participation and positive moods (e.g. contentment, satisfaction and enjoyment), while also linking negative mood states with disengagement (e.g. depression, anxiety and tension). Early reliance on only one measure, the Profile of Mood States Questionnaire (POMS), may have thwarted deeper exploration of the complexities of the relationships between sport participation and both positive and negative affect, operating as two independent factors. Furthermore, research has often disregarded the issue of causality – does being in a good mood encourage physical exercise or does exercise improve our mood? The answer is probably both, but later research using measures that make a clearer distinction between positive and negative states (e.g. Positive Affect Negative Affect Schedule or PANAS) has helped to advance our understanding. As one example, increased frequency of engagement in organised sport has been found to be associated with positive affect and overall mental health (Doré et al., 2019). Moreover, a meta-analysis by Panza et al. (2020) showed that symptoms of anxiety and depression were significantly lower among sport-involved adolescents than in those not involved in sport. Physical activity accumulated through sport may affect the links between mood state and sport participation, and the role played by mediating variables, both psychological (including self-efficacy) and structural (including significant others), would suggest that a complex interplay is at work where, for example, friendships can improve mood state, which in turn can increase the likelihood of taking part in sport, which in turn can enhance mood state even further.

ENJOYMENT

A construct closely related to positive mood is enjoyment (or fun) and, especially in youth sport, enjoyment is considered the greatest predictor of sustained engagement, with lack of enjoyment the most frequently cited predictor of sport withdrawal (Crane and Temple, 2015). Several large-scale surveys have shown that children's reasons for taking part in sport change as they grow older, with an increased emphasis on competition and fitness at the expense of enjoyment. Foster et al. (2007) found that factors such as a dislike of team sports, gender and cultural stereotyping of certain sports, the costs of participation in organised sports and an increasing emphasis on technical and performance issues at the expense of fun are all 'turn-offs' for young children (under 8 years old), while the 'turn-ons' were enjoyment, parental and peer support and age-appropriate activities. Among adults, the best predictors of enjoyment have been found to be mastery, good performance, effort, sports' importance and psychological wellbeing.

In contrast with affect and mood, enjoyment has only begun to receive theoretical and methodological attention in the past decade through, for example, Fun Integration Theory (FIT) (Visek et al., 2015). FIT distinguishes four fundamental factors for youth enjoyment: social (e.g. friendships), internal (e.g. learning and improving), external (e.g. positive coaching) and contextual (e.g. game time). Enjoyment is also integral in the recently developed Supportive, Active, Autonomous, Fair, Enjoyable (SAAFE) principles (Lubans et al., 2017). SAAFE is an evidence-based and theoretically informed framework designed to guide the planning, delivery and evaluation of organised physical activity sessions in school, community sport and after-school sports programmes.

SIGNIFICANT OTHERS

Other people often play a critical role in determining patterns of motivation and sport participation throughout life, and they are of critical importance in determining early initiation into a sport. Hellstedt (1987) first referred to the critical role played by the 'athletic triangle' of athlete, coach and parent. A recent review of 111 studies into youth sport (Howie et al., 2020) identified the significant role that parents play in facilitating youth sports participation, although Kim et al. (2018) also established that parents are becoming increasingly worried about placing their children in unsafe environments that may cause injuries such as concussion, and thus may discourage engagement.

Over time, research would suggest that the relative importance of significant others changes. While adults, including parents, teachers and coaches, may be critical in the early stages of engagement, peer influences become increasingly important into adolescence. Among adults it is work colleagues, health professionals, family and friends who exert the strongest influence. Notably, adults and particularly older adults, report that their responsibilities for the participation of significant others (e.g. children and grandchildren) may paradoxically hinder their own participation in sport (Jenkin et al., 2018).

HEALTH AND FITNESS

Research consistently points to the significance of health-related motives for participation, most especially as we grow older. However, according to Allender et al. (2006), health benefits *per se* are not usually cited as the primary motive but instead factors such as weight management, enjoyment, social interaction and support are more likely to exert a direct influence. Somewhat ironically, research has established that more relaxed, playful forms of sport and recreation, conceived as an end in and of themselves, have greater potential to enhance wellbeing as compared to sport participation aiming to achieve health outcomes such as weight regulation (Jetzke and Mutz, 2019). Some authors and policy makers have argued that, in order to increase societal health motives through sport participation, it is imperative that sporting structures and cultures be carefully tailored. That is, public health should be intentionally embedded in the delivery of sport, rather than the current approach of implanting health objectives into existing approaches that predominantly value performance and success (Haycock et al., 2020).

ACTIVITY CHOICE

The extensive literature describing leisure activity among young people reveals that choice of activity is an important predictor of sport participation. For example, in the aforementioned SAAFE principles, Lubans et al. (2017) cite the extensive research showing that young people who feel they can make meaningful sporting choices are more likely to be intrinsically motivated, and find sporting activities enjoyable and interesting. In addition, culturally valued sports often remain more attractive than others. For example, the native Irish sports of Gaelic football and hurling remain the most widely participated sports in Ireland, despite the attraction and availability of international sports such as soccer and rugby union.

A gender effect may also be present in activity choice such that, traditionally, boys have tended to opt for competitive team sports that emphasise competence and physical prowess, whereas girls have been more inclined to choose individual, non-competitive activities (see **7.37**). However, these historical trends are becoming less marked over time, with female participation in competitive team sports such as soccer, rugby and boxing steadily increasing. Furthermore, among young people in general there has been a shift away from organised activities and towards individual activity, for example, extreme sports and combat.

STRUCTURAL BARRIERS

Along with the psychological factors listed below, there are many real and concrete barriers that have an immediate impact on participation opportunities. Despite good intentions and strong motivations, it is these obstacles that in real terms often prevent regular participation. These include, for example, transport and the presence of a sporting/recreational infrastructure

(Davison and Lawson, 2006), life transitions, and cost and time (Somerset and Hoare, 2018). Among adolescents, lack of time and conflict with other activities are cited as the most important reasons for sport disengagement, while in adults, employment, socioeconomic factors and family responsibilities are most often mentioned (Jenkin et al., 2018).

Specifically, and with increased age, perceived risk of injury becomes increasingly important (Biddle and Nigg, 2000), with gender differences also remaining (see **7.37**). For example, in a review of UK sport policy and participation, Rowe et al. (2013) contended that gender factors often still stood in the way of regular participation for girls, fuelled by an early socialisation process that frames competitive sport as 'unfeminine'. Alongside gender, structural inequalities attached to class and income result in difficulty in accessing facilities, the poor state of those facilities and the costs attached to joining sporting clubs and fitness gyms. Also, critical stages in life (e.g. leaving school, having children, children leaving home, retirement) all had a significant impact on participation, drop-out and future reasons for participation.

KEY READINGS

Clancy, R., Herring, M., MacIntyre, T. and Campbell, M. (2016) 'A review of competitive sport motivation research', *Psychology of Sport and Exercise*, 27, 232–42.

Crane, J. and Temple, V. (2015) 'A systematic review of dropout from organized sport among children and youth', *European Physical Education Review*, 21, 114–31.

Fraser-Thomas, J., Falcão, W. and Wolman, L. (2018) 'Understanding take-up, drop-out and drop-off in youth sport', in K. Green and A. Smith (eds), *Routledge Handbook of Youth Sport*. London: Routledge. pp. 227–42.

Howie, K., Daniels, B. and Guagliano, M. (2020) 'Promoting physical activity through youth sports programs: It's social', *American Journal of Lifestyle Medicine*, 14 (1), 78–88.

PRACTICAL QUESTIONS

- Outline the key psychological reasons why young people drop out of sport, and what practical steps can be taken to reduce drop-out rates?
- How can positive and negative affect be robustly measured in practical sport settings over time, and how can these results be used to enhance motivation and performance levels?

REFERENCES

Allender, S., Cowburn, G. and Foster, C. (2006) 'Understanding participation in sport and physical activity among children and adults: A review of qualitative studies', *Health Education Research*, 21, 826–35.

Biddle, S.J.H. and Nigg, C.R. (2000) 'Theories of exercise behavior', *International Journal of Sport Psychology*, 31, 290–304.

Clancy, R.B., Herring, M.P., MacIntyre, T.E. and Campbell, M.J. (2016) 'A review of competitive sport motivation research', *Psychology of Sport and Exercise*, 27, 232–42.

Crane, J. and Temple, V. (2015) 'A systematic review of dropout from organized sport among children and youth', *European Physical Education Review*, 21, 114–31.

Davison, K. and Lawson, C. (2006) 'Do attributes in the physical environment influence children's physical activity? A review of the literature', *International Journal of Behavioral Nutrition and Physical Activity*, 3, 3–19.

Doré, I., Sabiston, C.M., Sylvestre, M.P., Brunet, J., O'Loughlin, J., Abi Nader, P., ... and Bélanger, M. (2019) 'Years participating in sports during childhood predicts mental health in adolescence: A 5-year longitudinal study', *Journal of Adolescent Health*, 64 (6), 790–96.

Foster, C., Cowburn, G., Allender, S. and Pearce-Smith, N. (2007) *Physical Activity and Children Review.* London: NICE Public Health Collaborating Centre – Physical Activity.

Fraser-Thomas, J., Falcão, W. and Wolman, L. (2018) 'Understanding take-up, drop-out and drop-off in youth sport', in K. Green and A. Smith (eds), *Routledge Handbook of Youth Sport*. London: Routledge. pp. 227–42.

Haycock, D., Jones, J. and Smith, A. (2020) 'Developing young people's mental health awareness through education and sport: Insights from the Tackling the Blues programme', *European Physical Education Review*, 26 (3), 664–681.

Hellstedt, J.C. (1987) 'The coach/parent/athlete relationship', *The Sport Psychologist*, 1 (2), 151–60.

Howie, E.K., Daniels, B.T. and Guagliano, J.M. (2020) 'Promoting physical activity through youth sports programs: It's social', *American Journal of Lifestyle Medicine*, 14 (1), 78–88. (Published online 2018.)

Hulteen, R.M., Smith, J.J., Morgan, P.J., Barnett, L.M., Hallal, P.C., Colyvas, K. and Lubans, D.R. (2017) 'Global participation in sport and leisure-time physical activities: A systematic review and meta-analysis', *Preventive Medicine*, 95, 14–25.

Jenkin, C.R., Eime, R.M., Westerbeek, H. and van Uffelen, J.G. (2018) 'Sport for adults aged 50+ years: Participation benefits and barriers', *Journal of Aging and Physical Activity*, 26 (3), 363–71.

Jetzke, M. and Mutz, M. (2019) 'Sport for pleasure, fitness, medals or slenderness? Differential effects of sports activities on well-being', *Applied Research in Quality of Life*, 1–16.

Kim, S., Connaughton, D.P., Leeman, R.F. and Lee, J.H. (2018) 'Concussion knowledge of youth sport athletes, coaches, and parents: A review', *Journal of Amateur Sport*, 4 (1), 82–107.

Lubans, D.R., Lonsdale, C., Cohen, K., Eather, N., Beauchamp, M.R., Morgan, P.J. and Smith, J.J. (2017) 'Framework for the design and delivery of organized physical activity sessions for children and adolescents: Rationale and description of the "SAAFE" teaching principles', *International Journal of Behavioral Nutrition and Physical Activity*, 14 (1), 1–11.

Panza, M.J., Graupensperger, S., Agans, J.P., Doré, I., Vella, S.A. and Evans, M.B. (2020) 'Adolescent sport participation and symptoms of anxiety and depression: A systematic review and meta-analysis', *Journal of Sport and Exercise Psychology*, 42 (3), 201–18.

Rowe, K., Shilbury, D., Ferkins, L. and Hinckson, E. (2013) 'Sport development and physical activity promotion: An integrated model to enhance collaboration and understanding', *Sport Management Review*, 16 (3), 364–77.

Sheehan, R.B., Herring, M.P. and Campbell, M.J. (2018) 'Associations between motivation and mental health in sport: A test of the hierarchical model of intrinsic and extrinsic motivation', *Frontiers in Psychology*, 9, 707.

Somerset, S. and Hoare, D.J. (2018) 'Barriers to voluntary participation in sport for children: A systematic review', *BMC Pediatrics*, 18 (1), 1–19.

Visek, A.J., Achrati, S.M., Mannix, H.M., McDonnell, K., Harris, B.S. and DiPietro, L. (2015) 'The fun integration theory: Toward sustaining children and adolescents sport participation', *Journal of Physical Activity and Health*, 12 (3), 424–33.

3.11 BURNOUT AND DROP-OUT

Definition: Burnout is a chronic psychological syndrome characterised by a reduced sense of accomplishment, a devaluing of or resentment towards sport, coupled with physical and emotional exhaustion. Drop-out is either total or partial disengagement from sport.

There can be few labels in sport more difficult to shoulder than 'The next …' Whether 'The next Rory McIlroy', or 'The next Lucy Bronze', all sports are littered with athletes who are tipped to be 'The next big thing' but sadly too often those athletes who have been earmarked for stardom end up failing to realise expectations and so become disenchanted with their sport and then leave. A word often invoked to describe this scenario is *burnout*, but what precisely do we mean by the term, how does it relate to motivation, is it automatically linked to *drop-out*, and, finally, and of most interest to practitioners, what can be done to prevent it?

In a thought-provoking article, Raedeke (1997) suggested that the term 'burnout' itself as a metaphor has intuitive appeal and resonance, and especially when coupled with descriptions of athletes as sports *stars*. Imagine a young star, burning bright in the firmament, before the talent fades and dies. In short, the term itself is poetic. However, poetic terms rarely make for quantifiable scientific phenomena, and so is the case with burnout. Many of the difficulties surrounding the definition and measurement of burnout in sport have been fuelled by the fact that the term originated outside the sport psychology literature. In fact, the early and influential studies into burnout are to be found in professional contexts that include drug rehabilitation volunteers and poverty lawyers. In these studies and contexts, burnout was often defined as the chronic experience of emotional exhaustion, depersonalisation and impaired performance, and while there may be parallels, it should not be assumed that there is necessarily a direct read-across to the world of sport.

In the early 2000s, sport-specific definitions of burnout began to emerge, along with the development and adoption of sport-specific measurements including the Athlete Burnout Questionnaire (ABQ). The broadly accepted definition of athlete burnout is: 'A chronic psychological syndrome characterised by a reduced sense of accomplishment; a devaluing of, or resentment towards sport; and physical and emotional exhaustion' (Raedeke et al., 2002). Within the literature there has been much debate as to the potential overlap between the concepts of overtraining and burnout, and also chronic stress and burnout. Although exhaustion is a core characteristic of burnout (Gustafsson et al., 2016), the multidimensional burnout definition extends beyond overtraining and stress alone. Most relevant to the present chapter, a recent expert statement on burnout (Madigan et al., 2019) indicated that there is sound evidence that burnout has deleterious consequences including depressed mood, reduced performance and sport withdrawal, and furthermore, the aetiology of burnout can in part stem from motivational processes.

To understand how such conclusions have been drawn, it is important to establish the theoretical and methodological underpinnings of the term burnout. Historically, explanations of burnout were rooted in stress models, with Smith's (1986) cognitive-affective model exerting perhaps the greatest influence. Stress was theorised as the physiological response to the perception that the athlete lacks the resources to meet the demands of a given situation. When the athlete consistently and repeatedly perceives an inability to cope with demands it may ultimately make them feel that they lack control over the situation, leading to feelings such as resentment and reduced accomplishment, as well as physical and emotional exhaustion associated with chronic stress (see **2.5** and **7.40**). While there is a widely accepted value in this account of burnout, it is not without its limitations. As Raedeke (1997) has pointed out, in the stress-based account of burnout, where is the line of demarcation between stress and burnout? Or to take the logic one step further, why does every stressed athlete not experience burnout, or ultimately drop out?

One of the key additional theoretical explanations of burnout that has emerged to address these dilemmas emphasises the importance of *commitment*. Schmidt and Stein (1991) proposed that athletes may *choose* to remain in a chronically stressful situation because of their high levels of commitment. Commitment is defined by the interplay of satisfaction, alternative courses of action and investments. It is at the point when commitment outweighs perceived stress (or vice versa) that the difference between drop-out and burnout may be delineated. In a stressful situation, an individual with better options and limited investment is likely to walk away while the individual who has invested a great deal in his/her sport may begin to feel trapped. This precludes drop-out, but may lead to the feelings associated with burnout. In support of this suggestion, Li et al. (2013) reported that athletes who presented higher levels of controlled extrinsic (rather than autonomous extrinsic or intrinsic) motivation went on to display higher levels of burnout. In short, a reliance on controlled motives refers to athletes who feel they *must* continue in their sport to solely satisfy an external outcome, rather than *wanting* to remain in their sport for the sake of personal congruence or intrinsic reasons.

A self-determination theory (SDT) perspective on burnout (Deci and Ryan, 2000) relates to how individuals are motivated to fulfil their basic psychological needs for autonomy, competence and relatedness, which in combination are assumed to be essential for wellness (see **3.14**). Specifically, sporting behaviours that are driven via controlled motives, and are engaged with so as to avoid negative outcomes (Lemyre et al., 2006), are more likely to result in burnout (Bartholomew et al, 2011), while behaviours motivated by high degrees of autonomy (or self-determination) are likely to reduce burnout symptoms (Hancox et al., 2018).

An additional theory of burnout was presented by Coakley (1992) who proposed that a narrowly defined identity may lead to a feeling of entrapment in the role of an athlete (see **7.38**). The premise of Coakley's model was that social organisation of sport was causing burnout in athletes due to a lack of control and identity constriction (see **5.31**). Some research has supported the tenets of Coakley's model, including the finding that a lack of perceived control is related to burnout. However, others (Gustafsson et al., 2016) have criticised Coakley's reliance solely on a convenience sample when formulating the tenets of the model.

Gustafsson et al. (2011, 2016) have acknowledged that each theoretical model of burnout has shown at least some predictive ulitity, while recognising that burnout had been modelled in a great many diverse and often contradictory ways. For example, some studies applied the term burnout to mean either a consequence or an antecedent of motivation. To reconcile these inconsistencies, Gustafsson et al. (2011) developed an integrated model (see Figure 3.3) that includes antecedents, early signs, consequences, as well as factors that influence the burnout process, including motivational climate and self-regulatory orientations.

While undoubtedly there has been progress towards the development of theoretical models of athlete burnout, an area receiving ongoing critical attention is the measurement of the burnout construct. The Athlete Burnout Questionnaire (ABQ; Raedeke and Smith, 2001) has shown sound internal psychometric properties, and practical utility in the monitoring and detection of burnout among athletes and coaches (Madigan et al., 2019). However, in one of the pioneering longitudinal measurement studies of the ABQ, Gerber et al. (2018) highlighted methodological concerns including the fact that the ABQ dimensions shared limited variance, did not predict each other across time and none of the ABQ subscales was suitable for the screening of clinically relevant burnout symptoms.

Aside from their heuristic or academic value, existing models of burnout have had limited success in helping frame positive and practical interventions in the field, with the exception of burnout prevention where the modelling of theoretical variables has helped

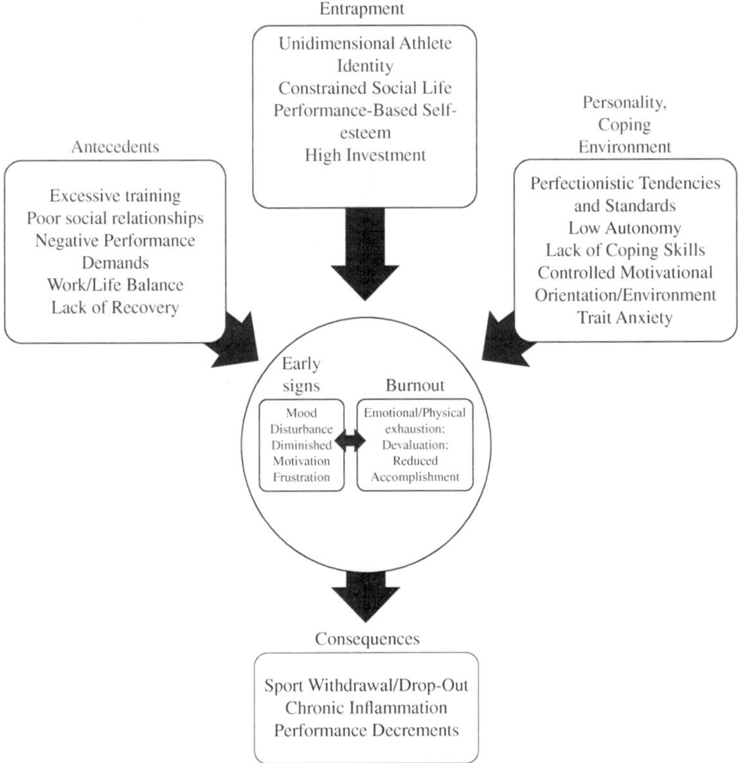

Figure 3.3 An Integrated Model of Athlete Burnout (adapted from Gustaffson et al., 2011; included with permission)

identify potential warning signs that burnout may be on the horizon. In an SDT-based intervention study, Langan et al. (2015) showed that athletes' burnout levels remained low to moderate and stable across a competitive season when their coaches received training in techniques that engendered a positive motivational climate. In terms of individual motivation, Lemyre et al. (2006) report that a shift towards extrinsic motivation is associated with feelings of burnout. In practice the picture is of an athlete who has forgotten the enjoyment that they first experienced when they started playing sport and have become consumed by other external factors, whether that be pressure from others, money, celebrity status or the other numerous potential distractions that young elite athletes face daily. Furthermore, a systematic review and meta-analysis of burnout from an SDT perspective (Li et al., 2013) also revealed that intrinsic motivation exerted a preventive role in burnout symptomology.

In terms of the stress models of burnout, two broad categories of burnout precursors have emerged: stressors and resources. In terms of stressors, Cresswell (2009) points to what he describes as 'hassles'. In particular, it is reported that in longitudinal studies sport-specific hassles (in his example, within rugby) and money hassles are associated with future feelings of burnout. In terms of resources, Cresswell also reports that the perception of a low level of social support can be associated with future feelings of burnout. Additional to this is the finding that exhaustion, in particular emotional exhaustion, is a central factor in burnout (Goodger et al., 2007). Other factors that have been associated with burnout include frustration due to injury or non-selection and feelings of limited performance improvement (Cresswell and Eklund, 2007). Finally, in terms of perceptions of entrapment, it has been reported that financial constraints, as well as a sense of loyalty, can lead athletes to remain locked in stressful situations, potentially leading to burnout (Boiché and Sarrazin, 2008).

Reflecting on the numerous athletes who become disenchanted with their sport and ultimately 'burned out', theories have helped us understand that some perceive overwhelming stress, feel pressured by external forces or actors, while some may feel sport provides limited satisfaction for their basic psychological needs. There can be little dispute that these stories of burnout are unfortunate and often tragic, not only on a sporting level but also on a human level. However, a review of the burnout literature (Gustafsson et al., 2016) gives some cause for optimism. Research has progressed to the point that there is now a broadly accepted definition of burnout and a useful validated measure to monitor burnout symptoms. Hence, future preventative work can now be well informed by a growing research base that is able to identify the precursors and mediators of burnout. What will serve the field, and athletes, well will be the appetite of practitioners and researchers to move towards the development of well validated intervention methods to help ensure that 'The next big thing' lives up to his or her potential, and if they do not, that they may continue to find solace in sport participation for its own sake.

KEY READINGS

Gustafsson, H., DeFreese, J.D. and Madigan, D.J. (2017) 'Athlete burnout: Review and recommendations', *Current Opinion in Psychology*, 16, 109–13.

Langan, E., Toner, J., Blake, C. and Lonsdale, C. (2015) 'Testing the effects of a self-determination theory-based intervention with youth Gaelic football coaches on athlete motivation and burnout', *The Sport Psychologist*, 29 (4), 293–301.

Madigan, D.J., Gustafsson, H., Smith, A., Raedeke, T. and Hill, A.P. (2019) 'The BASES expert statement on burnout in sport', *The Sport and Exercise Scientist*, 61, 6–7.

Raedeke, T.D. (1997) 'Is athlete burnout more than stress? A sport commitment perspective', *Journal of Sport and Exercise Psychology*, 19, 396–417.

PRACTICAL QUESTIONS

- Explain how stress and burnout are commonly confused in sport, and how is this reflected in the design of intervention programmes?
- What are the characteristics of the three constructs that constitute athlete burnout?

REFERENCES

Bartholomew, K.J., Ntoumanis, N., Ryan, R.M. and Thøgersen-Ntoumani, C. (2011) 'Psychological need thwarting in the sport context: Assessing the darker side of athletic experience', *Journal of Sport and Exercise Psychology*, 33 (1), 75–102.

Boiché, J. and Sarrazin, P.G. (2008) 'Proximal and distal factors associated with dropout versus maintained participation in organized sport', *Journal of Sports Science and Medicine*, 8 (1), 9–16.

Coakley, J. (1992) 'Burnout among adolescent athletes: A personal failure or social problem?', *Sociology of Sport Journal*, 9, 271–85.

Cresswell, S.L. (2009) 'Possible early signs of athlete burnout: A prospective study', *Journal of Science and Medicine in Sport*, 12, 393–8.

Cresswell, S.L. and Eklund, R.C. (2007) 'Athlete burnout: A longitudinal qualitative study', *The Sport Psychologist*, 21, 1–20.

Deci, E.L. and Ryan, R.M. (2000) 'The "what" and "why" of goal pursuits: Human needs and the self-determination of behavior', *Psychological Inquiry*, 11 (4), 227–68.

Gerber, M., Gustafsson, H., Seelig, H., Kellmann, M., Ludyga, S., Colledge, F. and Bianchi, R. (2018) 'Usefulness of the Athlete Burnout Questionnaire (ABQ) as a screening tool for the detection of clinically relevant burnout symptoms among young elite athletes', *Psychology of Sport and Exercise*, 39, 104–13.

Goodger, K., Gorely, T., Lavallee, D. and Harwood, C. (2007) 'Burnout in sport: A systematic review', *The Sport Psychologist*, 21, 127–51.

Gustafsson, H., Kenttä, G. and Hassmén, P. (2011) 'Athlete burnout: An integrated model and future research directions', *International Review of Sport and Exercise Psychology*, 4 (1), 3–24.

Gustafsson, H., Lundkvist, E., Podlog, L. and Lundqvist, C. (2016) 'Conceptual confusion and potential advances in athlete burnout research', *Perceptual and Motor Skills*, 123 (3), 784–91.

Gustafsson, H., DeFreese, J.D. and Madigan, D.J. (2017) 'Athlete burnout: Review and recommendations', *Current Opinion in Psychology*, 16, 109–13.

Hancox, J.E., Quested, E., Ntoumanis, N. and Thøgersen-Ntoumani, C. (2018) 'Putting self-determination theory into practice: Application of adaptive motivational principles in the exercise domain', *Qualitative Research in Sport, Exercise and Health*, 10 (1), 75–91.

Lemyre, P., Treasure, D.C. and Roberts, G.C. (2006) 'Influence of variability in motivation and affect on elite athlete burnout susceptibility', *Journal of Sport and Exercise Psychology*, 28, 32–48.

Langan, E., Toner, J., Blake, C. and Lonsdale, C. (2015) 'Testing the effects of a self-determination theory-based intervention with youth Gaelic football coaches on athlete motivation and burnout', *The Sport Psychologist*, 29 (4), 293–301.

Li, C., Wang, C.J. and Kee, Y.H. (2013) 'Burnout and its relations with basic psychological needs and motivation among athletes: A systematic review and meta-analysis', *Psychology of Sport and Exercise*, 14 (5), 692–700.

Madigan, D.J., Gustafsson, H., Smith, A., Raedeke, T. and Hill, A.P. (2019) 'The BASES expert statement on burnout in sport', *The Sport and Exercise Scientist*, 61, 6–7.

Raedeke, T.D. (1997) 'Is athlete burnout more than stress? A sport commitment perspective', *Journal of Sport and Exercise Psychology*, 19, 396–417.

Raedeke, T.D. and Smith, A.L. (2001) 'Development and preliminary validation of an athlete burnout measure', *Journal of Sport and Exercise Psychology*, 23, 281–306.

Raedeke, T.D., Lunney, K. and Venables, K. (2002) 'Understanding athlete burnout: Coach perspectives', *Journal of Sport Behavior*, 25, 181–206.

Schmidt, G.W. and Stein, G.L. (1991) 'A commitment model of burnout', *Journal of Applied Sport Psychology*, 8, 323–45.

Smith, R.E. (1986) 'Toward a cognitive-affective model of athlete burnout', *Journal of Sport Psychology*, 8, 36–50.

3.12 GOAL SETTING

Definition: Goal setting is a motivational technique based on the principle of establishing specific and challenging short-term goals in order to move towards the realisation of long-term targets or objectives.

In elite sport, setting goals is something that most athletes now generally believe in and practise (e.g. Burton et al., 1998). What is more, evidence has shown it to be effective in enhancing athletic performance such as strength capacity (Tod et al., 2015), as well as improving autonomous goal functioning motivation, and wellbeing (Healy et al., 2014). Reports by Ireland runner Ciara Mageen in 2020 highlight how her accomplishment as the first Irish woman to finish 800m in under two minutes (1:59.69), was, 'On my list for years and I finally ticked it off. Now I just want to go faster', neatly encapsulating the cyclical process of setting and meeting long- and short-term goals. However, despite its popularity, whether sound theory is guiding goal-setting practices among most athletes and coaches is unlikely, and it is difficult to underestimate the range, diversity and scope of goals that modern athletes typically incorporate into their career development plans. As a consequence, setting goals does not automatically result in performance gains, with many coaches and athletes unwittingly setting unregulated goals that end up as counterproductive to motivation and subsequent performance. Without question, goal setting has enjoyed a chequered history in sport, leaving many questions still unanswered, perhaps including the most critical of all: what is the ultimate goal of an athlete's career?

It is no coincidence that goals have been of longstanding interest in both the psychology of business and the psychology of sport. Indeed, empirical goal-setting research has been established for over a century (James, 1890). But what precisely constitutes a goal? Do the lessons of goal setting in the world of business apply to the world of sport? What are the various types of goals? Is it beneficial for an athlete to set goals and, if so, which type of goals? It is with these questions in mind that the goal-setting literature will now be examined.

To begin, defining what constitutes a goal is not difficult. A goal may be defined as an objective that an individual is seeking to achieve through a particular course of action. Goals may not always be conscious; indeed, it has been suggested that they are likely to drift in and out of conscious thought (Locke and Latham, 1990). Goals can also be short-, medium- and long-term, and can be categorised into three types: process goals, performance goals and outcome goals. Each goal category effectively builds on the other, with process goals typically characterised as forming the foundation of the athlete's career. Process goals are under the athlete's control and pertain to concerns such as technique and strategy that are thought to be needed to achieve a successful outcome. They are the *how* of sport. Performance goals reflect the athletes' own personal application of their athletic skill. They are the *what* of sport, for example, a basketball player's free-throw percentage. Outcome goals are, to a degree, the result of how well an athlete performs. They are victories, championships and financial rewards. Effectively, they are the *why* of sport.

Burton et al. (1998) emphasised that deliberate goal-setting techniques often appear straightforward but are usually far more complicated in practice. Historically, Locke and Latham's (1990) theory of goal setting (GST) was a watershed for the field as it provided the basis for goal setting to be widely applied in business settings. There are two core tenets of GST, namely: (a) a linear relationship exists between goal difficulty and performance, and this is moderated by four factors: ability, commitment (or acceptance), feedback and resources; and (b) specific, difficult goals are held to lead to higher performance compared to no goals or vague, unattainable goals. As such, Locke (2015) theorised that goal setting affects performance through four mediating mechanisms: by focusing attention; by activating appropriate levels of effort; by enhancing persistence; and by encouraging the development of strategies to achieve the stated goal. A further critical development of GST was the characterisation of both a learning goal and a performance goal, which may coexist or act independently of each other, depending on the context and circumstances (Locke, 2015).

Whilst GST was orginally developed for business settings, the unique characteristics of sport led to complementary developments with empirical insights that were increasingly sport-specific. For example, sport is likely to entail a more explicit focus on competition and individual athletes' desire to win. Business, by contrast, is more often characterised by corporate thinking, as well as a more hierarchical structure that can see certain goals dictated from above. This leads to the question, how effective is goal setting in sport-specific settings?

In practice, GST principles have been reflected in sport by interventions such as SMART Goal Setting: that is, the setting of goals that are Specific, Measurable, Action-Oriented, Realistic and Timely. Linked with further work on self-appraisal, Richard Butler popularised goal setting alongside *performance profiling* with his visually appealing profiling dartboard, first used with Olympic boxers (Butler, 1996). This involves listing the range of attributes around the rim of the dartboard and then shading each segment up to a maximum of ten with two colours, one showing 'where you are now', the other 'where you want to be'. This profile then acts as a masterplan for subsequent goal setting, and allows change or improvement over time to be easily recorded.

The addition of the Self Concordance Model (Sheldon and Elliott, 1999) with Achievement Goal Theory (AGT) revealed that self-selected goals are typically more effective for autonomous motivation, effort and goal attainment than prescribed goals, with the latter largely resulting in controlled motives which are short-lived. Moreover, the integration of GST with AGT and SDT has led to the proposition that athletes are more likely to pursue sporting goals for autonomous motives when their coaches use needs-supportive behaviours (e.g. offering choice, seeking athlete input) and avoid needs-controlling behaviours (e.g., controlling language, intimidation) (Healy et al., 2016).

In reviewing the vast literature that has developed around goal setting, Healy et al. (2018) concluded that, in the right hands, goal-setting can be an important and valuable process which is able to help athletes enhance their performance and experience within sport. Specifically, goals are effective when progressive (e.g., stepping-stone approach) and continuous (i.e. sequenced into short-, medium- and long-term timeframes), and athletes are given space to autonomously consider and choose their own goals, while accepting the dynamic, challenging, trajectory of goal pursuits. The evidence base for such a conclusion is broad, incorporating evidence from various sport settings and research designs, including the experimental.

Contemporary meta-analytic studies of goal setting remain somewhat limited but earlier reviews suggest that goal setting can be part of an effective intervention. Specifically, in their comprehensive review of 88 sport-specific studies into goal setting, Burton and Weiss (2008) reported that 80 per cent of these studies found a moderate to strong effect on performance. Butt and Weinberg (2020) further emphasised the positive perceptions of goals by elite athletes. However, when restricted to non-self-report performances (e.g. objective times, scores), effect sizes in sport-based goal-setting interventions are reported as mainly small (Van Yperen et al., 2014), with a cluster of elite athletes disregarding the effectiveness of goal setting (Burton et al., 2010).

Such findings underscore the question as to which particular considerations should be afforded prominence in an athlete's goal-setting programme? Clearly, one must be mindful that the context within which each goal-setting programme is applied will be different, and hence practitioners should be aware of the particular concerns, contextual demands and abilities of the athlete in question (Hall and Kerr, 2001). First and foremost, Burton and Weiss suggest what they call the Fundamental Goal Concept, namely that setting both process and performance goals builds a path to successful outcome goals. This is said to be the case for a number of reasons but chiefly because outcome goals are rarely within the complete control of an athlete. Other factors such as conditions, officials and opponents' skill are likely to play a role. The benefit for the athlete of focusing on process and performance goals derives from the fact that this ensures that the criteria for success remain under personal control, hopefully thereby limiting the damage attached to failures to achieve particular outcomes. Additionally, the focus encourages an emphasis on autonomous rather than controlled motivation. Crucially, the point is made that setting outcome goals is not to be discouraged; indeed, they are seen as vital components of an athlete's commitment. The question is one of priority and focus and how one judges the success of goal-setting interventions. The research to date would suggest that a focus on skills and their practical application is the most appropriate way by which to set and judge success.

Further characteristics of effective goals have been examined and tested in sport-specific contexts. Regarding Locke's suggestion that, the more difficult a goal, the greater the impact on performance, this relationship has not been consistently demonstrated in sport. Indeed, it has been reported that unattainable, vague and difficult goals may prove counterproductive by increasing stress and thereby impairing performance (Weinberg et al., 2001). Goal difficulty is more complex and requires association with further concepts of goal motives, disengagement and goal adjustment. It would appear that, particularly when approached with a controlled motivational orientation, athletes are likely to disengage from goals, but when driven by autonomous motives then the individual is likely to adapt and persist in his or her goal pursuits (Healy et al., 2018). Finally, a key consideration is the proximity of a goal, that is, how quickly can success be achieved and evaluated? While this is not an area that has received a great deal of attention, it would appear that the success of long-term goals is contingent on short-term markers of success (Kyllo and Landers, 1995; Healy et al., 2018). This proposition would sit comfortably with Locke's emphasis on the importance of regular feedback in achieving goals.

In summarising the literature on goal setting in sport, one broad conclusion would be that it remains an important performance-enhancing tool, but this endorsement comes with caveats attached. Consideration has to be afforded to the particular idiosyncrasies of each sporting context, the social nature of working with individual athletes across time and the levels of autonomy experienced by athletes during the goal-setting process. While the concept of setting goals would appear to be a relatively simple one, the process of guiding an athlete through the goal-setting process rarely is. Conceptualisations of goal setting as a process, such as the Competitive Goal Setting Model (CGS-3) (Burton and Weiss, 2008), or the integration of SDT and/or AGT with GST, each provide an insight into the complexities of the goal-setting process. The success or otherwise of any goal-setting intervention hinges on numerous important factors, including the cognitive (e.g. the athlete's beliefs regarding the nature of ability, perceptions of autonomous goal strivings); the social (e.g. the psychological needs-support an athlete receives from his/her coach); and the situational (e.g. performance outcomes and the athlete's reactions to them). The importance of each of these sets of factors should be recognised and none should be addressed in isolation.

Despite these caveats, the history of the goal-setting literature stands as testimony to the importance of the development of a sport-specific literature. There would now appear to be a degree of consensus that, while athletes should be supported to develop mindful, short-, medium- and longer-term outcome goals, their focus should never stray too far from the process by which they are achieved. Hence the key characteristic of effective goal setting in sport may be to continually focus athletes on the means by which to achieve their desired outcome goals, through the practice and successful application of the particular skills of their sport.

KEY READINGS

Burton, D. and Weiss, C. (2008) 'The fundamental goal concept: The path to process and performance success', in T. Horn (ed.), *Advances in Sport Psychology* (3rd ed.). Leeds: Human Kinetics. pp. 339–75.

Healy, L.C., Ntoumanis, N., van Zanten, J.J.V. and Paine, N. (2014) 'Goal striving and well-being in sport: The role of contextual and personal motivation', *Journal of Sport and Exercise Psychology*, 36 (5), 446–59.

Locke, E.A. (2015) 'Theory building, replication, and behavioral priming: Where do we need to go from here?', *Perspectives on Psychological Science*, 10, 408–14. http://dx.doi.org/10.1177/1745691614567231.

Tod, D., Edwards, C., McGuigan, M. and Lovell, G. (2015) 'A systematic review of the effect of cognitive strategies on strength performance', *Sports Medicine*, 45 (11), 1589–1602.

PRACTICAL QUESTIONS

- Using practical examples, illustrate how the characteristics of process goals and outcome goals differ, and indicate how each relates to motivation and performance.
- When, where and how can goals be counterproductive to successful sporting performance?

REFERENCES

Burton, D. and Weiss, C. (2008) 'The fundamental goal concept: The path to process and performance success', in T. Horn (ed.), *Advances in Sport Psychology* (3rd ed.). Leeds: Human Kinetics. pp. 339–75.

Burton, D., Pickering, M., Weinberg, R., Yukelson, D. and Weigand, D. (2010) 'The competitive goal effectiveness paradox revisited: Examining the goal practices of prospective Olympic athletes', *Journal of Applied Sport Psychology*, 22 (1), 72–86.

Burton, D., Weinberg, R.S., Yukelson, D. and Weigland, D. (1998) 'The goal effectiveness paradox in sport: Examining the goal practices of collegiate athletes', *The Sport Psychologist*, 12, 404–18.

Butler, R.J. (1996) *Sport Psychology in Action.* Oxford: Butterworth-Heinemann.

Butt, J. and Weinberg, R. (2020) 'Goal-setting' in D. Hackfort and R.J. Schinke (eds), *The Routledge International Encyclopedia of Sport and Exercise Psychology. Volume 2: Applied and Practical Measures*. Abingdon: Routledge. pp. 333–42.

Hall, K. and Kerr, A.W. (2001) 'Goal setting in sport and physical activity: Tracing empirical development and establishing conceptual direction', in G.C. Roberts (ed.), *Advances in Motivation in Sport and Exercise*. Champaign, IL: Human Kinetics. pp. 183–235.

Healy, L.C., Ntoumanis, N. and Duda, J.L. (2016) 'Goal motives and multiple-goal striving in sport and academia: A person-centered investigation of goal motives and inter-goal relations', *Journal of Science and Medicine in Sport*, 19 (12), 1010–14.

Healy, L.C., Ntoumanis, N., van Zanten, J.J.V. and Paine, N. (2014) 'Goal striving and well-being in sport: The role of contextual and personal motivation', *Journal of Sport and Exercise Psychology*, 36 (5), 446–59.

Healy, L., Tincknell-Smith, A. and Ntoumanis, N. (2018) 'Goal setting in sport and performance', *Oxford Research Encyclopedia of Psychology*.

James, W. (1890) *Principles of Psychology*. New York: Holt, Rinehart & Winston.

Kyllo, L.B. and Landers, D.M. (1995) 'Goal setting in sport and exercise: A research synthesis to resolve the controversy', *Journal of Sport and Exercise Psychology*, 17, 117–37.

Locke, E.A. (2015) 'Theory building, replication, and behavioral priming: Where do we need to go from here?', *Perspectives on Psychological Science*, 10, 408–14. http://dx.doi.org/10.1177/1745691614567231.

Locke, E.A. and Latham, G.P. (1990) *A Theory of Goal Setting and Task Performance.* Englewood Cliffs, NJ: Prentice Hall.

Locke, E.A. and Latham, G.P. (1994) 'Goal setting in theory', in H.F. O'Neill and M. Drillings (eds), *Motivation: Theory and Research*. Hillside, NJ: Lawrence Erlbaum. pp. 13–29.

Sheldon, K.M. and Elliot, A.J. (1999) 'Goal striving, need satisfaction, and longitudinal well-being: The self-concordance model', *Journal of Personality and Social Psychology*, 76 (3), 482.

Tod, D., Edwards, C., McGuigan, M. and Lovell, G. (2015) 'A systematic review of the effect of cognitive strategies on strength performance', *Sports Medicine*, 45 (11), 1589–1602.

Van Yperen, N.W., Blaga, M. and Postmes, T. (2014) 'A meta-analysis of self-reported achievement goals and nonself-report performance across three achievement domains (work, sports, and education)', *PloS One*, 9 (4), e93594.

Weinberg, R.S., Butt, J. and Knight, B. (2001) 'High school coaches' perceptions of the process of goal setting', *The Sport Psychologist*, 15, 20–47.

3.13 FEAR OF FAILURE AND NEED TO ACHIEVE

Definitions: Fear of failure describes the motive to avoid those occasions where the prospect of failure is a possibility, while the need to achieve characterises the desire to succeed in competitive situations.

Fear is a phenomenon that has long received substantial academic attention. As far back as 1915, Walter Cannon coined the key phrase that has characterised discussions of the psychology of fear – *fight or flight*. Cannon, a physiologist by training, examined animal responses to threat. His supposition was that the bodily reactions associated with the perception of threat, essentially the activation of the sympathetic nervous system, prepared the organism to make one of two responses, to meet it or to beat it (i.e. fight or to flight) (Cannon, 1915). This central consideration, that the arousal associated with the perception of threat may have an adaptive purpose, would later inform drive theories of motivation that sought to examine the effects of increased arousal on performance.

Once it is accepted that arousal may affect performance, the relevance to sport becomes immediately apparent. Arguably the key theory to emerge in this respect was McClelland-Atkinson's Need Achievement Theory (NAT). Building on Cannon's idea that the stress reaction can elicit one of two responses (flight or fight), the NAT posited two key psychological constructs that continue to influence the field to this day – fear of failure and need to achieve.

The NAT is a theory of motivation cast in the tradition of early approaches that focused on undifferentiated intrinsic drives or forces (see **3.14**, **3.15** and **3.16**). Within its framework, motivation is conceptualised as a drive to meet challenges or, as termed in the theory, a need to achieve (NAch). The strength of this need is dependent on three factors. The first factor is the relative strengths of two motives: the motive to achieve success (MS) and the motive to avoid failure (MAF), also known as fear of failure (FF). The second factor is the combination of two perceptions: the perception that success is likely (Ps) and the perception of the incentives available (Is). The final factors are resultant tendencies to approach success or avoid failure, which have a causal role in emotional reactions. Figure 3.4 summarises the key ingredients of NAT.

As an emotional reaction, the concept of fear of failure has received substantial attention across various domains within the psychological literature, including education, business and sport. It is now understood as a relatively stable disposition that may be first established in childhood (Conroy and Coatsworth, 2004). In general, younger athletes tend to have higher achievement motives and focus more on pride of success than fear of failure (Gardner et al., 2017) in comparison with adult athletes. With increasing age, there is a growing trend towards viewing evaluation as threatening (Conroy et al., 2002), and this trend is particularly salient during adolescence, a time when peer comparison and

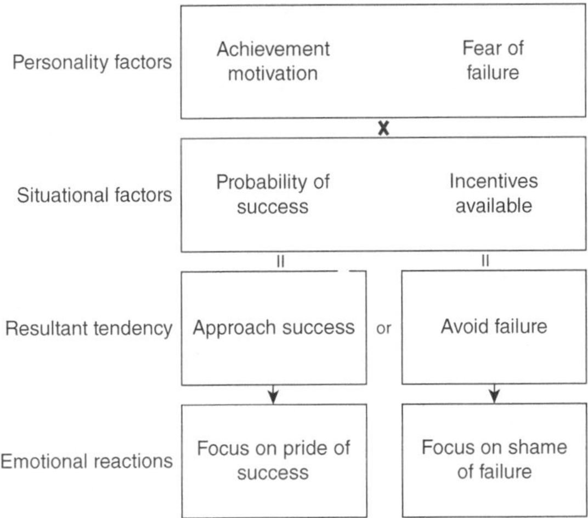

Figure 3.4 Need Achievement Theory

the establishment of identity is under constant negotiation. The perception of threat, or fear, is likely to have a restrictive effect on performance in such situations, leading to the adoption of avoidance-based goals (Birney et al., 1969). The adoption of these negative goals is in turn associated with a number of negative consequences, including worry, stress and anxiety (Conroy et al., 2002), less enjoyment and intentions to discontinue sport (Gardner et al., 2017), hostile self-concepts and lower self-esteem (Conroy at al., 2005). Especially in young athletes, this can affect interpersonal behaviour, school work, sporting performance and general wellbeing (Sagar et al., 2009). Furthermore, implicit beliefs of lower ability predict the adoption of avoidance-based goals and higher cognitive anxiety (Stenling et al., 2014).

In the light of these negative outcomes, recent years have witnessed increasing attempts to understand the developmental origins of fear of failure in young athletes (e.g. Gómez-López et al., 2020). The starting point for any discussion of the origin of fear of failure must be the recognition that fear itself is a natural reaction to perceived threat – the question then is why do some young athletes perceive competitive situations as more threatening than others? What has been suggested is that, while failure itself is unlikely to cause fear, what is likely is that the young athlete fears the *consequences* of failure. The central consequence highlighted by the literature has been that of *anticipatory shame* associated with failure (McGregor and Elliot, 2005). For example, an athlete with high anticipatory shame will avoid goals and behaviours during a game (e.g. less willingness to shoot, aim to gain possession), which ultimately results in diminished motivation, impaired performance and poorer wellbeing (Correia and Rosado, 2019). However, this contention raises a further question: why do some young athletes perceive failure as something to be ashamed of? This question may be answered by examining hierarchical models of fear of failure.

Conroy (2001) has identified five aversive consequences associated with failure – experiencing shame/embarrassment; devaluing one's self-estimation; being uncertain of the future; worry that significant others may lose interest; and concern that significant others may be upset. Of all these factors, the role played by significant others has emerged as central. For example, it has been reported that young athletes experiencing a high level of fear of failure are likely to perceive parents and coaches as hostile (Conroy, 2003), and perceive coaches as egocentric in their shaping of the motivational climate (Gómez-López et al., 2020). In terms of personal factors, athletes with a high fear of failure also report that they engage in critical self-talk that mirrors the criticism they receive from their coaches, suggesting that fear of failure may be socialised or transferred from important others (Moreno-Murcia et al., 2019). Self-esteem is undoubtedly a casualty in this process, with normative referencing (i.e. peer comparisons) further compounding fear of failure and impaired wellbeing, and ultimately avoidance/discontinuation of sport. Indeed, recent research (Gustafsson et al., 2017) has established that fear of failure is directly related to a reduced sense of accomplishment, a key component of burnout and psychological stress in athletes.

While intuitively the suggestion that an increased emphasis on competition will increase fear of failure is appealing, research has revealed various factors mediating this relationship, including the coach-created motivational climate (i.e. ego v. task-oriented), gender, sport type and the balance of intrinsic v. extrinsic goal aspirations (Conroy and Elliot, 2004; Correia et al., 2017).

Looking to the future, there remains limited research into the developmental origins of fear of failure, particularly among elite athletes (Sagar et al., 2009), and including the interaction between peer and coach climate (Gómez-López et al., 2020), and past failure appraisals and adaptive responses to failure such as self-compassion (Ceccarelli et al., 2019). While there remains work to be done in mapping the aetiological factors that contribute to fear of failure, once the importance of the behaviour of significant others has been duly acknowledged then practitioners have an obvious focus for their interventions. Programmes that target coach, parent and peer behaviours from a young age, when used in conjunction with appropriate self-appraisal techniques, are likely to promote healthy motivational orientations among athletes (Sagar et al., 2009).

At this point, it may be tempting to also conclude that fear of failure may be reduced by increasing the need to achieve. However, and as highlighted in Figure 3.4, the view that need to achieve and fear of failure are two sides of the same coin is misleading. The NAT posits that these two constructs are in fact independent. In practice this means that it is possible for an athlete to possess both a high need to achieve and a high fear of failure. In fact, four theoretical combinations are possible, each of which makes its own distinct predictions regarding motivation:

Type 1. *Low need to achieve and high fear of failure* – this athlete is highly likely to withdraw from competition, viewing the stress associated with possible failure as more pertinent than any potential achievements.

Type 2. *Low need to achieve and low fear of failure* – this athlete is likely to be quite indifferent to competition, being driven by neither fear nor a need to achieve.

Type 3. *High need to achieve and low fear of failure* – this athlete is likely to enjoy competitive situations and not perceive them as a threat to their self-concept.

Type 4. *High need to achieve and high fear of failure* – this athlete is likely to enjoy competition but perceive it as a potential threat to their self-concept.

The immediate question for practitioners is which of the above is preferable? It could certainly be suggested that Type 3 represents, in a sense, the *purest* form of motivation, and is likely to be associated with athletes in the early stages of their careers, before they are socialised into experiencing fear of failure. Indeed, studies of elite athletes would suggest that many possess a motivational profile associated with a high need to achieve, bolstered by intrinsic motivation and a focus on task goals (Mallett and Hanrahan, 2004). However, in the world of elite sport it would be naïve to ignore the role inevitably played by extrinsic factors, such as the opinions of others, potential loss of income and comparisons with other athletes (Duda et al., 1995). Evidence would suggest this is often the case, with elite athletes possessing goals of both an intrinsic and extrinsic nature (Roberts, 2001). In these instances, the motivational profile of an elite athlete may more closely reflect Type 4, a high need to achieve but accompanied by a high fear of failure. As such, while it is useful that practitioners seek to lessen fear in young athletes, there must also be a recognition that, in top-level sport, the ability to handle fear is likely to be as useful an asset as possessing a need to achieve. As Mark Twain famously put it, '*Courage is resistance to fear, mastery of fear – not the absence of fear.*'

KEY READINGS

Conroy, D.E. (2001) 'Fear of failure: An exemplar for social development research in sport', *Quest*, 53, 165–83.

Gardner, L., Vella, S. and Magee, C. (2017) 'Continued participation in youth sports: The role of achievement motivation', *Journal of Applied Sport Psychology*, 29 (1), 17–31.

Gómez-López, M., Chicau Borrego, C., Marques da Silva, C., Granero-Gallegos, A. and González-Hernández, J. (2020) 'Effects of motivational climate on fear of failure and anxiety in teen handball players', *International Journal of Environmental Research and Public Health*, 17 (2), 592. doi: 10.3390/ijerph17020592.

Stenling, A., Hassmén, P. and Holmström, S. (2014) 'Implicit beliefs of ability, approach/avoidance goals and cognitive anxiety among team sport athletes', *European Journal of Sport Science*, 14, 720–9. doi:10.1080/17461391.2014.901419.

PRACTICAL QUESTIONS

- Where does fear of failure typically stem from, and how does it impact on performance and motivation?
- Explain why fear of failure and need to achieve are best described as independent constructs, and outline the significance of this relationship for understanding performance and motivation.

REFERENCES

Birney, R.C., Budick, H. and Teevan, R.C. (1969) *Fear of Failure*. New York: Van Nostrand.

Cannon, W. (1915) *Bodily Changes in Pain, Hunger, Fear and Rage: An Account of Recent Researches into the Function of Emotional Excitement*. New York: Appleton.

Ceccarelli, L.A., Giuliano, R.J., Glazebrook, C.M. and Strachan, S.M. (2019) 'Self-compassion and psycho-physiological recovery from recalled sport failure', *Frontiers in Psychology, 10*, 1564.

Conroy, D.E. (2001) 'Fear of failure: An exemplar for social development research in sport', *Quest*, 53, 165–83.

Conroy, D.E. (2003) 'Representational models associated with fear of failure in adolescents and young', *Journal of Personality*, 71, 757–83.

Conroy, D.E. and Coatsworth, J.D. (2004) 'The effects of coach training on fear of failure in youth swimmers: A latent growth curve analysis from a randomized, controlled trial', *Journal of Applied Developmental Psychology*, 25, 193–214.

Conroy, D.E. and Elliot, A.J. (2004) 'Fear of failure and achievement goals in sport: Addressing the issue of the chicken and the egg', *Anxiety, Stress and Coping*, 17, 271–85.

Conroy, D.E., Willow, J.P. and Metzler, J.N. (2002) 'Multidimensional fear of failure measurement: The performance failure appraisal inventory', *Journal of Applied Sport Psychology*, 14, 76–90.

Conroy, D.E., Coatsworth, J.D. and Fifer, A.M. (2005) 'Testing dynamic relations between perceived competence and fear of failure in young athletes', *Revue Européenne de Psychologie Appliqué*, 55, 99–110.

Correia, M.E., Rosado, A., Serpa, S. and Ferreira, V. (2017) 'Fear of failure in athletes: Gender, age and type of sport differences', *Ibero-American Journal of Exercise and Sports Psychology*, 12 (2), 185–93.

Correia, M. and Rosado, A. (2019) 'Anxiety in athletes: Gender and type of sport differences', *International Journal of Psychological Research*, 12 (1), 9–17.

Duda, J.L., Chi, L., Newton, M.L., Walling, M.D. and Catley, D. (1995) 'Task and ego orientation and intrinsic motivation in sport', *International Journal of Sport Psychology*, 26, 40–63.

Gardner, L., Vella, S. and Magee, C. (2017) 'Continued participation in youth sports: The role of achievement motivation', *Journal of Applied Sport Psychology*, 29 (1), 17–31

Gómez-López, M., Chicau Borrego, C., Marques da Silva, C., Granero-Gallegos, A. and González-Hernández, J. (2020) 'Effects of motivational climate on fear of failure and anxiety in teen handball players',

International Journal of Environmental Research and Public Health, 17 (2), 592. doi: 10.3390/ijerph17020592.

Gustafsson, H., Sagar, S.S. and Stenling, A. (2017) 'Fear of failure, psychological stress, and burnout among adolescent athletes competing in high level sport', *Scandinavian Journal of Medicine & Science in Sports*, 27 (12), 2091–102.

Mallett, C.J. and Hanrahan, S.J. (2004) 'Elite athletes: Why does the "fire" burn so brightly?', *Psychology of Sport and Exercise*, 5, 183–200.

McGregor, H.A. and Elliot, A.J. (2005) 'The shame of failure: Examining the link between fear of failure and shame', *Personality and Social Psychology Bulletin*, 31, 218–31.

Moreno-Murcia, J.A., Huéscar Hernández, E., Conte Marín, L. and Nuñez, J.L. (2019) 'Coaches' motivational style and athletes' fear of failure', *International Journal of Environmental Research and Public Health*, 16 (9), 1563.

Roberts, G.C. (2001) 'Understanding the dynamics of motivation in physical activity: The influence of achievement goals on motivational processes', in G.C. Roberts (ed.), *Advances in Motivation in Sport and Exercise*. Champaign, IL: Human Kinetics. pp. 1–50.

Sagar, S.S., Lavallee, D. and Spray, C.M. (2009) 'Coping with the effects of fear of failure: A preliminary investigation of young elite athletes', *Journal of Clinical Sport Psychology*, 1, 1–27.

Stenling, A., Hassmén, P. and Holmström, S. (2014) 'Implicit beliefs of ability, approach/avoidance goals and cognitive anxiety among team sport athletes', *European Journal of Sport Science*, 14, 720–9. doi:10.1080/17461391.2014.901419.

3.14 SELF-DETERMINATION THEORY

Definition: A theory of human motivation and health that links our innate motivation to satisfy our psychological needs for autonomy, competence and social relatedness with autonomous and controlled motives.

Following from the early work of McClelland and Atkinson (see **3.13**), and set within the broader context of the social cognitive movement, Self-Determination Theory (SDT) emerged in the 1970s to offer an intricate framework for considering how our innate growth tendencies reflect in motivational quality, subsequent behaviours and wellbeing (Ryan and Deci, 2019). As a framework for understanding why we take part in both sport and physical exercise generally, and what we derive from that engagement, SDT has continued to enjoy support both in academia and a variety of practical settings (Vallerand, 2008; Ryan and Deci, 2017). Indeed, a relatively recent review found that SDT remains the most prominent theory with regard to sport motivation research (Clancy et al., 2016).

Overall, SDT encompasses several subtheories centred on the social environment's influence on our motivation, behaviour and wellbeing. A unifying concept between the subtheories is how social environments support or thwart the satisfaction of our innate psychological needs for autonomy, competence and social relatedness. Competence refers to an individual's capacity to impact on his/her environment, thereby experiencing environmental mastery; autonomy refers to self-endorsed volitional behaviour; and social relatedness refers to a sense of belonging, including caring for others and feeling cared for by others (Ryan and Deci, 2002).

SDT is typically represented as a hierarchical model, with psychological needs and subsequent motivation influenced by factors that can be either global (e.g. personality), contextual (e.g. coach behaviour) or situational (e.g., moment-to-moment feedback). Further, according to Vallerand (2007a), motivation is seen to exist at three levels of generality: the global (i.e. the environment as a whole), the contextual (i.e. usual response to a specific context, e.g. education, sport) and the situational (i.e. specific activity at a given time).

The theory includes a critical distinction between intrinsic and extrinsic motivation, and the relative degree of autonomy that these motives are derived from. Intrinsic motivation, the inherent pleasure or joy of doing something for its own sake, is qualitatively distinct from motivation derived from tangible rewards that we often automatically associate with success, known as extrinsic motives. In turn, extrinsic motivation can encompass various motives that regulate our behaviour including introjected motives (i.e. to avoid shame/ satisfy ego), identified motives (i.e. seeing personal benefit), and, the most autonomously regulated extrinsic motives, integrated motives (i.e. behaviour that is consistent with one's values and interests). The SDT continuum of motivation (see Figure 3.5) incorporates each of these motives and their relative degree of self-determination and needs-satisfaction, along with the state of amotivation, or the absence of motivation.

Among the subtheories now attached to SDT, Cognitive Evaluation Theory (CET) considers how various factors, in particular environmental or contextual influences,

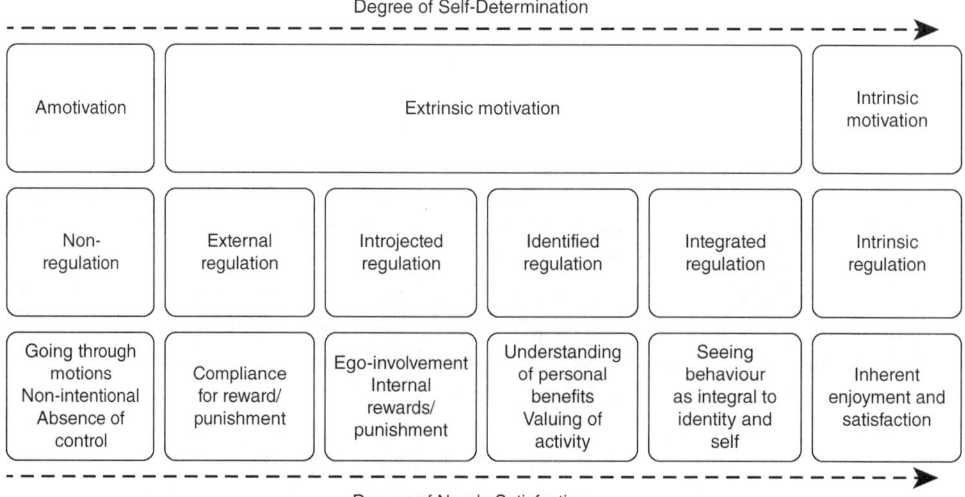

Figure 3.5 Self-Determination Theory Continuum of Motivation

impact on intrinsic motivation, with a particular focus on competence and autonomy. CET highlights the importance of good feedback on performance, linked to the ability of the athlete to control that performance. For example, the strength of intrinsic motivation is influenced principally by the person's degree of autonomy, which normally has been operationalised as their locus of causality (either internal or external). An external locus of causality ('Things happen to me') reflects low control and is likely to decrease intrinsic motivation, while an internal locus of causality ('I make things happen') reflects a high degree of perceived control and is more likely to enhance intrinsic motivation. Moreover, perceived competence (see **3.16**) and engagement with challenging activities also mediate our intrinsic motivation. This is because the level of challenge attached to an activity is critical in showing us how competent we actually are. Easy and difficult activities provide little feedback but a challenge that is both difficult and demanding yet also attainable seems to strike the right balance (see **3.12**). In support of CET, a number of studies have considered how different types of reward systems (e.g. task completion v. engagement contingent v. performance contingent) may influence future motivation in different ways (see Hagger and Chatzisarantis, 2007). Furthermore, specific coaching actions, including the provision of clear instructions and being supportive of player input, is related to athletes' self-determined motivation through the satisfaction of their basic needs (Clancy et al., 2016).

Another prominent subtheory, Organismic Integration Theory (OIT; Deci and Ryan, 1985), describes extrinsic motivation as having distinct dimensions that vary in motivational strength due to the degree to which behaviours support the athlete's psychological needs (see Figure 3.5). Applying this lens, an athlete could engage in sport for outcomes including to avoid punishment (i.e. external regulation), or to receive approval from others such as coaches (i.e. introjected regulation). Identified and integrated forms of motivation are autonomous forms of extrinsic motivation, in which behaviour is engaged in for the sake of valuing an activity (i.e. identified regulation) or for personal importance (i.e. integrated regulation). Importantly, across time one can shift from an initially controlled extrinsic sport participation motive such as 'I'm only going to satisfy my parents' to a more sustainable autonomous extrinsic motive, i.e., 'I now see the friendship and health benefits that sport brings to me'.

This multidimensional view of motivation has been measured in a variety of ways; one of the most popular and psychometrically valid is the Sport Motivation Scale II (Pelletier et al., 2013). Using such instruments, the OIT hypothesis that the more autonomously oriented extrinsic motives (i.e. integrated and identified regulation) predict continued engagement has been well supported in physical activity and health contexts (Owen et al., 2014; Ntoumanis et al., 2020), and in sport (Standage and Ryan, 2020). A recent classification of techniques derived from SDT (Teixeira et al., 2020) emphasised that, through time, by being receptive to an instructor's (or coaches') needs-supportive behaviours, an athlete can progress through a range of extrinsic motives and thereby experience a higher degree of volition.

Goal Contents Theory (GCT; Niemiec et al., 2009) also has significant links with OIT, such that it too concerns itself with the distinctions between intrinsic and extrinsic goal aspirations and their impact on motivational types. However, most research has been conducted from the perspective of life aspirations (e.g., money) and not sport *per se*, and hence is beyond the scope of this chapter.

A further prominent subtheory, Basic Psychological Needs Theory (BPNT; Ryan, 1995) considers how psychological need satisfactions (and frustrations) impact upon wellbeing, and has recently received significant support in the context of sport and exercise. However, BPNT is not explicity focused on motivation but on wellbeing, and is therefore once more outside this chapter's remit.

Lastly, and in an integration of passion theories with SDT (Sheldon, 2002), research has shown that passion is highly prevalent and influential in sport, and is internalised in two ways, as either obsessive or harmonious. Obsessive passion results from a controlled internalisation of the activity into the athlete's identity where the values and regulations associated with the sport activity are taken on board but are not embraced completely within the sense of self. This type of internalisation may develop because contingencies are attached to the activity, such as feelings of social acceptance or self-esteem, or because the sense of excitement derived from engagement is uncontrollable. According to Vallerand (2007b), an obsessive passion can fuel an uncontrollable and unhealthy urge to participate. In contrast, harmonious passion develops naturally from the internalisation of the activity into the person's identity. It occurs when the activity is freely accepted as important, unfettered by any contingencies. In a recent review of passion research in sport, Vallerand and Verner-Filion (2020) concluded that harmonious passion is associated with positive, long-term engagement in sport, including flexible persistence and high-level involvement. In stark contrast, obsessive passion may foster unhealthy and rigid persistence that may allow the athlete to remain fiercely competitive but can consume the athlete/coach and those around him/her in the process.

KEY READINGS

Ryan, R.M. and Deci, E.L. (2019) 'Brick by brick: The origins, development, and future of self-determination theory', in *Advances in Motivation Science*, 6, 111–56.

Standage, M. and Ryan, R.M. (2020) 'Self-determination theory in sport and exercise', in *Handbook of Sport Psychology*. New York: John Wiley & Sons, Inc. pp. 37–56.

Vallerand, R.J. (2007a) 'Intrinsic and extrinsic motivation in sport and physical activity: A review and a look at the future', in G. Tenenbaum and E. Eklund (eds), *Handbook of Sport Psychology* (3rd ed.). New York: Wiley. pp. 49–83.

Vallerand, R.J. (2008) 'On the psychology of passion: In search of what makes people's lives most worth living', *Canadian Psychology*, 49, 1–13.

PRACTICAL QUESTIONS

- We can hold multiple motives for why we participate in sport, and these fall into two broad categories of autonomous or controlled motivation. What are the key features of both motivational categories and how do they impact on commitment over time?
- Explain the ways in which one coach is able to promote needs satisfaction while another provokes needs frustration, and how do these styles impact on athletes in their charge over time?

REFERENCES

Clancy, R.B., Herring, M.P., MacIntyre, T.E. and Campbell, M.J. (2016) 'A review of competitive sport motivation research', *Psychology of Sport and Exercise*, 27, 232–42.

Deci, E.L. and Ryan, R.M. (1985) 'Toward an organismic integration theory', in E.L. Deci and and R.M. Ryan *Intrinsic Motivation and Self-determination in Human Behavior* (pp. 113–48). Boston, MA: Springer.

Hagger, M.S. and Chatzisarantis, N.L.D. (eds) (2007) *Intrinsic Motivation and Self-Determination in Exercise and Sport*. Champaign, IL: Human Kinetics.

Niemiec, C.P., Ryan, R.M. and Deci, E.L. (2009) 'The path taken: Consequences of attaining intrinsic and extrinsic aspirations in post-college life', *Journal of Research in Personality*, 43 (3), 291–306.

Ntoumanis, N., Ng, J.Y., Prestwich, A., Quested, E., Hancox, J.E., Thøgersen-Ntoumani, C., and Williams, G.C. (2020) 'A meta-analysis of self-determination theory-informed intervention studies in the health domain: Effects on motivation, health behavior, physical, and psychological health', *Health Psychology Review*, 1–31.

Owen, K.B., Smith, J., Lubans, D.R., Ng, J.Y. and Lonsdale, C. (2014) 'Self-determined motivation and physical activity in children and adolescents: A systematic review and meta-analysis', *Preventive Medicine*, 67, 270–9.

Pelletier, L. G., Rocchi, M. A., Vallerand, R. J., Deci, E. L., & Ryan, R. M. (2013). Validation of the revised sport motivation scale (SMS-II). *Psychology of Sport and Exercise*, *14*(3), 329–341.

Ryan, R.M. (1995) 'Psychological needs and the facilitation of integrative processes', *Journal of Personality*, 63 (3), 397–427.

Ryan, R.M. and Deci, E.L. (2002) 'An overview of self-determination theory', in E.L. Deci and R.M. Ryan (eds), *Handbook of Self-Determination Research*. Rochester, NY: University of Rochester Press. pp. 3–33.

Ryan, R.M. and Deci, E.L. (2017) *Self-Determination Theory: Basic Psychological Needs in Motivation, Development, and Wellness*. New York: Guilford Publications.

Ryan, R.M., and Deci, E.L. (2019) 'Brick by brick: The origins, development, and future of self-determination theory', in A.J. Eliot (ed.), *Advances in Motivation Science*, vol. 6. Amsterdam: Elsevier Press. pp. 111–56.

Sheldon, K.M. (2002) 'The self-concordance model of healthy goal-striving: When personal goals correctly represent the person', in E.L. Deci and R.M. Ryan (eds), *Handbook of Self-Determination Research*. Rochester, NY: University of Rochester Press. pp. 65–86.

Standage, M. and Ryan, R.M. (2020) 'Self-determination theory in sport and exercise', *Handbook of Sport Psychology*. New York: John Wiley & Sons. pp. 37–56.

Teixeira, P.J., Marques, M.M., Silva, M.N., Brunet, J., Duda, J.L., Haerens, L. and Hagger, M.S. (2020) 'Classification of techniques used in self-determination theory-based interventions in health contexts: An expert consensus study', *Motivation Science* (in press).

Vallerand, R.J. (2007a) 'Intrinsic and extrinsic motivation in sport and physical activity: A review and a look at the future', in G. Tenenbaum and E. Eklund (eds), *Handbook of Sport Psychology* (3rd ed.). New York: John Wiley & Sons. pp. 49–83.

Vallerand, R.J. (2007b) 'Passion for sport in athletics', in S. Jowett and D. Lavallee (eds), *Social Psychology in Sport*. Champaign, IL: Human Kinetics. pp. 249–64.

Vallerand, R.J. (2008) 'On the psychology of passion: In search of what makes people's lives most worth living', *Canadian Psychology*, 49, 1–13.

Vallerand, R.J. and Verner-Filion, J. (2020) 'Theory and research in passion for sport and exercise', *Handbook of Sport Psychology*. New York: John Wiley & Sons. pp. 206–29.

3.15 ACHIEVEMENT GOAL THEORY

Definition: A psychological theory of motivation that considers how beliefs and cognitions deliberately orient us towards achievement or success, especially in relation to two styles, task (mastery) and ego (performance).

As psychologists have become increasingly interested in social-cognitive approaches to understanding motivation, Achievement Goal Theory (AGT) has emerged to play a prominent role in the contemporary sport psychology literature and is now the second most applied theory after Self-Determination Theory (SDT; Clancy et al., 2016) (see **3.14**). AGT makes a distinction between how people vary in the types of motives or goals set, determined by the motivational climate within which they operate. This climate can be either harmful or helpful to future motivational processes and engagement.

As with many sport motivational models, the origins of AGT in the 1970s lie outside sport, in the world of educational psychology. However, it did not take long to see the potential application to sporting endeavours. The original exponents (Carole Ames, Carol Dweck, Martin Maehr and John Nicholls) emphasised the importance of situational, contextual and cultural influences on achievement goals, and argued that goals ultimately give an activity purpose and meaning. Furthermore, the relevance of success in achieving a goal can vary across contexts, a finding which has immediate implications for how a task is learnt and performed (Urdan and Kaplan, 2020). Hence, when an individual adopts an achievement goal, AGT describes the athletes' attitudes towards achievement, their motivation in achievement settings and their achievement performance (Wang and Biddle, 2007).

Sport psychologists have found the approach intuitively appealing for many reasons, not least because of its focus on achievement. In the early years at least, it also appeared to offer a clear way of distinguishing between those whose goal orientations are positive and concerned with mastery of skills, as opposed to those whose motives are more ego-oriented and less wholesome, such as being more concerned with self-advancement at the expense of others. The two styles are defined in AGT as representing two achievement goal orientations, either task (mastery) or ego (performance) which were hypothesised to be independent or orthogonal to each other. These orientations are not seen as fixed (or traits) but are more like cognitive schema (or mental representations) that tend to be quite stable over time, unless feedback on performance suggests that a radical reorientation is required (Duda, 2005). The two orientations are seen to be a function of three interacting factors: underlying disposition; the climate created by significant others (or motivational climate, see later); and developmental influences during childhood (White, 2007).

'Task orientation' refers to those occasions where the person focuses primarily on improvement and mastery of a skill. AGT suggests that those with a task (mastery) orientation are more likely to show persistence and to choose challenging activities that allow them to assess not only where they are but where they need to be. By contrast, those with an ego (performance) orientation use sport to prove their worth against others, and often have an unhealthy preoccupation with competition and winning. This approach can reveal itself in an arrogance that masks underlying insecurities, and where fear of failure can become the overriding concern (see **3.13**). AGT also recognises that task and ego goal orientations differ significantly in relation to how competence is construed. Those with a task orientation tend to use self-referenced criteria to assess their competence while those with an ego orientation are more inclined to use others as their primary reference point, thereby making them more vulnerable to dips in confidence (Roberts et al., 2007). Indeed, a meta-analysis in the context of competitive sport (Lochbaum et al., 2016) revealed that while both goal orentations correlated with competence, a significantly larger effect was evident for task orientation.

Early research on either side of the Atlantic, as initially pioneered by Nicholls (1984), appeared to confirm the practical utility of the theory in sport (Duda, 2005). For example, it was found that young people with a high task orientation believed that their engagement with sport improved cooperation and mastery skills, while those with a high ego orientation looked on sport as a way of gaining social acceptance, and of bolstering their ego through competition. Further, a task orientation linked effort to success, teamwork and experience, while an ego orientation saw success as being dependent on natural skill or ability above all else. Such findings were supported in a more recent meta-analysis (Lochbaum et al., 2016) wherein task orientation correlated positively with adaptive sporting and motivational factors, including intrinsic motivation, autonomous extrinsic motivation and prosocial behaviours. In contrast, ego orientation was positively correlated with amotivation and maladaptive sporting behaviours. Hence, those with a task orientation generally feel they can improve and are in control of their own destiny (an internal attribution style, see **5.24**), while those with an ego orientation feel themselves more as the victims of fate or circumstance (an external attribution style, see **5.24**). It should therefore come as no surprise to learn that those with an ego orientation are more likely to resort to cheating, aggression and foul play in order to succeed (Urdan and Kaplan, 2020).

To this point, the picture may look straightforward. Someone with a task orientation is a better sporting prospect and is likely to be more highly motivated, and successful, over time. However, through adopting contemporary advances in statistical modelling, some have cast doubt on this simple explanation, with research indicating that both task and ego orientations can be helpful in the right circumstances (Harwood, 2002). For example, when profiling children as individuals (rather than an homogeneous group), researchers found that children with both high task and ego orientation displayed better perceived competence, and had higher intrinsic autonomous motivation than those in other groups (Wang et al., 2002). Furthermore, a cluster analysis involving Finnish children showed that those with high task and ego orientations displayed the most adaptive motivational profiles for sport (Kallinen et al., 2019). Indeed, evidence suggests that many elite athletes see an ego orientation as complementing, not competing with, a task orientation as, in concert, the two help to give them the edge that is necessary to ensure continued success and to sustain motivation in the longer term. This finding refutes original theorising in AGT, and confirms that both orientations must be seen as independent and complementary constructs, i.e. a person can be high on both, low on both or any high/low combination of the two.

An extensive research literature has now grown to consider the many variables that interact with goal orientation, and also the relationship between participation motives and goal orientation. For example, those who are task oriented tend to choose to participate in sport in order to develop or master skills, or for social reasons or fun. In contrast, those with a strong ego orientation tend to take part principally for recognition and social status. Such findings suggest that those with an ego-oriented outlook will tend to find competition more meaningful as it provides an opportunity for social comparison (Harwood et al., 2000). However, those with either a high task or an ego orientation have been shown to place a similar emphasis on competition, and it appears that it is their subjective evaluation of the competitive context that is important rather than the context itself (Treasure et al., 2001).

AGT suggests that early influences will make an impression not only on the goal orientation of the young person but also the perceived motivational climate within which sport takes place (Parish and Treasure, 2003; Duda, 2005). Significant others, including parents, teachers and coaches, help create this climate which is typically characterised as being either mastery (task) or performance (ego) oriented (Ntoumanis and Biddle, 1999), and has, in turn, been shown to correlate with various autonomous motivational types (Lochbaum et al., 2016). By way of example, it has been found that parents and teachers high in task orientation tend to emphasise a mastery climate that values a team orientation, whereas those with an ego orientation nurture a climate or culture that focuses more on outcomes, competition and winning. In time, the dominant orientation of the significant other can be internalised by the young person, and so the climate is passed down to the next generation. The interplay between the motivational climate and the person's own goal orientation profile then becomes of primary concern, along with how the individual orientation changes depending on context, for example in and out of competition (Harwood, 2002).

Interestingly, a relatively recent review by Harwood et al. (2015) concluded that neither parents nor children are always accurate in assessing what the achievement goal orientation of their respective parent/child actually is, but it is their *perception* that matters most and which comes to have the most profound influence on the person's own style. Those who perceive that their parents or coaches have an ego orientation are more likely to worry about making mistakes and winning at all costs, whereas significant others who are seen to have a task orientation generally place a greater emphasis on learning and fun. Moreover, over time there is some evidence that our goal orientation may shift from a task orientation in early childhood to an ego orientation in adolescence. At the same time, large individual differences have been noted, depending on the predominant motivational climate during childhood. Differences have also been noted between boys and girls, with boys (and men) being viewed as generally more ego oriented than girls (or women).

Contemporary reviews have shown a steady growth of interest in AGT, coupled with a critical appraisal of earlier findings and methodologies (e.g. Harwood et al., 2015; Lochbaum et al., 2016). For example, it is argued that there is now a need to consider simultaneously multiple achievement goals and how these interact, in contrast with many earlier studies that focused exclusively on specific sporting goals (Urdan and Kaplan, 2020).

Second, and as discussed previously, the assumed orthogonal structure of task and ego orientation has been questioned, and recent person-centred modelling approaches have provided renewed insight to the relationships between AGT's central tenets. Indeed, and in terms of measurement, traditionally the Perception of Sport Questionnaire (POSQ) or the Task and Ego Orientation Sports Questionnaire (TEOSQ) have been used, the latter measuring both sport-specific and domain-general goal orientation. Both measures treat the two orientations as either entirely independent or orthogonally related constructs, with scores on one not necessarily related to scores on the other. Authors of recent systematic reviews have questioned this assumed structure, and due to item dissimilarities between the dominant measures in the field, outlined the need to concurrently test the validity and reliability of both the TEOSQ and POSQ.

Third, due to a paucity of longitudinal research, it is not clear as to whether goal orientations change through the course of a sporting season or career and, if they do, what factors act as antecedents and which are influenced by goal orientation. Sport provides constant sources of feedback and information on performance which undoubtedly will change perceptions of competence, enjoyment and satisfaction over time, and hence orientation.

Lastly, and despite an accumulation of research evidence, Elliot's 2 × 2 Achievement Goal framework (Elliot and Conroy, 2005) linking task and ego orientation with approach and avoidance goals has received limited support from contemporary meta-analyses, with some arguing for a reconfiguration of this framework to help accommodate conflicting findings (see Lochbaum et al., 2016).

KEY READINGS

Elliot, A.J. and Conroy, D.E. (2005) 'Beyond the dichotomous model of achievement goals in sport and exercise psychology', *Sport and Exercise Psychology Review*, 1, 17–25.

Kallinen, V., Jaakkola, T., Mononen, K., Blomqvist, M., Tolvanen, A. and Konttinen, N. (2019) 'Relationships between achievement goal orientation, perceived competence, and organized sports', *International Journal of Sport Psychology*, 50, 485–502.

Lochbaum, M., Zazo, R., Kazak Çetinkalp, Z., Graham, K., Wright, T. and Konttinen, N. (2016) 'A meta-analytic review of achievement goal orientation correlates in competitive sport: A follow-up to Lochbaum et al. 2016', *Kinesiology*, 48, 159–73.

Urdan, T. and Kaplan, A. (2020) 'The origins, evolution, and future directions of achievement goal theory', *Contemporary Educational Psychology*, 101862. doi.org/10.1016/j.cedpsych.2020.101862.

PRACTICAL QUESTIONS

- What are the key distinctions between a task-oriented and an ego-oriented environment in sport and how do these environments reveal themselves in an athlete's attitudes and behaviour?
- What are the key reasons why an ego-oriented athlete would choose to participate in sport, and what forms of intervention are likely to be most successful with this type of athlete?

REFERENCES

Clancy, R.B., Herring, M.P., MacIntyre, T.E. and Campbell, M.J. (2016) 'A review of competitive sport motivation research', *Psychology of Sport and Exercise*, 27, 232–42.

Duda, J.L. (2005) 'Motivation in sport: The relevance of competence and achievement goals', in A.J. Elliot and C.S. Dweck (eds), *Handbook of Competence and Motivation.* New York: Guilford Publications. pp. 318–35.

Elliot, A.J. and Conroy, D.E. (2005) 'Beyond the dichotomous model of achievement goals in sport and exercise psychology', *Sport and Exercise Psychology Review*, 1, 17–25.

Harwood, C.G. (2002) 'Assessing achievement goals in sport: Caveats for consultants and a case for contextualisation', *Journal of Applied Sport Psychology*, 14, 106–19.

Harwood, C., Hardy, L. and Swain, A. (2000) 'Achievement goals in sport: A critique of conceptual and measurement issues', *Journal of Sport and Exercise Psychology*, 22, 235–55.

Harwood, C.G., Keegan, R.J., Smith, J.M. and Raine, A.S. (2015) 'A systematic review of the intrapersonal correlates of motivational climate perceptions in sport and physical activity,' *Psychology of Sport and Exercise*, 18, 9–25.

Kallinen, V., Jaakkola, T., Mononen, K., Blomqvist, M., Tolvanen, A. and Konttinen, N. (2019) 'Relationships between achievement goal orientation, perceived competence, and organized sports', *International Journal of Sport Psychology*, 50, 485–502.

Lochbaum, M., Zazo, R., Kazak Çetinkalp, Z., Graham, K., Wright, T. and Konttinen, N. (2016) 'A meta-analytic review of achievement goal orientation correlates in competitive sport: A follow-up to Lochbaum et al. 2016', *Kinesiology*, 48 (2), 159–73.

Nicholls, J.G. (1984) 'Achievement motivation: Conceptions of ability, subjective experience, task choice, and performance', *Psychological Review*, 91 (3), 328–46.

Ntoumanis, N. and Biddle, S.J.H. (1999) 'A review of motivational climate in physical activity', *Journal of Sport Sciences*, 17, 643–65.

Parish, L.E. and Treasure, D.C. (2003) 'Physical activity and situational motivation in physical education: Influence of the motivational climate and perceived ability', *Research Quarterly of Exercise and Sport*, 74, 173–82.

Roberts, G.C., Treasure, D.C. and Conroy, D. (2007) 'Understanding the dynamics of motivation in sport and physical activity: An achievement goal interpretation', in G. Tenenbaum and R.C. Eklund (eds), *Handbook of Sport Psychology*. Hoboken, NJ: Wiley. pp. 3–30.

Treasure, D.C., Duda, J.L., Hall, H.K., Roberts, G.C., Ames, C. and Maehr, M.L. (2001) 'Clarifying misconceptions and misrepresentations in achievement goals research in sport: A response to Harwood, Hardy and Swain', *Journal of Sport and Exercise Psychology*, 23, 317–29.

Urdan, T. and Kaplan, A. (2020) 'The origins, evolution, and future directions of achievement goal theory', *Contemporary Educational Psychology*, 101862.

Wang, C.J., Chatzisarantis, N.L., Spray, C.M. and Biddle, S.J. (2002) 'Achievement goal profiles in school physical education: Differences in self-determination, sport ability beliefs, and physical activity', *British Journal of Educational Psychology*, 72 (3), 433–45.

Wang, C.K.J. and Biddle, S.J.H. (2007) 'Understanding young people's motivation toward exercise: An integration of sport ability beliefs, achievement goals theory, and self-determination theory', in M. Hagger and N.L.D. Chatzisarantis (eds), *Self-Determination Theory in Exercise and Sport*. Champaign, IL: Human Kinetics. pp. 193–208.

White, S.A. (2007) 'Parent-created motivational climate', in S. Jowett and D. Lavallee (eds), *Social Psychology in Sport*. Champaign, IL: Human Kinetics. pp. 131–44.

3.16 SELF-EFFICACY AND PERCEIVED COMPETENCE

Definitions: Self-efficacy is a person's judgement of his or her capabilities to organise and execute courses of action required to attain designated types of performance. Perceived competence is an innate need to seek out challenges and feel effective in one's environment.

Alongside the growth of interest in intrinsic influences on sport participation during the 1970s, it was inevitable that a focus would fall on the self, and in particular on aspects of the self that have a direct bearing on our confidence and ability to perform well. At that time there were major developments regarding the self within psychology, typically driven from within the field of education, and these new ideas resonated strongly in the world of sport. Chief among such influences were the constructs of self-efficacy and perceived competence, the former most closely associated with social learning theory and Albert Bandura, the latter with Susan Harter. Although based on quite distinct research literatures, the underlying themes are not dissimilar. Both deal with our confidence or perceived ability to deal with new experiences and challenges, and both form an integral part of our self-concept.

Before looking at key research findings it may be useful to define each term and to see how they interrelate. To begin, self-concept is defined as a person's self-perceptions that are formed through experience with, and interpretations of, his or her environment, including both the academic and non-academic (social, emotional, physical). This encompasses all self-perceptions, both positive and negative. In contrast, perceived competence and self-efficacy focus attention on the positive, or what is commonly known as confidence or self-confidence. Perceived competence is characterised as the extent to which we feel we possess the necessary attributes (including social, emotional, physical and intellectual/cognitive skills) in order to succeed, while self-efficacy concerns our personal evaluation of our ability to perform, defined by Bandura as 'people's judgements of their capabilities to organise and execute courses of actions required to attain designated types of performance' (Bandura, 1997).

How do these constructs interrelate? Not an easy question and one which the majority of authors have sidestepped, perhaps because of the degree of overlap. To some the terms are used interchangeably, while others have at least attempted to map out their connections more systematically (Sundström, 2006; Feltz et al., 2008), or to highlight distinctions, however subtle. According to Reeve (2014) self-efficacy relates to state-specific perceptions of ability that either vary across tasks or within tasks (depending on difficulty and context) and fluctuate as new information is collected and processed. Further, self-efficacy addresses what you perceive you *are* able to do with your abilities, rather than what you are objectively capable of. Perceived competence is more of a developmental constant about feeling effective in one's environment, and relates to our innate tendency to seek out new challenges. By way of illustration, a young footballer kicking a ball against a wall for hours on end is satisfying his or her need for competence. In contrast, his or her ability to kick certain shots such as volleying the ball against the wall without the ball hitting the ground on the way back will be more directly affected by self-efficacy information that is collected and will fluctuate from ongoing attempts. Due to perceptions of self-efficacy, the footballer may choose to continue, change or stop the volleying attempts and move to alternative practices. After some time and depending on perceived self-efficacy, the young person may stop playing football altogether to continue their Playstation game, and thus seek out new experiences, thereby satisfying their need for competence in another domain.

SELF-EFFICACY

In Bandura's original formulation (Self-Efficacy Theory), self-efficacy was regarded as a stable attribute that was determined by four primary sources of information (performance or past accomplishment; vicarious experience; verbal persuasion; and physiological state), with the first, performance accomplishment, seen as the most significant. As identified in Figure 3.6, self-efficacy has direct effects on outcomes necessary to sustain and enhance motivation, including persistence, effort and emotional reactions (e.g. pride, joy). Indeed, Bandura (1997) contends that an individual's perception of self-efficacy is typically a better predictor of behaviour and performance than what they are objectively capable of.

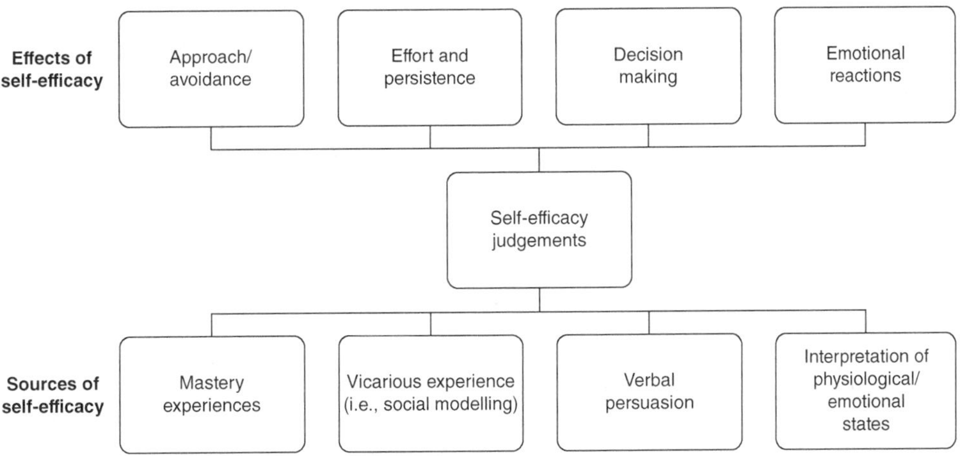

Figure 3.6 Sources and Effects of Self-Efficacy

Later writers have modified the theory (see Maddux and Volkmann, 2010), for example adding a further two potential sources of information (imaginal experiences – i.e. seeing ourselves succeeding – and emotional states), while Vealey (2001) postulated that as many as nine separate sources of information in sport could be identified: mastery; demonstration of ability; physical and mental preparation; physical self-presentation; social support; coaches' leadership; vicarious experience; environmental comfort; and situational favourableness.

In a later reformulation (Social-Cognitive Theory; Bandura, 1997), self-efficacy was broken down further into two components. The first relates to our ability to actually perform the skill or task in the first place (*efficacy expectations*), while the second concerns our judgements about the outcomes attaching to that performance, otherwise known as *outcome expectations*. He also argued that, rather than being a stable predisposition, our self-efficacy may be more context-dependent, suggesting that cognitions (including self-efficacy), actions and the environment interact in a reciprocal manner over time. Bandura also maintained that any measure of self-efficacy must consider three dimensions: level (expected level of attainment); strength (certainty that the level will be attained); and generality (the domains across which the person feels capable). For example, someone with a high sense of general physical self-efficacy would expect to perform well at subdomains such as catching and running.

Since that time, and given the importance that athletes attach to confidence, it is no surprise that sport psychologists have attempted to consider how self-efficacy reflects in performance (Feltz et al., 2008). For example, research has shown that self-efficacy predicts engagement with specific physical activities and that those who are more physically efficacious tend to exercise more regularly, expend greater effort, persist longer, enjoy greater success and achieve better health-related benefits from exercise than adults with a low sense of physical self-efficacy (Reeve, 2014). That is, with high expectations of a successful outcome to participation and repeated success, a person will be more likely to repeat and sustain their involvement. In contrast, low self-efficacy and unfavourable experiences are more likely to lead to withdrawal. However, in a recent critique of self-efficacy theory and research, Beauchamp et al. (2019) present emerging evidence that, on occasion, the relationship between self-efficacy and performance can be negative and in particular when a person has overestimated his/her objective capabilities because of past accomplishments – and thus future performances suffer.

Several variables including prior experience, social support and personality have been shown to impact on self-efficacy prior to engagement with the activity, while during participation itself the person's confidence is influenced by prior self-efficacy, personal goals, feedback and rewards; in turn these then influence self-efficacy and motivation toward sustained involvement (Bruton et al., 2013). Overall, the influence of self-efficacy on exercise and sports participation appears to be stronger in the early stages of skill development. With repeated experience the activity often becomes more routine and the psychological demands are less taxing; in these circumstances the person relies less on self-efficacy and more on feedback (McAuley et al., 2001; Bruton et al., 2013).

Bandura (1997) posited socio-structural factors as mediators between self-efficacy and behaviour, suggesting self-efficacy is the primary causal driver of behaviour. However, Beauchamp et al. (2019) presented evidence that socio-structural factors can in fact precede self-efficacy. In terms of demographic variables, men and those with higher socio-economic status are often characterised by greater self-efficacy, while among adults self-efficacy tends to peak up to middle age. Extant evidence indicates that, during childhood and adolescence, it would appear that different age groups rely on different sources of self-efficacy. For example, encouragement from coaches and peers is the most important source of self-efficacy for adolescents while performance accomplishment remains significant for all ages.

The literature on self-efficacy continues to show the practical utility of the construct (Beauchamp et al., 2019), and strongly suggests the positive role that significant others, including parents and coaches, can play in improving self-efficacy. Also, the construct of self-efficacy increasingly makes an appearance in many contemporary theoretical perspectives, including recent integrated models of behaviour change (Hagger and Chatzisarantis, 2014).

An approach that borrows heavily from both the work of Bandura and Achievement Goal Theory (see **3.15**) is Vealey's Theory of Sport Confidence (Vealey, 2001). This approach tracks the effect that underlying trait confidence (self-efficacy) will have on state confidence and ultimately performance, mediated by the competitive orientation (either task or ego) that the athlete brings to his or her sport. Additionally, a quite separate literature has developed considering not *personal* self-efficacy but *collective* efficacy. This deals with not the individual's but the team's belief in its combined capabilities to perform collective tasks (Beauchamp, 2007), and has been shown to have a considerable bearing on team performance and success (see **5.22** and **5.23**).

Despite the valuable contributions cited, questions still remain in relation to measurement, within-persons effects (i.e. can too much self-efficacy come at a price?), and causal directionality (Beauchamp et al., 2019), with some evidence suggesting that existing measures may be unintentionally tapping into outcome expectations that could be considered either as a precursor or an outcome of self-efficacy.

PERCEIVED COMPETENCE

As with Albert Bandura's work on self-efficacy, the origins of research on perceived competence lie far outside the world of sport but again it did not take long for the ideas to be borrowed to help understand sport performance and motivation. According to Susan Harter (Harter, 1999), human motivation is mediated by the influence of our perceptions of competence and control in various domains, including the cognitive, the social and the physical (Weiss and Amorose, 2006). During the 1970s, work on perceived competence in a sporting context flourished, where it was found to exert an influence both on the initiation of activity and then on its continuation, a bi-directional pattern now commonly referred to as 'the success circle'.

According to Harter, once the individual has engaged in a mastery attempt, that person will receive feedback on competence from a variety of sources, including significant others. This information will influence the individual's perceptions of competence, control and their emotional reactions, which then go on to influence the likelihood of the person choosing to either repeat or avoid the experience. In an emotional capacity, success is accompanied by pleasure which raises perceived competence which in turn increases achievement-striving behaviour and so the success circle grows. In contrast, failure leads to dissatisfaction and shame, and a perception of incompetence, decreasing the likelihood of future attempts at mastery.

In common with Social-Cognitive Theory, Harter's theory suggests that perceptions of competence are strongly influenced by the feedback provided by significant others including coaches, teachers, parents and peers. The available evidence strongly suggests that the nature of such feedback, following from either success or failure, is critical in nurturing perceptions of competence, and subsequent engagement in sport and exercise.

In addition to theoretical overlaps with Bandura's Social Cognitive Theory, and Ryan and Deci's Self-Determination Theory, Expectancy-Value Theory (Eccles and Wigfield, 2002) supports the contention that competence is central in determining motivation. Expectancy-value theorists consider perceived competence in terms of two belief systems, those relating to expectancy (of a certain performance) and those linked to ability or perceived competence in certain domains. Ability beliefs represent an individual's broad beliefs about their competence in a given domain (e.g. the physical), while expectancy beliefs for task performance are more domain-specific. Ability beliefs thus are distinguished conceptually from expectancy beliefs in at least two ways. First, ability beliefs are broad beliefs about one's competence while expectancy beliefs are domain-specific. Second, ability beliefs focus on present ability while expectancy beliefs focus on the future (Eccles and Wigfield, 2002). The widely held assertion that perceived competence positively links to sports participation has consistent support in the evidence; however, the reported effect sizes are now generally smaller than once thought. For example, a meta-analysis of 59 studies among young people (Babic et al., 2014) revealed an r of 0.30 for physical competence and physical activity, while a further meta-analysis of the relationship between motor competence and physical fitness during the transition from early childhood to early adulthood showed an r of 0.43 (Utesch et al., 2019). Interestingly, a recent systematic review showed a mismatch, such that the strength of the association between actual motor competence and perceived motor competence/physical self-perception in youth was found to be low to moderate. In general terms, the available research does still suggest that perceived competence may be significant but not exclusive; instead, it acts as one of many reasons that individuals routinely cite for taking part in sport (Weiss et al., 2009).

KEY READINGS

Bandura, A. (1997) *Self-Efficacy: The Exercise of Control*. Basingstoke: Freeman.

Beauchamp, M.R., Crawford, K.L. and Jackson, B. (2019) 'Social cognitive theory and physical activity: Mechanisms of behavior change, critique, and legacy', *Psychology of Sport and Exercise*, 42, 110–17.

Feltz, D.L., Short, S.E. and Sullivan, P.J. (2008) *Self-Efficacy in Sport: Research and Strategies for Working with Athletes, Teams and Coaches*. Champaign, IL: Human Kinetics.

Hagger, M.S. and Chatzisarantis, N.L. (2014) 'An integrated behavior change model for physical activity', *Exercise and Sport Sciences Reviews*, 42 (2), 62–9.

PRACTICAL QUESTIONS

- How do self-efficacy and competence overlap, in what ways do they differ and why are these differences important in framing an intervention with an under-performing young athlete?
- What does high self-efficacy predict in sport?

REFERENCES

Babic, M.J., Morgan, P.J., Plotnikoff, R.C., Lonsdale, C., White, R.L. and Lubans, D.R. (2014) 'Physical activity and physical self-concept in youth: Systematic review and meta-analysis', *Sports Medicine*, 44 (11), 1589–601.

Bandura, A. (1997) *Self-Efficacy: The Exercise of Control*. Basingstoke: Freeman.

Beauchamp, M.R. (2007) 'Efficacy beliefs within relational and group contexts in sport', in S. Jowett and D. Lavallee (eds), *Social Psychology in Sport*. Champaign, IL: Human Kinetics. pp. 181–93.

Beauchamp, M.R., Crawford, K.L. and Jackson, B. (2019) 'Social cognitive theory and physical activity: Mechanisms of behavior change, critique, and legacy', *Psychology of Sport and Exercise*, 42, 110–17.

Bruton, A.M., Mellalieu, S.D., Shearer, D., Roderique-Davies, G. and Hall, R. (2013) 'Performance accomplishment information as predictors of self-efficacy as a function of skill level in amateur golf', *Journal of Applied Sport Psychology*, 25 (2), 197–208.

Eccles, J.S. and Wigfield, A. (2002) 'Motivational beliefs, values, and goals', *Annual Review of Psychology*, 53, 109–32.

Feltz, D.L., Short, S.E. and Sullivan, P.J. (2008) *Self-Efficacy in Sport: Research and Strategies for Working with Athletes, Teams and Coaches*. Champaign, IL: Human Kinetics.

Harter, S. (1999) *The Construction of the Self: A Developmental Perspective*. New York: Guilford Press.

Hagger, M.S. and Chatzisarantis, N.L. (2014) 'An integrated behavior change model for physical activity', *Exercise and Sport Sciences Reviews*, 42 (2), 62–9.

Maddux, J.E. and Volkmann, J.R. (2010) 'Self-efficacy and self-regulation', in R. Hoyle (ed.), *Handbook of Personality and Self-Regulation*. New York: Wiley-Blackwell. pp. 210–45.

McAuley, E., Pena, M.M. and Jerome, G. (2001) 'Self-efficacy as a determinant and an outcome of exercise', in G.C. Roberts (ed.), *Advances in Motivation in Sport and Exercise*. Champaign, IL: Human Kinetics. pp. 235–61.

Reeve, J. (2014) *Understanding Motivation and Emotion*. New York: John Wiley & Sons.

Sundström, A. (2006) *Beliefs about Perceived Competence: A Literature Review*. Educational Measurement Report (EMR), 55. Umeå, Sweden: University of Umeå.

Utesch, T., Bardid, F., Büsch, D. and Strauss, B. (2019) 'The relationship between motor competence and physical fitness from early childhood to early adulthood: A meta-analysis', *Sports Medicine*, 49(4), 541–51.

Vealey, R.S. (2001) 'Understanding and enhancing self-confidence in athletes', in R.A. Singer, H.A. Hausenblas and C. Jannelle (eds), *Handbook of Sport Psychology* (2nd ed.). New York: Wiley. pp. 550–65.

Weiss, M.R. and Amorose, A.J. (2006) 'Motivational orientations and sport behavior', in T.S. Horn (ed.), *Advances in Sport Psychology* (3rd ed.). Champaign, IL: Human Kinetics. pp. 115–55.

Weiss, M.R., Amorose, A.J. and Wilko, A.M. (2009) 'Coaching behaviors, motivational climate, and psychosocial outcomes among female adolescent athletes', *Journal of Pediatric Exercise Science*, 21, 475–92.

Cognitive Processes in Sport

Chapter Summary: In this chapter, significant topics in sport psychology that emphasise how cognitive processes enhance sport performance will be reviewed. The chapter begins with an outline of how athletes have used mental imagery and mental practice to enhance performance, along with a consideration of relevant hypotheses, theories and models. Attentional styles and concentration are then reflected on, as are the benefits associated with positive self-talk and thought control. Finally, the chapter ends with a discussion of the key characteristics of mental toughness, conceptual problems inherent in its definition and how mental toughness can be enhanced.

4.17 Mental Imagery 106
4.18 Mental Practice 111
4.19 Attention and Concentration 117
4.20 Positive Self-Talk and Thought Control 122
4.21 Mental Toughness 127

4.17 MENTAL IMAGERY

Definition: Mental imagery is the ability to simulate in the mind information that is not currently being perceived by the senses.

One of the most remarkable capacities of the mind is its ability to simulate sensations, actions and other types of experience, in the immediate absence of that experience. For example, if you close your eyes you should be able to imagine the appearance of a tennis racket (a visual image), the sound of a tennis ball bouncing on the strings of the racket (an auditory image) and perhaps even the 'feeling' or weight of this racket in your hand (a kinaesthetic image).

Mental imagery (or visualisation) is the ability to simulate in the mind information that is not currently being perceived by the senses. It is a cognitive process that enables us to 'see', 'hear' and 'feel' things in our imagination. At a theoretical level, imagery involves perception without sensation. To explain: whereas *perception* occurs when we interpret sensory input obtained from the outside world, *imagery* arises from our interpretation of stored, memory-based information. So, the process of generating a mental image is rather like running perception backwards. Not surprisingly, different types of mental imagery exist – depending on the sensory modality involved. Apart from visual and auditory imagery, the most recent type of imagery investigated in sport psychology and cognitive neuroscience is motor imagery (also known as kinaesthetic imagery), which is used whenever people imagine actions without engaging in the actual physical movements involved (see also **4.18**).

At least three strands of evidence confirm the importance of mental imagery for the learning and performance of sport skills (Moran and Toner, 2017). First, anecdotal testimonials to the value of imagery come from world-class athletes such as Dottie Pepper (golf), Ronaldinho (soccer) and Michael Phelps (swimming). Second, descriptive evidence (e.g. survey data) suggests that elite athletes, coaches and psychologists use imagery extensively for a variety of purposes, including skill-learning (see **6.35**), anxiety management and mental preparation for competitive performance. Third, experimental research on mental practice shows that the systematic use of mental imagery can improve skill-learning and skilled performance (see **4.18**).

Although mental imagery processes are unobservable, they are measurable indirectly. In general, three different approaches or paradigms have been used for this task: the psychometric, qualitative and chronometric. To begin with, researchers using the psychometric approach have developed standardised self-report scales designed to measure athletes' imagery abilities and their imagery use (see review by Morris et al., 2005). Typically, imagery ability tests ask participants to evaluate certain aspects of their imagery experience (e.g. the *vividness* of an image or its clarity or sensory richness). Among the most popular and psychometrically impressive tests of imagery skills in athletes are the Vividness of Movement Imagery Questionnaire (VMIQ) (Isaac et al., 1986) and the revised version of the Movement Imagery Questionnaire (MIQ-R) (Hall and Martin, 1997). The VMIQ is a 24-item measure of 'visual imagery of movement itself and imagery of kinaesthetic sensations' (Isaac et al., 1986: 24). Each of the items presents a different movement or action to be imagined (e.g. riding a bicycle). Respondents are required to rate these items in two ways: 'watching somebody else' and 'doing it yourself'. The ratings are given on a five-point scale where 1 = 'perfectly clear and as vivid as normal vision' and 5 = 'no image at all'. The MIQ-R was designed to assess individual differences in *kinaesthetic* as well as visual imagery of movement. Briefly, this test contains eight items which assess people's ease of imaging specific movements either visually or kinaesthetically. In order to complete an item, respondents must execute a movement and rate it on a scale ranging from 1 (very hard to see/feel) to 7 (very easy to see/feel). Imagery scores are calculated as separate sums of the two subscales of visual and kinaesthetic imagery skills. Available evidence indicates that the MIQ-R displays adequate reliability and validity. The most recent psychometric test of imagery ability is the Vividness of Movement Imagery Questionnaire-2 (VMIQ-2) (Roberts et al., 2008). This test consists of 12 items and assesses the ability to form mental images of a variety of movements visually and kinaesthetically. The visual component is further subdivided into 'external' and 'internal' visual imagery. Respondents are required to 'imagine' each of the 12 movements and to rate the vividness of each item on a Likert-type scale from 1 (perfectly clear and vivid) to 5 (no image at all). The VMIQ-2 displays impressive factorial validity and acceptable concurrent and discriminate validity.

Turning to imagery use, the *Sport Imagery Questionnaire* (SIQ) (Hall et al., 1998) is a popular, theory-based and reliable tool for measuring the frequency with which athletes employ imagery for motivational and cognitive purposes. Based on Paivio's (1985) theory that imagery affects behaviour through motivational and cognitive mechanisms operating at general and specific levels, the SIQ is a 30-item instrument (with five subscales) that asks respondents to rate on a seven-point scale (where 1 = 'rarely' and 7 = 'often') how often they use five specific categories of imagery:

- Motivation general – mastery (e.g. imagining appearing confident in front of others)
- Motivation general – arousal (e.g. imagining the stress and/or excitement associated with competition)
- Motivation specific (e.g. imagining winning a medal)
- Cognitive general (e.g. imagining various strategies for a competitive event)
- Cognitive specific (e.g. mentally practising a skill)

Sample items from these subscales include:

- 'I imagine myself appearing self confident in front of my opponents' (motivational general-mastery)
- 'I imagine the stress and anxiety associated with competing' (motivation general-arousal)
- 'I imagine myself winning a medal' (motivation specific)
- 'I imagine alternative strategies in case my event/game plan fails' (cognitive general)
- 'I can mentally make corrections to physical skills' (cognitive specific)

The six items that comprise each subscale are averaged to yield a score that indicates the extent to which respondents use each of the five functions of imagery.

Unfortunately, subjective self-report scales of imagery have certain limitations. For example, the movements that participants are required to perform in these tests are quite complex and time-consuming, thereby making such tests administratively burdensome.

Also, these tests are subject to contamination from response sets such as social desirability. Put simply, most people are eager to portray themselves as having a good or vivid imagination regardless of their true skills in that area. To overcome this tendency, objective tests of imagery have been developed. Thus, the controllability dimension of a visual mental image (which refers to the ease and accuracy with which it can be transformed symbolically) can be measured objectively by requesting people to complete tasks that are known to require visualisation abilities. For example, in the Group Mental Rotations Test (GMRT) (Vandenberg and Kuse, 1978), people have to make judgements about whether or not the spatial orientation of certain three-dimensional target figures matches (i.e. is congruent with) or does not match (i.e. is incompatible with) various alternative shapes. The higher a person scores on this test, the stronger are his or her image control skills.

The second approach to measuring mental imagery skills in sport is derived from the qualitative paradigm. Using this method, in-depth interviews are employed to investigate the meaning and richness of people's imagery experiences. Although such methods have obvious weaknesses (e.g. they depend on introspective access to conscious awareness), they can provide valuable insights into athletes' *meta-imagery* processes – or their knowledge of, and control over, their *own* mental imagery skills and experiences (Moran, 2002; Moran and Toner, 2017). For example, MacIntyre and Moran (2007a, 2007b) investigated whether or not expert athletes have greater insight into, and control over, their use of imagery than their less successful counterparts. In particular, athletes were asked about their knowledge of some common motor imagery effects. Results indicated that athletes were aware both of *mental practice* effects (see **4.18**) and *mental travel* effects – the fact that when one imagines a movement it should last the same duration as the actual executed action. Unfortunately, a weakness of the qualitative approach is that it is inherently subjective and hence difficult to validate empirically (Ely et al., 2020).

The final approach to measuring mental imagery is the chronometric paradigm (see reviews by Guillot and Collet, 2005, 2010). This approach allows researchers to investigate motor imagery objectively by comparing the duration required to execute real and imagined actions. The logic here is as follows. According to the functional equivalence hypothesis (e.g. Jeannerod, 1994), imagined and executed actions rely on similar motor representations and activate some common brain areas (e.g. the parietal and prefrontal cortices, and the pre-motor and primary cortices). As the temporal organisation of imagined and actual actions is similar, there should be a close correspondence between the time required to mentally perform simulated actions and that required for actual performance. In a typical study, Calmels et al. (2006) examined the temporal congruence between actual and imagined movements in gymnastics. They found that the overall times required to perform and imagine a complex gymnastic vault were broadly similar – regardless of whether participants used 'first person' or 'third person' imagery perspectives. However, the temporal congruence between actual and imagined actions is mediated by a number of factors. For example, Guillot and Collet (2005) concluded that when the skills in question are largely automatic (e.g. reaching or grasping) or occur in cyclical movements (e.g. walking, rowing), there is usually a high degree of temporal congruence between actual and imagined performance. However, when the skill being performed involves complex, attention-demanding movements (e.g. golf putting, tennis serving), people tend to *overestimate* imagined duration. Guillot and Collet (2010) have shown that methods based on recording motor imagery times and measuring the temporal congruence between imagery and actual times are powerful and versatile tools for the assessment of mental imagery ability. However, a limitation of this approach is that it does not consider imagery vividness (Moran and Toner, 2017).

Although considerable progress has been made in understanding the mechanisms underlying, and measuring, mental imagery processes in athletes, a potentially important gap in this field cannot be ignored. Specifically, although a wealth of evidence has been gathered on imagery use in athletes (e.g. see Weinberg, 2008, Ely et al., 2020), imagery researchers in sport have largely neglected *meta-imagery* processes or athletes' knowledge of, and control over, their *own* mental imagery skills and experiences. However, MacIntyre and Moran (2007a, 2007b) explored such meta-imagery processes in elite athletes. An interesting discovery from these studies was that these athletes sometimes deliberately generated *negative* imagery content based on the belief that it would help them to cope with possible future adversity. Looking to the future, the use of both negative and positive imagery may represent one important part of broader metacognitive and action pathways, whose exploration should further our understanding of performance expertise in sport (MacIntyre et al., 2014).

KEY READINGS

Ely, F.O., Munroe-Chandler, K.J., Jenny, O. and McCullagh, P. (2020) 'The practice of imagery: A review of 25 years of applied sport imagery recommendations', *Journal of Imagery Research in Sport and Physical Activity*, 15 (1). DOI: 10.1515/jirspa-2020-0018.

Hall, C., Mack, D., Paivio, A. and Hausenblas, H.A. (1998) 'Imagery use by athletes: Development of the Sport Imagery Questionnaire', *International Journal of Sport Psychology*, 29, 73–89.

MacIntyre, T.E., Igou, E.R., Campbell, M.J., Moran, A.P. and Matthews, J. (2014) 'Metacognition and action: A new pathway to understanding social and cognitive aspects of expertise in sport', *Frontiers in Psychology*, 5, 1155.

Moran, A. and Toner, J. (2017) *Sport and Exercise Psychology: A Critical Introduction*. London: Taylor & Francis. pp. 165–200.

PRACTICAL QUESTIONS

- Using each of the five functions described in the Sport Imagery Questionnaire, consider what should be included in an imagery script to support the enhancement of an athlete's imagery skills.
- A football player is having difficulties with taking penalty shots and especially during important games where she experiences high pressure to perform well. How could imagery be employed to help the player in these situations?

REFERENCES

Calmels, C., Holmes, P., Lopez, E. and Naman, V. (2006) 'Chronometric comparison of actual and imaged complex movement patterns', *Journal of Motor Behavior*, 38, 339–48.

Ely, F.O., Munroe-Chandler, K.J., Jenny, O. and McCullagh, P. (2020) 'The practice of imagery: A review of 25 years of applied sport imagery recommendations', *Journal of Imagery Research in Sport and Physical Activity*, 15(1). DOI: 10.1515/jirspa-2020-0018.

Guillot, A. and Collet, C. (2005) 'Duration of mentally simulated movement: A review', *Journal of Motor Behavior*, 37, 10–20.

Guillot, A. and Collet, C. (eds) (2010) *The Neurophysiological Foundations of Mental and Motor Imagery*. Oxford: Oxford University Press.

Hall, C.R. and Martin, K.A. (1997) 'Measuring movement imagery abilities: A revision of the Movement Imagery Questionnaire', *Journal of Mental Imagery*, 21, 143–54.

Hall, C., Mack, D., Paivio, A. and Hausenblas, H.A. (1998) 'Imagery use by athletes: Development of the Sport Imagery Questionnaire', *International Journal of Sport Psychology*, 29, 73–89.

Isaac, A., Marks, D. and Russell, E. (1986) 'An instrument for assessing imagery of movement: The Vividness of Movement Imagery Questionnaire (VMIQ)', *Journal of Mental Imagery*, 10, 23–30.

Jeannerod, M. (1994) 'The representing brain: Neural correlates of motor intention and imagery', *Behavioral and Brain Sciences*, 17, 187–245.

MacIntyre, T. and Moran, A. (2007a) 'A qualitative investigation of imagery use and meta-imagery processes among elite canoe-slalom competitors', *Journal of Imagery Research in Sport and Physical Activity*, 2, 1–23.

MacIntyre, T. and Moran, A. (2007b) 'A qualitative investigation of meta-imagery processes and imagery direction among elite athletes', *Journal of Imagery Research in Sport and Physical Activity*, 2, 1–20.

MacIntyre, T.E., Igou, E.R., Campbell, M.J., Moran, A.P. and Matthews, J. (2014) 'Metacognition and action: a new pathway to understanding social and cognitive aspects of expertise in sport', *Frontiers in Psychology*, 5, 1155.

Moran, A.P. (2002) 'In the mind's eye', *The Psychologist*, 15, 414–15.

Moran, A. and Toner, J. (2017) *Sport and Exercise Psychology: A Critical Introduction*. London: Taylor & Francis. pp. 165–200.

Morris, T., Spittle, M. and Watt, A.P. (2005) *Imagery in Sport*. Champaign, IL: Human Kinetics.

Paivio, A. (1985) 'Cognitive and motivational functions of imagery in human performance', *Canadian Journal of Applied Sport Science*, 10, 22–8.

Roberts, R., Callow, N., Hardy, L., Markland, D. and Bringer, J. (2008) 'Movement imagery ability: Development and assessment of a revised version of the Vividness of Movement Imagery Questionnaire', *Journal of Sport and Exercise Psychology*, 30, 200–21.

Vandenberg, S. and Kuse, A.R. (1978) 'Mental rotations: A group test of three-dimensional spatial visualization', *Perceptual and Motor Skills*, 47, 599–604.

Weinberg, R.S. (2008) 'Does imagery work? Effects on performance and mental skills', *Journal of Imagery Research in Sport and Physical Activity*, 3 (1), 1–21.

4.18 MENTAL PRACTICE

Definition: Mental practice is the systematic use of mental imagery to rehearse an action in one's imagination without engaging in the actual physical movements involved.

The term 'mental practice' (MP) refers to the systematic use of mental imagery to 'see' and 'feel' an action in one's imagination without engaging in the actual physical movements. Because it relies on *simulated* movements, MP is sometimes known as 'symbolic rehearsal', 'covert rehearsal' or 'imaginary practice'. Psychological interest in mental practice is as old as the discipline of psychology itself. For example, William James (1890) suggested, rather counter-intuitively, that by anticipating experiences imaginatively, people actually learn to skate in the summer and to swim in the winter! For well over a century, the effects of MP on skilled performance have been investigated by psychology researchers with several reviews (e.g Driskell et al., 1994) and a 24-year follow-up meta-analysis showing that MP has an enduring positive influence on performance (Toth et al., 2020).

Typically, investigators use an experimental paradigm that involves a comparison of the pre- and post-intervention performance of four groups of participants: those who have been engaged only in physical practice of the skill in question (the physical practice group, PP); those who have mentally practised it (the mental practice group, MP); those who have alternated between physical and mental practice (PP/MP); and participants in a non-practice control condition. After a pre-treatment baseline test has been conducted on a designated skill, participants are randomly assigned to one of these conditions (PP, MP, PP/MP or control). Normally, the cognitive rehearsal that occurs in the MP treatment condition is guided by a mental imagery 'script' that describes the motor actions to be executed in clear and vivid detail (see Morris et al., 2005). After this MP intervention has been applied, the participants' performance on the target skill is tested again. If the performance of the MP group is significantly superior to that of the control group, then a positive effect of mental practice is deemed to have occurred.

Using this experimental paradigm, imagery researchers have established a number of conclusions about the efficacy of mental practice. First, MP has been shown to improve the learning and performance of a variety of motor skills in sport (e.g. self-paced skills such as golf-putting and 'reactive' skills such as tackling in rugby) (Moran and Toner, 2017), music (Miksza et al., 2018) and medical surgery (Anton et al., 2017). MP has also been found to increase physical strength performance and to facilitate rehabilitation from physical injury or neurological damage. Second, research suggests that MP, when combined and alternated with physical practice, tends to produce superior skill-learning to that resulting from either mental or physical practice alone. Third, there is evidence that mental practice improves the performance of cognitive skills (i.e. those that involve sequential processing activities, e.g. mirror drawing tasks) more than it does for motor skills (e.g. balancing on a stabilometer). Fourth, expert athletes tend to benefit more from MP than do novices, regardless of the type of skill being practised (either cognitive or physical). Fifth, the positive effects of MP on task performance tend to decline sharply over time. Indeed, according to Driskell et al. (1994), the beneficial effects of motor imagery training are reduced to *half* of their original value after approximately two weeks have elapsed. A practical implication of this finding is that, in order to gain optimal benefits from mental practice, 'refresher' training should be implemented after this critical two-week period. In a review of 37 studies and 115 effects, mental practice has been shown to have a stronger effect for externally cued movement tasks compared to internally cued movement tasks, and was more effective in programmes lasting between one and six weeks (Toth et al., 2020). Finally, there is evidence that imagery ability mediates the relationship between MP and motor skill performance. Thus, athletes who are proficient in generating and controlling vivid images tend to benefit more from visualisation than do their counterparts who lack such abilities.

Despite the proliferation of research on MP, a key validation problem afflicts many studies in this field. Specifically, how do we know that people who *claim* to be using imagery when engaged in mental practice are actually doing so? Put differently, how can we validate people's subjective reports about their imagery experiences? One way of addressing this issue is to use custom-designed 'manipulation checks' or verification procedures that attempt to assess the ease and accuracy with which participants adhered to the imagery instructions/script that they had received. Another potential solution to this validation problem comes from research on the *mental travel* chronometric paradigm (see review by Guillot and Collet, 2005). To explain, according to the functional equivalence hypothesis (see **4.17**), imagined and executed actions rely on similar motor representations and activate common brain areas (e.g. the pre-motor and primary cortices). Because the temporal organisation of imagined and actual actions is similar, there should be a close correspondence between the time required to *mentally* perform simulated actions and that required for *actual* performance, and indeed this hypothesis has been tested and corroborated empirically (Guillot and Collet, 2005, 2010). Using this mental chronometry approach, Moran and MacIntyre (1998) validated the veracity of canoe-slalomists' imagery reports by comparing the congruence between the imagined time and 'real' time required by these athletes to navigate their courses in competition.

In general, four main theories have been postulated to explain MP effects: the neuromuscular model (e.g. Jacobson, 1932); the cognitive or symbolic approach (e.g. Denis, 1985); the bio-informational theory (e.g. Lang, 1979); and, most recently, the PETTLEP approach (Holmes and Collins, 2001). These theories are summarised briefly as follows (for further detail, see Moran, 2016).

To begin with, the neuromuscular model proposes that mental practice effects are mediated by faint activity in the peripheral musculature. This theory postulates that there is a strong positive relationship between the muscular activity elicited by imagining a given skill and that detected during the actual execution of this skill. Unfortunately, there is little empirical support for this hypothesis or, more generally, for neuromuscular theories of mental practice.

Next, the cognitive approach suggests that mental practice facilitates the coding and rehearsal of key elements of the skilled task. By contrast with neuromuscular accounts of MP, cognitive models attach little importance to what happens in the *peripheral* musculature of the performer. Instead, they focus on the possibility that mental rehearsal strengthens the brain's *central* representation or cognitive 'blueprint' of the skill being imagined. Although this approach has a plausible theoretical rationale, it is challenged by evidence that MP can improve people's performance of strength tasks which, by definition, contain few cognitive components. Another problem for symbolic theories is that they find it difficult to explain how MP can enhance the performance of expert athletes who, presumably, already possess well-established blueprints, mental representations or motor schemata for the movements being imagined (Moran, 2016).

Third, the bio-informational theory postulates that MP effects reflect an interaction of three different factors: the environment in which a given movement is performed ('stimulus' information such as 'feeling' the soft ground as one imagines teeing up a ball in golf); what is felt by the performer while the movement occurs ('response' information such as feeling a slow, smooth practice swing on the imaginary tee-box); and the perceived importance of this skill to the performer ('meaning' information such as feeling slightly anxious because other people are watching as one prepares to drive the ball). Of these factors, the *response* propositions are held to be especially significant because they are believed to reflect how a person would *actually* react in the real-life situation being imagined. Therefore, bio-informational theorists postulate that imagery scripts that are heavily laden with response propositions should elicit greater MP effects than those without such information. Despite a dearth of empirical evidence to support this hypothesis, the bio-informational approach has been influential among imagery researchers in highlighting the value of 'individualising' imagery scripts so that they take account of the personal meaning which people attribute to the skills or movements that they wish to rehearse.

Fourth, a theoretical approach to describe mental practice is called PETTLEP (Holmes and Collins, 2001) – an acronym referring to *P*hysical, *E*nvironment, *T*ask, *T*iming, *L*earning, *E*motion and *P*erspective aspects of mental imagery (Collins and Carson, 2017). In this model, 'P' refers to the athlete's physical response to the sporting situation imagined, 'E' is the environment in which the imagery is performed, 'T' is the imagined task, 'T' refers to timing (i.e. the pace at which the imagery is performed), 'L' is a learning or memory component of imagery, 'E' refers to the emotions elicited by the imagery and 'P' designates the type of visual imagery perspective used by the practitioner (i.e. whether he or she imagines the movement from a 'first-person' perspective or from a 'third-person' perspective). Overall, the PETTLEP model proposes that, in order to produce optimal functional equivalence (see **4.17**) between imagery and motor production, and thereby to enhance subsequent sport performance, imagery interventions should replicate not only the athletes' sporting situation but also the emotions that they experience when performing their skills. Although the predictions of the PETTLEP model have not been tested extensively to date, available empirical results have been generally supportive. For example, Smith et al. (2007) compared the use of PETTLEP imagery training with traditional mental practice techniques and also with physical practice in developing gymnastics jump skills. Results showed that the PETTLEP group improved its proficiency in these skills whereas the traditional imagery group did not.

Unfortunately, few studies have been conducted to arbitrate empirically between the preceding theories of mental practice. However, progress has been made in identifying some of the neural substrates of MP effects. For example, neuroimaging studies indicate that there is a great deal of overlap between the neural substrates of physical and imagined movement execution. Specifically, motor imagery and movement execution both activate neural regions such as the premotor cortex, primary motor cortex, basal ganglia and cerebellum (Jeannerod, 2001). It has also been suggested that motor imagery and movement execution share neural mechanisms related to visual, parietal lobe and frontal cortex (Dijkstra et al., 2019) but the overlap of neural substrates between the two functions is not absolute. Overall, based on available neuroscientific evidence, and allowing for data gaps, it still seems plausible to propose that mental practice (MP) is best understood as a centrally mediated cognitive activity that mimics perceptual, motor and certain emotional experiences in the brain.

KEY READINGS

Dijkstra, N., Bosch, S.E. and van Gerven, M.A. (2019) 'Shared neural mechanisms of visual perception and imagery', *Trends in Cognitive Sciences*, 23 (5), 423–34.

Holmes, P. and Collins, D. (2001) 'The PETTLEP approach to motor imagery: A functional equivalence model for sport psychologists', *Journal of Applied Sport Psychology*, 13, 60–83.

Moran, A. (2016) 'Expertise and mental practice', in R.J. Schinke, K.R. McGannon and B. Smith (eds), *Routledge International Handbook of Sport Psychology* London: Routledge/Taylor & Francis Group. pp. 421–8.

Toth, A.J., McNeill, E., Hayes, K., Moran, A.P. and Campbell, M. (2020) 'Does mental practice still enhance performance? A 24 year follow-up and meta-analytic replication and extension', *Psychology of Sport and Exercise*, 48. DOI: 10.1016/j.psychsport.2020.101672.

PRACTICAL QUESTIONS

- Using the PETTLEP approach how would you support a golfer who would like to improve putting performance?
- Angie plays basketball for her local club team which has qualified for the semi-finals of the Senior Cup. During regular games Angie plays well but gets anxious before big games. How could imagery be used to support her? Apply PETTLEP to your approach with Angie and describe the contents of an imagery script.

REFERENCES

Anton, N.E., Bean, E.A., Hammonds, S.C. and Stefanidis, D. (2017) 'Application of mental skills training in surgery: A review of its effectiveness and proposed next steps', *Journal of Laparoendoscopic and Advanced Surgical Techniques*, 27 (5), 459–69.

Collins, D. and Carson, H.J. (2017) 'The future for PETTLEP: A modern perspective on an effective and established tool', *Current Opinion in Psychology*, 16 (1), 12–16. DOI: 10.1016/j.copsyc.2017.03.007.

Denis, M. (1985) 'Visual imagery and the use of mental practice in the development of motor skills', *Canadian Journal of Applied Sport Sciences*, 10, 4s–16s.

Dijkstra, N., Bosch, S.E. and van Gerven, M.A. (2019) 'Shared neural mechanisms of visual perception and imagery', *Trends in Cognitive Sciences*, 23 (5), 423–34.

Driskell, J., Copper, C. and Moran, A. (1994) 'Does mental practice enhance performance? A meta-analysis', *Journal of Applied Psychology*, 79, 481–92.

Guillot, A. and Collet, C. (2005) 'Duration of mentally simulated movement: A review', *Journal of Motor Behavior*, 37, 10–20.

Guillot, A. and Collet, C. (eds) (2010) *The Neurophysiological Foundations of Mental and Motor Imagery*. Oxford: Oxford University Press.

Holmes, P. and Collins, D. (2001) 'The PETTLEP approach to motor imagery: A functional equivalence model for sport psychologists', *Journal of Applied Sport Psychology*, 13, 60–83.

Jacobson, E. (1932) 'Electrophysiology of mental activities', *American Journal of Psychology*, 44, 677–94.

James, W. (1890) *Principles of Psychology*. New York: Holt, Rinehart & Winston.

Jeannerod, M. (2001) 'Neural simulation of action: A unifying mechanism for motor cognition', *NeuroImage*, 14, S103–S109.

Lang, P.J. (1979) 'A bio-informational theory of emotional imagery', *Psychophysiology*, 17, 495–512.

Miksza, P., Watson, K. and Calhoun, I. (2018) 'The effect of mental practice on melodic jazz improvisation achievement', *Psychomusicology: Music, Mind, and Brain*, 28 (1), 40.

Moran, A. (2016) 'Expertise and mental practice', in R.J. Schinke, K.R. McGannon and B. Smith (eds), *Routledge International Handbook of Sport Psychology* London: Routledge/Taylor & Francis Group. pp. 421–8.

Moran, A.P. and MacIntyre, T. (1998) '"There's more to an image than meets the eye": A qualitative analysis of kinaesthetic imagery among elite canoe-slalomists', *Irish Journal of Psychology*, 19, 406–23.

Moran, A. and Toner, J. (2017) *Sport and Exercise Psychology: A Critical Introduction*. London: Taylor & Francis. pp. 165–200.

Morris, T., Spittle, M. and Watt, A.P. (2005) *Imagery in Sport*. Champaign, IL: Human Kinetics.

Smith, D., Wright, C.J., Allsopp, A. and Westhead, H. (2007) 'It's all in the mind: PETTLEP-based imagery and sports performance', *Journal of Applied Sport Psychology*, 19, 80–92.

Toth, A.J., McNeill, E., Hayes, K., Moran, A.P. and Campbell, M. (2020) 'Does mental practice still enhance performance? A 24 year follow-up and meta-analytic replication and extension', *Psychology of Sport and Exercise*, 48. DOI: 10.1016/j.psychsport.2020.101672.

4.19 ATTENTION AND CONCENTRATION

Definitions: Attention is the process of exerting mental effort on specific features of the environment or on certain thoughts or activities. Concentration is one example of an attentional process that involves the ability to focus on the task at hand while ignoring distractions.

The ability to concentrate, or focus on the task at hand while ignoring distractions (Moran and Toner, 2017), is a crucial prerequisite of successful performance in sport. Evidence to support this claim comes from anecdotal accounts from athletes, descriptive reflections and experimental studies, and these will now be looked at in turn.

First, anecdotally, athletes will often highlight the role that concentration has played in their success. For example, Trevor Immelman (South Africa) attributed his victory in the US Open golf championship in 2008 to the fact that he had been 'totally in the present' in his final round (McRae, 2008: 6). Jonathan Rae from Northern Ireland, the six-time World Superbike Champion, attributed his winning in wet conditions to: 'I just tried to keep my concentration at a maximum and the only way I could do that was keep my pace and not back off or be conservative' (Bike Sport News, 2020).

Second, correlational studies indicate that the capacity to become absorbed in the present moment is a key component of peak performance experiences in athletes (Jackson and Kimiecik, 2008).

Third, laboratory experiments show that there is a relationship between people's focus of attention and skilled performance. Specifically, Wulf (2007) showed that an external focus of attention (where performers direct their attention to the effects that their movements have on the environment) is usually more effective than an internal one (where performers focus on their own body movements) in the learning and performance of motor skills (see also Abdollahipour et al., 2017).

For psychologists, concentration (i.e. the decision to invest mental effort in what is most important in any situation to the exclusion of other stimuli and/or distractions) is one component of the multidimensional construct of 'attention', or the process of exerting mental effort 'on specific features of the environment, or on certain thoughts or activities' (Goldstein, 2008: 100). Two other dimensions of this construct are *selective attention* and *divided attention*. Selective attention is the perceptual ability to 'zoom in' on task-relevant information while ignoring distractions. For example, a goalkeeper who is preparing to defend against a corner-kick has to learn to focus only on the flight of the incoming ball, rather than on the movements of players in the penalty area. Divided attention is a form of mental time-sharing or multi-tasking through which performers learn, as a result of extensive practice, to perform two or more concurrent actions equally well. To illustrate:

a skilled basketball player can dribble with the ball while simultaneously looking around for a team-mate who is in a good position to receive a pass. In summary, attention refers to three different cognitive processes: concentration or effortful awareness; selectivity of perception; and/or the ability to coordinate two or more actions at the same time.

As scientists, psychology researchers often use metaphors to frame the unknown in terms of the known. Of the various metaphors of attention postulated since the 1950s, the 'spotlight' approach (Posner, 1980) has probably been the most influential in sport psychology. According to this metaphor, concentration resembles a mental spotlight that we shine at things that are important to us at a given moment. These targets of our concentration beam can be *external* (i.e. in the world around us) or *internal* (i.e. in the private domain of our own thoughts and feelings). For example, aiming an arrow at a target involves an external focus of attention, whereas concentrating on rhythm or the feeling of loosing the arrow from the bowstring involves an internal focus of attention. Although the spotlight metaphor has several weaknesses (e.g. it neglects emotional influences on attentional processes; see **2.8**), it has two important and positive practical implications. First, it shows us that our concentration is never truly 'lost' because our mental spotlight is always shining somewhere – externally or internally. Second, it suggests that whenever we focus on the 'wrong' target (i.e. something irrelevant to the task at hand or that lies outside our control), our performance is likely to deteriorate. This latter point raises the issue of distractions in sport.

Competitive sport offers an abundance of distractions that can divert athletes' mental spotlight from its intended target. Whereas external distractions are objective stimuli from the world around us, internal distractions include a vast array of thoughts, feelings and/or bodily sensations (e.g. fatigue) that can disrupt our focus. Typical external distractions include factors such as spectator movements, sudden changes in ambient noise levels (e.g. the click of a camera), gamesmanship (e.g. trying to block a goalkeeper in soccer from seeing the ball at a corner-kick) and unpredictable weather conditions (e.g. golfers can become distracted when windy conditions affect the flight of the ball). Usually, these distractions impair athletic performance. For example, Roger Federer's victory over Robin Söderling in the final of the 2009 French Open tennis championship was jeopardised by the sudden appearance of a spectator who jumped on to the court and approached him. Clearly rattled by this distraction, Federer lost the next three points and admitted afterwards, 'It definitely threw me out of my rhythm' (cited in Sarkar, 2009). Fortunately, he regained his concentration and won the match.

In football, noisy supporters can distract players. For example, fans of the Turkish soccer club, Galatasaray, are infamous for using flares, drums, smoke and incessant shouting to intimidate visiting teams at their home ground, which is known to visitors as 'Hell'! Not surprisingly, some of the world's leading soccer teams (e.g. AC Milan, Barcelona, Manchester United, Real Madrid) have come unstuck in this hostile environment (see **5.29**). Interestingly, during the COVID-19 pandemic when crowds were not allowed to attend games, the home advantage effect was reduced. The visiting team was given fewer yellow and red cards, with the referee feeling less pressure than when a home crowd was present (Bryson et al., 2020).

Internal distractions stem mainly from thoughts such as wondering what might happen in the future, regretting what has happened in the past or worrying about what other people might think, say or do. A classic example of a costly internal distraction occurred in the case of the golfer Doug Sanders who missed a putt of less than three feet that prevented him from winning the 1970 British Open Championship in St Andrews, Scotland, his first major tournament, and also deprived him of millions of pounds in prize money, tournament invitations and advertising endorsements. Remarkably, Doug's attentional lapse was precipitated by thinking too far ahead, 'I had the victory speech prepared before the battle was over' (cited in Moran, 2005: 21).

Unfortunately, despite such dramatic lapses, little research has been conducted to date on the mechanisms by which internal distractions disrupt performance. Nevertheless, Wegner (1994) developed a model which attempted to explain why attentional lapses occur 'ironically' – or precisely at the most inopportune moment for the person involved. Briefly, this model postulated that when our working memory system is overloaded because we are anxious or tired, trying *not* to think about something may paradoxically increase the prominence of this idea in our consciousness. This ironic rebound effect applies to actions as well as thoughts. For example, trying *not* to miss a penalty or basketball free throw can cause the exact opposite of what was intended. Thus Woodman and Davis (2008) discovered that when golfers were in pressure situations (arising from the opportunity to win a financial prize), they made more ironic errors in a putting task than when no pressure was evident.

In an effort to achieve a focused state of mind where there is no difference between what they are thinking about and what they are doing, athletes tend to use some of the following concentration strategies (Kremer et al., 2019; Moran and Toner, 2017). First, they set specific performance or action goals for themselves every time they compete. These goals (e.g. 'keep up with play' in football or 'first serve in' in tennis) encourage athletes to focus on task-relevant information and on controllable actions. Second, athletes make extensive use of pre-performance routines (PPRs) (Cotterill, 2010) or characteristic sequences of preparatory thoughts and actions before executing self-paced skills (i.e. actions that are carried out largely at one's own speed and without interference from other people) such as place-kicking in rugby or taking a short corner in hockey. PPRs are helpful because they encourage performers to focus, step-by-step, on task-relevant information. For example, many soccer goalkeepers follow pre-kick routines in an effort to block out any jeering that is directed at them by supporters of opposing teams. Cotterill et al. (2010) investigated PPR use among amateur international golfers. Results showed that these players used routines for attentional purposes such as attempting to 'switch on and off' (p. 55) and 'staying in the present and not dwelling on the past or engaging in fortune telling' (p. 55). A third concentration strategy used by athletes involves 'trigger words' or short, vivid and positively phrased verbal reminders to focus on a specific target or action. For example, the British Olympic athlete Paula Radcliffe, who won the 2007 New York City Marathon, reported counting her steps silently to herself in an effort to maintain her concentration in a race. As she explained afterwards, 'When I count to 100 three times, it's a mile. It helps me to focus on the moment and not to think about how many miles I have to go. I concentrate on breathing and striding, and I go within myself' (cited in Kolata, 2007: 1). The fourth popular concentration technique is mental practice (see **4.18**) or the systematic use of mental imagery (see **4.17**) to 'see' and 'feel' a skill in one's imagination before actually executing it. For example, Mike Atherton, the former England cricket captain, used to prepare to concentrate in test matches by going to the match venue and visualising, 'Who's going to bowl, how they are going to bowl … so that nothing can come as a surprise' (cited in Selvey, 1998: 2). From this quote it seems that imagery can help athletes to anticipate hypothetical scenarios, thereby ensuring that they will not be distracted by unexpected events on the day itself. The final concentration strategy that is used increasingly by athletes and coaches alike is simulation training (i.e. practising under conditions that replicate key aspects of an impending competitive situation). For example, the renowned US swimming coach Bob Bowman admitted deliberately breaking the goggles of Michael Phelps (who has won more Olympic gold medals than any other athlete in history, 28) during practice so that he could learn to swim calmly without them if necessary in a competition. Remarkably, this later situation actually arose in the 2008 Olympics when Phelps won the 200m butterfly event even though his goggles had been broken for the last 100m of the race (Whitworth, 2008).

In summary, attentional processes such as concentration are vital determinants of athletic success. Although considerable progress has been made in understanding the principles underlying an optimal focus for sport performance (see Pons et al., 2020) research is urgently required to evaluate which concentration strategies work best in enhancing different types of sport skills, especially when athletes are under pressure to succeed, or experience anxiety.

KEY READINGS

Cotterill, S.T. (2010) 'Pre-performance routines in sport: Current understanding and future directions', *International Review of Sport and Exercise Psychology*, 3, 132–53.

Kremer, J., Moran, A.P. and Kearney, C.J. (2019) *Pure Sport: Sport Psychology in Action*. London: Routledge.

Moran, A.P. (2016) *The Psychology of Concentration in Sport Performers: A Cognitive Analysis*. London: Psychology Press.

Zachry, T., Wulf, G., Mercer, J. and Bezodis, N. (2005) 'Increased movement accuracy and reduced EMG activity as the result of adopting an external focus of attention', *Brain Research Bulletin*, 67 (4), 304–9.

PRACTICAL QUESTIONS

- Selecting a sport of your choice, an athlete reports losing concentration during performance. What suggestions can you provide to the athlete to regain concentration?
- Declan is captain of his basketball club team and is very consistent in his performance. His long-term goal is to represent his country in basketball. However, on several occasions the national team coach has attended his games and Declan then loses concentration and makes simple mistakes. What advice would you offer to Declan?

REFERENCES

Abdollahipour, R., Nieto, M.P., Psotta, R. and Wulf, G. (2017) 'External focus of attention and autonomy support have additive benefits for motor performance in children', *Psychology of Sport and Exercise*, 32, 17–24.

Bike Sport News (2020) 'Rea kept concentration at maximum to win wet race', www.bikesportnews.com/news/news-detail/lausitz-wsbk-rea-kept-concentration-at-maximum-to-win-wet-race. Accessed 19 January 2020.

Bryson, A., Dolton, P., Reade, J.J., Schreyer, D. and Singleton, C. (2020) 'Causal effects of an absent crowd on performances and refereeing decisions during Covid-19', *Economics Letters*, 109664.

Cotterill, S.T. (2010) 'Pre-performance routines in sport: Current understanding and future directions', *International Review of Sport and Exercise Psychology*, 3, 132–53.

Cotterill, S.T., Sanders, R. and Collins, D. (2010) 'Developing effective pre-performance routines in golf: Why don't we ask the golfer?', *Journal of Applied Sport Psychology*, 22, 51–64.

Goldstein, E.B. (2008) *Cognitive Psychology: Connecting Mind, Research, and Everyday Experience* (2nd ed.). Belmont, CA: Thompson/Wadsworth.

Jackson, S.A. and Kimiecik, J.C. (2008) 'The flow perspective of optimal experience in sport and physical activity', in T.S. Horn (ed.), *Advances in Sport Psychology* (3rd ed.). Champaign, IL: Human Kinetics. pp. 377–99, 474–7.

Kolata, P. (2007) 'I'm not really running, I'm not really running …' *The New York Times*, 6 December, available at www.nytimes.com/2007/12/06/health/nutrition/06Best.html.

Kremer, J., Moran, A.P. and Kearney, C.J. (2019) *Pure Sport: Sport Psychology in Action*. London: Routledge.

McRae, D. (2008) 'Even great players have tortured minds'. *The Guardian* (Sport), 15 July, p. 6.

Moran, A. and Toner, J. (2017) *Sport and Exercise Psychology: A Critical Introduction*. London: Taylor & Francis.

Moran, G. (2005) 'Oh dear, so near but yet so far away', *The Irish Times*, 12 July, p. 2.

Pons, J., Ramis, Y., Viladrich, C. and Checa, I. (2020) 'Anxiety levels and coping styles depending on the perceptual-motor skills of the sport', *Journal of Sport Psychology*, 29 (2), 105–15.

Posner, M.I. (1980) 'Orienting of attention: The VIIth Sir Frederic Bartlett lecture', *Quarterly Journal of Experimental Psychology*, 32A, 3–25.

Sarkar, P. (2009) 'Open – Federer unnerved by spectator intrusion', *The Guardian*, 7 June, available at www.guardian.co.uk/sport/feedarticle/8546123.

Selvey, M. (1998) 'Getting up for the Ashes'. *The Guardian* (Sport), 20 November, p. 2.

Wegner, D.M. (1994) 'Ironic processes of mental control', *Psychological Review*, 101, 34–52.

Whitworth, D. (2008) 'On the waterfront'. *The Times* (magazine), 13 September, pp. 20–5.

Woodman, T. and Davis, P.A. (2008) 'The role of repression in the incidence of ironic errors', *The Sport Psychologist*, 22, 183–96.

Wulf, G. (2007) 'Attentional focus and motor learning: A review of 10 years of research', *Bewegung and Training*, 1, 4–14.

4.20 POSITIVE SELF-TALK AND THOUGHT CONTROL

Definition: Self-talk is a cognitive self-regulation strategy which involves the use of vividly phrased cue-words to help athletes to control their thoughts and to instruct and motivate themselves.

It has long been known that athletes talk to themselves either silently or out loud when they train and compete – usually in an effort to improve their thinking, concentration and performance. For example, during the 2002 Wimbledon ladies' singles tennis final between the Williams sisters, Serena Williams (who defeated Venus 7–6, 6–3) was observed by millions of viewers to be reading hand-written notes as she sat down during the change-overs between games. Afterwards, she explained that she had been reading notes as reminders to think about cues such as 'hit in front' or 'stay low' during the match (Williams, 2002: 6). Supporting such anecdotal examples, empirical research has confirmed the relationship between self-talk and athletic success. For example, Taylor et al. (2008) discovered that instructional self-talk (e.g. 'I have specific cue words or phrases that I say to myself to help my performance during competition') was one of the strongest predictors of successful Olympic performance among US athletes. Not surprisingly, in light of such evidence a great deal of research has been conducted on the nature, functions and efficacy of self-talk by athletes. A recent review distinguished between three time periods: (1) the 1990s, with the early foundations of self-talk research; (2) the 2000s and the development of systematic self-talk research; and (3) post-2011 characterised by the modern-day maturation of self-talk research (Hardy et al., 2018). Before we summarise this research, however, a brief clarification of terminology may be useful.

The term 'self-talk' refers to 'Those automatic statements reflective of, and deliberate techniques (e.g. thought stopping) athletes use, to direct, sports-related thinking' (Hardy et al., 2009a: 38). Put simply, self-talk is a cognitive self-regulation strategy. More precisely, it involves the use of vividly phrased cue-words to help athletes to control their thoughts and to instruct and motivate themselves (Zinsser et al., 2010). In sport psychology, self-talk is regarded as a multidimensional construct with at least three dimensions: overtness (i.e. whether self-talk is expressed explicitly or covertly); valence (i.e. whether self-talk is positive or negative); and functions (e.g. either cognitive/instructional or motivational) (Hardy, 2006). Two main types of self-talk have been identified. *Instructional* self-talk (as exemplified by Serena Williams) refers to covert self-directed statements that are intended to enhance athletic performance through adoption of a task-relevant attentional focus (see also **4.19**). *Motivational* self-talk involves similar statements intended to facilitate performance by increasing effort and energy expenditure and by boosting one's confidence and mood. With regard to instructional self-talk, considerable research has accumulated on the use of 'associative' thinking in sport or the use of attentional strategies whereby athletes deliberately focus on bodily signals such as breathing, heart-beat and kinaesthetic sensations when competing in arduous endurance events.

This research was spawned by Morgan and Pollock's (1977) discovery that elite marathon runners tended to use *associative* cognitive strategies whereas non-elite runners tended to prefer *dissociative* strategies which involved attempting to block out sensations of pain and discomfort. For Morgan (1978: 39), an athlete who dissociates, 'purposefully cuts himself [*sic*] off from the sensory feedback he normally receives from his body'. Early research on this topic showed that associative attentional strategies, when compared with dissociative equivalents, were linked with faster performance in sports such as running and swimming. From such evidence, Masters and Ogles (1998) concluded that whereas associative techniques facilitated comparatively faster performances by athletes, dissociative techniques were linked to a reduction in perceived exertion in endurance events. However, this conclusion was challenged by Salmon et al. (2010) in a review of the relevant research literature. Briefly, these latter investigators pointed out that studies have been hampered by conceptual confusion (e.g. inconsistency in the definitions of association and dissociation) and methodological problems (e.g. the use of unvalidated measures of key constructs). Despite such difficulties, the use of associative and dissociative cognitive strategies has attracted increasing research interest in exercise endurance settings (e.g. see Brick et al., 2019; Lind et al., 2009 for a review), as have meta-cognitive processes in reacreational endurance runners (Brick et al., 2020).

The efficacy of self-talk in enhancing athletic performance has been demonstrated using observational studies (e.g. Van Raalte et al., 1994), laboratory-based experiments (e.g. Van Raalte et al., 1995), intervention studies (e.g. Johnson et al., 2004) and research using single-case designs (e.g. Hamilton et al., 2007). To illustrate, in a study of the dimensions of overtness and valence, Van Raalte et al. (1994) found that a large proportion of the overt self-talk of young tennis players was negative in content. Furthermore, such negative self-talk was associated with losing. These researchers also noted that players who reported believing in the utility of self-talk won more points than players who did not share this belief. Hamilton et al. (2007) showed that time-trial cyclists who used *positive* self-talk consistently rode faster than did their counterparts who used *negative* self-talk.

Theoretically, the content of self-talk may involve praise (e.g. 'Well done! That's good'), criticism ('You idiot – that's a stupid mistake') and/or instruction ('Swing slowly'). Accordingly, self-talk may be positive, negative or neutral. Exploring this idea psychometrically, Zourbanos et al. (2009) developed an instrument titled the Automatic Self-Talk Questionnaire for Sports (ASTQS) in an effort to measure the content of athletes' self-talk. Factor analysis revealed eight factors or distinct dimensions of thoughts in athletes – four measuring positive self-talk, three tapping negative self-talk and one indicating neutral self-talk. Among the positive self-talk items were statements used by athletes to 'psych up' (e.g. 'Let's go'), boost confidence (e.g. 'I can make it'), instruct themselves (e.g. 'Concentrate on your game') and control their anxiety levels (e.g. 'Relax', 'Calm down'). For the factors measuring negative self-talk, typical items reflected worrying (e.g. 'I am going to lose'), disengagement (e.g. 'I can't keep going') and feeling somatic fatigue (e.g. 'I am tired'). Finally, a sample item from the neutral self-talk factor concerned irrelevant thoughts (e.g. 'What will I do later tonight?'). Preliminary analyses have indicated that this test possesses adequate psychometric characteristics, with a recent study showing that the measure is valid and can be converted to other languages effectively (Latinjak et al., 2016).

In summary, there is substantial evidence that positive self-talk helps performance and should be encouraged while negative self-talk can be detrimental to performance and should be discouraged. But how can this latter objective be achieved? Logically, the first step in changing self-talk is to become more aware of it (Zinsser et al., 2010). So, Hardy et al. (2009b) evaluated the efficacy of two intervention strategies purported to increase athletes' awareness of their negative self-talk. The intervention strategies involved a thought awareness logbook and an exercise requiring athletes to transfer paper-clips from one pocket to another whenever they used a negative self-statement. Results showed that, although both treatment groups showed increased awareness of the content of their negative self-talk, the logbook group showed greater awareness of the use of negative self-talk than the control group. Accordingly, Hardy et al. recommended that logbook maintenance may be a useful tool for increasing awareness of negative self-talk among athletes in applied settings.

Unfortunately, as Hardy et al. (2009b) acknowledged, if applied sport psychology consultants seek to build on increased awareness of negative self-talk with the use of a thought control technique such as 'thought stopping' (whereby a verbal cue such as 'stop' is stated aloud every time an undesired thought is encountered), problems may occur. Specifically, research based on Wegner's (1994) ironic processes model shows that when our working memory is overloaded due to anxiety or fatigue, the attempt to suppress a thought may paradoxically increase the prominence of that thought in our consciousness. In such circumstances, the attempt to engage in thought stopping may lead to a 'rebound' experience whereby the suppressed thought becomes even more prominent and conscious. This tendency for a suppressed thought to come to mind more readily than a thought that is the focus of intentional concentration is called 'hyperaccessibility' and is especially likely to occur under conditions of heavy mental load. In summary, a key implication of the theory of ironic processes is that thought stopping should only ever be used with great caution when attempting to reduce negative self-talk by athletes.

To conclude, research on self-talk is a vibrant and fertile ground for the future study of cognitive self-regulation. With regard to research directions in this field, a potentially fruitful line of inquiry concerns research on the comparative evaluation of instructional and motivational self-talk on skilled performance. For example, Kolovelonis et al. (2011) found partial support for the hypothesis (Hardy et al., 2009b) that whereas instructional self-talk is especially beneficial for the performance of tasks that require precision or timing, motivational self-talk is beneficial for the performance of tasks that require strength or endurance. Research is also required urgently to establish the precise theoretical mechanisms that underlie the effects of self-talk on athletic performance. Some researchers have used fMRI and other brain assessment tools to examine brain function and self-talk, but current brain imaging technology does not always lend itself to use in sport settings (see Van Raalte and Vincent, 2017). Further development of technology that can facilitate a reliable assessment of the brain while an athlete actually performs will provide invaluable insight into the real-life performance merits attached to self-talk.

KEY READINGS

Brick, N., MacIntyre, T. and Schücker, L. (2019) 'Attentional focus and cognitive strategies during endurance activity', in C. Meijen (ed.), *Endurance Performance in Sport: Psychological Theory and Interventions*. London: Routledge. pp. 113–24.

Hardy, J., Comoutos, N. and Hatzigeorgiadis, A. (2018) 'Reflections on the maturing research literature of self-talk in sport: Contextualizing the special issue', *The Sport Psychologist*, 32 (1), 1–8.

Van Raalte, J.L., Vincent, A. and Brewer, B.W. (2016) 'Self-talk: Review and sport-specific model', *Psychology of Sport and Exercise*, 22, 139–48.

Weinberg, R. (2018) 'Self-talk theory, research, and applications: Some personal reflections', *The Sport Psychologist*, 32 (1), 74–8.

PRACTICAL QUESTIONS

- Self-talk and the use of mantras can be effective in enabling an athlete to remain focused on performance. Gerry is an accomplished marathon runner but can lose concentration towards the end of a race due to internal distraction (e.g. leg muscle pain). How could you implement a positive self-talk intervention with Gerry, and what would it contain?
- When working with athletes on self-talk, questionnaires as well as discussions are useful. Access at least two of the self-talk questionnaires described above and consider their practical utility in three different sports (i.e. running, football, tennis).

REFERENCES

Brick, N., MacIntyre, T. and Schücker, L. (2019) 'Attentional focus and cognitive strategies during endurance activity', in C. Meijen (ed.), *Endurance Performance in Sport: Psychological Theory and Interventions*. London: Routledge. pp. 113–24.

Brick, N.E., Campbell, M.J., Sheehan, R.B., Fitzpatrick, B.L. and MacIntyre, T.E. (2020) 'Metacognitive processes and attentional focus in recreational endurance runners', *International Journal of Sport and Exercise Psychology*, 18 (3), 362–79.

Hamilton, R.A., Scott, D. and MacDougall, M.P. (2007) 'Assessing the effectiveness of self-talk interventions on endurance performance', *Journal of Applied Sport Psychology*, 19, 226–39.

Hardy, J. (2006) 'Speaking clearly: A critical review of the self-talk literature', *Psychology of Sport and Exercise*, 7, 81–97.

Hardy, J., Oliver, E. and Tod, D. (2009a) 'A framework for the study and application of self-talk within sport', in S. Mellalieu and S. Hanton (eds) *Advances in Applied Sport Psychology: A Review*. London: Routledge. pp. 37–74.

Hardy, J., Roberts, R. and Hardy, L. (2009b) 'Awareness and motivation to change negative self-talk', *The Sport Psychologist*, 23, 435–450.

Hardy, J., Comoutos, N. and Hatzigeorgiadis, A. (2018) 'Reflections on the maturing research literature of self-talk in sport: Contextualizing the special issue', *The Sport Psychologist*, 32 (1), 1–8.

Johnson, J.J.M., Hrycaiko, D.W., Johnson, G.V. and Halas, J.M. (2004) 'Self-talk and female youth soccer performance', *The Sport Psychologist*, 18, 44–59.

Kolovelonis, A., Goudas, M. and Dermitzaki, I. (2011) 'The effects of instructional and motivational self-talk on students' motor task performance in physical education', *Psychology of Sport and Exercise*, 12, 153–8.

Latinjak, A.T., Viladrich, C., Alcaraz, S. and Torregrosa, M. (2016) 'Spanish adaptation and validation of the Automatic Self-Talk Questionnaire for Sports', *International Journal of Sport and Exercise Psychology*, 14 (4), 402–13.

Lind, E., Welch, A.S. and Ekkekakis, P. (2009) 'Do "mind over muscle" strategies work? Examining the effects of attentional association and dissociation on exertional, affective and physiological responses to exercise', *Sports Medicine*, 39, 743–64.

Masters, K.S. and Ogles, B.M. (1998) 'Associative and dissociative cognitive strategies in exercise and running: 20 years later, what do we know?', *The Sport Psychologist*, 12, 253–70.

Morgan, W.P. (1978) 'The mind of the marathoner', *Psychology Today*, 11, 38–49.

Morgan, W.P. and Pollock, M.L. (1977) 'Psychological characterization of the elite distance runner', *Annals of the New York Academy of Sciences*, 301, 382–403.

Salmon, P., Hanneman, S. and Harwood, B. (2010) 'Associative/dissociative cognitive strategies in sustained physical activity: Literature review and proposal for a mindfulness-based conceptual model', *The Sport Psychologist*, 24, 127–56.

Taylor, M.K., Gould, D. and Rolo, C. (2008) 'Performance strategies of US Olympians in practice and competition', *High Ability Studies*, 19, 19–36.

Van Raalte, J.L. and Vincent, A. (2017) 'Self-talk in sport and performance', in O. Braddick (ed.), *Oxford Research Encyclopedia of Psychology*. Oxford: Oxford University Press. pp. 1–20.

Van Raalte, J., Brewer, B.W., Rivera, P.M. and Petitpas, A.J. (1994) 'The relationship between observable self-talk and competitive junior tennis players' match performance', *Journal of Sport and Exercise Psychology*, 16, 400–15.

Van Raalte, J., Brewer, B.W., Lewis, B.P., Linder, D.E., Wildman, G. and Kozimor, J. (1995) 'The effects of positive and negative self-talk on dart throwing performance', *Journal of Sport Behavior*, 18, 50–7.

Wegner, D.M. (1994) 'Ironic processes of mental control', *Psychological Review*, 101, 34–52.

Williams, R. (2002) 'Sublime Serena celebrates the crucial difference', *The Guardian*, 8 July, p. 6 (Sport).

Zinsser, N., Bunker, L. and Williams, J. (2010) 'Cognitive techniques for building confidence and enhancing performance', in J.M. Williams (ed.), *Applied Sport Psychology: From Personal Growth to Peak Performance* (6th ed.). New York: McGraw-Hill. pp. 305–35.

Zourbanos, N., Hatzigeorgiadis, A., Chroni, S., Theodorakis, Y. and Papaioannou, A. (2009) 'Automatic Self-Talk Questionnaire for Sports (ASTQS): Development and preliminary validation of a measure identifying the structure of athletes' self-talk', *The Sport Psychologist*, 23, 233–51.

4.21 MENTAL TOUGHNESS

Definition: Mental toughness is a multidimensional personality construct that defines the ability to persevere towards goal accomplishment through the display of hardiness, and irrespective of circumstance, adversity, success or failure.

The study of mental toughness has been popular within sport and exercise psychology over the past two decades (Gucciardi, 2017). As Sheard (2010) suggests, mental toughness is a term associated with the greatest champions and appears in numerous guises across the sporting media (such as 'spine', 'grit', 'guts', 'cojones' or 'character'). Indeed, at times the construct has been synonymous with lay perceptions of what sport psychology seeks to achieve with an athlete (Pain and Harwood, 2004). Given the much heralded association between mental toughness and sporting success, as a construct it would appear to have much to offer the discipline of sport psychology; however, over the years the relationship between the public or lay understanding of the concept and the academic attention it has received has been complex, and at times fraught with difficulty and ambiguity (Gucciardi, 2017). The difficulty lies in part because the term is used in so many different guises, and a consensus on any one definition remains elusive. Like sand running through the fingers of the discipline, a strong grasp of this vital concept has often slipped away, with uncertainty and conceptual blurring being the result (see Gucciardi, 2017). Perhaps in an attempt to untangle this Gordian knot, the past decade has witnessed a growth in the academic attention directed towards the concept, in particular seeing it as more than a *personality trait*, and instead as a *psychological state*.

The starting point for the discussion of any academic concept typically has to be its definition. The difficulty is that, for writers in this particular field, definition has become a bête noire. As mentioned previously, mental toughness makes an appearance in a variety of guises across the sporting media. Any sports fan will have an understanding of what phrases such as 'resolve', 'desire' and 'steel' refer to, but each will have their own individualised theories of what that may involve. Similarly, each sport psychologist will know what the term 'mental toughness' means – but ask them to agree on a common definition and you are likely to be disappointed. Furthermore, there appears to be a lack of expert consensus on what mental toughness is, with some researchers suggesting a good point to start would be to come to a consensus using the delphi method (Gucciardi, 2017). A comprehensive review of these definitions is beyond the remit of this chapter (see Sheard, 2010; Gucciardi, 2017), however, typical phrases associated with mental toughness include belief (Bull et al., 2005), resilience (Clough et al., 2002), persistence (Cashmore, 2002), unshakeable perseverance (Middleton et al., 2011), and performing despite significant adversity (Gucciardi et al., 2015). The difficulty with so many definitions is that each is so narrow in scope and, by consequence, circular. In other words, if mental toughness is resilience (see **7.42**), does this mean resilience is mental toughness? The danger of such circularity is that it can render the concept in question (in this case, mental toughness) meaningless. Further to this, when examining discussions of what characterises mental toughness it becomes apparent why a shared definition of the concept has proven so elusive.

One of the first domains within the psychology literature to make mention of mental toughness was personality theory. In his seminal theory of personality, Cattell (1957) made reference to tough mindedness (as the polar opposite of tender mindedness) as a trait of the personality factor of sensitivity. That mental toughness makes an appearance in such a prominent, historical psychological theory of personality hints towards why it has proved to be such a difficult concept to define within the sport psychology literature; namely, it is a pervasive concept that may not be restricted to sport but is more likely reflective of wide-ranging aspects of the athlete's (or any individual's) personality. Indeed, investigations into the characteristics of mental toughness have confirmed this assumption. Qualitative investigations of 'super-elite' athletes, coaches and sport psychologists' understandings of mental toughness have highlighted four common dimensions: attitude/mindset (including belief and focus); training (including motivation); competition (including coping with pressure); and post-competition (including perceptions of success and failure) (Jones et al., 2007).

Reflection on these four dimensions suggests that any narrow definition will be partial and, instead, a multidimensional, hierarchical and flexible model of the construct is called for. Recognition of this fact is not new. In particular, Loeher's (1986) highly influential description of mental toughness suggested seven characteristics: self-confidence; negative energy control; attention control; imagery control; motivation; positive energy; and attitudinal control. Recent years have witnessed attempts to subsume these numerous dimensions into hierarchical models of mental toughness, allowing for the classification of the key characteristics of a mentally tough athlete. Much of this work had its genesis outside the sport psychology literature, being influenced by models from developmental psychology, including Michael Rutter's (1999) work on resilience and Kobasa's (1979) theory of hardiness. Essentially, resilience and hardiness as psychological constructs help us understand the capacity to deal with difficult circumstances. Kobasa suggested three key aspects to an individual's worldview that will allow them to meet difficult circumstances with courage and a belief that they can cope. In applied sport psychology, they are commonly referred to as 'the three Cs':

- *Commitment* – how prepared the individual is to become involved and attempt to tackle the circumstances they find themselves in.
- *Control* – the extent to which the individual wants to, and believes they can, influence their circumstances.
- *Challenge* – the tendency to see unexpected events as exciting and to feel unthreatened by evaluative situations.

The '3 Cs' model has proven particularly influential in sport psychology, later being adapted by Clough et al. (2002) to a '4 Cs' sport-specific model that incorporates *Confidence* and has been used to inform the development of a measurement tool for mental toughness, The Mental Toughness Questionnaire-48 (MTQ-48), and more recently an 18-item version (MTQ-18). Middleton et al. (2005) have also provided a hierarchical model that takes on board the numerous characteristics that have been associated with mental toughness over time. This model is at once a summation and a consolidation of previous work on the construct. Through its definition of mental toughness as 'perseverance towards a goal in the face of adversity', it incorporates much of the general understanding of what mental toughness actually *is*. However, this model moves further, by highlighting not only what it is but what it *does*. The 12 characteristics listed are: self-efficacy; a belief in one's own potential; a positive mental self-concept; task familiarity; task value; intrinsic motivation to achieve one's own personal best; goal commitment; perseverance; task-specific attention; positivity; stress minimisation; and positive self-comparison to opponents. Again a now familiar theme re-emerges, namely that mental toughness touches on almost every aspect of the athlete's life. This has been taken a step further by Sheard's (2010) suggestion that mental toughness is about more than dealing with adversity, that it is in fact present during the good times as well as the difficult times and is not only an *outcome* but a *process* or integral part of a sporting journey. This is an appealing suggestion, particularly when one reflects on those athletes who have continued to dominate their respective fields over long periods of time. Mental toughness, in all probability, enables the athlete who reaches the top to stay there. Famous examples must include Michael Schumacher's seven world Formula One titles, Roger Federer's 23 consecutive tennis Grand Slam semi-final appearances, Phil Taylor's 16 world darts championships, Tony McCoy's incredible 4,358 winners and 20 consecutive national hunt jockey titles, and Jonathan Rae's six World Superbike Championship victories. Even at the peak of their careers, with all seemingly well in their sporting world, few would argue that these athletes had not remained mentally tough.

A central theme within the literature is the role that mental toughness plays in enabling the athlete to cope with stress. Increasingly athletes, particularly at the elite level, are required to cope with stress in both the good and the challenging times on a daily basis (see **7.40**). As such, any suggestion that mental toughness may serve as a moderator of an athlete's reaction to stress is worthy of investigation. It is perhaps the case that an element of mental toughness is to be open to acceptance of psychological weakness, and to be confident enough to know when to ask for help and support if required (see **7.40**).

It has also been suggested that mental toughness may serve as a composite or global reflection of an athlete's stress coping skills (Fletcher, 2005). In other words, we may deem an athlete as mentally tough if they have a capacity to cope with stress. Indeed, it may be suggested that the mentally tough athlete does not only *cope* with stress, they actually *thrive* on stress (see **2.5**). This is suggestive of the athlete who deliberately seeks out challenges, who values skill improvement, has a low fear of failure and who is committed to their sport (Mischel and Shoda, 1995). Again, consideration should be given to the suggestion that attributes of this nature, while undoubtedly useful in sport, may also be characterised as life skills (Connaughton et al., 2008). Particularly at the highest levels of sport, it can be difficult to delineate where an athlete's sporting life ends and his or her private life begins. In such a sporting world it may be contended that an athlete will require mental toughness in every domain of life if s/he is to maximise potential. In many respects this brings us to the crux of any discussion of mental toughness. Much of the debate surrounding the concept has seen the field jumping through its own definitional, and at times tautological and circular, hoops. However, any athlete or coach will be seeking the bottom line to this debate, namely, can mental toughness, as it is generally understood, be increased?

Over recent years, much of the progress towards an answer to this intriguing question has rested with the development of valid and reliable measures of mental toughness. Two particular measures, the Psychological Performance Inventory (Golby et al., 2007) and the Sports Mental Toughness Questionnaire (Sheard et al., 2009), appear to have gone some way towards addressing Moran and Toner's (2017) contention that mental toughness as a concept requires an independent index. The development of such indices allows for greater measurement of the effect of interventions on mental toughness. Returning to the contention that mental toughness reflects an athlete's coping skills, Sheard and Golby (2006) report promising findings regarding the impact of psychological skills training on the development of mental toughness. It is reported that athletes who receive training in goal setting (see **3.12**), visualisation (see **4.17**), relaxation (see **2.9**), concentration (see **4.19**) and thought stopping (see **4.20**) display higher levels of mental toughness post-intervention. While research in this field remains in its infancy, there can be no doubting the potential importance of such findings; they suggest that mental toughness can be practised and improved. There can be few individuals working in sport who have not heard sentiments such as 'He lacks the bottle' or 'She doesn't have the winning mentality'. The great promise of mental toughness research is that it appears to offer a means to address, and overcome, such labels and stereotypes. Indeed, it has been suggested that the development of mental toughness should be placed in the context of the overall development of the athlete's career (Connaughton et al., 2008), although more recently the term resilience has been recommended over mental toughness (see **7.42**).

Whether using the term resilience or the broader construct of mental toughness, the athlete's early years should be characterised by a supportive environment that allows him or her to learn from critical early experiences in a positive and constructive manner. Moving into their middle years the athlete will learn to apply the skills and lessons learnt, allowing them to reach their optimum mental toughness in their later years, at a time when they should be reaching peak performance. Of course, there are numerous factors that will determine when athletes begin to display optimum levels of resilience or mental toughness, including their innate temperament, the significant others surrounding them and the skills they are taught. A further factor that is yet to receive much attention, but which remains intriguing nonetheless, is the possibility that mental toughness may be socialised. As Sheard (2010) suggests, it would appear that certain sporting institutions exude mental toughness. The Australian cricket team of the late 1990s and early part of this century and the New Zealand rugby union team would be two such examples. The mechanisms by which these institutions or cultures manage to transmit their apparent mental toughness to new members are likely to prove fertile ground for investigation.

In conclusion, answering the question, 'Can mental toughness be increased?', the answer would appear to be a tentative 'yes'. That the mechanisms for doing so are so broad, incorporating general psychological skills training, the athlete's developmental profile and socialisation, returns us to a familiar theme – the pervasive nature of mental toughness in the life of the athlete. Mental toughness is not characterised as a distinct, singular skill; as Sheard (2010: 61) suggests, it is more likely 'a lived and experienced philosophy, applied to each situation encountered'. To succinctly define such a philosophy is a difficult challenge. This is not to suggest that sport psychologists should abandon any attempts to develop mental toughness, far from it. Rather, it is a call to recognise the importance of mental toughness not only for an athlete's profession but also for life. As the American football coach Tom Landry famously remarked, 'First become a winner in life – then it's easier to become a winner on the field.'

KEY READINGS

Bauman, N.J. (2016) 'The stigma of mental health in athletes: Are mental toughness and mental health seen as contradictory in elite sport?', *British Journal of Sports Medicine*, 50, 135–6.

Clough, P., Earle, K. and Sewell, D. (2002) 'Mental toughness: The concept and its measurement', in I. Cockerill (ed.), *Solutions in Sport Psychology*. London: Thomson. pp. 32–46.

Fletcher, D. (2005) '"Mental toughness" and human performance: Definitional, conceptual and theoretical issues', *Journal of Sports Sciences*, 23, 1246–7.

Gucciardi, D.F., Hanton, S., Gordon, S., Mallett, C.J. and Temby, P. (2015) 'The concept of mental toughness: Tests of dimensionality, nomological network, and traitness', *Journal of Personality*, 83 (1), 26–44.

PRACTICAL QUESTIONS

- Martin is 14 years old and has been competing in karate for six years. He has had success in local competitions and is well respected in his club. He has his sights set on competing at national level. To do so he feels he needs to become more 'mentally tough'. How would you describe mental toughness to Martin and what would you do to develop his mental toughness?
- Read the short editorial by Bauman (2016) listed in the Key Readings. In your view, are mental toughness and good mental health mutually exclusive or contradictory? What should you consider when developing a mental toughness intervention for Martin given what you have read?

REFERENCES

Bull, S.J., Shambrook, C.J., James, W. and Brooks, J.E. (2005) 'Towards an understanding of mental toughness in elite English cricketers', *Journal of Applied Sport Psychology*, 17, 209–27.

Cashmore, E. (2002) *Sport Psychology: The Key Concepts*. London: Routledge.

Cattell, R.B. (1957) *Personality and Motivation Structure and Measurement*. New York: Harcourt, Brace & World.

Clough, P., Earle, K. and Sewell, D. (2002) 'Mental toughness: The concept and its measurement', in I. Cockerill (ed.), *Solutions in Sport Psychology*. London: Thomson. pp. 32–46.

Connaughton, D., Wadney, R., Hanton, S. and Jones, G. (2008) 'The development and maintenance of mental toughness', *Journal of Sports Sciences*, 26, 83–95.

Fletcher, D. (2005) '"Mental toughness" and human performance: Definitional, conceptual and theoretical issues', *Journal of Sports Sciences*, 23, 1246–7.

Golby, J., Sheard, M. and van Wersch, A. (2007) 'Evaluating the structure of the Psychological Performance Inventory', *Perceptual and Motor Skills*, 105, 309–25.

Gucciardi, D.F. (2017) 'Mental toughness: Progress and prospects'. *Current Opinion in Psychology*, 16, 17–23.

Gucciardi, D.F., Hanton, S., Gordon, S., Mallett, C.J. and Temby, P. (2015) 'The concept of mental toughness: Tests of dimensionality, nomological network, and traitness', *Journal of Personality*, 83 (1), 26–44.

Jones, G., Hanton, S. and Connaughton, D. (2007) 'A framework of mental toughness in the world's best performers', *The Sport Psychologist*, 21, 243–64.

Kobasa, S.C. (1979) 'Stressful life events, personality, and health: An inquiry into hardiness', *Journal of Personality and Social Psychology*, 37 (1), 1–11.

Loeher, J.E. (1986) *Mental Toughness Training for Sports: Achieving Athletic Excellence*. Lexington, MA: Stephen Greene Press.

Middleton, S.C., Marsh, H.W., Martin, A.J., Richards, G.E. and Perry, C. (2005) 'Discovering mental toughness: A qualitative study of mental toughness in elite athletes', *Psychology Today*, 22, 60–72.

Middleton, S.C., Martin, A.J. and Marsh, H.W. (2011) 'Development and validation of the mental toughness inventory (MTI)', *Mental Toughness in Sport: Developments in Theory and Research*, 1, 91.

Mischel, W. and Shoda, Y. (1995) 'A cognitive-affective system theory of personality: Reconceptualizing situations, dispositions, dynamics, and invariance in personality structure', *Psychological Review*, 102, 246–68.

Moran, A. and Toner, J. (2017) *Sport and Exercise Psychology: A Critical Introduction*. London: Taylor & Francis.

Pain, M.A. and Harwood, C.G. (2004) 'Knowledge and perceptions of sport psychology within English soccer', *Journal of Sports Sciences*, 22, 813–26.

Rutter, M. (1999) 'Resilience concepts and findings: Implications for family therapy', *Journal of Family Therapy*, 21, 119–44.

Sheard, M. (2010) *Mental Toughness: The Mindset behind Sporting Achievement*. London: Routledge.

Sheard, M. and Golby, J. (2006) 'Effect of a psychological skills training program on swimming performance and positive psychological development', *International Journal of Sport and Exercise Psychology*, 4, 149–69.

Sheard, M., Golby, J. and van Wersch, A. (2009) 'Progress toward construct validation of the Sports Mental Toughness Questionnaire (SMTQ)', *European Journal of Psychological Assessment*, 25, 184–91.

Social Psychology of Sport

Chapter Summary: The wide-ranging literature within sport psychology addressing social psychological themes is summarised in ten sections, beginning with a consideration of the construct of team cohesion, including distinctions between task and social cohesion, before reflecting on the efficacy of a variety of team-building techniques. The focus then shifts to a consideration of social cognition, and in particular theoretical explanations offered for performance outcomes in sport, i.e. causal attributions. The impact of audiences and other athletes/players on performance is next reviewed, including both social facilitation and social loafing effects, before looking at leadership in sport, including both captaincy and coaching. A separate section is devoted to the well-known phenomenon of home advantage before turning to the literature that considers aggression in sport, and including the critical distinction between reactive and instrumental aggression. Further sections address research on the role of fans and spectators, and a theoretical perspective that has had a significant impact on the subdiscipline of sport psychology over recent times: social identity theory.

5.22 Team Cohesion 136

5.23 Team Building 142

5.24 Causal Attribution 148
5.25 Social Facilitation and Social Loafing 154
5.26 Leadership and Management 159
5.27 Effective Coaching Styles 165
5.28 Home Advantage 171
5.29 Aggression 177
5.30 Fans and Spectators 182
5.31 Social Identity Theory 190

5.22 TEAM COHESION

Definition: A dynamic process which is reflected in the tendency for a group to stick together and remain united in the pursuit of its instrumental objectives and/or the satisfaction of member affective needs (Carron et al., 1998).

Watch any team sport and it becomes immediately obvious that a good team dynamic is crucial to success. In the words of the legendary baseball star, Babe Ruth: 'The way a team plays as a whole determines its success. You may have the greatest bunch of individual stars in the world, but if they don't play together, the club won't be worth a dime.' In many respects this quotation encapsulates why team dynamics are afforded so much attention in sport. Time and again it is not the team that is made up of the most talented individuals that succeeds but instead the team that functions most effectively as a unit. The history of sport is littered with examples of tournaments where individual superstars failed to shine and instead those teams in which the sum was greater than its parts eventually took home the silverware. The biannual Ryder Cup in golf between the USA and Europe is a classic example where the form of individual players as a predictor of success seems to pale into insignificance against the forces binding the team together.

How and why collectivism tends to supersede individualism is one of the most fascinating issues in sport psychology (Beauchamp et al., 2020). Every team in every team sport represents a unique combination of elements, but often successful and unsuccessful teams in general can be distinguished from each other depending on factors including the degree to which team members identify with the team and share common goals. However, as with many issues in sport, discussions regarding the positives and negatives of team dynamics are prone to over-simplification. Often the importance of these complex, dynamic and unique entities is boiled down to only two ill-defined words, 'team spirit'. The purpose of this chapter is to deconstruct these two words through the lens of the sport psychology literature and theoretical perspectives, thereby identifying the mechanisms and concepts that make team dynamics such an intriguing aspect of sport, past, present and future.

Perhaps the first task should be to clarify precisely what is meant by the word 'team'. A team is more than simply a collection of individuals who are mutually connected (e.g. a yoga group); a team is a collection of individuals who share a purpose, whether this is characterised by a specific goal or the nature of the relationships within the team (e.g. providing support for each other). Implicit in this definition are a number of additional features that must be present in order to facilitate the pursuit of a common purpose. These are the nature of interactions within the team, the structure of the team, how cohesive the team is, the goals that the team is pursuing and the team identity (Forsyth, 2017). Each of these factors contributes to the team dynamic and ultimately success but one central factor has dominated the psychological literature over many years: team cohesion.

There is a widely held belief within sport that cohesion and team spirit go hand in hand. There is also a view that cohesion is all or nothing; in other words a team is either cohesive (i.e. has a good team spirit) or it is not. In reality, team cohesion is a far more complex concept and, at times, is one that contradicts conventional sporting wisdom.

Team cohesion has been defined as a process that sees a group of individuals stick together to pursue a common goal and/or satisfy group member needs (Carron and Hausenblas, 1998). A key distinction is then normally made between two types of cohesion: task and social. *Task cohesion* is a measure of how well integrated the team is when they are working towards their goals; *social cohesion* is how well integrated the team is on a personal level. Further work by Albert Carron and his colleagues then subdivided the categories of cohesion yet further by adding the distinction between attraction to the group and group integration (see Table **5.1**).

Both task and social cohesion are subdivided into members' perceptions of group integration (GI) and the extent to which members feel they are attracted to the group (ATG) (Widmeyer et al., 1992). Hence, in terms of individual member's attraction to the group, social cohesion (*ATG – Social*, top right) is an indicator of team members' perceptions about personal involvement, acceptance and social interaction, while team members' perceptions of task integration (*ATG – Task*, top left) concern perceptions about personal involvement with group tasks, productivity and goals. Regarding group integration, the social dimension (*GI – Social*, bottom right) refers to perceptions about similarity, closeness and bonding concerning social aspects of the team, while the task

Table 5.1 Social and Task Attraction to the Group

		Dimension	
		Task	*Social*
Orientation	*Attraction to the Group*	ATG – Task	ATG – Social
	Group Integration	GI – Task	GI – Social

dimension (*GI – Task*, bottom left) relates likewise to similarity, closeness and bonding – but on this occasion with reference to the team's tasks.

Previously, both researchers and practitioners had considered numerous indicators of cohesion (Hogg, 1992) but the delineation of these four subtypes now enjoys widespread acceptance, and in turn has spawned the development of a well validated and respected measure of team cohesion, the Group Environment Questionnaire (GEQ). The GEQ includes 18 items, five relating to both *ATG – Social* and *GI – Task*, and four items relating to both *ATG – Task* and *GI – Social*. However, arriving at the point where a concept such as team cohesion may be defined and measured is not the end of the story; it then becomes important to explain what influences team cohesion, and ultimately to determine how important it really is to sporting performance.

Turning first to the question of what exactly influences team cohesion, Carron (1982) originally proposed four categories of factors: situational, leadership, personal and team. While these may provide a useful framework for structuring research, empirical support for the importance of each of these factors remains limited (Lavallee et al., 2004; Eys and Kim, 2017). This is not to suggest that there is no empirical evidence but rather that conclusive evidence remains elusive. For example, numerous correlates of team cohesion have been reported, including group size, the pursuit of shared goals, and role clarity. However, the difficulty in building a comprehensive evidence base is at least partly due to the methodological problems associated with capturing team dynamics over time. Studies into cohesion tend, by necessity, to be correlational in design. It is a well-worn phrase that correlation does not imply causality, and so it proves here. In short, is a team cohesive because it shares goals, or does it share goals because it is cohesive? This question of causality (which came first?) also impacts on a second key issue: just how important is team cohesion in determining team performance?

In answering this second question, the primary concern has typically been the relationship between team cohesion and team success. It has been argued that this is a somewhat narrow focus and fails to take into account variables such as player mood and team stability (Lavallee et al., 2004), and team satisfaction and team identity (Biber, 2019). However, given the continued professionalisation of sport, it is not surprising that the bottom line remains – does greater cohesion produce better results? Evidence suggests that there is a relationship of some kind between cohesion and success, even if the nature of this relationship is equivocal and, at times, contradictory (Filho et al., 2014). For example, Widmeyer et al. (1992) reported that 83 per cent of studies which they had reviewed showed a positive relationship between cohesion and success. At the same time this finding should be tempered by the conclusion reached by Mullen and Copper (1994) that, while collectively significant, each of these effects in isolation is best characterised as small. Furthermore, the type of sport under consideration cannot be ignored, one key distinction being whether the sport is co-active (members perform individually to achieve a team outcome, e.g. athletics, golf, tennis), interactive (team members interact to achieve their goal, e.g. football, basketball) or a blend of the two (e.g. cricket, baseball) (D'souza et al., 2018). Equally, while Carron et al.'s (2002) meta-analysis reported a moderate to large effect overall, when examining professional sports, as compared to high-school sports, the relationship between cohesion and performance was much weaker.

With this in mind, there are also a number of other mediating factors to be considered when examining the strength of the relationship, not least age (Martin et al., 2013), where younger teams in particular gain benefit from higher levels of cohesion, and gender, where the link between cohesion and success often appears stronger for women's teams than for men's (Eys et al., 2015).

In another important twist, Mullen and Copper (1994) reported that the relationship between cohesion and performance is explicable only with reference to task cohesion, while Carron et al. (2002) contested that the relationship also holds for social cohesion. Suffice it to say, to this day, while the link between task cohesion and success is well established, the jury is still out on the connection between social cohesion and performance, and even if a relationship is present, the question of causality remains a difficult one to answer (Gioldasis et al., 2016). Mullen and Copper first reported that the direction of the effect appears to be from success to cohesion, that is, a successful team is more likely to create a cohesive team, as compared to a cohesive team creating a successful team. Indeed, several laboratory studies have revealed that team cohesion and performance display a bi-directional association, with the role of cohesion becoming ever more significant with increased team interactions (Braun et al., 2020). However, Albert Carron and later commentators have argued that there is no tendency in either direction. In answering the question of how beneficial cohesion is, the literature provides few clear findings. A relationship appears to exist, but it seems more likely that, if anything, social cohesion follows success, rather than vice versa.

Any discussion of the potential benefits of cohesion should also be balanced with a recognition of the potential pitfalls of cohesion. There is certainly enough evidence in the psychological literature to suggest that there is such a thing as too much cohesion. Regarding social cohesion, it has been reported that athletes see high levels as potentially damaging to team performance, citing factors such as a loss of focus on task goals and the added pressure of not wanting to disappoint peers (Hardy et al., 2005). In a related vein, it is vital to be mindful of the suggestion that a cohesive group will be unproductive if group members do not have high expectations of each other (Forsyth, 2017). In other words, in a socially cohesive group there is a danger that individuals will not wish to stand out or belittle their teammates. This brings into focus the role of conflict in teams. While historically, cohesion and conflict have been seen as mutually exclusive, it would now appear that the relationship between the two is much more subtle. In particular, it has been suggested that a constructive attitude towards conflict resolution within a team may increase cohesion, whereas avoiding disputes (perhaps due to an overly socially cohesive environment) may in fact damage task cohesion in the longer term (Sullivan and Feltz, 2001).

Research dealing with collective efficacy within sport teams, or the shared belief among team members of their collective capabilities (Beauchamp, 2007), would suggest that, along with factors including success, appropriate leadership behaviours, group size, vicarious experiences and motivational climate, team cohesion also impacts on perceptions of collective efficacy. This would appear to be a relationship that is worthy of further consideration (Chow and Feltz, 2007; Beauchamp et al., 2020), along with broader considerations of individual team player's wellbeing and cohesion (Teymori et al., 2014).

In seeking to reach a conclusion on the role played by team cohesion in sporting success, it is important to bear in mind the suggestion made at the outset, each team represents a unique entity. There is no such thing as a 'good' team, or the right type of team spirit. However, in practice, the key priority for practitioners and coaches alike should be to constantly review the team dynamic, ensuring that it is fit for purpose in that time and at that place, and acknowledging that the impact of team cohesion on performance will constantly vary (Gioldasis et al., 2016). Available evidence would suggest that it is task, rather than social cohesion, that is likely to be of most importance. Should an appropriate level of social cohesion follow, this may be of longer term benefit – but only to a point, and practitioners should be mindful of the potential damage to task cohesion of an excess of 'team spirit'. And finally, in terms of the salience of task cohesion, hard and fast rules cannot be applied – each situation is likely to vary as a factor of the individuals involved and the tasks they are involved with. The possible bi-directional role of success in building team cohesion is also likely to be of continued interest to researchers and practitioners alike (see **5.23**).

No easy answers here, and none in sight, with the subtleties of team dynamics continuing to make teams such a fascinating part of the sporting landscape. And the task for those working with teams? To find the right blends and balances that will help the team grow in order hopefully to be greater than the sum of its parts.

KEY READINGS

Beauchamp, M., McEwan, D. and Wierts, C. (2020) 'Psychology of group dynamics: Key considerations and recent developments', in G. Tenenbaum and R. C. Eklund (eds), *Handbook of Sport Psychology* (4th ed.). London: John Wiley & Sons. pp. 321–343.

Carron, A.V., Colman, M.M., Wheeler, J. and Stevens, D. (2002) 'Cohesion and performance in sport: A meta analysis', *Journal of Sport and Exercise Psychology*, 24, 168–88.

Filho, E., Dobersek, U., Gershgoren, L., Becker, B. and Tenenbaum, G. (2014) 'The cohesion–performance relationship in sport: A 10-year retrospective meta-analysis', *Sport Sciences for Health*, 10, 165–77.

Eys, M. and Kim, J. (2017) 'Team building and group cohesion in the context of sport and performance psychology', retrieved from *Oxford Research Encyclopedia of Psychology*: http://psychology.oxfordre.com/view/10.1093/acrefore/9780190236557.001.0001/acrefore-9780190236557-e-186.

PRACTICAL QUESTIONS

- If you are asked by a team coach to help create the right 'group climate' within his or her team, what advice would you give, and how would you then go about establishing and maintaining that climate?
- If a team shows signs of not working well together, how would you try to identify where the problem lies, and what steps could be taken to remedy the problem?

REFERENCES

Beauchamp, M.R. (2007) 'Efficacy beliefs within relational and group contexts in sport', in S. Jowett and D. Lavallee (eds), *Social Psychology in Sport. Champaign, IL*: Human Kinetics. pp. 181–95.

Beauchamp, M., McEwan, D. and Wierts, C. (2020) 'Psychology of group dynamics: Key considerations and recent developments', in G. Tenenbaum and R.C. Eklund (eds), *Handbook of Sport Psychology* (4th ed.). London: John Wiley & Sons. pp. 321–343.

Biber, D. (2019) 'Creating team cohesion and sport identity', *Strategies*, 32 (6), 40–2.

Braun, M.T., Kozlowski, S.W., Brown, T.A. and DeShon, R.P. (2020) 'Exploring the dynamic team cohesion–performance and coordination–performance relationships of newly formed teams', *Small Group Research*. https://doi.org/10.1177/1046496420907157.

Carron, A.V. (1982) 'Cohesiveness in sports groups: Interpretations and considerations', *Journal of Sport Psychology*, 4, 123–8.

Carron, A.V. and Hausenblas, H.A. (1998) *Group Dynamics in Sport* (2nd ed.). Morgantown, WV: Fitness Information Technology.

Carron, A.V., Brawley, L.R. and Widmeyer, W.N. (1998) 'The measurement of cohesiveness in sport groups', in J.L. Duda (eds), *Advances in Sport and Exercise Psychology Measurement*. Morgantown, WV: Fitness Information Technology. pp. 213–26.

Carron, A.V., Colman, M.M., Wheeler, J. and Stevens, D. (2002) 'Cohesion and performance in sport: A meta analysis', *Journal of Sport and Exercise Psychology*, 24, 168–88.

Chow, G.M. and Feltz, D.L. (2007) 'Exploring new directions in collective efficacy and sport', in M.R. Beauchamp and M.A. Eys (eds), *Group Dynamics in Exercise and Sport Psychology: Contemporary Themes. New York: Routledge*. pp. 221–48.

D'souza, H., Walmiki, R. and Mane, M. (2018) 'Relevance of team cohesion in training of track and field athletes: A review', Preprints. 2018070513 DOI: 10.20944/preprints201807.0513.v1.

Eys, M. and Kim, J. (2017) 'Team building and group cohesion in the context of sport and performance psychology', retrieved from *Oxford Research Encyclopedia of Psychology*: http://psychology.oxfordre.com/view/10.1093/acrefore/9780190236557.001.0001/acrefore-9780190236557-e-186.

Eys, M., Evans, M.B., Martin, L.J., Ohlert, J., Wolf, S.A., Van Bussel, M. and Steins, C. (2015) 'Cohesion and performance for female and male sport teams', *The Sport Psychologist*, 29, 97–109.

Filho, E., Dobersek, U., Gershgoren, L., Becker, B. and Tenenbaum, G. (2014) 'The cohesion–performance relationship in sport: A 10-year retrospective meta-analysis', *Sport Sciences for Health*, 10, 165–77.

Forsyth, D. (2017). *Group Dynamics* (7th ed.). Belmont, CA: Wadsworth Cengage Learning. pp. 7–11.

Gioldasis, A., Stavrou, N., Mitrotasios, M. and Psychountaki, M. (2016) 'Cohesion and performance in soccer: A causal model', *Sport Science Review*, 97–112.

Hardy, J., Eys, M.A. and Carron, A.V. (2005) 'Exploring the potential disadvantages of high cohesion in sports teams', *Small Group Research*, 36, 166–87.

Hogg, M.A. (1992) *The Social Psychology of Group Cohesiveness: From Attraction to Social Identity*. London: Harvester Wheatsheaf.

Lavallee, D., Kremer, J., Moran, A. and Williams, M. (2004) *Sport Psychology: Contemporary Themes*. London: Palgrave Macmillan.

Martin, L.J., Paradis, K.F., Eys, M.A. and Evans, B. (2013) 'Cohesion in sport: New directions for practitioners', *Journal of Sport Psychology in Action*, 4(1), 14–25. https://doi.org/10.1080/21520704.2012.702710.

Mullen, B. and Copper, C. (1994) 'The relation between group cohesiveness and performance: An integration', *Psychological Bulletin*, 115, 210–27.

Sullivan, P.J. and Feltz, D.L. (2001) 'The relationship between intra-team conflict and cohesion within hockey teams', *Small Group Research*, 32, 342–55.

Teymori, S., Khaki, A.A. and Nikbhakhsh, R. (2014) 'The relationship between team cohesion and anxiety on team sports student athletes', *Bulletin of Environment, Pharmacology and Life Sciences*, 414–17.

Whitton, S.M. and Fletcher, R.B. (2014) 'The Group Environment Questionnaire: A multilevel confirmatory factor analysis', *Small Group Research*, 45(1), 68–88.

Widmeyer, W.N., Brawley, L.R. and Carron, A.V. (1992) 'Group cohesion in sport and exercise', in R. Singer, M. Murphy and L. Tennant (eds), *Handbook on Research in Sport Psychology*. New York: Macmillan. pp. 672–92.

5.23 TEAM BUILDING

Definition: The use of a range of techniques to help foster a sense of collective efficacy within the team and to strengthen relationships between team members.

'There may be no 'I' in team … but there is 'a me'. (Unattributed)

Finding quotes from top coaches on the key role they attach to team building is not hard. It is a firmly established maxim within sport that one of the primary tasks for a coach/manager is to build a team; indeed, this is an expectation that coaches seem to be highly aware of (Bloom et al., 2003). When teams do not appear to be functioning to their maximum capacity it is the manager who is held to account, often by the use of well-worn clichés such as 'S/he has lost the dressing room'.

Over the years this sense of responsibility has drawn coaches to experiment with numerous strategies that fall under the umbrella term of 'team building'. From a practical perspective, an understanding of team-building strategies that are more or less beneficial is likely to be invaluable to sport in general, and to effective coaching in particular (see 5.27) (Bruner et al., 2013). Sadly, too often in the past quality control of these interventions has not always been a high priority, and the world of sport is littered with examples of interventions that relied more on showmanship and gimmickry than genuine evidence-based efficacy (Kremer et al., 2019: 147).

The term 'team building' has come to encompass a diverse array of activities often loosely associated with team dynamics. Indeed, in the broadest sense, team building could be defined as any intervention that aims to improve the functioning of a team. However, the difficulty with such a broad definition is that it borders on the tautological, in other words it is close to saying that team building is building a team. Schein (1999) provides a more fruitful working definition where team building is taken to be a means of both analysing and changing intergroup relations and behaviours. However, there are then numerous opinions as to how precisely teams should be analysed and how behaviour should be changed. For example, some definitions make explicit reference to cohesion (task and social) while others refer to the importance of satisfying group member needs (Brawley and Paskevich, 1997). Such ambiguity may reflect on the differences that exist in the focus of team-building interventions, the means of delivery and the outcome measures that are employed. Therefore, when referring to any team-building activity it is important to be clear what exactly it is seeking to achieve, and how it is seeking to achieve it. Veach and May (2005) have provided a useful framework known as MAPS (Mission; Assessment; Plan; Systematic evaluation) within which any team-building intervention can operate and be assessed. MAPS involves four steps, as shown in Table **5.2**.

Regarding the actual content of each intervention, across the literature three broad categories can be identified. First are interventions that are broadly task-focused; second are activities that are socially focused; and third are those based on outdoor pursuits and/or shared experiences (Martin et al., 2009). Within each category a variety of different approaches can be found. For example, in terms of task-focused interventions, there may be a concern with either one or more factors that influence team functioning, such as

Table 5.2 A Description of MAPS to Assess Team Building

MISSION	Map out the team's identity values and objectives
ASSESSMENT	Assess the team's synergy, communication and response to feedback
PLAN	Develop a masterplan to coordinate team and individual efforts through use of goal-setting procedures.
SYSTEMATIC EVALUATION	Review where you have been, where you are and where you are going.

cohesiveness, team identity, goal setting and team communication (Yukelson, 1997). In the past, the socially focused category has accommodated an eclectic mix of approaches, from the traditional team night out or bonding weekend to specific forms of ongoing social support within a team. However, there is a difficulty in allowing team building to be such an all-embracing term. Without carefully defined parameters it will be difficult to measure the effectiveness of team building and in turn make sensible recommendations as to which approaches have been more or less effective.

This danger has been acknowledged in recent years, leading to clearer definitions as to what exactly constitutes team building. First, there has been a growing consensus as to the main approaches adopted, with the four widely accepted techniques appearing to involve: goal-setting interventions; the development of interpersonal relationships; clarifying roles; and creating a capacity for problem-solving (Salas et al., 1999). Second, there are now clearer lines of distinction regarding the methods of delivering team building. For example, it is recognised that interventions may be formally or informally delivered (Klein et al., 2009), and that they may be directly delivered (i.e. by the sport psychologist) or indirectly (i.e. through the coach under the guidance of the sport psychologist) (Eys and Kim, 2017). A further distinction then relates to the duration of the intervention (Martin et al., 2009). Finally, there is a need for clarity as to precisely what the intervention is trying to achieve. Four primary outcomes have been suggested: cognitive (including knowledge of team processes); team (e.g. cohesion); performance; and affective (Klein et al., 2009).

It should be borne in mind that while there has been undoubted progress in clarifying what is meant by the term team building at a theoretical level, in practice, interventions are rarely 'pure' in their approach (Buller, 1986). Often this is by necessity as teams are such complex, interactive entities and hence interventions designed to improve their functioning end up being characterised by a more hands-on, pragmatic and problem-solving approach. Team-building interventions are therefore tailored to suit individual situations – but the question still remains, does team building really work?

In answering this question it is important to take cognisance of how team-building interventions have been chronicled across the psychological literature. Team building has long been seen as an important aspect of the psychology of business and organisational behaviour, where any intervention that may increase the productivity of workers, or more specifically teams of workers, is highly valued (Proctor and Mueller, 2000). As such, team building is often considered de rigueur in corporate and industrial settings (Fapohunda, 2013). While there are undoubtedly comparisons to be drawn between work teams and sport teams, there is a danger in the wholesale export of principles from one setting to another. Instead, what is required is a careful appraisal of the concrete evidence for effectiveness in both settings before any cast iron judgements can be reached. Sadly, in both the business and sport domains there remains a shortage of systematic research dealing specifically with the effectiveness of team building (Bloom et al., 2003; Klein et al., 2009). Thankfully, more recent studies, particularly those employing meta-analytic techniques, are starting to address this issue. In terms of team building in the business setting, there is now evidence to suggest that it can have a positive effect (Fapohunda, 2013). More specifically it has been reported that the strongest effects appear to be associated with interventions using goal-setting and/or role-clarification approaches and that, in terms of outcome measures, the largest effects appear to be associated with team processes and affective outcomes (Klein et al., 2009). The general message to be gleaned from this evidence would therefore appear to be that task-focused approaches to team building reap the greatest rewards.

Increasingly it would appear that the evidence of team-building efficacy from the sporting world mirrors that from the business world. In their comprehensive meta-analysis Martin et al. (2009) report that goal setting is the most effective of the team-building approaches (see **3.12**). Again it is notable that this type of intervention is distinctly task-oriented in nature. It should be borne in mind, though, that a smaller but statistically significant effect was also found to exist for interventions with an outdoor pursuits/adventure focus. A recent team-building intervention study (Bruner et al., 2020) involving an elite hockey team showed the programme had a positive effect on task cohesion. The intervention focused on enhancing role acceptance and leadership through a newly developed *T*eam *E*nvironment *A*ssess*M*ent (TEAM) procedure, and demonstrated the utility of specific tools in helping guide the team-building process.

In terms of outcome measures that are positively related to team-building interventions, Martin et al. (2009) report the greatest impacts are in relation to cognitive and performance outcomes. Interestingly, it is also reported that team building has little effect on task cohesion (see **5.22**). While the authors suggest this may be due to difficulties in measuring task cohesion, an alternative explanation may be advanced. Task cohesion is about how well a team carries out its duties on the court or pitch. In a sporting context it may be that this is something that is learnt on the training pitch, not in a conference room. In terms of method of delivery, it was found that there was little difference in effectiveness between direct and indirect methods.

What appeared more important was intervention length. Interventions of fewer than two weeks were found to be ineffective, with effectiveness rising after 20 weeks. This tallies with previous suggestions that team building should not be regarded as a 'one-off' endeavour but should be carried out across the entire season (Brawley and Paskevich, 1997). Furthermore, such findings support the previously cited study (Bruner et al., 2020) indicating that the importance of team cohesion to performance becomes more significant with increased team member interactions. Intriguingly, it is also reported that greater effects are evident in individual sports as compared with team sports. While this finding is at first glance counter-intuitive, it is perhaps understandable as, by definition, team sports require some degree of interaction between members, whereas in individual sports, players may co-act without necessarily interacting (e.g. golf, tennis, see **5.22**). In this respect there may be more to be gained from any form of team building, as the level of support and engagement within a team of individuals is starting from such a low point.

In examining the evidence above, one thing is clear – many of the activities that have been associated with team building in the past need not necessarily be taken as a priority for the coach seeking to 'build' his or her team. Traditional views of teams being built by bonding or socialising together, particularly where alcohol or 'enjoying the craic' is involved, do not appear to be validated by careful scrutiny of the evidence. Instead there are many examples where the 'jolly' did more harm than good, not only to team performance but also team reputation! Ultimately, the purpose of a team is to achieve defined goals. The evidence would suggest that assisting teams in clarifying those goals, the team members' role in those goals, assessing the steps required to achieve those goals and assisting teams in developing a healthy and helpful focus on those goals, is likely to improve the team's ability to achieve their goals. When coaches and managers speak of drawing on the resources of teammates, what is being referred to is what happens on the pitch, not what happened in the bar. It is unsurprising then that, for coaches and sports psychologists alike, a focus on task concerns appears the most effective path towards building a successful team.

KEY READINGS

Carron, A.V. and Eys, M.A. (2012) *Group Dynamics in Sport* (4th ed.). Morgantown, WV: Fitness Information Technology.

Klein, C., DiazGranados, D., Salas, E., Huy Le, C., Burke, S., Lyons, R. and Goodwin, G.F. (2009) 'Does team building work?', *Small Group Research*, 40 (2), 181–222.

Martin, L.J., Carron, A.V. and Burke, S.M. (2009) 'Team building interventions in sport: A meta-analysis', *Sport and Exercise Psychology Review*, 5 (2), 3–18.

Veach, T.L. and May, J.R. (2005) 'Teamwork: For the good of the whole', in S. Murphy (ed.), *The Sport Psych Handbook*. Champaign, IL: Human Kinetics. pp. 171–89.

PRACTICAL QUESTIONS

- A team coach approaches you seeking advice on organising a team weekend away. What advice would you offer as to how the weekend should be structured, and what activities would you recommend?
- Based on the available research evidence, suggest how, where and when a team-building intervention should be introduced with a football team made up of a diverse group of players of different ages and backgrounds.

REFERENCES

Bloom, G., Stevens, D. and Wickwire, T. (2003) 'Expert coaches' perceptions of team building', *Journal of Applied Sport Psychology*, 15 (2), 129–43.

Brawley, L.R. and Paskevich, D.M. (1997) 'Conducting team building research in the context of sport and exercise', *Journal of Applied Sport Psychology*, 9, 11–40.

Bruner, M.W., Eys, M.A., Beauchamp, M.R. and Côté, J. (2013) 'Examining the origins of team building in sport: A citation network and genealogical approach', *Group Dynamics: Theory, Research, and Practice*, 17, 30–42.

Bruner, M.W., Eys, M., Carreau, J.M., McLaren, C. and Van Woezik, R. (2020) 'Using the Team Environment AssessMent (TEAM) to enhance team building in sport', *The Sport Psychologist*, 34 (1), 62–70.

Buller, P.F. (1986) 'The team building–task performance relation: Some conceptual and methodological refinements', *Group and Organization Studies*, 11, 147–68.

Eys, M. and Kim, J. (2017) 'Team building and group cohesion in the context of sport and performance psychology', retrieved from *Oxford Research Encyclopedia of Psychology*: http://psychology.oxfordre.com/view/10.1093/acrefore/9780190236557.001.0001/acrefore-9780190236557-e-186.

Fapohunda, T.M. (2013) 'Towards effective team building in the workplace', *International Journal of Education and Research*, 1 (4), 1–12.

Klein, C., DiazGranados, D., Salas, E., Huy Le, C., Burke, S., Lyons, R. and Goodwin, G.F. (2009) 'Does team building work?', *Small Group Research*, 40 (2), 181–222.

Kremer, J., Moran, A. and Kearney, C. (2019) *Pure Sport: Sport Psychology in Action* (3rd ed.). London: Routledge.

Martin, L.J., Carron, A.V. and Burke, S.M. (2009) 'Team building interventions in sport: A meta-analysis', *Sport and Exercise Psychology Review*, 5 (2), 3–18.

Proctor, S. and Mueller, F. (2000) *Teamworking.* Houndmills, Hants: Palgrave Macmillan.

Salas, E., Rozell, D., Mullen, B. and Driskell, J.E. (1999) 'The effect of team building on performance: An integration', *Small Group Research*, 30, 309–29.

Schein, E.H. (1999) *Process Consultation Revisited: Building the Helping Relationship.* Reading, MA: Addison-Wesley.

Veach, T.L. and May, J.R. (2005) 'Teamwork: For the good of the whole', in S. Murphy (ed.), *The Sport Psych Handbook.* Champaign, IL: Human Kinetics. pp.171–89.

Yukelson, D. (1997) 'Principles of effective team building interventions in sport: A direct services approach at Penn State University', *Journal of Applied Sport Psychology*, 9, 73–96.

5.24 CAUSAL ATTRIBUTION

Definition: The psychological processes involved in helping us explain why events take place, normally with reference to either internal or external dimensions that vary in relation to factors including stability and control.

Success and failure in sport reflect a unique blend of factors, factors that are not only associated with those who are taking part but also the circumstances within which they take part, some of which are under the control of participants and some which aren't. That is the reality of sport, but the focus of this chapter is not necessarily on reality *per se* but on the cognitive explanations that we employ when interpreting the outcome, be it win, lose or draw. Sometimes we are rational in our explanations but more often research reveals significant biases that distort our view of reality, sometimes to protect us, sometimes to protect others, but rarely to protect the truth. The purpose of this chapter is to place these explanations, or attributions, under close examination, to help understand why and how they are made, and why they matter so much.

As conscious and reflective beings with a unique sense of self, it is adaptive and functionally valuable for human beings to seek out explanations as to why things happen, and to perceive ourselves to be the authors of our destiny. When an event can be attributed to a cause it provides us with the opportunity to understand future events and so to increase our capacity to predict and control, the twin tenets of science. Essentially this is an attribution, the perceived cause of an event which may, of course, be different from the actual cause (Hanrahan and Biddle, 2008). The process of making attributions is such a fundamentally human characteristic that it is not surprising that it has occupied centre stage across various psychology subdisciplines for a considerable number of years.

Over 75 years ago, Fritz Heider first highlighted our desire to understand causality, or what caused what to happen. Heider (1944) cast humans as lay psychologists or naïve scientists, seeking to understand and predict the behaviour of others. Building on this work, Jones and Davis (1965) then examined the importance of attributions in how we make inferences about the personalities of others. This would lead to one of the key findings of attribution theory and one which remains significant in the context of sport: the fundamental attribution error. This states that, as observers or spectators, we tend to attribute the behaviour of those we are watching to ability, skill or disposition rather than circumstance, while as actors or players ourselves, we are more inclined to blame circumstances. Little wonder that such attributions are a source of conflict between spectators, coaches and athletes.

As the field developed the emphasis began to move away from examining the attributions that people make about others and their world, and towards understanding the attributions that they make about themselves (Kelley, 1972). Kelley's covariation model suggests that we examine how accompanying conditions or events vary as outcomes vary. This information is then analysed in terms of three factors in particular: consistency, distinctiveness and consensus. For example, a golfer who plays distinctively worse in the rain, and on a consistent basis, and who is told by her caddy and significant others that she struggles in the rain, is then likely to form the attribution that rain affects her game. This example also hints at a further key distinction that is made in the attribution literature: the difference between internal and external attributions (Weiner, 1972). Weiner (1986), in his slowly evolving attributional theory of emotion and motivation, suggested that when we make attributions we are faced with something of a dilemma – do we look inwards, to ourselves, or do we look outwards, to external factors?

The distinction between an internal and external 'locus of control' then informed a key finding derived from his attributional theory known as the attributional or self-serving bias (e.g. Miller and Ross, 1975), an issue which is yet again so salient in a sporting context (Allen et al., 2020). This bias is our general tendency to attribute success to internal factors (such as ability) and failure to external factors (typically luck, the pitch, the referee, the weather, our opponents, teammates, etc.). From a practical sport psychology perspective, this finding is so important for recognising those who fail to learn from past failures, often because their powers of externalising, or blaming/rationalising without taking personal responsibility, are so well honed.

Further to this formulation, Weiner then suggested a second dimension to attributions: stability. This concerns the likelihood of the perceived cause remaining consistent. For example, ability is likely to be perceived as fairly constant, whereas individuals may perceive an abstract concept, such as luck or even mood state, to be more variable. Weiner explicitly applied his theory to achievement settings, initially focusing on academia but later adopted enthusiastically in the world of sport. Weiner maintained that outcomes (e.g. test results) lead to emotions (positive or negative), which in turn lead to a search for reasons for the outcome. Our understanding of the reasons will in turn affect our psychological state. For example, if a bad result is perceived to be due to a lack of ability, this may lead to the conclusion that there is no point in trying. This will ultimately have a behavioural consequence; in this instance it may be a lack of effort in the future (see Figure 5.1).

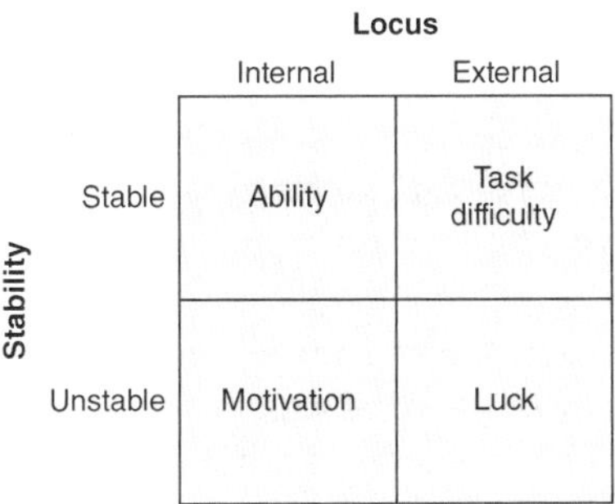

Figure 5.1 Weiner's Attribution Model – Showing Locus of Control and Stability Factors

While earlier studies of attribution had tended to focus on discrete factors such as ability, effort, task difficulty and luck (see above), Weiner's theory helped shift attention to other attributional dimensions. Initially this consisted of two, internality and stability, with the further dimensions of globality, universality, intentionality and controllability only later receiving attention (Hanrahan and Biddle, 2008; Rees et al., 2005). 'Globality' refers to the perceived breadth of effect of the perceived cause, that is, how likely it is to remain a factor across different settings. 'Universality' refers to whether the cause is common to all people (a universal attribution) or unique to the individual (a personal attribution). 'Intentionality' refers to whether or not the cause was present through the desire of the individual, in turn overlapping with 'controllability' or the degree of control that the individual perceives to exist.

By conceptualising attribution dimensions in this way, it becomes possible to reflect on the considerable number of discrete factors that athletes may perceive as important in helping explain and understand events. Not that this is always an easy task. As Hanrahan and Biddle suggest, grey areas still exist. For example, in certain closed-skill sports (e.g. diving, darts, pistol shooting), task difficulty remains generally stable. However, in a sport such as golf or motor racing, task difficulty could be seen as unstable, being influenced by both the course and the conditions. This highlights the strength of the dimensional concept of attribution theory; it provides a mechanism to recognise the influence of the particular sport in question and the influence of the athlete's perception of attribution dimensions. It is through the lens of these dimensions that attribution research in sport continues to be conducted (Allen et al., 2020), and it is through this lens that we will now turn to consider how attributions are made and why they are so important.

In understanding how attributions are made, traditionally the primary focus has been on seeking to identify factors that predict the types of attributions which individuals are likely to make. For example, in children's sport, self-worth has been identified as an important factor. It is reported that children with higher levels of self-esteem are more likely to make attributions that are internal, stable and controllable. Additionally, children with higher levels of self-efficacy are more likely to attribute failures to a lack of effort, rather than a lack of ability (see **3.16**). A further factor that has been identified as a predictor of attributions is goal orientation (see **3.15**) (Hanrahan and Gross, 2005). In this instance it is reported that a higher task orientation is likely to reflect in global and stable attributions. It is also reported that expertise is likely to affect attributions, with expert basketball players appearing more likely to make strategic attributions (i.e. blaming poor strategy for failures) than novice basketball players (Clearly and Zimmerman, 2001). A particularly interesting finding is that intelligence does not appear to influence attributional style (Kozub, 2002). This would support the assertion made earlier that explanations in sport are often lacking in logic or rationale, but instead are driven primarily by emotion. Of course, these findings only matter if the attributions that athletes make have a direct effect on their performance, that is, if attributions have consequences. It is with this in mind that we move to examine why attributions are so important.

One of the primary reasons that attributions are so important is that they influence future expectancies, and therefore motivation. For example, an athlete who attributes his or her failures to internal, unstable and controllable causes is likely to have more positive expectancies of future performance. They are likely to form the belief that they are capable of altering the circumstances that led to their failure. In this way, players who attribute failure to a lack of effort (an internal, unstable and controllable factor) are more likely to believe that they can perform better in the future. This contrasts with attributions that cite external, stable and uncontrollable factors for failure. The classic example is the player who believes 'my name was never on the trophy'. In such an example the athlete is likely to feel helpless and at the mercy of fate when it comes to future performances. Stability in particular seems important in this regard in that it has been found to influence athlete self-efficacy, with those who attribute success to stable factors displaying higher levels of self-efficacy (see **3.16**) (Bond et al., 2001). A similar effect has been noted on perceptions of performance, with both athletes and coaches displaying increased perceptions of performance and higher levels of persistence when they attribute success to internal, stable, controllable and intentional causes.

In practical terms, what these findings mean is that athletes' attributions are likely to prove fertile ground for intervention and, in particular, around cognitive restructuring (see **4.20**) (Allen, 2012). If certain attributions lead to more desirable outcomes, then it would make sense that athletes should learn how best to explain their successes and failures. Across the discipline of psychology this type of intervention has been labelled as 'attribution retraining' (Sinnott and Biddle, 1998). The central premise of attribution retraining is that objective information may be used to challenge unhelpful attributions. In sport this has tended to focus on ensuring that athletes attribute failure to something which they believe they can change, as opposed to more stable causes such as ability (Rees et al., 2005). One potential attribution that athletes may be encouraged to make is that failure was due to a lack of effort, as this is something they can change. Good coaches employ this technique on a regular basis (see **5.27**). Instead of telling players that they are not good enough, coaches may encourage them to try harder or sharpen key skills, in the belief that this will lead to improved results. However, this suggestion comes with a warning that, at times, failure may actually be due to uncontrollable circumstances (including superior opposition) and the athlete may have tried as hard as they could. In this instance, an attribution associated with lack of effort is likely to prove demoralising to the athlete. As such, positive results have been reported for programmes which focus on other unstable, controllable factors, in particular, strategy. An example of this type of thinking is the coach who tells her players that they are good enough but that they need to stick to the game plan in order to win. Such attributions are designed to protect self-efficacy and self-esteem while at the same time ensuring that athletes still believe success is under their control.

Such a viewpoint stands in stark contrast to the type of superstitions that are so often found in sport (see **2.7**) (Dömötör et al., 2016). However, the attribution literature does provide us with some clues as to why sport is littered with such irrational attributions

(Allen, 2012). Faulkner and Finlay (2002) point out that attributions occur in a social context and as such should be seen as much as an action as a belief. In other words, attributions often serve a social function: for example, justifying oneself to the media (or a psychologist!). With this in mind it may suit to blame failures on a curse rather than admit that your team is simply not good enough! Hence, attributions are important not only to the people who make them but also to the people who hear them. This is a central distinction in attribution theory. While we may make excuses to others, our appraisal of ourselves must be both accurate and helpful. This is the challenge for practitioners and athletes alike when they seek to put attribution theory into practice.

KEY READINGS

Allen, M.S. (2012) 'A systematic review of content themes in sport attribution research: 1954–2011', *International Journal of Sport and Exercise Psychology*, 10 (1), 1–8. DOI: 10.1080/1612197X.2012.645130.

Allen, M.S., Robson, D.A., Martin, L.J. and Laborde, S. (2020) 'Systematic review and meta-analysis of self-serving attribution biases in the competitive context of organized sport', *Personality and Social Psychology Bulletin*, 46 (7), 1027–43.

Hanrahan, S.J. and Biddle, S.J.H. (2008) 'Attributions and perceived control', in T.S. Horn (ed.), *Advances in Sport Psychology* (3rd ed.). Leeds: Human Kinetics. pp. 99–114.

Rees, T., Ingledew, D.K. and Hardy, L. (2005) 'Attribution in sport psychology: Seeking congruence between theory, research and practice', *Psychology of Sport and Exercise*, 6, 189–204.

PRACTICAL QUESTIONS

- Try to identify a range of superstitions that top athletes have used in the past and the present. What are the pros and cons of relying on superstitions in sport?
- When working with a player who has an exaggerated external attribution style, describe techniques that you could use to attempt to shift the attribution style to one which accepts greater personal responsibility. What are the advantages of changing this external attribution style?

REFERENCES

Allen, M.S. (2012) 'A systematic review of content themes in sport attribution research: 1954–2011', *International Journal of Sport and Exercise Psychology*, 10 (1), 1–8. DOI: 10.1080/1612197X.2012.645130.

Allen, M.S., Robson, D.A., Martin, L.J. and Laborde, S. (2020) 'Systematic review and meta-analysis of self-serving attribution biases in the competitive context of organized sport', *Personality and Social Psychology Bulletin*, 46 (7), 1027–43.

Bond, K.A., Biddle, S.J.H. and Ntoumanis, N. (2001) 'Self-efficacy and causal attribution in female golfers', *International Journal of Sport Psychology*, 32, 243–56.

Clearly, T.J. and Zimmerman, B.J. (2001) 'Self-regulation differences during athletic practice by experts, non-experts, and novices', *Journal of Applied Sport Psychology*, 13, 185–206.

Dömötör, Z., Ruíz-Barquín, R. and Szabo, A. (2016) 'Superstitious behavior in sport: A literature review', *Scandinavian Journal of Psychology*, 57 (4), 368–82.

Faulkner, G. and Finlay, S.J. (2002) 'It's not what you say, it's the way you say it! Conversation analysis: A discursive methodology for sport, exercise, and physical education', *Quest*, 54, 49–66.

Hanrahan, S.J. and Biddle, S.J.H. (2008) 'Attributions and perceived control', in T.S. Horn (ed.) *Advances in Sport Psychology* (3rd ed.). Leeds: Human Kinetics. pp. 99–114.

Hanrahan, S.J. and Gross, J. (2005) 'Attributions and goal orientations in masters athletes: Performance versus outcome', *Revista de Psicologia del Deporte*, 14 (1), 43–56.

Heider, F. (1944) 'Social perception and phenomenal causality', *Psychological Review*, 51, 358–74.

Jones, E.E. and Davis, K.E. (1965) 'From acts to dispositions: The attribution process in person perception', in L. Berkowitz (ed.), *Advances in Experimental Social Psychology*, vol. 2. London: Academic Press. pp. 219–66.

Kelley, H.H. (1972) 'Causal schemata and the attribution process', in E.E. Jones, D.E. Kanouse, H.H. Kelley, R.E. Nisbett, S. Valins, and B. Weiner (eds), *Attribution: Perceiving the Causes of Behaviour*. Morristown, NJ: General Learning Press. pp. 1–26.

Kozub, F.M. (2002) 'Expectations, task persistence, and attributions in children with mental retardation during integrated physical education', *Adapted Physical Activity Quarterly*, 19, 334–49.

Miller, D.T. and Ross, M. (1975) 'Self-serving biases in the attribution of causality: Fact or fiction?', *Psychological Bulletin*, 82 (2), 213–25.

Rees, T., Ingledew, D.K. and Hardy, L. (2005) 'Attribution in sport psychology: Seeking congruence between theory, research and practice', *Psychology of Sport and Exercise*, 6, 189–204.

Sinnott, K. and Biddle, S. (1998) 'Changes in attributions, perceptions of success and intrinsic motivation after attribution retraining in children's sport', *International Journal of Adolescence and Youth*, 7, 137–44.

Weiner, B. (1972) *Theories of Motivation: From Mechanism to Cognition*. Chicago, IL: Rand McNally.

Weiner, B. (1986) *An Attributional Theory of Motivation and Emotion*. New York: Springer-Verlag.

5.25 SOCIAL FACILITATION AND SOCIAL LOAFING

Definitions: Social facilitation is a change in individual effort and subsequent performance in the real or imagined presence of either co-actors or an audience. Social loafing is a reduction in individual effort when acting as part of a group or collective.

For more than a century (see **1.1**), the world of sport and exercise has presented itself as a natural laboratory for exploring how the presence of other people, whether as spectators, competitors or teammates, impacts on motivation and performance. Social influence can reveal itself in many ways but the primary focus of much of this work has been on two related social phenomena: social facilitation and social loafing. That is, how the presence of others either helps or hinders individual effort and, in turn, performance.

Is it mere coincidence that so many world records and outstanding feats don't occur in training but in front of millions of spectators, or at venues which players and athletes recognise as 'special' for undefined reasons? Equally, in team sports, do we subconsciously ease back on the throttle when we know we can hide ourselves in the group or team? In actual fact, answers to these intriguing questions have been sought since the very earliest days of experimental psychology. In the case of social facilitation, this can be traced to Norman Triplett's pioneering fishing-line experiment with children in 1898 (see **1.1**), while the first social loafing experiment was carried out by a French agricultural engineer called Max Ringelmann in 1913 (Kravitz and Martin, 1986). Using a weighing scale attached by a rope to a tree, he measured the force exerted by either one, two, three or up to eight men. By the time that eight men were pulling on the rope the average force that each exerted (31 kg) was less than half that they had shown they were capable of when acting alone (63 kg). Later experiments have confirmed this effect by taking account of coordination losses; even so the losses that could be explained by social loafing alone accounted for between 10 per cent and 15 per cent reduction in effort.

Both experiments generated a great deal of interest and started long research traditions, while also triggering other lines of enquiry. For example, Triplett was aware that the presence of others did not have the same effect on everyone, with some coping better than others (Triplett, 1898). Some children wound faster alongside another child while others went to pieces, suggesting the significant role that arousal or stress had played (see **2.5**). Equally, later work on social influence across social psychology, including that dealing with topics such as conformity, compliance and obedience, all point to the non-conscious ways in which the presence of others influences our motives and behaviour.

SOCIAL FACILITATION

Triplett's work was taken up by eminent social psychologists including Floyd Allport in the 1920s and from that time until the 1980s there followed a multitude of human and animal studies, both in the field and the laboratory (Aiello and Douthill, 2001; Strauss, 2002). Some were truly ingenious. For example, one involved looking at the speed with which cockroaches ran from a bright light, either alone or in pairs, and either in a straight line (a dominant response) or around a corner (a non-dominant response). Across this research the results have been generally consistent, if not spectacular. In a nutshell, the presence of others leads to enhanced performance on certain tasks, and specifically tasks which call for well-learnt, dominant responses. If you can do something well, the presence of others will improve performance. On the other hand, if you are incompetent, learning a skill or attempting something for the first time, then you may perform worse in company than alone. Such a view is apparent in early childhood years, where a focus on sport competition at the expense of enjoyment and learning can disengage children and be a source of social anxiety (Chronis-Tuscano et al., 2018).

While the phenomenon of social facilitation is very important in the context of competitive sport, the number of applied studies is surprisingly small. One notable exception involved secretly rating players in a US pool hall according to their shot accuracy. Four spectators (confederates of the experimenter) then stood and watched games. As you may expect, those who were above average improved in front of an audience (from 71 per cent accuracy to 80 per cent), while those who were below average potted even fewer shots (from 36 per cent to 25 per cent) (Michaels et al., 1982). More recently, Edwards et al. (2018) demonstrated that the presence of a vocal audience had a significant effect not only on the effort exerted in a cycling task but also the willingness to return to exercise the following day.

Despite these isolated examples, from the 1980s onwards interest in researching the phenomenon has waned, while interest has grown in trying to explain not the *what* but the *why* of social facilitation in the broader context of work on social influence generally (Strauss, 2002). Zajonc's original explanation (Zajonc, 1965) held sway for some time, arguing that the *mere presence* of an audience (or co-actors) was somehow sufficient to increase drive or motivation, and this would improve well-learnt performance but at the same time interfere with newly acquired skills, whatever the circumstance. Later work suggested that the type of audience was critical and raised the possibility that the role played by *evaluation apprehension* could not be ignored. Cottrell et al. (1968) maintained that social facilitation increased in proportion to the extent that the person felt he or she was being evaluated by either spectators or competitors. While evaluation apprehension does appear to be important to some degree (and hence explains why some teams have always played better away from the critical gaze of home 'supporters'), the larger 'why' questions still remain more elusive. Evaluation apprehension has been connected at different times with a host of 'self' variables such as self-awareness, self-consciousness, self-presentational concern, self-monitoring and self-attention. Meanwhile it was also suggested that the effect could be explained by anxiety linked to the conflict generated when we are performing in the presence of others (Chronis-Tuscano et al., 2018) – the conflict between attending to the task and attending to other people (Baron, 1986).

As to which theory offers the most valid explanation, the answer probably lies in the fact that all contain a kernel of truth – but fundamentally the effect may not be as profound as some would have suggested. In a meta-analysis of over 241 studies and involving nearly 24,000 participants, Bond and Titus (1983) concluded that the presence of others had only marginal effects on performance overall, to the order of only 2–3 per cent. They concluded that the presence of others may increase arousal but only if the individual is performing a complex task, and this may lead to a knock-on effect on both speed (increased) and accuracy (decreased). However, the effect of evaluation on performance was not shown to be strong across these published experiments.

SOCIAL LOAFING

On the other side of the coin from social facilitation lies social loafing, where the presence of others does not increase drive or arousal but instead provides an opportunity to exert less effort. A substantial literature shows a variety of factors that impact on the extent of social loafing (Hardy, 1990). Factors that have been shown to decrease loafing effects include: smaller group size; the extent to which individual effort can be identified; the strength of group identity; the nature and attractiveness of the task; the degree of trust between group members; the interdependence of group members; the extent of involvement with the group; group cohesiveness; intergroup comparisons; collective efficacy; and personal responsibility.

More recently, Heuze and Brunel (2003) found that when playing darts against opponents of varying degrees of ability, loafing was greatest when the opponent was superior and least when the other player was thought to be of a similar standard and hence competition was most fierce. Other factors have also been shown to impact on the extent of loafing. For example, Czyż et al. (2016) replicated the original Ringelmann experiment but used participants who did or did not have previous involvement in team sports. Interestingly, they found that experience of team sports effectively eliminated social loafing. Haugen et al. (2016) also found that a personal attribute, mental toughness, could ameliorate the effects of social loafing, with those scoring highly on a mental toughness questionnaire (see **4.21**) showing few signs of social loafing in a cycling time-trial task (akin to Triplett's), in contrast with those with lower scores.

Standing back from the literature, and including the interpretations commonly offered for both social facilitation and loafing effects, the overlap between the constructs becomes very obvious. Hence it should come as no surprise to learn that there have been repeated calls to integrate the findings in the broader context of the social influence literature (Karau and Williams, 1993; Carron and Brawley, 2008).

As to why social loafing occurs, a number of explanations have been offered, all generally pointing to two dominant concerns. First, the potential to share responsibility when individual effort is not identifiable and, in particular, on tasks or in games that are not seen as important. Second, the extent to which the person identifies with the collective and feels bound to the values and goals of the group or team.

By now it should be apparent that there are obvious connections between the two phenomena, social loafing and social facilitation, as both deal with how we are influenced by others in social situations, including teams. With this in mind a number of approaches have emerged to try to offer an overarching framework. For example, both Harkins and Szymanski (1987) and Mullen and Baumeister (1987) describe social faciliation and social loafing in relation to self-concept; the former emphasising evaluation by self and others, the latter our self-awareness in a variety of social contexts. In a very different way, Sanna (1992) used self-efficacy theory (see **3.16**) to model four possible outcomes attaching to the interaction between loafing and facilitation. They proposed that when the presence of others *increases* evaluation then dominant responses will be enhanced (social facilitation) but difficult tasks will be impaired (social inhibition). However, when the presence of others *decreases* evaluation then we will be inclined to 'take the foot off the pedal' on less demanding or easy tasks (social loafing) but our performance may actually improve on more difficult tasks as we are less anxious (social security).

In a similar vein, Karau and Williams (2001) developed their Collective Effort Model to help explain both social phenomena, arguing that effort will only be expended when the individual values the task and their personal contribution to the group, and when their performance is being evaluated. At the same time, Aiello and Douthill (2001) outlined an integrative unifying theory, principally to consider social facilitation effects but with the potential to include social loafing as well. The model considers how situational (e.g. sensory cues, proximity of others, feedback and climate), presence (e.g. type of presence, roles of others, salience of presence, relationships and length of presence) and task (e.g. difficulty, cognitive/motor characteristics and time) factors combine to influence the individual's perceptions, cognitions, reactions and performance.

KEY READINGS

Bond, C.F. and Titus, L.J. (1983) 'Social facilitation: A meta-analysis of 241 studies', *Psychological Bulletin*, 94 (2), 265–92.

Czyż, S.H., Szmajke, A., Kruger, A. and Kübler, M. (2016) 'Participation in team sports can eliminate the effect of social loafing', *Perceptual and Motor Skills*, 123, 754–68.

Karau, S.J. and Williams, K.D. (1993) 'Social loafing: A meta-analytic review and theoretical integration', *Journal of Personality and Social Psychology*, 65, 681–706.

Strauss, B. (2002) 'Social facilitation in motor tasks', *Psychology of Sport and Exercise*, 3, 237–56.

PRACTICAL QUESTIONS

- With reference to two sports involving fine motor skills (e.g. archery, shooting, golf), outline how both audiences and co-actors will influence performance, and what circumstances should be created to maximise potential performance in these sports?
- With reference to two sports involving gross motor skills (e.g. powerlifting, rowing, tug-of-war), outline how both audiences and co-actors will influence performance, and what circumstances should be created to maximise potential performance in these sports?

REFERENCES

Aiello, J.R. and Douthill, E.A. (2001) 'Social facilitation from Triplett to electronic performance monitoring', *Group Dynamics*, 5, 163–80.

Baron, R.A. (1986) 'Distraction-conflict theory: Progress and problems'. in L. Berkowitz (ed.), *Advances in Experimental Social Psychology*, vol. 19. Orlando, FL: Academic Press. pp. 1–39.

Bond, C.F. and Titus, L.J. (1983) 'Social facilitation: A meta-analysis of 241 studies', *Psychological Bulletin*, 94 (2), 265–92.

Carron, A.V. and Brawley, F.R. (2008) 'Group dynamics in sport and physical activity', in T.S. Horn (ed.), *Advances in Sport Psychology*. Champaign, IL: Human Kinetics. pp. 213–38.

Cottrell, N.B., Sekerak, G.J., Wack, D.L. and Rittle, R.H. (1968) 'Social facilitation of dominant responses by the presence of an audience and the mere presence of others', *Journal of Personality and Social Psychology*, 9 (3), 245–50.

Chronis-Tuscano, A., Danko, C.M., Rubin, K.H., Coplan, R.J. and Novick, D.R. (2018) 'Future directions for research on early intervention for young children at risk for social anxiety', *Journal of Clinical Child and Adolescent Psychology*, 47 (4), 655–67.

Czyż, S.H., Szmajke, A., Kruger, A. and Kübler, M. (2016) 'Participation in team sports can eliminate the effect of social loafing', *Perceptual and Motor Skills*, 123, 754–8.

Edwards, A.M., Dutton-Challis, L., Cottrell, D., Guy, J.H. and Hettinga, F.J. (2018) 'Impact of active and passive social facilitation on self-paced endurance and sprint exercise: Encouragement augments performance and motivation to exercise', *BMJ Open Sport and Exercise Medicine*, 4, e000368. doi: 10.1136/bmjsem-2018-000368.

Hardy, C.J. (1990) 'Social loafing: Motivational losses in collective performance', *International Journal of Sport Psychology*, 21, 305–27.

Harkins, S.G. and Szymanski, K. (1987) 'Social loafing and social facilitation: New wine in old bottles', in C. Hendrick (ed.), *Review of Personality and Social Psychology: Group Processes and Intergroup Relations*. Newbury Park, CA: SAGE. pp. 167–88.

Haugen, T., Reinboth, M., Hetlelid, K.J., Peters, D.M. and Høigaard, R. (2016) 'Mental toughness moderates social loafing in cycle time-trial performance', *Research Quarterly in Exercise and Sport*, 87 (3), 305–10.

Heuze, J.-P. and Brunel, P.C. (2003) 'Social loafing in a competitive context', *International Journal of Sport and Exercise Psychology*, 1 (3), 246–63.

Karau, S.J. and Williams, K.D. (1993) 'Social loafing: A meta-analytic review and theoretical integration', *Journal of Personality and Social Psychology*, 65, 681–706.

Karau, S.J. and Williams, K.D. (2001) 'Understanding individual motivation in groups: The Collective Effort Model', in M.E. Turner (ed.) *Groups at Work: Theory and Research*. Mahwah, NJ: Erlbaum. pp. 113–41.

Kravitz, D.A. and Martin, B. (1986) 'Ringelmann rediscovered: The original article', *Journal of Personality and Social Psychology*, 50, 936–41.

Michaels, J.W., Blommel, J.M., Brocato, R.M., Linkous, R.A. and Rowe, J.S. (1982) 'Social facilitation and inhibition in a natural setting', *Replications in Social Psychology*, 2, 21–4.

Mullen, B. and Baumeister, R.F. (1987) 'Group effects on self-attention and performance: Social loafing, social facilitation, and social impairment', in C. Hendrick (ed.), *Review of Personality and Social Psychology: Group Processes and Intergroup Relations*. Newbury Park, CA: SAGE. pp. 189–205.

Sanna, L.J. (1992) 'Self-efficacy theory: Implications for social facilitation and social loafing', *Journal of Personality and Social Psychology*, 62, 774–86.

Strauss, B. (2002) 'Social facilitation in motor tasks', *Psychology of Sport and Exercise*, 3, 237–56.

Triplett, N. (1898) 'The dynamogenic factors in pacemaking and competition', *American Journal of Psychology*, 9, 507–33.

Zajonc, R.B. (1965) 'Social facilitation', *Science*, 149, 269–74.

5.26 LEADERSHIP AND MANAGEMENT

Definition: The delivery of effective sport leadership and management that accommodates the contingencies of the situation, the demands of the sport and the characteristics of those being led.

The role occupied by leaders in sport has long been a preoccupation within sport psychology, deriving in the early years from Coleman Griffith's pioneering work with the Chicago Cubs in the 1930s (Green, 2003) (see **1.1**). This interest is probably not surprising given the prominence afforded to leaders in sports media and wider sport literature, whether acting as coaches, managers or captains.

At the same time, not all aspects of the leadership role have been afforded equal attention within the subdiscipline. As one example, the relationship between leadership and playing position has only attracted sporadic attention. Perhaps this is because the available research has merely served to confirm the intuitive and significant relationship between leadership, influence and the *interactional centrality* of certain playing positions, irrespective of sex, sport or skill level (Fransen et al., 2016). Those occupying central positions in team sports are not only afforded greater leadership opportunities when playing but they are also more likely then to go on to become managers and coaches (see **5.27**).

Equally, there remains a strong yet unsubstantiated assumption that those who excel as players will also succeed as coaches or managers, and yet there is little evidence to support this proposition. Indeed, Marcotti (2001) found that of the 26 soccer managers who led English Premiership winning teams between 1945 and 2000, fewer than one in five had represented their country more than six times. Being good at sport is not necessarily a prerequisite for helping others to become good at sport, and many of the world's most accomplished coaches and managers only shone when their playing days were a distant memory. Indeed, several current high-profile English Premiership football managers are renowned for not actually playing football at a professional level. Furthermore, some of the greatest team captains were not necessarily those with outstanding sporting ability but with the acumen to harness and steer their teammates to success.

Leaving these issues aside, according to a recent review by Arthur and Bastardoz (2020), the extant leadership literature in sport psychology can be best characterised with reference to four strands: models and theories of leadership that have been developed and applied within sport; models and theories that have been developed in other disciplines and then applied in a sporting context; observational studies of the characteristics of good coaches and managers; and stand-alone measures of leadership/coach behaviours, often with little reference to theory. It is the first two strands that will be the primary concern of this section, while a closer consideration of the role of the coach will be the focus of the next (see **5.27**).

It should come as no surprise that sport psychology first turned to organisational and occupational psychology when searching for theories and models to apply to understanding the sport leader (Kremer and Scully, 1994: 134–42). Within industrial and business settings, the longstanding concern with how best to manage people and teams is reflected in a burgeoning industry examining leadership and leaders. Current definitions now characterise leadership as a process, a process during which a group is influenced towards achieving its goals by an individual (Northouse, 2001). Much of this work can be traced back to Kurt Lewin's (1951) highly influential research into leadership styles of more than 70 years ago, and when the distinction between task and socio-emotional orientations was first mooted.

Lewin's was the first of many theories to be developed within the occupational psychology literature and then purloined and applied in a sporting context. Other influential models included Fiedler's Contingency Model of Situational Control, Normative Theory, Path-Goal Theory and Situational Leadership Theory. Expositions of these theories are well rehearsed and numerous, and while there remains undoubted applied value in elements of these non-sport specific theories, it was not until the early 1990s that a comprehensive model of leadership in the sporting setting was proposed, the highly influential Multidimensional Model of Leadership (MML; Chelladurai, 2007).

The model was an attempt to synthesise existing work but specifically tailored to the context of sport (Riemer, 2008). The MML posited three central elements to leadership in sport: first, circumstantial requirements placed on the leader; second, the behaviour displayed by the leader; and third, the preferences of the athletes being led. The interplay between these factors ultimately determines the two primary outcomes of leadership behaviour, athlete performance and athlete satisfaction. Of central importance is how closely the leader's preferred behaviour corresponds with both the demands of the situation and the preference of the athlete. So, for example, an expert youth coach may find that his or her approaches and preferences may not square with the requirements of managing a highly experienced, elite-level squad. This is not to say that a change in approach is not possible in different situations; rather it is to say that it is *required.*

More recently, Arthur and Bastardoz (2020) have elaborated on Chelladurai's model by including reference to potential explanatory (e.g. confidence and motivation) and moderating (e.g. sex, age and personality) variables in the determination of both satisfaction and performance, while also downplaying the significance of circumstantial requirements until such time as there is greater clarity on both definition and measurement (see Figure **5.2**).

The measurement tool that was developed in conjunction with MML is the Leadership Scale for Sports (LSS; Chelladurai and Saleh, 1980). Developed by the same authors, the LSS identifies five dimensions of leadership behaviour in sport, namely: Training and Instruction; Democratic Behaviour; Autocratic Behaviour; Social Support; and Positive Feedback. Zhang et al. (1997) later revised the LSS to include two further dimensions of leader behaviour, Group Maintenance and Situational Consideration, while keeping the original format and instructions intact.

Although appealing in both its intuition and scope, the research literature surrounding MML remains far from definitive, and the model has spawned little research over recent times. Instead, it would appear to have been superseded by alternative approaches or offshoots (Riemer and Toon, 2001), albeit ones that tend to share similar tenets. One

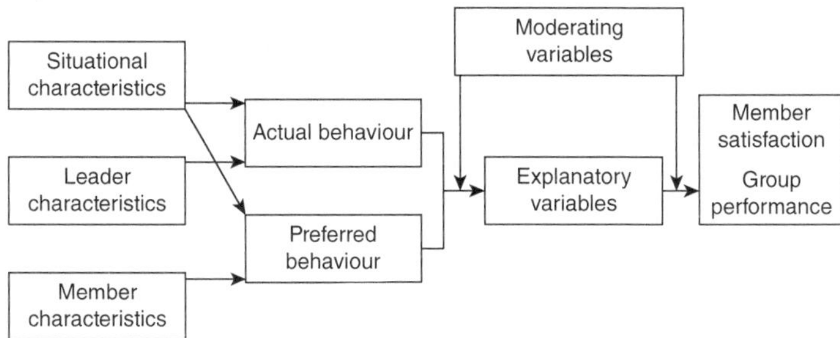

Figure 5.2 Modified Multidimensional Model of Leadership (Arthur and Bastardoz, 2020)

adaptation to MML is represented in the extensive work centred on *transformational leadership* (Hoption et al., 2007; Arthur et al., 2017). Transformational leadership highlights the importance of the manager, coach or captain's ability to ensure that athletes buy into their vision. 'Charisma', 'inspiration' and 'vision' are terms typically associated with this approach to leadership, and are terms that resonate strongly with many commentaries on successful coaching and managing. In many respects, this marks a return to the concept of the coach, manager or captain as *leader* in the almost mystical sense of the word, and is a long way removed from modern conceptualisations of leadership as a dynamic process of social exchange between those who lead and those who are led (Hollander and Offermann, 1990).

Despite the widespread attention that charisma continues to receive in both the media and supporters' attributions of team performance, the concept of transformational leadership remains under-researched in sport. In truth this is unsurprising. The mystical figures of sport leadership are afforded this status because they are perceived to be 'one in a million'. In some respects this is a throwback to the early days of leadership research, when leadership was couched crudely as either a reflection on the leader (i.e. the great man [*sic*] approach) or the situation/circumstances within which s/he led (i.e. the zeitgeist or spirit of the times approach), when in fact neither approach tells the full story. This is not to say that transformational leadership is an undesirable characteristic in a coach – far from it. The danger is in concentrating on such a nebulous concept as charisma without affording due regard to context and so many other elements that may be salient to the leadership function beyond personality alone.

As one example, in their expansive reflection on the future of group dynamics research in sport, Eys and Spink (2016) called for a widening of horizons in many research domains, including leadership, where so many topics remain unexplored, not least the construct of *followership*. With this in mind, over recent years it has been implicitly acknowledged that any consideration of leadership in sport needs to move beyond a focus on the role of the coach or manager to include all those ways in which leadership is manifest. For example, recent research has suggested that some of the leadership functions expected of the coach may be fulfilled by other leadership figures within a team. Specifically, it has been reported that teams may recognise up to a quarter of their members as informal leaders (Loughead and Hardy, 2005), and Fransen et al. (2014) go further, suggesting that formal roles, including coach, manager and specifically, the captain, are vastly overrated. In their words: 'It can be concluded that leadership is spread throughout the team; informal leaders rather than the captain take the lead, both on and off the field' (2014: 1389).

Research suggests that it is these informal leaders who are more likely to fulfil the roles of social support, positive feedback and democratic decision-making than those in formal positions of authority. Indeed, Fransen et al. (2014) argue that attention should shift to the various ways in which non-formal as well as formal leadership operates within sport teams, and that an exclusive focus on those with designated responsibility may only be telling a small part of the story as to how teams operate and are influenced. Acknowledging and utilising alternative or non-formal leadership systems can be of considerable practical benefit, as this then frees time to concentrate on training and instruction, in other words, the bigger strategic picture. This highlights an important and final point. Leadership is not static and is not something to be guarded by the coach but rather something to be fostered among those they 'lead', to be given away freely as a sign of natural progression, and of a job well done (Kremer et al., 2019: 183). By doing this they are likely to increase the effectiveness of their coaching and to have empowered those they are entrusted to lead.

KEY READINGS

Arthur, C.A. and Bastardoz, N. (2020) 'Leadership in sport', in G. Tenenbaum and R.C. Eklund (eds), *Handbook of Sport Psychology* (4th ed.). Hoboken, NJ: John Wiley & Sons. pp. 113–35.

Beauchamp, M., Jackson, B. and Loughead, T. (2018) 'Leadership in physical activity contexts', in T. Horn and A. Smith (eds), *Advances in Sport and Exercise Psychology* (4th ed.). Champaign, IL: Human Kinetics. pp. 151–70.

Cotterill, S.T. and Fransen, K. (2016) 'Athlete leadership in sport teams: Current understanding and future directions', *International Review of Sport and Exercise Psychology*, 9 (1), 116–33. doi: 10.1080/1750984X.2015.1124443.

Fransen, K, Vanbeselaere, N., De Cuyper, B, Vande Broek, G. and Boen, F. (2014) 'The myth of the team captain as principal leader: Extending the athlete leadership classification within sport teams', *Journal of Sports Sciences*, 32 (14), 1389–97. doi: 10.1080/02640414.2014.891291. Epub 2014 Mar 24. PMID: 24660668.

PRACTICAL QUESTIONS

- When selecting a team captain for the new season, identify the criteria that should be applied to decide which player is likely to be best suited to the role.
- Discuss the term 'charisma' and its relevance to our understanding of what contributes to successful leadership in sport.

REFERENCES

Arthur, C.A. and Bastardoz, N. (2020) 'Leadership in sport', in G. Tenenbaum and R.C. Eklund (eds), *Handbook of Sport Psychology* (4th ed.). Hoboken, NJ: John Wiley & Sons. pp. 113–35.

Arthur, C.A., Bastardoz, N. and Eklund, R. (2017) 'Transformational leadership in sport: Current status and future directions', *Current Opinion in Psychology*, 16, 78–83.

Chelladurai, P. (2007) 'Leadership in sports', in G. Tenenbaum and R.C. Eklund (eds), *Handbook of Sport Psychology* (3rd ed.). Hoboken, NJ: Wiley. pp. 113–35.

Chelladurai, P. and Saleh, S.D. (1980) 'Dimensions of leader behaviour in sports: Development of a leadership scale', *Canadian Journal of Applied Sports Sciences*, 3, 85–90.

Eys, M.A. and Spink, K.S. (2016) 'Forecasts to the future: Group dynamics', in R.J. Schinke, K.R. McGannon and B. Smith (eds), *Routledge International Handbook of Sport Psychology*. London: Routledge/Taylor & Francis Group. pp. 572–80.

Fransen, K., Haslam, S.A., Mallett, C.J., Steffens, N.K., Peters, K. and Boen, F. (2016) 'Leading from the centre: A comprehensive examination of the relationship between central playing positions and leadership in sport. *PLoS ONE* 11 (12): e0168150. https://doi.org/10.1371/journal.pone.0168150.

Fransen, K., Vanbeselaere, N., De Cuyper, B., Vande Broek, G. and Boen. F. (2014) 'The myth of the team captain as principal leader: Extending the athlete leadership classification within sport teams', *Journal of Sports Sciences*, 32 (14), 1389–97. doi: 10.1080/02640414.2014.891291.

Green, C. (2003) 'Psychology strikes out: Coleman R. Griffith and the Chicago Cubs', *History of Psychology*, 6 (3), 267–83.

Hollander, E.P. and Offermann, L.R. (1990) 'Power and leadership in organizations: Relationships in transition', *American Psychologist*, 45 (2), 179–89. https://doi.org/10.1037/0003-066X.45.2.179.

Hoption, C., Phelan, J. and Barling, J. (2007) 'Transformational leadership in sport', in M.R. Beauchamp and M.A. Eys (eds), *Group Dynamics in Exercise and Sport Psychology: Contemporary Themes. New York: Routledge*. pp. 45–60.

Kremer, J. and Scully, D. (1994). *Psychology in Sport*. London: Taylor & Francis. pp. 134–42.

Kremer, J., Moran, A. and Kearney, C. (2019) *Pure Sport: Sport Psychology in Action* (3rd ed.). London: Routledge.

Lewin, K. (1951) *Field Theory in Social Science*. New York: Harper.

Loughead, T.M. and Hardy, J. (2005) 'A comparison of coach and peer leader behaviours in sport', *Psychology of Sport and Exercise*, 6, 303–12.

Marcotti, G. (2001) 'Made not born', *The Sunday Tribune* (Sport), 7 October, p. 9.

Northouse, P.G. (2001) *Leadership: Theory and Practice* (2nd ed.). Thousand Oaks, CA: SAGE.

Riemer, H.A. (2008) 'Multidimensional model of coach leadership', in T.S. Horn (ed.), *Advances in Sport Psychology* (3rd ed.). Champaign, IL: Human Kinetics. pp. 58–73.

Riemer, H.A. and Toon, K. (2001) 'Leadership and satisfaction in tennis: Examination of congruence, gender and ability', *Research Quarterly for Exercise and Sport*, 72, 243–56.

Zhang, J., Jensen, B.E. and Mann, B.L. (1997) 'Modification and revision of the Leadership Scale for Sport', *Journal of Sport Behavior*, 20 (1), 105–21.

5.27 EFFECTIVE COACHING STYLES

Definition: The delivery of effective sport leadership and coaching styles that accommodate the contingencies of the situation and the sport along with the characteristics of those being coached or managed.

Whether stalking the sidelines in designer clothing, staring at a computer screen up in the stand or barking out instructions on a windy training ground, one of the most enigmatic and fascinating figures in sport has to be the coach or manager. In many professional and some amateur sports, leading an elite squad has evolved into a high-profile, high-pressure, multifaceted vocation. Never was President Truman's phrase 'The buck stops here!' more appropriate than when applied to the modern-day sports coach or manager. Coaches' careers stand or fall on results, and the modern sporting media place a huge onus on the importance of the leadership role in the determination of success. But is this fair? What exactly is the role of the coach, and what makes an effective coach? It is the last question in particular towards which we will now turn.

As mentioned previously, over several decades there has been evidence of a rift between the leadership and coaching literatures in sport psychology and sport science. This is due, at least in part, to the fact that coaching spans numerous disciplines, including teaching, management and psychology. While there is undoubted strength in drawing information from such a broad base, it would appear that this tendency has often contributed to a lack of focus (Gilbert and Trudel, 2004).

Historically, examinations of coaching within sport psychology have tended to be largely descriptive, focusing on discrete coaching behaviours: for example, how often the coach gives positive feedback. This work can appear somewhat piecemeal but has helped lay the foundations for more recent endeavours that tried to paint a bigger and more comprehensive picture. The most significant model to have attempted to marshal this descriptive work is the mediational model of leadership (Smoll et al., 1978). The model has three constructs at its core: coaches' behaviours; players' perception of these behaviours; and players' evaluations of these behaviours. It also accommodates a host of personal and situational variables in the determination of attitudes and behaviours, and ultimately what makes for good coaching. Over time this model has expanded as an increasing number of personal, situational, attitudinal and behavioural variables have been taken on board in order to reflect more accurately on the complexities of the dynamic relationship between a coach and his/her charges. While the model has intuitive appeal, it remains to be tested in its entirety (see Figure **5.3**).

In essence, the model characterises how situational, personal, and behavioural factors interact in the determination of a coach's behaviour, along the way introducing a plethora of personal and situational variables that either influence or are influenced. Specifically, the

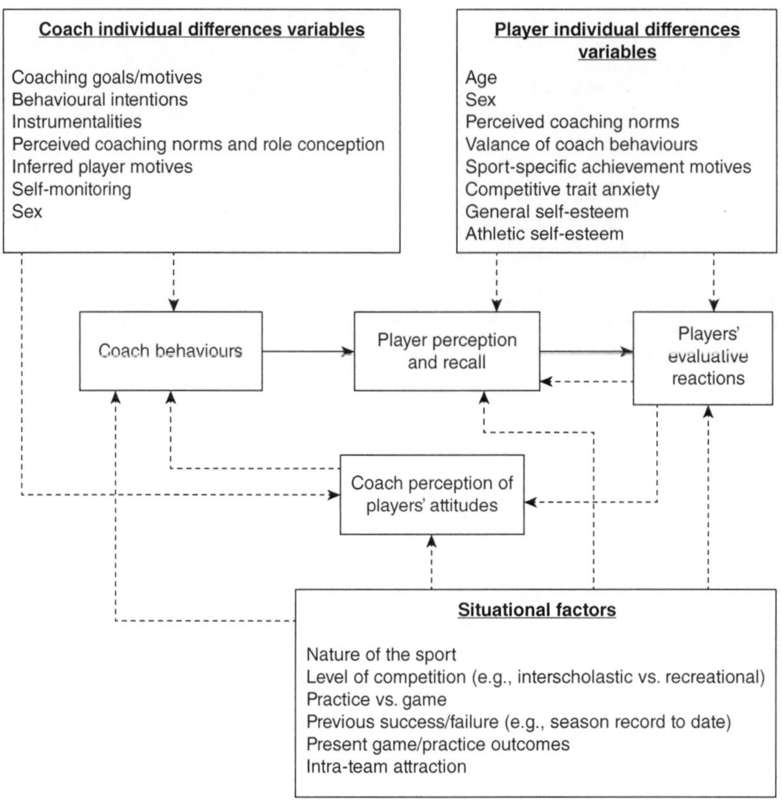

Figure 5.3 The Mediational Model of Leadership (adapted from Chelladurai, 2007)

model identifies three critical antecedent factors of coach behaviours (coaches' individual differences; situational factors; and coaches' perceptions of their athlete's attitude), while players' perception and recall, along with players' evaluative reactions, are also seen to hinge on a further three antecedents (athlete individual differences, situational factors and coaches' behaviours). Finally, a coach's perceptions of players' attitude is also seen to be contingent on three factors (coaches' individual differences, situational factors and players' evaluative reactions), which in turn then also impacts on the coach's behaviours.

It is understandable that the complexity of the model has not acted as a spur for primary research, in particular as statistical modelling of any findings would require considerable sample sizes. Instead, discrete elements of the model have been subject to scrutiny, and the findings, though somewhat limited in scope, have been encouraging. For example, it has been found that styles based on positive reinforcement and encouragement, along with sound technical advice, are more effective for remedying mistakes and for enhancing effort over the longer term, while also helping to foster an environment characterised by trust and liking (Smith and Smoll, 2007).

The Coach Behaviour Assessment System or CBAS (Smith et al., 1977) was developed by the same team of researchers as a tool to record coaches' behaviour in real time and as they went about their coaching. The CBAS has generally confirmed a number of speculations regarding the ingredients of good coaching, including, most importantly, the need for targeted positive reinforcement to enhance both performance and sustained effort.

The model has been useful in highlighting the complex two-way interactions between situational demands, personality traits and the nature of the particular sport but, at the same time, the central focus on coach behaviour may have led to a neglect of theoretical frameworks that attempt to understand the 'why' of coaching, as opposed to the 'what, where and how' (Gilbert and Trudel, 2004).

Perhaps in response to this deficit, recent years have seen the emergence of theories that have sought to clarify the dynamic and changing nature of the relationship between coaches and athletes over time (Arthur and Bastardoz, 2020). Jowett and Poczwardowski (2008) proposed an integrated research model of four of these theories. This framework recognises the complexity of the coaching relationship, delineating three key categories of concern. First, recognition is given to the role of antecedents to the coach–athlete relationship. Factors such as age, ability, experience and cultural norms will all play a role in determining which coaching approaches are appropriate in which circumstance. Second, consideration is given to the nature of the coach–athlete relationship. Specifically, Jowett's (2005) categorisation of the key components of the coach–athlete relationship (closeness, commitment, coordination and complementarity) is incorporated at this stage of the model. This factor also incorporates actual coaching behaviour. Third, the relative importance of the desired outcomes is considered. In other words, appropriate coaching behaviour will be determined collectively by what both the coach and athlete are seeking to achieve. For example, is the relationship mainly a social one, or is it predicated on achieving a specific sporting goal? Underpinning these three factors is the nature of communication between the coach and the athlete, communication being identified as the key driving force within the relationship, and having influence over every aspect of it.

The scale of this framework highlights the challenge facing the coaching literature. Any research into effective coaching must be placed in context, making recognition of the particular demands and outcomes relevant in any given situation. As one small but highly important example: there is a growing literature which reflects on the uphill battle faced not only by women but also by those from minority ethnic cultures in establishing a foothold within the coaching ranks, and the historical absence of those from minority communities in coaching roles does not reflect well on inherent biases at work within the fabric of many sports (see **7.31**) (Bradbury et al., 2018). To ignore such factors in any consideration of coaching and coaching behaviour will be to leave an analysis unfinished and inadequate.

More recently, a number of these ingredients have been integrated into Jowett and Shanmugan's (2016) model of 'relational coaching', a model which prioritises the relationship between coach and athlete above technical know-how when defining good coaching practice. As with the previous model, four properties lie at the heart of the relationship between coach and athlete (closeness, commitment, complementarity and co-orientation). Closeness reflects on the emotional bond, respect and liking between coach and athlete. Commitment concerns the long-term orientation and investment in the relationship by both parties. Complementarity considers two distinct sets of behaviours (corresponding and reciprocal) that in combination ensure harmony and stability in the relationship, while Co-orientation relates to the interdependence of feelings, thoughts and behaviours which ensure both 'sing from the same songsheet' at all times.

These constructs (The '3+1 Cs') combine to define the core quality of the relationship between the coach and athlete or a team but a number of other factors (i.e. individual differences; socio-cultural factors; relationship factors) then play a role in determining both wellbeing (i.e. depression; anxiety; satisfaction; life quality) and performance (i.e. motivation; passion; team cohesion; collective efficacy). Indeed, in the context of athlete wellbeing, the construct of complementarity has been found to be highly predictive of basic needs satisfaction (Felton et al., 2020), demonstrating the two-way, reciprocal manner in which coach–athlete relationships help to foster positive outcomes.

In terms of the elite sporting context, some interesting work has been carried out examining the cognitive demands that this complex relationship places on the coach. Particularly in sports that require the coach to take major decisions during competition, problem-solving skills are likely to be an important ingredient of effective coaching. Indeed, research has borne this out. It has been reported that higher level coaches possess greater problem-solving competence than lower-level coaches (Hagemann et al., 2008). Perhaps most interestingly, it is reported that this reflects on a general capacity for effective problem-solving and is not dependent on sporting experience or knowledge. The idea of problem-solving being crucial in effective coaching has also been reflected in observational studies which have reported that elite-level coaches spend the majority of game time deliberately engaging in silent monitoring before intervening as and when required (Smith and Cushion, 2006).

It is not a surprising finding that good coaches are often highly reflective and, as this review suggests, there is no shortage of advice and information for them to reflect on! Recent years have seen much progress in the development of sport-specific models of both leadership and effective coaching, and the identification of factors that contribute to successful coaching and leadership more generally. While the further testing and elaboration of models is crucial, the next step for the field should be the systematic gathering and placement of empirical findings within these frameworks. By doing so, further clarity will emerge regarding the role of the coach and the precise influence exerted by various situational and personal factors acting in concert. At the same time, further examination of the role of the coach must be tempered with some caution. While he or she undoubtedly remains an important, and often enigmatic, figure in the wide world of sport, the best coach can achieve nothing on his or her own. Coaching is a two-way relationship. As one of the most decorated and enigmatic soccer coaches, Brian Clough, once put it, 'Players lose you games, not tactics'. Whether monitoring from the sidelines or instructing on the training pitch, the success of any coach ultimately depends on the players or athletes they are leading. Given the broad range of expectations placed on the shoulders of the coach, their ultimate frustration is likely to remain that theirs is a vicarious experience and they remain dependent on the performance of others for their success or failure. Considered in this light, it is perhaps a little unfair that the buck should always stop with them.

KEY READINGS

Arthur, C.A. and Bastardoz, N. (2020) 'Leadership in sport', in G. Tenenbaum and R.C. Eklund (eds), *Handbook of Sport Psychology* (4th ed.). Hoboken, NJ: John Wiley & Sons. pp. 113–35.

Gilbert, W.D. and Trudel, P. (2004) 'Analysis of coaching science research published from 1970–2001', *Research Quarterly for Exercise and Sport*, 75 (4), 388–99.

Jowett, S. and Shanmugam, V. (2016) 'Relational coaching in sport: Its psychological underpinnings and practical effectiveness', in R. Schinke, K.R. McGannon and B. Smith (eds), *Routledge International Handbook of Sport Psychology*. Abingdon, Oxon: Routledge. pp. 471–84.

Smith, R.E. and Smoll, F.L. (2007) 'Social-cognitive approach to coaching behaviors', in S. Jowette and D. Lavallee (eds), *Social Psychology in Sport. Champaign, IL*: Human Kinetics. pp. 75–90.

PRACTICAL QUESTIONS

- As a newly qualified coach, working with a team for the first time, outline the steps that the coach should follow to become familiar with the team and to ensure that the team stay on message throughout the season.
- Which coaching styles are likely to be most appropriate for a young team that is newly formed? And for a team of seasoned professionals who have played together for many seasons?

REFERENCES

Arthur, C.A. and Bastardoz, N. (2020) 'Leadership in sport', in G. Tenenbaum and R.C. Eklund (eds) *Handbook of Sport Psychology* (4th ed.). Hoboken, NJ: John Wiley & Sons. pp. 113–35.

Bradbury, S., Van Sterkenburg, J. and Mignon, P. (2018) 'The under-representation and experiences of elite level minority coaches in professional football in England, France and the Netherlands', *International Review for the Sociology of Sport*, 53 (3), 313–34.

Chelladurai, P. (2007) 'Leadership in sports', in G. Tenenbaum and R.C. Eklund (eds), *Handbook of Sport Psychology* (3rd ed.). Hoboken, NJ: Wiley. pp. 113–35.

Felton, L., Jowett, S., Begg, C. and Zhong, X. (2020) 'A multistudy examination of the complementarity dimension of the coach–athlete relationship', *Sport, Exercise, and Performance Psychology. Advance online publication.* https://doi.org/10.1037/spy0000209.

Gilbert, W.D. and Trudel, P. (2004) 'Analysis of coaching science research published from 1970–2001', *Research Quarterly for Exercise and Sport*, 75 (4), 388–99.

Hagemann, N., Strauss, B. and Busch, D. (2008) 'The complex problem-solving competence of team coaches', *Psychology of Sport and Exercise*, 9, 301–17.

Jowett, S. (2005) 'On repairing and enhancing the coach–athlete relationship', in S. Jowett and M. Jones (eds), *The Psychology of Coaching.*Leicester: British Psychological Society. pp. 14–26.

Jowett, S. and Poczwardowski, A. (2008) 'Understanding the coach–athlete relationship', in T.S. Horn (ed.), *Advances in Sport Psychology* (3rd ed.). Champaign, IL: Human Kinetics. pp. 4–14.

Jowett, S. and Shanmugam, V. (2016) 'Relational coaching in sport: Its psychological underpinnings and practical effectiveness', in R. Schinke, K.R. McGannon and B. Smith (eds), *Routledge International Handbook of Sport Psychology*. Abingdon, Oxon: Routledge. pp. 471–84.

Smith, M. and Cushion, J. (2006) 'An investigation of the in-game behaviours of professional, top-level youth soccer coaches', *Journal of Sports Sciences*, 24, 355–66.

Smith, R.E. and Smoll, F.L. (2007) 'Social-cognitive approach to coaching behaviors', in S. Jowette and D. Lavallee (eds), *Social Psychology in Sport. Champaign, IL*: Human Kinetics. pp. 75–90.

Smith, R.E., Smoll, F.L. and Hunt, E. (1977) 'System for behavioral-assessment of athletic coaches', *Research Quarterly*, 48 (2), 401–7.

Smoll, F.L., Smith, R.E., Curtis, B. and Hunt, E. (1978) 'Toward a mediational model of coach–player relationships', *Research Quarterly*, 49 (4), 528–41.

5.28 HOME ADVANTAGE

Definition: The advantages, actual and/or perceived, that teams and individual athletes associate with playing at home venues.

As the COVID-19 global pandemic continued to redefine the experience of international sport for players and spectators alike, it provided the ideal conditions for natural experiments exploring the influence of empty stadia on team performance. For example, does playing 'at home' matter more or less than playing in front of home supporters? Has the 'magic' attached to certain home venues or fortresses dissipated during government-enforced lockdown periods? Historically many legendary stadia have carried an aura that was seen as intimidating and, anecdotally at least, added points to the scoreline before the whistle was blown. But is this effect typically more apparent than real, and will it survive the pandemic?

To begin this discussion, we need to establish what is actually meant by the term *home advantage*. In the simplest of terms, home advantage means that home teams win more than half of their games (Courneya and Carron, 1992). Fuelled by statisticians' and sports fans' fascination with such matters, over many decades there has been a plethora of studies looking at home advantage in relation to an array of sports including speed skating (Koning, 2005), athletics (Jamieson, 2010), tennis (Koning, 2011) and baseball (Jones, 2015), together with meta-analyses and literature reviews across a range of sports (e.g. Jones, 2013; Legaz-Arrese et al., 2013).

In an earlier example, Nevill and Holder (1999) provided an overview of home win percentages (hwp) across five sports, and found some evidence of home advantage in them all, albeit to varying degrees (i.e. baseball, 54.3 hwp; American football, 57.3 hwp; ice hockey, 61.2 hwp; basketball, 64.4 hwp; and soccer, 68.3 hwp). Other research has revealed that all six teams in rubgy union's Six Nations tournament scored more points at home than away (Thomas et al., 2008), and that teams who played the second leg in the

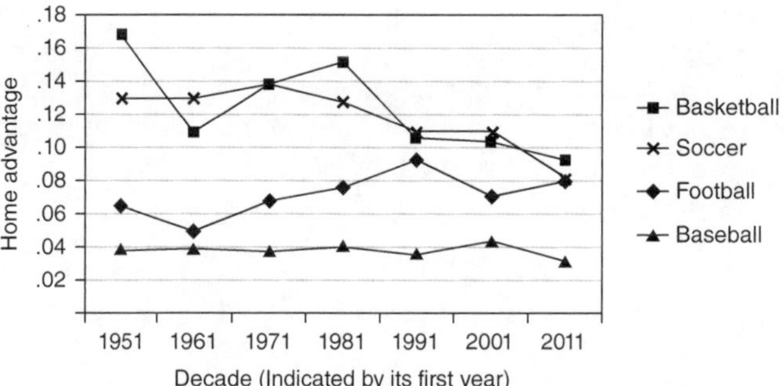

Figure 5.4 Home Advantage Effects across Team Sports and Time

Union of European Football Associations (UEFA) Champions League ties at home were more likely to progress (Page and Page, 2007).

In combination, these studies undoubtedly confirm the robustness of the home advantage effect but also highlight how difficult it can be to explain why, and, in particular, given idiosyncratic variations over sport, time and place. For example, Jones (2015) considered the extent of home advantage over seven decades for the four team sports of basketball, soccer, American football and baseball (home advantage defined as the proportion of home wins among decided games or matches minus 0.5, except for soccer which is based on win, lose or draw points). As Figure **5.4** above demonstrates, while baseball showed a small but consistent home advantage (.04), the effect in basketball and soccer was much higher but declined over the years, while the advantage for American football rose from a relatively low base (.06) to join basketball and soccer by 2011 (see Figure **5.4**).

Intriguing differences also emerged when home advantage was considered over the course of a competition, with the effect generally diminishing as the tournament progresses, or if the team in question is defending a title (Benjafield et al., 1989). Courneya and Carron (1991) demonstrated that home advantage grew along with the distance travelled by the opposing team, while other work has shown that players' behaviour became less controlled and more dysfunctionally aggressive the further from home they performed (Glamser, 1990). Home advantage has further been shown to be more prevalent in elite sport (Madrigal and James, 1999) and where subjective judgements are made by officials, for example boxing (Balmer et al., 2005), while other work suggests that the pressure of playing at home may negatively affect performance (Bray and Martin, 2003) and, in particular, when home supporters have a reputation for being overly judgmental.

In their much-cited literature review, Courneya and Carron (1992) concluded that the existence of a home advantage was now so well established that researchers should no longer be looking for it (the *what* and the *where*), and instead their attention should shift to trying to explain it (the *why*). To this end they suggested potential avenues of investigation which may be divided into two broad categories: location effects and psychological effects.

The first potential location factor is the influence of travel. Anyone who has travelled in a cramped minibus to a sporting fixture can attest to the particular challenges associated with playing away from home but, given the continued professionalisation of sports, do we expect mundane factors such as travel to still exert an influence at the highest level? Travel factors have been found to play a small role in explaining home advantage, even when taking into account the distance travelled and the number of time zones crossed by away teams (Glamser, 1990; Varca, 1980). A potential second location factor is familiarity; that is, does already knowing a venue carry an immediate advantage? The available evidence questions the significance of this factor. For example, when English soccer was examined between 1981–4, only minimal effects of pitch size and even the use of an artificial surface were found to impact on performance (Pollard, 1986, 2006).

The location effect which has received the most attention, and is perhaps the most salient in relation to COVID-19, is the effect of the *actual* crowd performance (Nevill and Holder, 1999). While some studies have failed to identify an influence of crowd size (Dowie, 1982), it now appears that the key factor mediating the influence of a crowd is its *density*. Crowd density is essentially a measure of how full a stadium is. Intuitively, this is unsurprising – after all, 15,000 spectators at Wembley Stadium is an entirely different proposition to 15,000 spectators at Wimbledon Centre Court. Schwartz and Barsky (1977) reported that hwp rose from 48 per cent for matches played in front of a less than 20 per cent full stadium, to 57 per cent in front of a stadium that was more than 40 per cent full. Such findings have obvious implications for stadium design, as perhaps does the finding that playing in a stadium with a roof may lead to a greater hwp. The data from matches played in 2020 should be of considerable interest.

Overall, evidence that impassioned and vocal home supporters will automatically drive their team on to better performance is equivocal (Legaz-Arrese et al., 2013). Linked to Albert Bandura's (1997) concept of verbal persusasion, the mechanism may be that increased persuasion links to increased team or individual's self-efficacy, which in turn may improve performance. Some evidence has suggested that higher motivation is present when athletes perform at home, while others have found higher testosterone levels.

This has led to the territoriality argument (Neave and Wolfson, 2003), the suggestion that home advantage is related to a primitive desire to defend one's own territory. However, positive findings on individual responses to home advantage have not been consistently demonstrated (Carron et al., 2005), suggesting that it may be that the psychological effects of playing at home are more subtle and idiosyncratic. According to Jones (2013), home advantage across a range of sports operates most noticeably not at the individual but at the team level. He maintains that when *embedded individual efforts*, such as penalty kicks in soccer or hockey or free throws in ice hockey, are considered in isolation from the team result, then home advantage virtually disappears. In other words, home advantage is gained by an enhancement of the team dynamic as a whole (e.g. effort or synergy), rather than by individual prowess, and can have both a positive effect on the home team as well as a negative effect on the away side.

For other commentators, the explanation rests primarily with perception or belief; in other words if players, managers and coaches commonly believe that familiarity with the home pitch is an advantage, then it becomes one (Gayton et al., 2001). While the accuracy of this assessment may be questioned, the perception cannot be – believing you have an advantage may be enough to give you an advantage.

The final psychological factor that has been examined is the effect of home advantage on match officials. Soccer provides two main indicators of referee bias that are easily examinable: the extra time added to matches and disciplinary actions (e.g. yellow cards and penalties). In terms of the extra time added on to the end of matches, research has clearly indicated home advantage (otherwise known colloquially as 'Fergie time', after the former Manchester United manager, Alex Ferguson). On average, it has been shown that Spanish referees add around two more minutes of extra time when the home team is trailing by a goal, compared to when they are leading by a goal. Nevill et al. (1996) report that home teams receive more penalties than away teams. The obvious response to this finding is that home teams receive more penalties as they attack more. However, Sutter and Kocher (2004) report that home teams receive a penalty from 81 per cent of their penalty appeals, whereas away teams receive a penalty from 51 per cent of their appeals. Common sense suggests what may be at play here. At a packed Old Trafford, 70,000 people will be calling for a home penalty, compared to around 5,000 calling for an away one. The research supports this view, but not as equivocally as may be expected. Using television replays of tackles from an English Premier League match, Nevill et al. (2002) asked qualified referees to decide whether the footage shown constituted a foul or not. Half the referees heard the accompanying crowd noise, half heard silence. This study found that crowd noise reduced the number of fouls given against the home team but did not significantly increase the number of fouls given against the away team. The authors take this as evidence that referees may avoid making decisions that may be unpopular. It is also suggested that this may relate to the *star player effect*, the finding that fewer fouls are given against star players (compared to non-star players) at home (Lehman and Reifman, 1987). Interestingly, Nevill et al. (2002) report that the effect of crowd noise appears to decrease as refereeing experience increases. It may be the case that increased experience provides referees with the confidence to make unpopular decisions.

Taking all of the research reported above, it is likely that partisan crowd noise influences officials and, in sports where subjective judgement is critical, this influence is then reflected in home advantage. However, whether this is the entire answer is highly debatable but, instead, a whole range of factors, both individual, team and situational, come together to favour the home team. In this regard, one particularly interesting finding is that home advantage appears to disappear during a team's first season in a new stadium (Wilkinson and Pollard, 2006), and before it has become established as 'home'.

To conclude, home advantage appears to entail something more than simply referees making biased decisions ('Homers'), and instead an array of factors including familiarity, perceived advantage, travel, experience, competition phase, evaluation apprehension, territoriality and the crowd dynamic (or its absence) may all influence the thoughts, feelings and behaviours of coaches, officials and athletes alike, and in turn, the advantage of being at home.

KEY READINGS

Carron, A.V., Loughhead, T.M. and Bray, S.R. (2005) 'The home advantage in sport competitions: Courneya and Carron's (1992) conceptual framework a decade later', *Journal of Sports Sciences*, 23, 395–407.

Courneya, K.S. and Carron, A.V. (1992) 'The home advantage in sport competitions: A literature review', *Journal of Sport and Exercise Psychology*, 14, 13–27.

Jones, M.B. (2013) 'The home advantage in individual sports: An augmented review', *Psychology of Sport and Exercise*, 14, 397–404.

Legaz-Arrese, A., Moliner-Urdiales, D. and Munguía-Izquierdo, D. (2013) 'Home advantage and sports performance: Evidence, causes and psychological implications', *Universitas Psychologica*, 12 (3), 933–43.

PRACTICAL QUESTIONS

- Under what circumstances is home advantage most likely to occur and why?
- Looking across a range of sports, discuss the factors that may influence where and when home advantage is likely to be found, and how its influence can be limited?

REFERENCES

Balmer, N.J., Nevill, A.M. and Lane, A. (2005) 'Do judges enhance home advantage in European championship boxing?', *Journal of Sport Sciences*, 23, 409–16.

Bandura, A. (1997) *Self-Efficacy: The Exercise of Control*. New York: Freeman.

Benjafield, J., Liddell, W.W. and Benjafield, I. (1989) 'Is there a homefield advantage in professional sports championships?', *Social Behavior and Personality: An International Journal*, 19, 264–80.

Bray, S.R. and Martin, K.A. (2003) 'The effect of competition location on individual athlete performance and psychological states', *Psychology of Sport and Exercise*, 4 (2), 117–23.

Carron, A.V., Loughhead, T.M. and Bray, S.R. (2005) 'The home advantage in sport competitions: Courneya and Carron's (1992) conceptual framework a decade later', *Journal of Sports Sciences*, 23, 395–407.

Courneya, K.S. and Carron, A.V. (1991) 'Effects of travel and length of home stand/road trip on the home advantage', *Journal of Sport and Exercise Psychology*, 13, 42–9.

Courneya, K.S. and Carron, A.V. (1992) 'The home advantage in sport competitions: A literature review', *Journal of Sport and Exercise Psychology*, 14, 13–27.

Dowie, J. (1982) 'Why Spain should win the world cup', *New Scientist*, 94, 693–5.

Gayton, W.F., Broida, J. and Elgee, L. (2001) 'An investigation of coaches' perceptions of the causes of home advantage', *Perceptual and Motor Skills*, 92 (3), 933–6.

Glamser, F.D. (1990) 'Contest location, player misconduct, and race: A case from English soccer', *Journal of Sport Behaviour*, 13, 41-49.

Jamieson, J. (2010) 'The home field advantage in athletics: A meta-analysis', *Journal of Applied Social Psychology*, 40, 1819–48.

Jones, M.B. (2013) 'The home advantage in individual sports: An augmented review', *Psychology of Sport and Exercise*, 14, 397–404.

Jones, M.B. (2015) 'The home advantage in major league baseball', *Perceptual and Motor Skills: Motor Skills and Ergonomics*, 121 (3), 791–804. DOI 10.2466/26. PMS.121c25x1.

Koning, R.H. (2005) 'Home advantage in speed skating: Evidence from individual data', *Journal of Sports Sciences*, 23, 417–27.

Koning, R.H. (2011) 'Home advantage in professional tennis', *Journal of Sports Sciences*, 29, 19–27.

Lehman, D.R. and Reifman, A. (1987) 'Spectator influence on basketball officiating', *Journal of Social Psychology*, 127, 673–5.

Legaz-Arrese, A., Moliner-Urdiales, D. and Munguía-Izquierdo, D. (2013) 'Home advantage and sports performance: Evidence, causes and psychological implications', *Universitas Psychologica*, 12 (3), 933–43.

Madrigal, R. and James, J. (1999) 'Team quality and home advantage', *Journal of Sport Behavior*, 22 (3), 381–98.

Neave, N. and Wolfson, S. (2003) 'Testosterone, territoriality, and the "home advantage"', *Physiology and Behavior*, 78, 269–75.

Nevill, A.M. and Holder, R. (1999) 'Home advantage in sport: An overview of studies on the advantage of playing at home', *Sports Medicine*, 28, 221–36.

Nevill, A.M., Newell, S.M. and Gale, S. (1996) 'Factors associated with home advantage in English and Scottish football', *Journal of Sports Sciences*, 14, 181–6.

Nevill, A.M., Balmer, N.J. and Williams, A.M. (2002) 'The influence of crowd noise and experience upon refereeing decisions in football', *Psychology of Sport and Exercise*, 3, 261–72.

Page, L. and Page, K. (2007) 'The second leg home advantage: Evidence from European football cup competitions', *Journal of Sports Sciences*, 25 (14), 1547–56.

Pollard, R. (1986) 'Home advantage in football: A retrospective analysis', *Journal of Sports Sciences*, 4, 237–48.

Pollard, R. (2006) 'Home advantage in soccer: Variations in its magnitude and a literature review of the inter-related factors associated with its existence', *Journal of Sport Behavior*, 29 (2), 169–89.

Schwartz, B. and Barsky, S.F. (1977) 'The home advantage', *Social Forces*, 55, 641–61.

Sutter, M. and Kocher, M.G. (2004) 'Favoritism of agents – the case of referees' home bias', *Journal of Economic Psychology*, 25, 461–9.

Thomas, S., Reeves, C. and Bell, A. (2008) 'Home advantage in the Six Nations Rugby Union Tournament', *Perceptual and Motor Skills*, 106, 113–16.

Varca, P.E. (1980) 'An analysis of home and away game performance of male college basketball teams', *Journal of Sport Psychology*, 2, 245–57.

Wilkinson, T. and Pollard, R. (2006) 'A temporary decline in home advantage when moving to a new stadium', *Journal of Sport Behavior*, 29 (2), 190–7.

5.29 AGGRESSION

Definition: Aggression in sport involves those occasions where the person has (or conveys) intent of hurting or intimidating another, where the other is motivated to avoid that behaviour, and is normally categorised as either instrumental or reactive.

'Serious sport has nothing to do with fair play. It is bound up with hatred, jealousy, boastfulness, disregard of all rules and sadistic pleasure in witnessing violence. In other words: it is war minus the shooting.' This infamous quote by George Orwell (1945) strikes to the heart of a key paradox in competitive sport. While fair play is lauded, at the highest level it is ruthlessness and a 'win at all costs' mentality that is often encouraged. No aspect of sport illustrates this paradox more vividly than the role played by aggression. In many sports, aggression, even to the point of physical violence, is encouraged and is often deemed legal (Russell, 1993). Indeed, an aggressive approach to sport may, in the eyes of some, be nothing more than a reflection of genuine passion, or a hunger for success. While healthy passion in sport is to be encouraged and welcomed, many now also acknowledge the dangers that lie in store when passion spills over into destructive aggression. Indeed, the International Society of Sport Psychology (ISSP) have issued a position paper on this very issue (Tenenbaum et al., 1997), albeit a paper that has attracted a degree of controversy within sport psychology (Kerr, 2002; Sacks et al., 2003). But what precisely is meant by aggression? Where does it come from? Should it be encouraged in sport? And finally, what can be done to appropriately manage aggression?

Aggression is a ubiquitous element of human life, and is a topic that has been studied from numerous perspectives, including from within social and sport psychology, the primary focus of this section. In global terms, aggression has been defined as 'any form of behaviour directed toward the goal of harming or injuring another living being who is motivated to avoid such treatment' (Baron and Richardson, 1994: 7). This definition warrants closer examination for a number of reasons. First, it is not restricted exclusively to physical acts as it may also be verbal, or even passive. Second, aggression cannot be directed to an inanimate object. This precludes acts such as racket abuse in tennis or squash being defined as aggression; rather, they are indicators of frustration (Maxwell, 2004). Third, there is also the implication that aggressive behaviour carries with it a certain degree of intent. However, while this definition captures much of what is meant by aggression in sport, as with many concepts brought from outside the sport psychology literature, there are sport-specific considerations. For example, how does one characterise aggressive behaviour in boxing? (Maxwell, 2004).

Clearly, outside of a sporting context, deliberately striking another person is aggressive, and typically deemed an illegal use of violence. However, when entering a boxing ring, can it accurately be said that the other individual is 'motivated to avoid such treatment'? After all, they have purposefully put themselves in harm's way, and consented to the ordeal. Having said that, there are clearly unsanctioned behaviours even in boxing that should be categorised as naked aggression. Take for example Mike Tyson deliberately spitting out his mouthguard before biting a piece out of Evander Holyfield's ear. This is without question unbridled aggressive behaviour as it goes beyond what Holyfield may have reasonably expected when he entered the ring, and what the agreed rules of boxing permit. The question in this instance is one of acceptability. This leads us to a key distinction in the understanding of sport aggression. In the sport psychology literature, two types of aggression are normally described - *reactive* and *instrumental* (e.g. Bredemeir, 1985), often along with a distinction between *sanctioned* and *unsanctioned* aggression (Kerr, 2006).

Given the acceptance of aggression in some sports, the need to clarify the difference between reactive and instrumental aggression is vital. Reactive aggression is akin to many lay definitions of aggression. It occurs solely with the aim of harming the other and is typically associated with anger or retaliation (Wann, 2005). Instrumental aggression, on the other hand, is motivated by a higher strategic purpose rather than designed only to harm (Donahue et al., 2009). In practice, the archetypal example of instrumental aggressive behaviour is the professional foul. The act may hurt the opponent but its purpose is to prevent a goal-scoring opportunity. However, this distinction may not be as clear-cut as it first appears. A professional foul, by its definition, implies a certain degree of necessity, that it is part of the job and, ultimately, understandable. Yet other acts of instrumental aggression may not be seen in the same light. For example, a spear tackle in rugby (where a player is up-ended and then driven into the ground head first) may be an instrumental act to take out a threatening player, yet it is judged much more harshly than a professional foul.

Such ambiguity can be resolved through consideration of an important distinction, the difference between sanctioned and unsanctioned aggression. This distinction becomes particularly important when considering acts of violence, whether they be physical or verbal. So, for example, throwing punches in boxing is sanctioned physical violence, in much the same way that sledging in cricket is sanctioned verbal aggression. While much of what is meant by sanctioned aggression is incorporated into the understanding of what is legal, the term is broader than this, expanding to incorporate the unwritten conventions of each particular sport (Kerr, 2006). Hence, while official abuse is aggressive, and considered illegal in most sports, each sport has its own conventions as to what is acceptable. Although it may be argued that the focus for psychologists should be on controlling unsanctioned aggression, the difficulty lies in the fact that the line between sanctioned and unsanctioned aggression is often blurred and ill-defined. For example, in ice hockey, a sport where fist fighting has historically been sanctioned, these fights have been governed by unwritten conventions (Colburn, 1986), for example involving the removal of equipment. The danger is that, in an aggressive mindset, a player may violate these unwritten conventions, leading them to commit acts that are viewed as unsanctioned (see for example Kerr's (2006) analysis of the Bertuzzi-Moore incident). In view of this, the central consideration when dealing with aggression would appear to be the ability to control and direct aggression into instrumental, and sanctioned, behaviours. This leads on to the next issue to be considered: from a social perspective, where does aggression come from and how can it be managed?

Historically, the major theories to have dominated the aggression literature have been the psychodynamic (or Freudian), Frustration Aggression (Revised) Theory (e.g. Berkowitz, 1989) and Social Learning Theory (e.g. Bandura, 1973). According to Freud, human aggression is linked to a basic instinct, *thanatos*, and is unavoidable; we are 'hard wired' to be aggressive. Sport provides a socially acceptable release valve for this basic instinct and, according to this perspective, those who take part in sport (both players and spectators) will be less aggressive having 'let off steam' (i.e. sport has a cathartic effect). Suffice it to say, there is little evidence to suggest that this is true (see **5.30**) and so the theory now enjoys little support.

As an alternative approach, the Frustration Aggression Hypothesis proposes that aggression is the inevitable behavioural outcome of frustration. However, this account has been criticised for its sense of inevitability. While on occasion frustration may lead to aggression, this account fails to explain why frustration does not always lead to aggression. For this reason the theory has been revised to take into account the influence of cognitive factors, situational cues and learned responses. Particularly in this final regard, there is an overlap between Frustration Aggression Theory and Social Learning Theory. While Bandura's theory recognises the importance of physiological and motivational factors, it is best known for highlighting the importance of observation/experience of aggression and the perceived/actual approval of aggression. This was famously illustrated by the Bobo Doll study which reported that children will imitate the aggressive behaviour of adults, in this case striking a large blow-up doll. In a similar vein, sport-specific studies have reported evidence that watching aggressive role models may lead to a more aggressive approach to sport (Smith, 1988).

While these theories each contribute valuable elements to understanding aggressive behaviour, later models instead have turned their attention towards delineating and explaining the numerous interacting factors, including the cognitive, affective, social, behavioural and emotional that likely underlie aggression, as with many psychological tendencies (Geen, 2001).

This leads to consideration of the specific antecedents of aggressive behaviour in sport. These may be divided into two main categories - *situational* and *cognitive*. Historically, research has tended to focus on the former, situational factors. For example, it has been reported that increased temperatures are associated with more aggressive pitching in baseball (Reifman et al., 1991). Additionally, it has been reported that aggressive behaviour by opposing teams is associated with increased aggression in the team playing at home (Harrell, 1980). While such findings are undoubtedly interesting, there now appears to be a move towards examining cognitive antecedents of aggression, and including the role played by *passion*, and in particular *obsessive passion* (see **3.14**) (Donahue et al., 2009). This makes practical sense. While an athlete may not be able to control situational variables, he or she should be able to control cognitive reactions to them. The idea of the importance of the cognitive interpretation of events is illustrated by the finding that anger rumination increases the likelihood of aggressive behaviour, a finding reported both in the general aggression literature and the sport psychology literature (Maxwell, 2004). So, while an athlete may be angered by an event during competition (e.g. a bad tackle), it is the propensity to dwell on this anger that ultimately leads to an increased possibility of retaliation. It is possible to call to mind examples of professional soccer players who have dwelt on perceived injustices for months before responding with physical aggression at a later date.

The role of *passion* in aggression is an interesting subject that has been picked up by the media who often cite athlete aggression as an inevitable companion of passion. However, the research would only partially support this assertion. It is reported that a high level of passion need not necessarily lead to an increased incidence of aggression but when an athlete derives a high degree of social acceptance and self-esteem from their sport, passion may be linked with a higher incidence of aggressive behaviour (Donahue et al., 2009). In terms of a potential role for psychologists in managing aggression, the implication of cognitive factors such as rumination and the role of self-esteem appear important as they point to potential avenues of intervention, such as those associated with cognitive behavioural models (Maxwell, 2004).

However, any conception of aggression management intervention must be balanced against the possibility that aggression may bring with it benefits. Unfortunately the literature remains inconclusive on this vital issue (e.g. Gill, 1986; Wann, 1997). While it would appear that certain sports require some degree of instrumental, sanctioned aggression, what would appear crucial is the idea of *control*. Whether aggression is beneficial or not, any loss of control ultimately may lead to suspensions and other disciplinary proceedings. Where control is lost, when the infamous 'red mist' descends, the possibility is that aggression may be misdirected into reactive, unsanctioned violence. It may have been incidents of this nature that Orwell was referring to when he dwelt on the more nefarious aspects of sport, but it remains the responsibility of sport psychologists not only to report but also to remedy and regulate the worst excesses of sport (Sacks et al., 2003).

KEY READINGS

Donahue, E.G., Rip, B. and Vallerand, R.J. (2009) 'When winning is everything: On passion, identity, and aggression in sport', *Psychology of Sport and Exercise*, 10, 526–34.

Sacks, D.N., Petscher, Y., Stanley, C.T. and Tenenbaum, G. (2003) 'Aggression and violence in sport: Moving beyond the debate', *International Journal of Sport and Exercise Psychology*, 1 (2), 167–79. https://doi.org/10.1080/1612197X.2003.9671710.

Tenenbaum, G., Stewart, E., Singer, R.N. and Duda, J. (1997) 'Aggression and violence in sport: An ISSP position stand', *The Sport Psychologist*, 11, 1–7.

Wann, D.L. (2005) 'Aggression in sport', *The Lancet*, 366, S31–S32.

PRACTICAL QUESTIONS

- With reference to a sport of your choice, consider how the taxonomy of instrumental/reactive and sanctioned/unsanctioned forms of aggression can be used to categorise typical behaviours in that sport, both verbal and physical.
- As an applied sport psychologist, you have been asked to work with a player who has a long history of reactive aggression, which he describes as the 'red mist'. Outline strategies that you could employ to help remedy this problem.

REFERENCES

Bandura, A. (1973) *Aggression: A Social Learning Analysis*. Englewood Cliffs, NJ: Prentice-Hall.

Baron, R.A. and Richardson, D.R. (1994) *Human Aggression* (2nd ed.). New York: Plenum Press.

Berkowitz, L. (1989) 'Frustration–aggression hypothesis: Examination and reformulation', *Psychological Bulletin*, 106, 59–73.

Bredemeier, B.J. (1985) 'Moral reasoning and the perceived legitimacy of intentionally injurious sport acts', *Journal of Sport Psychology*, 7, 110–24.

Colburn, K. (1986) 'Deviance and legitimacy in ice hockey: A micro-structural theory of violence. *The Sociological Quarterly*, 27, 63–74

Donahue, E.G., Rip, B. and Vallerand, R.J. (2009) 'When winning is everything: On passion, identity, and aggression in sport', *Psychology of Sport and Exercise*, 10, 526–34.

Geen, R.G. (2001) *Human Aggression* (2nd ed.). Milton Keynes: Open University Press.
Gill, D.L. (1986) *Psychological Dynamics of Sport*. Champaign, IL: Human Kinetics.
Harrell, W.A. (1980) 'Aggression by high school basketball players: An observational study of the effects of opponent aggression and frustration-inducing factors', *International Journal of Sport Psychology*, 11, 290–8.
Kerr, J.H. (2002) 'Issues in aggression and violence in sport: The ISSP position stand revisited', *The Sport Psychologist*, 16, 68–78.
Kerr, J.H. (2006) 'Examining the Bertuzzi–Moore NHL ice hockey incident: Crossing the line between sanctioned and unsanctioned violence in sport', *Aggression and Violent Behavior*, 11, 313–22.
Maxwell, J.P. (2004) 'Anger rumination: An antecedent of athlete aggression?', *Psychology of Sport and Exercise*, 5, 279–89.
Orwell, G. (1945) 'The sporting spirit', *Tribune*, 14 December.
Reifman, A.S., Larrick, R.P. and Fein, S. (1991) 'Temper and temperature on the diamond: The heat–aggression relationship in Major League Baseball', *Personality and Social Psychology Bulletin*, 17 (5), 580–5.
Russell, G.W. (1993) *The Social Psychology of Sport*. New York: Springer-Verlag.
Sacks, D.N., Petscher, Y., Stanley, C.T. and Tenenbaum, G. (2003) 'Aggression and violence in sport: Moving beyond the debate', *International Journal of Sport and Exercise Psychology*, 1 (2), 167–79. https://doi.org/10.1080/1612197X.2003.9671710.
Smith, M.D. (1988) 'Interpersonal sources of violence in hockey: The influence of parents, coaches and teammates', in F.L. Smoll, R.A. Magill and M.J. Ash (eds), *Children in Sport* (3rd ed.). Champaign, IL: Human Kinetics. pp. 301–13.
Tenenbaum, G., Stewart, E., Singer, R.N. and Duda, J. (1997) 'Aggression and violence in sport: An ISSP position stand', *The Sport Psychologist*, 11, 1–7.
Wann, D.L. (1997) *Sport Psychology*. Upper Saddle River, NJ: Prentice Hall.
Wann, D.L. (2005) 'Aggression in sport', *The Lancet*, 366, S31–S32.

5.30 FANS AND SPECTATORS

Definitions: Spectators are those who watch sport, either directly (in person) or indirectly (via the media), while fans not only watch but have an affiliation in which aspects of identity, emotional significance and value are derived from group membership.

As already mentioned (see **5.28**), the COVID-19 pandemic has thrown the world of sport as we knew it into disarray, and nowhere is this revealed more starkly than in the way that sport is now consumed. Gone are the days when crowds stood cheek by jowl on packed terraces. Instead, matches have an almost surreal air as they are played out in front of empty seats along with piped music and crowd noise designed to somehow convey a sense of business as usual. Existing research already shows that factors such as stadium occupancy impact on the perceived quality of the game by television viewers

(Oh et al., 2017), while the negative impact on people's lives and wellbeing of not being able to attend live sport should not be underestimated. For example, it has been shown that life satisfaction correlates positively with the number of visits to live sporting events by fans (Inoue et al., 2017) and that this effect is not as evident when the event is viewed indirectly via media (Oh et al., 2020). What is more, even the wellbeing of a nation can fluctuate according to international success and failure, and especially in team sports such as soccer (Kavetsos and Szymanski, 2010).

In so many ways the sporting deficit attached to COVID-19 has brought into focus what attracts fans to sport, and what can hopefully continue to keep fans involved and engaged through changed times. So much of this reflection must be speculative at the time of writing, but perhaps lessons can be learned from sport's history, which is where we will begin.

Sport psychology has generally paid far more attention to those who *do* rather than those who *watch*, i.e. the fans and spectators, but from its earliest days there has also been an interest in those on the other side of the fence, whether as direct (physically present) or indirect (via the media) sport consumers (McPherson, 1976). This literature has considered many issues, not least speculation as to the psychology that drives spectators to become so engrossed in their chosen sports.

In one of the earliest examples, Patrick (1903) reflected on the US public's obsession with American football, declaring that little had changed from Neolithic times. In his own words: 'Evidently there is some great force, psychological or sociological, at work here which science has not yet investigated' (1903: 115). In keeping with the dominant psychoanalytic tradition of the times, to him sport stirred our base instincts, 'The game thus acts as a sort of Aristotelian catharsis, purging our pent up feelings and enabling us to return more placidly to the slow upwards toiling' (p. 116). In a similar vein, Howard (1912: 43) described the 'mob-mind of the athletic spectator'. His disapproving tone leaps from the page, 'Violent shouts and epithets give notice that the cave-man is up' (p. 45).

As section **5.29** demonstrates, psychoanalytic predictions based on catharsis have not stood the test of time well. Indeed, a recent study of drinking behaviour among rugby fans showed that it was the followers of the winners rather than the losers who were more aggressive, and more likely to drink to excess (Moore et al., 2007). Catharsis would predict the opposite effect.

Today, millions of people have an extremely intense and time-consuming engagement with sport and yet they may never have kicked a ball, run on an athletics track or seen the inside of a snooker hall. According to an unpublished British Market Research Bureau (BMRB) survey (carried out for the Newspaper Marketing Agency in 2004), 54 per cent of tabloid newspaper readers turn first to the sports pages, rising to an impressive 69 per cent of all readers when those who merely scanned the first page are included.

Despite the significant role that sport plays in so many people's lives, up until recently, the majority of sport psychologists have only turned their attention to spectators infrequently. Historically, most sport psychology texts and journals rarely feature this work, and the contrast between how much effort has been devoted to understanding participation motivation and how little has been spent on spectator motivation could not be more obvious. Where spectator research has typically appeared it has often been in the guise of a contextual variable that impacts on the sportsperson, for example in relation to home advantage (see **5.28**), social facilitation (see **5.25**), causal attribution (see **5.24**) or the role of significant others with regard to sport socialisation and participation motivation (see Chapter 3).

In a notable study, Daniel Wann and his colleagues reflected on the range of factors that can impact on the decision to become a 'fan' (as opposed to a spectator), and subsequent fan behaviour, including violence, along with the functions that fan behaviour serves for both individuals, clubs and society in general (Wann et al., 2001). Their work drew on earlier formulations and including the work of McPherson (1976) on sport consumer socialisation.

McPherson considered four agents that impact on the fledgling consumer – peers, family, school and community – with peers having the greatest impact on young men and the family on young women. Sport consumption was then considered in relation not only to behaviour (attendance and buying) but also affect (including mood state and loyalty or 'fandom') and cognition (knowledge). This research highlights the distinction between those who merely watch and those who become involved as sport fans, and it is the latter who have attracted greatest interest. In reviewing various definitions and distinctions between the two terms, Jacobson (2003) concludes that the most critical difference lies in perceived interest and personal importance, hence the degree of emotional investment in the team and its performance. In other words, spectators *watch* but fans *care*. She also reminds us that the word 'fan' itself is an abbreviation of 'fanatic', implying excessive, even obsessional, enthusiasm. With this in mind, Wann et al. (2001) also argue the need to distinguish between fans in terms of the extent of their identification with the team, ranging from high to low. Not surprisingly, it is the former that are often the focus of research.

According to Wann (1995), having been socialised into a sport or sports, fans are then galvanised by one or more of eight possible motives: group affiliation, family, escape, entertainment, eustress, aesthetics, self-esteem and economics (i.e. gambling). The strength of each is typically gauged by using the Sport Fan Motivation Scale (SFMS), a 23-item self-report Likert-scale that contains eight subscales reflecting the eight motives. Typically, entertainment and eustress score highest, with the economic motive being the least important (Wann, 1995).

Of these motives, the one which has attracted greatest attention is group affiliation, or more correctly, *team identification*. Drawing on theories of social identity from within social psychology, and including social identity theory and identity theory (see **5.31**) (Stets and Burke, 2000), research has considered the degree to which fans come to adopt the team's identity as part of their self-concept, the factors that impact on the extent of identification, and how identification can manifest itself in behaviour towards both ingroup and outgroup members.

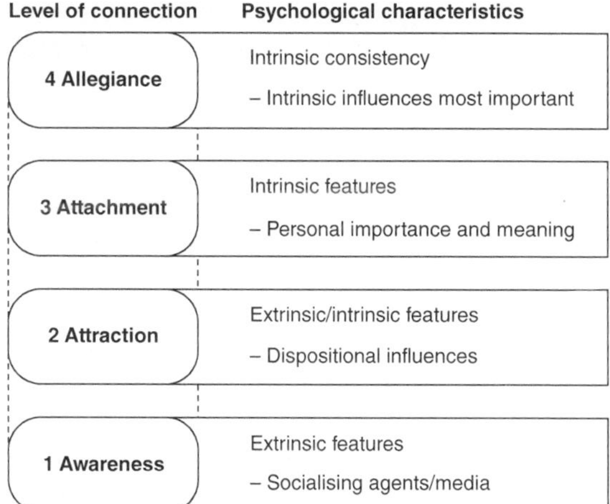

Figure 5.5 Psychological Continuum Model (PCM) (adapted from Funk and James, 2001)

This research suggests that individual differences (e.g. gender, Dietz-Uhler et al., 2000) and events both on and off the field can influence loyalty (Wann et al., 2001) but the most important factor is team success. According to Mahony et al. (2000), our inclination to either 'bask in reflected glory' (BIRG) or 'cut off reflective failures' (CORF) will go a long way towards helping explain variations in fan support over time. Those with a high level of identification are likely to be those whose loyalty will carry them through the bad times as well as the good (Madrigal, 1995).

In order to quantify the connection that exists between a fan and his or her team, Funk and James (2001) developed the Psychological Continuum Model (PCM) (see Figure **5.5**). The model outlines the parameters within which this relationship is mediated, and charts the development and strengthening of that involvement over time through four stages, and a movement from extrinsic to intrinsic psychological characteristics:

Awareness: The person first learns that certain sports, and/or teams exist, but does not have a specific favourite;

Attraction: Acknowledgement of a favourite team or sport based on various social-psychological and demographic-based motives;

Attachment: A psychological connection begins to crystallise, creating various degrees of association between the individual and the sport object, the strength of this association being based on the perceived importance attached to physical and psychological features associated with it;

Allegiance: The person becomes a loyal (or committed) fan of the sport or team, along with influential attitudes that produce consistent and durable behaviour.

The model proposes that the psychological connections between an individual and a sport or team are governed by the complexity and strengthening of sport-related mental associations, and provides a useful mechanism for synthesising previous research findings.

Other work continues to explore what may lie behind a team 'brand' which makes it more or less appealing to its fans. Working with various major sports (i.e. soccer, baseball, basketball, American football and ice hockey) and drawing on previous measures, Stadler Blank et al. (2017) have developed the Sport Team Personality Scale (STPS), made up of 18 items that load onto six factors (success, talent, entertainment, dedication, admiration and care). The authors have used the STPS to explore team identification and team identities, and interestingly have found that a team's 'character' (i.e. the admiration and care factors) is more important than its performance (i.e., success and talent) as a source of team identification, and hence loyalty.

From a business perspective, fan loyalty is key. However, there is a darker side to fan loyalty which has been revealed throughout the history of sport, crowd violence or hooliganism, a social phenomenon that, contrary to popular opinion, is far from new (Pearson, 1983). The topic has attracted considerable attention from a wide range of disciplines, including sport sociology and sport psychology. While longstanding concerns with hooliganism are never far from the headlines, sometimes particular events or tragedies have acted as a catalyst for research. One prime example was the research that fed into the 1986 *Popplewell Inquiry into Crowd Safety and Control at Sports Grounds*. The inquiry was set up following the tragic events in early 1985, including the West Stand fire at Bradford City Football Club and the Heysel stadium disaster in Brussels. In their subsequent book *Football in its Place*, Canter et al. (1989) used their background in environmental psychology to offer practical insight and advice on the interaction between structural and psychological issues, including stadia design, spectators' attitudes and experiences, soccer club cultures, crowd and emergency behaviour and violence in sport. These ideas were acted on by the Popplewell Inquiry (Popplewell, 1986) and were also taken into account during the subsequent Taylor Report (1989) into the Hillsborough Stadium disaster when 95 Liverpool supporters tragically died.

In contrast with sport psychology, sport sociology does have a long history of spectator research, with a particular emphasis on fan violence. This includes Eric Dunning's research on the sport socialisation process and the development of habits consistent with casual acceptance of violence in sport (Murphy et al., 2003). Using a combination of historical, observational, quantitative and qualitative techniques, various authors have tried to help understand why hooliganism and fan violence should have such a long and ignoble history in Europe and, in particular, Britain (hence commonly known as the 'English Disease'). It is suggested that the interplay between personal, interpersonal, intergroup, cultural, socioeconomic and political forces may help determine why particular anti-social behaviours manifest themselves at certain times and in certain sports. For example, neither rugby league nor rugby union have typically been associated with fan violence, yet soccer has. At the same time, it is argued that the media may distort perceptions of what may or may not have taken place, a classic example being the presentation of England soccer fans' behaviour during Euro 2000 (Weed, 2001).

While soccer violence may be hyped up, there is evidence that crowd disorder at other sports, including American football, may have been hidden from view for both political and economic reasons, along with other unsavoury associations (Young, 1991). One example is a study by White (1989) which considered the incidence of murders in US cities that had American football teams through to the National Football League playoff games. In those cities where the team lost a playoff there was an increase in reported homicides in the subsequent six days, but the crime rate remained unchanged if the team was successful.

Over the years various approaches have been proposed to explain fan violence (Weed, 2001). In their figurational approach, Dunning and his colleagues (see Murphy et al., 2003) place emphasis on the culture of violence still prevalent among young, working-class men in Britain, while Kerr (2005) has adapted Reversal Theory to try to understand hooliganism, arguing that it is the switch between motivational states (telic – goal-oriented; paratelic – playful) that best explains why trouble 'kicks off' at particular games. According to Simons and Taylor (1992) there is a need to accommodate a wide range of variables, and any approach that fails to account for all these variables is likely to be partial. Variables include:

- potentiating or general predisposing factors (socioeconomic conditions, politics and geography, media influences and community norms);
- critical factors (social and personal identification, group solidarity, de-individuation, dehumanisation of the opposition, leadership);
- on-field contributing factors (type of sport, modelling, score configuration and competitive events);
- off-field contributing factors (alcohol, crowd density, frustration and role modelling).

This model offers a useful framework for understanding fan violence at a great many levels of analysis, and sits easily with developments across social psychology as a whole.

Over recent years there has been a growing literature devoted to a related historical blight of the British game (i.e. soccer), but not confined exclusively to the UK: racism (Hylton, 2018). In previous years, tales of endemic racism within the game were widespread. Lawrence and Davis (2019) point to the fact that, in response to a number of initiatives designed to tackle racism, including Stamp It Out, there had been some positive signs of a decline in overt racism on the terraces. Working from within Critical Race Theory (CRT), the same authors argue that football fandom and spectatorship remain predominantly 'white' activities, and go on to suggest that the problem of racism may not have disappeared but may instead have mutated and gone underground in more 'sanitised' and 'acceptable' forms (Cleland and Cashmore, 2016). At the same time, the absence of large sections of the BAME community as fans still warrants due regard as tangible evidence of institutionalised racism still latent within the game (Cleland and Cashmore, 2014; Gibbons, 2016).

KEY READINGS

Funk, D.C. and James, J. (2001) 'The psychological continuum model: A conceptual framework for understanding an individual's psychological connection to sport', *Sport Management Review*, 4, 119–50. doi:10.1016/S1441-3523(01)70072-1.

Hylton, K. (2018) *Contesting 'Race' and Sport: Shaming the Colour Line*. London: Routledge.

Simons, Y. and Taylor, J. (1992) 'A psychosocial model of fan violence in sports', *International Journal of Sport Psychology*, 23, 207–26.

Wann, D.L., Melnick, M.J., Russell, G.W. and Pease, D.G. (2001) *Sport Fans: The Psychology and Social Impact of Spectators*. London: Routledge.

PRACTICAL QUESTIONS

- With reference to relevant research, what advice would you give to a football club with regard to the design of its new stadium, to encourage fan safety and also loyalty?
- Why do certain sports tend to attract more fan violence and what measures can be taken to prevent such violence?

REFERENCES

Canter, D., Comber, M. and Uzzell, D.L. (1989) *Football in its Place: An Environmental Psychology of Football Grounds*. London: Routledge.

Cleland, J. and Cashmore, E. (2014) 'Fans, racism and British football in the twenty-first century: The existence of a "colour-blind" ideology', *Journal of Ethnic and Migration Studies*, 40 (4), 638–54. doi:10.1080/1369183X.2013.777524.

Cleland, J. and Cashmore, E. (2016) 'Football fans' views of violence in British football: Evidence of a sanitized and gentrified culture', *Journal of Sport and Social Issues*, 40 (2), 124–42. doi:10.1177/0193723515615177.

Dietz-Uhler, B., Harrick, E., End, C. and Jacquemotte, L. (2000) 'Sex differences in sport fan behavior and reasons for being a sports fan', *Journal of Sport Behavior*, 23, 219–31.

Funk, D.C. and James, J. (2001) 'The psychological continuum model: A conceptual framework for understanding an individual's psychological connection to sport', *Sport Management Review*, 4, 119–50. doi:10.1016/S1441-3523(01)70072-1.

Gibbons, T. (2016) *English National Identity and Football Fan Culture: Who are Ya?* London: Routledge.

Howard, G. (1912) 'Social psychology of the spectator', *American Journal of Sociology*, 18, 33–50.

Hylton, K. (2018) *Contesting 'Race' and Sport: Shaming the Colour Line*. London: Routledge.

Inoue, Y., Sato, M., Filo, K., Du, J. and Funk, D.C. (2017) 'Sport spectatorship and life satisfaction: A multi-country investigation', *Journal of Sport Management*, 31 (4), 1–40.

Jacobson, B. (2003) 'The social psychology of the creation of a sports fan identity: A theoretical review of the literature', *Athletic Insight*, 5 (2), 1–14.

Kavetsos, G. and Szymanski, S. (2010) 'National well-being and international sports events', *Journal of Economic Psychology*, 31 (2), 158–71.

Kerr, J.H. (2005) *Rethinking Aggression and Violence in Sport*. London: Routledge.

Lawrence, S. and Davis, C. (2019) 'Fans for diversity? A critical race theory analysis of Black, Asian and Minority Ethnic (BAME) supporters' experiences of football fandom', *International Journal of Sport Policy and Politics*. DOI: 10.1080/19406940.2019.1627481.

Madrigal, R. (1995) 'Cognitive and affective determinants of fan satisfaction with sporting event attendance', *Journal of Leisure Research*, 27, 205–27.

Mahony, D., Howard, D. and Madrigal, R. (2000) 'BIRGing and CORFing behaviors by sport spectators: High self-monitors versus low self-monitors', *International Sports Journal*, 4, 87–106.

McPherson, B.D. (1976) 'Socialization into the role of sport consumer: A theory and causal model', *Canadian Review of Sociology and Anthropology*, 13 (2), 165–77.

Moore, S.C., Shepherd, J.P., Eden, S. and Sivarajasingam, V. (2007) 'The effect of rugby match outcome on spectator aggression and intention to drink alcohol', *Criminal Behaviour and Mental Health*, 17, 118–27.

Murphy, P., Williams, J. and Dunning, E. (2003) *Football on Trial: Spectator Violence and Developments in the Football World*. London: Taylor & Francis.

Oh, T., Sung, H. and Kwon, K.D. (2017) 'Effect of the stadium occupancy rate on perceived game quality and visit intention', *International Journal of Sports Marketing and Sponsorship*, 18 (2), 166–79.

Oh, T., Kang, J-H. and Kwon, K. (2020) 'Is there a relationship between spectator sports consumption and life satisfaction?', *Managing Sport and Leisure*. DOI: 10.1080/23750472.2020.1784035.

Patrick, G.T.W. (1903) 'The psychology of football', *American Journal of Psychology*, 14, 104–17.

Pearson, G. (1983) *Hooligan: A History of Respectable Fears*. Basingstoke: Macmillan.

Popplewell, Mr Justice (1986) *Popplewell Inquiry into Crowd Safety and Control at Sports Grounds*. London: HMSO.

Simons, Y. and Taylor, J. (1992) 'A psychosocial model of fan violence in sports', *International Journal of Sport Psychology*, 23, 207–26.

Stadler Blank, A., Koenigstorfer, J. and Baumgartner, H. (2017) 'Sport team personality: It's not all about winning!', *Sport Management Review*, 21 (2), 114–32.

Stets, J.E. and Burke, P.J. (2000) 'Identity theory and social identity theory', *Social Psychology Quarterly*, 63 (3), 224–37.

Taylor, Lord Justice (1989) *Interim Report into the Hillsborough Stadium Disaster*. London: HMSO.

Wann, D. (1995) 'Preliminary validation of the sport fan motivation scale', *Journal of Sports and Social Issues*, 19, 377–96.

Wann, D.L., Melnick, M.J., Russell, G.W. and Pease, D.G. (2001) *Sport Fans: The

Psychology and Social Impact of Spectators. London: Routledge.

Weed, M. (2001) 'Ing-ger-land at Euro 2000: How handbags at 20 paces was portrayed as a full scale riot', *International Review for the Sociology of Sport*, 36 (4), 407–24.

White, G.F. (1989) 'Media and violence: The case of professional football championship games', *Aggressive Behavior*, 15, 423–33.

Young, K. (1991) 'Sport and collective violence', *Exercise and Sport Sciences Review*, 19, 539–86.

5.31 SOCIAL IDENTITY THEORY

Definition: Social Identity Theory (SIT) refers to an 'individual's knowledge that he/she belongs to certain social groups together with some emotional and value significance to him/her of this group membership' (Tajfel, 1982: 292). Being part of an in-group, compared to not being a member (out-group) according to the theory can impact motivation, belonging and sense of value.

Over recent years, there has been a growing recognition of the potential relevance to sport of one theory from within social psychology in particular, Social Identity Theory (SIT). The fundamental tenets of SIT are now well established. In essence, it is argued that feeling a sense of belonging, purpose and being able to identify with others is important for psychosocial development. Sharing this sense of identity creates cohesion within a group and motivates individuals to defend and take pride in the group, thereby enhancing a positive identity for themselves and their group (in-group) in contrast with other groups (out-groups). In this way, the role of social identification through group membership is incorporated into our self-concept, and can impact group and individual experiences and outcomes (Cassidy et al., 2014; Hogg, 2001; Hogg and Abrams, 1990; Hornsey, 2008).

According to SIT, in order to become an effective in-group member, s/he needs to share the same values, attitudes, beliefs and desires of the group (e.g. when joining a new football or basketball team). Also, other team members of the in-group will assess new members using a mental description or prototype of what it is to be a 'good' group member. The closer an individual matches the description held of what a group member is, the more likely it is that the person in question will be perceived as socially attractive, be welcomed and respected. This combination of matching the mental description of other members of the in-group as well as being socially attractive enables individuals to function within the group, and to exert social influence (Hogg, 2001).

In brief, the three central factors or sequential mental processes that characterise what occurs when associating with an in-group are: (a) social categorisation; (b) social identification; and (c) social comparison (see Figure **5.6**). Although most SIT research has been conducted within the subdiscipline of social psychology, recently, SIT processes have been articulated in sport as: (a) *cognitive centrality*, which refers to the perception

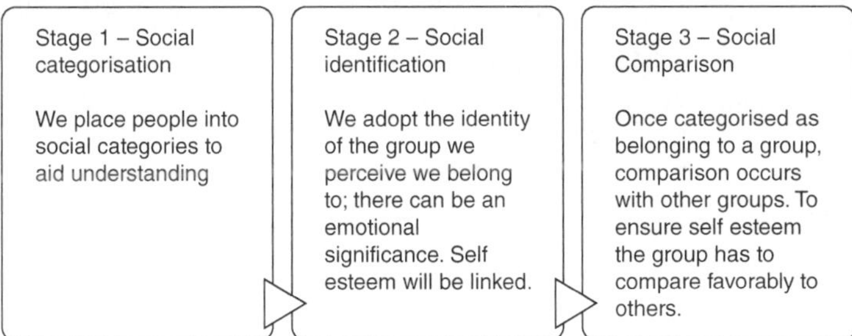

Figure 5.6 Three Central Tenets or Stages that Characterise Associating with an In-group

or salience of group membership; (b) *in-group ties*, which represent perceptions of the similarities and connectedness that one has with other in-group members; and (c) *in-group affect* which refers to the emotional component of a person's social identity as a member of the group in question (Bruner et al., 2020).

SIT now enjoys considerable popularity across sport and exercise psychology and has been tested in numerous studies, mainly in the area of team development and leadership (Ellemers et al., 2004; Haslam et al., 2011; Haslam and Platow, 2001), where it has been shown to impact on motivation, performance and team cohesion. The alignment of SIT to the study of team cohesion in sport is also intuitively appealing as sport includes a complex interplay of relationships: coach–athlete, athlete–athlete, athlete to support team and parent–coach–athlete (see **5.22**). This view is supported by Vella et al. (2010: 425) who describe coaching as a 'complex social process that is constituted and maintained by a set of reciprocal, interpersonal relationships and permeated by contextual constraints' (see **5.27**). Given the complexity of the relationships and links between social identity and self-esteem, recent advances have seen the theory applied to athlete health and wellbeing (Bruner et al., 2020; Haslam et al., 2020). For instance, Bruner et al. (2020) investigated the relationship between social identification and perceived social support from coaches, family, and friends of athletes. Social support was defined as 'the perceived comfort, caring, assistance, and information that a person receives from others' (Lox et al., 2010: 102). The authors showed that athletes who had higher social support in turn displayed an increased sense of social identity when compared to athletes with average or lower support. Other researchers have shown associations between high social identity and low perceived stress, injury (Levine and Reicher, 1996) and mood (Henderson et al., 1998; Lowther and Lane, 2002). With the increased awareness of mental health issues in sport (see **7.40**), it is apparent that social groups represent a key resource that can be harnessed to support athletes. Indeed, belonging to multiple social groups can be beneficial for broadening identity beyond a single athlete identity (see **5.22)**, and hence decreasing an athlete's potential vulnerability (Haslam et al., 2020), especially during times of high pressure to perform, or following retirement.

A recent study that assessed whether participant's social identification with their team moderated self-determined motivation and mental health showed some promising results (Vella et al., 2020). The researchers demonstrated that those with average and higher levels of social identification and self-determined motivation exhibited lower psychological distress, while at high levels of social identification, self-determined motivation was positively associated with wellbeing. The authors concluded that mental health outcomes may be magnified when sport participants strongly identify with their sports teams. That said, there remains a paucity of intervention studies, so further applied research underpinned by SIT is required, along with a consideration of how SIT research previously carried out in occupational settings could be transposed to the world of sport.

A recent review of SIT measurement scales (Cassidy et al., 2014) showed that from a potential 13 that are available, six could be readily applied in sport. These were: (a) the Collective Self-Esteem Scale (CSES) (Luhtanen and Crocker, 1992); (b) three-component Social Identification Measure (Ellemers et al., 1999); (c) two-component measure of social identity (Karasawa, 1991); (d) six-item measure of global organisational identification (Mael and Ashforth, 1992); (e) four-item global identification measure (Doosje et al., 1995); and (f) the three-component Social Identity Measure (Hinkle et al., 1989). Linking some of these scales to wellbeing outcome measures in sport, after providing interventions based on SIT, may prove interesting, and fruitful, in the future.

Overall, SIT shows some significant promise for integrating many areas of sport and, according to some recent reviews and special issues in journals and textbooks, some would argue that SIT provides the basis on which to consider a new psychology of sport and exercise (Haslam et al., 2020). We may watch the trajectory of SIT research and applied practice in sport with great interest.

KEY READINGS

Bruner, M.W., McLaren, C., Swann, C., Schweickle, M. J., Miller, A., Benson, A., … and Vella, S.A. (2020) 'Exploring the relations between social support and social identity in adolescent male athletes', *Research Quarterly for Exercise and Sport*, 1–7. DOI: 10.1080/02701367.2020.1737629.

Cassidy, T., Cummins, P., Breslin, G. and Stringer, M. (2014) 'Perceptions of coach social identity and team confidence, motivation and self-esteem', *Psychology*, 5 (10), 1175–84.

Haslam, S.A., Fransen, K. and Boen, F. (eds) (2020) *The New Psychology of Sport and Exercise: The Social Identity Approach*. London: SAGE.

Tajfel, H. and Turner, J.C. (1979) 'An integrative theory of intergroup conflict', in W.G. Austin and S. Worchel (eds), *The Social Psychology of Intergroup Relations*. Monterey, CA: Brooks/Cole. pp. 33–47.

PRACTICAL QUESTIONS

- How can sport psychologists support athlete transition and integration into a new team using Social Identity Theory?
- How could Social Identity Theory be helpful in supporting athlete mental health or wellbeing?

REFERENCES

Bruner, M.W., McLaren, C., Swann, C., Schweickle, M.J., Miller, A., Benson, A.... and Vella, S.A. (2020) 'Exploring the relations between social support and social identity in adolescent male athletes', *Research Quarterly for Exercise and Sport*, 1–7.

Cassidy, T., Cummins, P., Breslin, G. and Stringer, M. (2014) 'Perceptions of coach social identity and team confidence, motivation and self-esteem', *Psychology*, 5 (10), 1175–84.

Doosje, B., Ellemers, N. and Spears, R. (1995) 'Perceived intragroup variability as a function of group status and identification', *Journal of Experimental Social Psychology*, 31, 410–36. http://dx.doi.org/10.1006/jesp.1995.1018.

Ellemers, N., Korkenaas, P. and Ouwerkerk, J. (1999) 'Self-categorisation, commitment to the group and group self-esteem as related but distinct aspects of social identity', *European Journal of Psychology*, 29, 371–89.

Ellemers, N., De Gilder, D. and Haslam, S.A. (2004) 'Motivating individuals and groups at work: A social identity perspective on leadership and group performance', *Academy of Management Review*, 29, 459–78.

Henderson, J., Bourgeois, A.E., Leunes, A. and Meyers, M.C. (1998) 'Group cohesiveness, mood disturbance, and stress in female basketball players', *Small Group Research*, 29 (2), 212–25.

Hogg, M.A. (2001) 'A social identity theory of leadership', *Personality and Social Psychology Review*, 5, 184–200. http://dx.doi.org/10.1207/S15327957PSPR0503_1.

Hogg, M.A. and Abrams, D. (1990) 'Social motivation, self-esteem and social identity', in D. Abrams and M.A. Hogg (eds), *Social Identity Theory: Constructive and Critical Advances. London: Harvester Wheatsheaf.* pp. 28–47.

Haslam, S.A. and Platow, M.J. (2001) 'Your wish is our command: The role of shared social identity in translating a leader's vision into followers' action', in M.A. Hogg and D.J. Terry (eds), *Social Identity Processes in Organizational Contexts*. Philadelphia, PA: Psychology Press. pp. 213–28.

Haslam, S.A., Reicher, S. and Platow, M.J. (2011) *The New Psychology of Leadership: Identity, Influence, and Power*. Hove: Psychology Press.

Haslam, S.A., Fransen, K. and Boen, F. (eds) (2020) *The New Psychology of Sport and Exercise: The Social Identity Approach*. London: SAGE.

Hinkle, S., Taylor, L.A., Fox-Cardamone, D.L. and Crook, K.F. (1989) 'Intragroup identification and intergroup differentiation: A multicomponent approach', *British*

Journal of Social Psychology, 28, 305–17. http://dx.doi.org/10.1111/j.2044-8309.1989.tb00874.x.

Hornsey, M.J. (2008) 'Social identity theory and self-categorization theory: A historical review', *Social and Personality Psychology Compass*, 2 (1), 204–22.

Karasawa, M. (1991) 'Towards an assessment of social identity: The structure of group identification and its effects on in-group evaluations', *British Journal of Social Psychology*, 30, 293–307. http://dx.doi.org/10.1111/j.2044-8309.1991.tb00947.x.

Levine, R.M. and Reicher, S.D. (1996) 'Making sense of symptoms: Self-categorization and the meaning of illness and injury', *British Journal of Social Psychology*, 35 (2), 245–56.

Lox, C., Martin Ginis, K. and Petruzzello, S.J. (2010) *The Psychology of Exercise: Integrating Theory and Practice* (3rd ed.). Scotsdale, AZ: Holcomb Hathaway Publishers.

Lowther, J. and Lane, A. (2002) 'Relationships between mood, cohesion and satisfaction with performance among soccer players.' *Athletic Insight*, 4 (3), 57–69.

Luhtanen, R. and Crocker, J. (1992) 'A collective self-esteem scale: Self-evaluation of one's social identity', *Personality and Social Psychology Bulletin*, 18, 302–18. http://dx.doi.org/10.1177/0146167292183006.

Mael, F. and Ashforth, B.E. (1992) 'Alumni and their alma mater: A partial test of the reformulated model of organizational identification', *Journal of Organizational Behavior*, 13, 103–23. http://dx.doi.org/10.1002/job.4030130202.

Tajfel, H. (1982) 'Social psychology of intergroup relations', *Annual Review of Psychology*, 33, 1–59. http://dx.doi.org/10.1146/annurev.ps.33.020182.000245

Vella, S.A., Oades, L.G. and Crowe, T.P. (2010) 'The application of coach leadership models to coaching practice: Current state and future directions', *International Journal of Sports Science & Coaching*. 5 (3), 425–34.

Vella, S.A., Benson, A., Sutcliffe, J., McLaren, C., Swann, C., Schweickle, M.J.... and Bruner, M. (2020) 'Self-determined motivation, social identification and the mental health of adolescent male team sport participants', *Journal of Applied Sport Psychology*, 1–15.

Motor Skills

Chapter Summary: Although our ability to control our movements is at the heart of all sporting activity, it is often overlooked. This chapter focuses on the importance of motor skills and starts by looking at their development, drawing the important distinction between motor development and motor learning. Expertise, the key characteristic that underpins elite performance, is then considered in light of different theoretical explanations. This review highlights the importance of using ecologically valid tasks to ensure that any conclusions drawn can be extrapolated to sport. The role of practice for the development of expertise and how practice should be structured is also considered. Finally, in this digital age, the importance of technology to help us understand and improve motor performance is considered.

6.32 Motor Development 196

6.33 Expertise 201

6.34 Decision-Making 206

6.35 Practising Motor Skills 212

6.36 Analysis and Measurement of Motor Performance 219

6.32 MOTOR DEVELOPMENT

Definition: Motor development is the sequential, continuous, age-related process whereby movement behaviour changes over time with practice.

When we observe sports skills such as a golf swing, a tennis serve, a high jump or a cricket shot, we are observing highly complex motor skills. We are not born with the innate ability to swing a golf club, nor are we born with the most 'basic' of motor skills, such as locomotion (walking, running), that we later simply take for granted as our skill repertoire increases. Such motor skills are necessary not only in sport but for survival in everyday life. Locomotive, ballistic and interceptive motor skills are learned and continue to develop across the lifespan. Unsurprisingly the development of these skills begins in infancy and continues into older adulthood. Take for example a new-born baby sucking. This is not a reflex but a coordinated, goal-directed and skilled action which is practised *in utero* (i.e. thumb sucking). Our capability to carry out skilled movements also changes across our lifetime and this is often well reflected in the modern structure of sports competitions. Take Wimbledon for example. There is a junior tennis tournament, an adult tournament and a seniors' tournament, separated according to age ranges. But does motor skill develop in parallel with age? What are the processes underlying motor development? What theoretical approaches are taken when studying motor development? This section will attempt to address these various questions.

Before continuing, it is necessary to define several of the terms that will appear in this and the following sections, namely motor learning, motor development, motor behaviour and motor control. *Motor learning* is defined by Schmidt and Lee (1999) as 'the relatively permanent gains in motor skill capability associated with practice or experience'. Note that this definition refers to experience rather than age. *Motor development*, on the other hand, is defined as the sequential, continuous, age-related process whereby movement behaviour changes over time (Haywood and Getchell, 2005). This definition of motor development describes a *process* where the emphasis is on the underlying mechanisms of change, while other definitions focus more on the *product* of motor development (namely changes in motor performance). Irrespective of this, an undeniable key characteristic of motor development is how growth, maturation and opportunities to practise impact on motor skills, and can be seen as the main difference between motor development and motor learning.

The study of motor development is principally concerned with the developmental change in movement behaviour: both the processes that underlie the change and the resultant movement outcome (product). Let's use an example to illustrate the difference between motor learning and motor development. If a professional golfer tweaks her swing by altering her grip, we do not refer to this change as motor development, but instead it is motor learning involving a change in technique that affects how the motor skill is executed. Motor behaviour, on the other hand, is a term that we use to include both motor learning and motor development, while motor control refers to the neural, physical and behavioural aspects of movement. The remainder of this section will focus on theoretical perspectives which are currently used to study and account for *motor development*.

In terms of motor development, many skills such as locomotive (moving), ballistic (exerting force on an object in order to project it) and interceptive (catching) skills are fundamental to any sport performance. But how do these skills change from childhood to adulthood? Take throwing as an example. Optimum performance of this motor skill is characterised by movements that obey mechanical principles that are required to yield the correct force and speed to hit a target and achieve a goal. As children develop into adults and performance in throwing improves, changes in their movements are consistent with such mechanical principles. For example, a forward step transfers momentum into the direction of the throw and sequential movements of the projecting limb transfer momentum and increase speed. In catching, development from childhood to adulthood will gradually see different movements employed in order to become more proficient. For example, when we learn to catch, we have to learn to tune into and read the ball's movement, so we close the gap between where we are and where the ball is going to land. In other words, we need to get to the right place at the right time in order to intercept the ball. But once we are in the right place, we also need to learn how to use our hands, so they absorb the ball's force by 'giving'. This often involves us dynamically manipulating the position of our fingers to improve our catching technique (e.g. pointing up for a high ball) (see **6.33** and **6.34**).

Current theories that attempt to explain motor development fall under three overarching perspectives: the maturational perspective, the information-processing perspective and the ecological perspective. We will first describe the fundamental differences between the perspectives and then present specific theories in more detail. The maturational perspective emphasises the importance of genetics and inheritance as the primary driving forces behind motor development, which is seen primarily as a series of maturational processes. It assumes motor development to be 'an internal or innate process driven by a biological or genetic time clock' (Haywood and Getchell, 2005). There is therefore little emphasis placed on the role of the environment as it is thought to have little effect on the biologically determined course. The popular information-processing model (often referred to as the cognitive approach) sees the brain akin to a computer where symbolic knowledge structures mediate the translation of sensory input to motor output. The ecological approach, on the other hand, places emphasis on the interrelationships between the individual, the environment and the task (Thelen, 1995). According to this approach, all three of these systems interact resulting in the emergence of a motor skill. The fundamental difference between these perspectives therefore relates to the role of internal processes. The information-processing approach sees perception of the world and movement production as separate processes whereby the brain receives perceptual information, performs calculations on it and then translates the information into movement of the muscles. The ecological approach, however, emphasises the role of the environment in shaping actions directly, rather than focusing on internalised knowledge structures. The distinction between these two perspectives and how they account for various aspects of motor behaviour will be a recurrent theme throughout the following sections.

The maturational approach was spearheaded in the 1930s by Arnold Gesell, who conducted co-twin control research in order to test the different effects of environment and inheritance on development. This paradigm saw one twin given special training while the other was allowed to develop naturally. This line of research allowed maturationists to begin to identify the sequence of skill development. Following this, Myrtle McGraw in 1943 began to look at changes in the nervous system that accounted for the emergence of new skills. In the 1950s, Anna Espenschade, Ruth Glasgow and Lawrence Rarick led a period of research that was focused on describing normative movement and biomechanics in school-aged children. Standardised tests were used to record scores in activities such as running, throwing and jumping. Although this approach was significant in describing naturally occurring sequences of change, the underlying mechanisms behind such changes were not addressed.

The most prominent theory that attempts to address how motor development comes about from an information-processing perspective is Schema Theory (Schmidt, 1975). According to this theory, through practice, a learner develops expansive and flexible 'generalised motor programmes' that are called upon for a variety of similar activities. Each class of skills (e.g. throwing a ball) has its own general motor programme which has both invariant (e.g. relative timing) and changeable (e.g. overall force) parameters. For example, aspects of a throwing movement, such as the relative timing of joint flexion and extension, will remain the same for any throwing task; however, overall force applied would vary according to the particular throw in question. This theory could account for cases of athletes excelling in more than one sport. For example, Ellyse Perry is the youngest sportswoman to represent Australia in World Cups for two different sports (cricket and soccer), while Sonny "Bill" Williams has won two World Cups with the New Zealand All Black rugby team and has also won seven professional boxing matches. These examples suggest that there is a repertoire of flexible and adaptable schemata that allow these athletes to perform skilled movements effectively and to a very high level in each of these sports. Motor development according to this approach is as a result of practice and the formation of more flexible, adaptable schemata.

The most significant model for studying motor development from an ecological perspective remains Newell's Constraints Model (Newell, 1986). This model suggests that movements emerge through the dynamic, constantly changing interactions of the individual, the environment and the task. Newell refers to individual, environmental and task 'constraints' – characteristics that either facilitate or restrict movement. Individual constraints are related to the individual's physical and mental characteristics and can be structural (related to the body's structure) or functional (related to behavioural function). For example, disabled limbs would be an individual constraint as this will affect the way that the person will move. Environmental constraints are related to the world around us. They may be physical (e.g. surfaces, weather) or sociocultural (e.g. societal constraints such as sexism discouraging female participation in sports) and are not task specific. Task constraints are also external and refer to goals and rules we use. For example, the cricket bowling action is constrained by the fact that the arm must be straight during delivery of the ball. Motor development from this perspective is therefore a result of changing constraints across the lifespan. Throughout development, individuals become more refined at mapping perceptual information onto the dynamics of the system in a way that is consistent with constraints. Another constraint-led approach – the dynamic systems approach – introduced in the 1980s by Peter Kugler, Scott Kelso and Michael Turvey, also suggests that motor behaviour 'self-organises' according to constraints (Clark, 1995). This approach highlights the role of 'rate limiters' – systems within an individual that hold back or slow the emergence of a motor skill, e.g. muscular strength is a rate limiter for walking as a certain level of muscular strength must be gained in order to support the body weight. Thelen developed this theory further, emphasising how the self-organising nature of developmental change is influenced by exploration, which pushes the selection of new emergent behaviours (Thelen, 1995).

Finally, another theory from within the ecological perspective is James Gibson's (1979) perception-action approach. Gibson famously wrote, 'we move to perceive and perceive to move', highlighting the strong link between perception and action and strongly suggesting the need to study together the two systems that have evolved together. Central to this theory is the concept of *affordances* which we directly perceive through our interactions with the environment. An affordance is often described as an opportunity for action that a particular object affords, with the same object affording different actions (e.g. a ball may afford kicking, throwing or catching). Most importantly, what an environmental property offers in terms of action is specific to that individual. For example, a standard rugby ball might afford catching for an adult but not a 4-year-old child who has smaller hands. Gibson therefore proposed that we perceive the world relative to our own body scale (body-scaled affordances) and action capabilities (action-scaled affordances). As we develop, our bodies grow (e.g. longer legs) and our action capabilities change (e.g. can run faster), which means our opportunities for action (affordances) will also change.

This is illustrated nicely in a study by Warren (1984) who demonstrated that the ratio between the height of the stair and the hip height was the body-scaled affordance which was used to determine whether or not a stair is climbable. Other research has shown how exposure to different environments that present different affordances, or opportunities for action, are also very important for a child's motor development. These environments shape the development of motor skills, and are present in home, school and sports contexts (Luz et al., 2017). Taking these ideas further, Whitagen and Caljouw (2016) have shown how the environment can also influence levels of physical activity, with certain home environments promoting more sedentary behaviours than was the case two decades ago. As development continues into late adulthood, affordances continue to change. While maturationists tend to focus on infants and children, a constraint-led or affordance-based ecological approach accounts for motor development across the entire lifespan.

To summarise, this section has made the distinction between terminologies often used in motor skill research, defined motor development as an age-related process before going on to discuss theoretical perspectives which offer descriptions and explanations as to what accounts for motor development.

KEY READINGS

Haywood, K.M. and Getchell, N. (2005) *Life Span Motor Development* (4th ed.). Champaign, IL: Human Kinetics.

Newell, K.M. (1986) 'Constraints on the development of coordination', in M.G. Wade and H.T.A. Whiting (eds.) *Motor Development in Children: Aspects of Coordination and Control*. Amsterdam: Martin Nijhoff. pp. 341–61.

Schmidt, R. and Lee, T. (1999) *Motor Control and Learning: A Behavioural Emphasis* (3rd ed.), Champaign, IL: Human Kinetics.

Thelen, E. (1995) 'Motor development: A new synthesis', *American Psychologist*, 50 (2), 79–95.

PRACTICAL QUESTIONS

- From your understanding of motor development, how could you improve the design of your local play park?
- In New Zealand junior rugby is played according to the weight of the players. From a motor development perspective, note down three advantages and disadvantages of this approach.

REFERENCES

Clark, J.E. (1995) 'On becoming skilful: Patterns and constraints', *Research Quarterly*, 66, 173–83.

Gibson, J.J. (1979) *An Ecological Approach to Visual Perception*. Boston, MA: Houghton-Mifflin.

Haywood, K.M. and Getchell, N. (2005) *Life Span Motor Development* (4th ed.). Champaign, IL: Human Kinetics.

Luz, C., Rodrigues, L.P., De Meester, A. and Cordovil, R. (2017) 'The relationship between motor competence and health-related fitness in children and adolescents', *PLoS ONE*, 12, e0179993.

Newell, K.M. (1986) 'Constraints on the development of coordination', in M.G. Wade and H.T.A. Whiting (eds.) *Motor Development in Children: Aspects of Coordination and Control*. Amsterdam: Martin Nijhoff. pp. 341–61.

Schmidt, R.A. (1975) 'A schema theory of discrete motor skill learning', *Psychological Review*, 82, 225–60.

Schmidt, R. and Lee, T. (1999) *Motor Control and Learning: A Behavioural Emphasis* (3rd ed.), Champaign, IL: Human Kinetics.

Thelen, E. (1995) 'Motor development: A new synthesis', *American Psychologist*, 50 (2), 79–95.

Warren, W.H. (1984) 'Perceiving affordances: Visual guidance of stair climbing', *Journal of Experimental Psychology: Human Perception and Performance*, 10 (5), 683–703.

Withagen, R. and Caljouw, S. R. (2016) '"The end of sitting": An empirical study on working in an office of the future', *Sports Medicine*, 46 (7), 1019–27.

6.33 EXPERTISE

Definition: Expertise is consistent and superior athletic performance displayed over an extended period of time; it is based on practice and encompasses the physiological, technical, cognitive and emotional domains.

Several times a year, millions of sports enthusiasts watch in awe as elite athletes compete in world-class competition. Be it the Superbowl, a golf or tennis major, or the Champions League final in soccer, these events are an opportunity to watch sports men and women perform at the top of their game. But what separates Serena Williams and Rory McIlroy from the rest of us who try so hard to emulate their performances? The answer: they are experts … we are not! Of the millions of people around the globe playing soccer, only a relatively tiny number will ever make it to the World Cup, just like a tiny number of the world's golfers will ever win a major. Those that do make it seem to possess superior abilities compared with those who don't. Researchers in sport expertise have, for decades, attempted to answer fundamental questions regarding these superior abilities. What makes an expert an expert? How and why do we study expertise? And finally, can anyone become an expert through training and practice?

The first question to consider is what exactly is expertise and what are its determinants? Frank Lloyd Wright, the famous American architect, once said, 'An expert is a man who has stopped thinking – he knows'. This could be said of an expert in any domain, referring to what seems to onlookers like second-nature performance in whatever the task. A more scientific definition proposed by Starkes (1993) states that expertise in sport involves the consistent presentation of superior athletic performance over an extended period of time. For authors Janelle and Hillman (2003), athletes obtain expert status when they excel in no less than four different domains: physiological, technical, cognitive (tactical/strategic; perceptual/decision making), and emotional (regulation/coping; psychological). In terms of physiological components of expertise, factors such as muscle fibre type and aerobic capacity, although malleable to an extent through training, are largely genetically determined (Swallow et al., 1998). Experts are often said to be 'built' for a certain sport, e.g. rowers with long levers and a naturally high level of aerobic fitness. Emotional and psychological expertise refers to social-cognitive determinants such as the ability of experts to regulate and exert control over their emotions in competition and to maintain motivation and a positive mental attitude. Since the focus of this section is on motor skills and considering that previous sections have dealt with many social-cognitive factors (e.g. anxiety and stress, cognitive processes), we will not expand further on these domains but instead focus on the two that have most relevance to motor skill: the expert's superior ability to know *how* (technical) and *when* (cognitive/perceptual) to perform *what* actions. Technical expertise refers to the skill execution or movement patterns involved when carrying out coordinated actions in sport, such as pitching in baseball, the golf swing or the tennis backhand, i.e. knowing *how to perform the action.* The expert performer will execute such techniques in a more refined, efficient and effective way than the non-expert performer. For example, Rory McIlroy is widely considered to have the 'best swing' in the game of golf. Cognitive and perceptual expertise refers to the superior ability of expert performers to know *what* and *when* to carry out a certain action. Williams et al. (1999) note the increasing recognition of the relationship between skilful perception and skilful action in successful sports performance.

Experts are able to attend to relevant information within their environment, ignore irrelevant information and use anticipatory cues, meaning they consistently seem to be doing 'the right thing, at the right time'. For example, a quote often attributed to Wayne Gretzky states that, 'A good hockey player plays where the puck is. A great hockey player plays where the puck is going to be.' This highlights the importance of anticipation and game knowledge to be in the right place at the right time in order to perform a given action. Research into perceptual and cognitive expertise in sport is an area that has received the most attention in sport expertise research. In sum, there is not a single determinant of expertise but rather an interaction of several components which contribute to expert performance. The challenge for researchers is to describe and account for expertise phenomena through scientific study. Having now addressed definitions and determinants of expertise, we will now consider why researchers study expertise, what theories exist that account for expert performance and, finally, the methods used to study expertise.

Why study expert performance in sport? On top of providing a window through which to enhance the understanding of skill acquisition in sport, it allows for the identification of factors distinguishing experts from non-experts. This in turn can highlight limiting factors to high-level performance and has implications for developing training programmes, practice regimes and the identification and selection of talent.

In terms of theoretical frameworks surrounding expertise research, the dominant approach in the past few decades has been the cognitive approach, underpinned by the information-processing metaphor which sees the mind as being akin to a computer. According to this approach, expert performers are thought to differ from novices in the amount and type of information pertaining to specific sport situations that they remember and/or recognise. Paradigms used to explore these differences were imported directly from cognitive expertise research following famous work with chess players where both recall (de Groot, 1965; Chase and Simon, 1973; cited in Williams et al., 1999) and recognition (Charness, 1976; cited in Williams et al., 1999) tasks were used to assess differences between experts and novices. Typically, these studies involved presenting chess players with game configurations via slides for a period of time and asking them to recall the piece positions afterwards. So as not to attribute results to differences in 'hardware' of visual short-term memory, control trials were introduced where the pieces were laid out randomly and not structured. Results from these studies suggested that experts had an advanced task-specific knowledge base and were able to retrieve this information more efficiently than novices. Using a similar paradigm, expertise effects have been demonstrated in various sports (e.g. soccer; Williams and Davids, 1995), with efforts made to present more realistic game configurations that involve dynamic film sequences presented on large screens. The notion that experts possess more sport-specific knowledge from which to draw was incorporated into an approach adopted by Anderson (1982) in his 'active control of thought' model. This proposed that expert performers possess a larger reservoir of 'IF … THEN … DO' statements stored in their declarative memory, allowing them to initiate appropriate responses under certain conditions: for example in rugby, if a line of defenders approaches leaving space behind, then kick the ball into that space.

A related line of research to the recognition and recall paradigm is that of advanced cue utilisation. This paradigm has demonstrated the ability of an expert performer to pick up information more quickly from a dynamic sport-specific action sequence through the recognition and utilisation of advanced cues. Bruce Abernethy has carried out extensive work incorporating the popular temporal occlusion paradigm where stimuli (e.g. a film of an action sequence) are segmented and occluded according to the duration of presentation (temporal occlusion: e.g. a tennis serve is occluded before contact with the ball and the participant must guess the direction of the serve). This technique has highlighted an expertise effect in various sports insofar as an elite athlete can successfully anticipate subsequent actions, with less information than a non-expert (e.g. rugby union; Brault et al, 2012).

More recently, and based on ecological psychology, an alternative framework to the information-processing one has been proposed to account for expertise. This approach is reluctant to resort to cognitive constructs such as memory structures and internal representations to explain behaviour. James Gibson's (1979) 'Ecological Approach to Visual Perception' proposes the notion that humans and animals perceive and interact with surfaces (e.g. grass), places (e.g. pitch), objects (e.g. ball) and events (e.g. set-play). These so-called properties of the surrounding environment provide opportunities for action. This relationship between the environment and athlete and the ensuing action possibilities are known as *affordances* (see **6.32**). Affordances are invitations to act and are defined by information that is constantly available to us via the visual system. For example, the soccer player Luka Modrić knows exactly when the environment *affords* passing the ball and has the action capability to execute the pass at the right time, with the right amount of pace. Using this conceptualisation, differences in novice and expert performance are thought to 'reflect, in part, differences in the informational variables upon which they rely' (Fajen et al., 2008: 85), rather than differences in task-specific knowledge structures which the cognitive approach would suggest. That is to say, novices' and experts' abilities to tune into and use relevant informational variables available to them within the environment may differ.

This approach to expertise has been likened to that of tuning a radio: the expert can tune in straight away to the correct frequency, while the non-expert will experience noise while passing through other frequencies. Although quite different in their accounts for expertise, both the information-processing and the ecological approach recognise and demonstrate differences in expert and non-expert performance. Considering this as well as the determinants of expertise discussed, the final question to address concerns the development of expertise. Can the acquisition of sport expertise be facilitated?

It is most likely the case that expert performance is a result of some combination of genetic and environmental interactions. Is it the case that the Williams sisters were born with an innate tennis ability or is their success the result of the military-like practice regime that they underwent while growing up? While a hard-line naturist perspective would suggest that you have to be born with innate talent, this argument has been all but abandoned in recent times. The more popular approaches include the strict 'nurturist' perspective which suggests that, through practice, anyone can achieve expertise, or the 'interactionist' approach, which suggests that the level of expertise achievable through practice is limited by innate hereditary factors. Ericsson et al. (1993) introduced the theory of deliberate practice, proposing that expertise will emerge through an extended period of deliberate practice which is structured, systematic, effortful and done often; typically ten years or 10,000 hours. The theory of deliberate practice is described in more detail elsewhere (see **6.35**), but here it suffices to say that this theory recognises a relationship between practice and level of attainment. This has been demonstrated in both individual and team sports. Although often criticised, the theory of deliberate practice has guided sport psychologists toward determining what type of practice will be effective for skill acquisition.

Some research exists where techniques have been employed in order to examine whether perceptual skills can be trained. This work is approached from the dominant cognitive perspective and much of it has used video simulation methods in an attempt to train decision-making or anticipation skills, i.e. to pick up relevant cues further in advance. Although some studies provide examples of improved performance using pre- and post-tests following video simulation (e.g. for novice tennis players, Williams et al., 2002), a meaningful treatment effect is difficult to isolate as results could be attributed to greater familiarity with the test environment. Another difficulty, which may explain why this approach has not been adopted in elite sports, is that the tests used in the laboratory setting lack the ecological validity necessary to transfer to real-world applications. While video simulation is by far the most popular tool used in this research, it lacks many of the features necessary to recreate a realistic sporting environment, (e.g. a player perspective viewpoint and depth information). The recent emergence of interactive, immersive virtual reality systems as a methodological tool in sport science provides exciting advantages over video presentation for this type of work, and with it there is the potential to develop more ecologically valid training environments that combine perception and action (for a review, see Craig, 2014).

KEY READINGS

Craig C.M. (2014) 'Understanding perception and action in sport: How can virtual reality technology help?', *Sports Technology*, 6, 161–9.

Ericsson, K.A., Krampe, R.T. and Tesch-Römer, C. (1993) 'The role of deliberate practice in the acquisition of expert performance', *Psychological Review*, 100 (3), 363–406.

Fajen, B.R., Riley, M.A. and Turvey, M.T. (2008) 'Information, affordances and the control of action in sport', *International Journal of Sport Psychology*, 40 (1), 79–107.

Janelle, C.M. and Hillman, C.H. (2003) 'Expert performance in sport: Current perspectives and critical issues', in J.L. Starkes and K.A. Ericsson (eds), *Expert Performance in Sports: Advances in Research on Sport Expertise*. Champaign, IL: Human Kinetics. pp. 49–83.

PRACTICAL QUESTIONS

- Recent research has criticised theories that place a heavy emphasis on the role of memory and pattern recognition to explain expertise in sport (see Craig 2014 – the indirect v. direct approach). Are these critiques justified? Provide reasons to support your answer.
- What are the advantages and disadvantages of using video to train perceptual expertise in soccer players?

REFERENCES

Anderson, J.R. (1982) 'Acquisition of cognitive skill', *Psychological Review*, 89 (4), 369–406.

Brault, S., Bideau, B., Kulpa, R. and Craig, C. (2012) 'Detecting deception in movement: The case of the sidestep in rugby', *PloS ONE.* Doi: 10.1371/journal.pone.0037494.

Craig C.M. (2014) 'Understanding perception and action in sport: How can virtual reality technology help?', *Sports Technology*, 6, 161–9.

Ericsson, K.A., Krampe, R.T. and Tesch-Römer, C. (1993) 'The role of deliberate practice in the acquisition of expert performance', *Psychological Review*, 100 (3), 363–406.

Fajen, B.R., Riley, M.A. and Turvey, M.T. (2008) 'Information, affordances and the control of action in sport', *International Journal of Sport Psychology*, 40 (1), 79–107.

Gibson, J.J. (1979) *An Ecological Approach to Visual Perception*. Boston, MA: Houghton-Mifflin.

Janelle, C.M. and Hillman, C.H. (2003) 'Expert performance in sport: Current perspectives and critical issues', in J.L. Starkes and K.A. Ericsson (eds), *Expert Performance in Sports: Advances in Research on Sport Expertise*. Champaign, IL: Human Kinetics. pp. 49–83.

Starkes, J.L. (1993) 'Motor experts: Opening thoughts', in J.L. Starkes and F. Allard (eds), *Cognitive Issues in Motor Expertise*. Amsterdam: Elsevier. pp. 3–16.

Swallow, J.G., Garland, T., Carter, P.A., Zhan, W.Z. and Sieck, G.C. (1998) 'Effects of voluntary activity and genetic selection on aerobic capacity in house mice (Mus domesticus)', *Journal of Applied Physiology*, 69–76.

Williams, A.M. and Davids, K. (1995) 'Declarative knowledge in sport: A by-product of experience or a characteristic of expertise?' *Journal of Sport and Exercise Psychology*, 17 (3), 259–75.

Williams, A.M., Davids, K. and Williams, J.G. (1999) *Visual Perception and Action in Sport*. London: E and FN Spon.

Williams, A.M., Ward, P., Knowles, J.M. and Smeeton, N.J. (2002) 'Perceptual skill in a real-world task: Training, instruction and transfer in tennis', *Journal of Experimental Psychology: Applied*, 8, 259–70.

6.34 DECISION-MAKING

Definition: Decision-making is a dynamic process, based on previous experience, that combines visual search, recognition, recall and anticipation in choosing the most appropriate option in a given situation and within available time constraints.

Decision-making in sport is a term that encompasses many different scenarios. It could refer to the strategic decision-making of the golfer Michelle Wie when selecting an approach shot or to Owen Farrell making a decision to kick for goal when his team is awarded a penalty. It could also refer to more temporally constrained 'in game' decisions such as Stephen Curry making the correct decision to pass, shoot or dribble the basketball or Manuel Neuer deciding to dive right when faced with a penalty kick in soccer. This section will focus most especially on occasions linked to the two latter examples as they both relate to the execution of motor skills under tight temporal constraints.

Decision-making is as equally important an aspect of sport as physical prowess, yet is somewhat less obvious. This is probably due to the apparent ease with which great decision-makers perform under time pressure. Indeed, great decision-makers often seem to 'have all the time in the world' when executing a manoeuvre. What theories exist to account for decision-making? What methods are used to study and analyse decision-making? And finally, can research inform practice in terms of improving decision-making through training?

To begin with, defining or classifying decisions is a challenge in itself. A 'right' decision is one that results in a favourable outcome for the performer or the performer's team. For example, in attack, a rugby player may decide to be tackled in order to take the ball to ground and set up another phase of play. Equally s/he may decide to kick the ball and gain territory. Research has therefore concentrated on trying to identify the processes and mechanisms that underlie decisions and judgements. The most popular approach for understanding how these decisions come about is embedded within the information-processing perspective. Decision-making from this perspective is seen as a process, underpinned by the same concepts as outlined earlier (see **6.33**), i.e. visual search, recognition, recall and anticipation. According to Tenenbaum (2003), skilled performers first search the environmental display when planning a motor response, and then eliminate irrelevant information and utilise advanced cues to select the appropriate response. This consists of an ongoing elaboration between the environmental information and the knowledge base which resides in memory. Finally, when a decision is made a course of action is taken. Wickens (1992) proposes that expert decision-makers possess three advantages which distinguish them from non-experts with regard to these processes. Experts can (a) use perceptual chunking to select relevant information/cues from a displayed action sequence; (b) calibrate their decisions to situational probabilities due to a more extensive knowledge base; and (c) couple cue recognition, hypothesis formation and decision outcomes more effectively (i.e. improved stimulus-response compatibility based on recognition and matching processes). These advantages allow for faster and more accurate expert decision-making under tight time constraints. To account for the inefficient and costly nature of serial processing under extreme temporal conditions, this conceptualisation argues that, under these conditions, the cognitive and motor systems operate faster and depend on motor schema and knowledge structures which are accessed automatically, i.e. without relying on conscious awareness (Tenenbaum and Bar-Eli, 1993).

In terms of methodology for studying decision-making from this approach, similar techniques that were used in recognition and anticipatory judgement paradigms (see **6.33**) are often adopted. For example, static or dynamic sequences of play would be displayed and occluded or cut off before the decision was behaviourally expressed. Participants would be asked to choose one of several decision options delivering a response verbally or by pressing a button. Response accuracy and response time would typically be recorded. Using these methods, several studies have shown that skill level affects decision-making (e.g. soccer; Helsen and Pauwels, 1988). However, this paradigm has been criticised because of the often unrealistic nature of the task constraints and stimulus presentation. Static presentations of game situations do not capture the space/time pressures of real game play where players and the ball are in a continual state of motion. The nature of the game means decisions will be directly influenced by the dynamics of the unfolding event. Presenting dynamic video sequences also has limitations that prevent it from truly capturing an in-game situation. The video is usually captured from a fixed viewpoint (allocentric) and not from the would-be decision-maker's viewpoint (egocentric). This means that the presentation of the patterns of visual information that the participant is using to make a decision is not the same visual information that they would have access to and use in a game scenario. This phenomenon also explains why many of us believe we are 'expert' players when we watch soccer games on television as we have access to a superior visual viewpoint (allocentric) that allows us to see 'options' that players on the pitch cannot physically see. Also, when displayed on small screens there is a loss of dimensionality with no depth information being present.

An alternative framework for considering decision-making and judgement is offered from within the ecological approach to visual perception (Gibson, 1979). One of the key concepts within this approach (see **6.33**) is the idea that people directly perceive meaningful information in the form of affordances within the environment (opportunities for action, e.g. a ball affords kicking), which does not require mediating cognitive processes. Perceiving affordances allows us to determine which actions are possible and which are not (Turvey, 1992) and therefore provides an appropriate framework under which to study sporting behaviour, where so many actions are possible within constantly changing environments. As Fajen et al. (2008) point out, 'to perceive an affordance, in Gibson's view, is to perceive how one can act when confronted with a particular set of environmental conditions' (p.87). Decisions from this perspective are therefore not seen as a series of cognitive processes but rather a result of what behaviour an environment affords at a given moment in time, combined with the action capabilities of the performer. For example, when deciding whether a volleyball shot is 'blockable' or not, Pepping and Li (2000) showed that both geometric (body-scaled – i.e. player's eye height) and kinetic (action-scaled – i.e. how high they can jump) properties of a player influenced their decision. This research shows that these types of action choices are not just determined by physical properties of the environment such as height or time, but also by the performer's perception of their own action capabilities, namely how high they can jump. Therefore affordances, and by default decisions, are both body-scaled (i.e. constrained by body dimensions) and action scaled (i.e. constrained by an actor's action capabilities).

Being able to perceive an affordance allows the performer to determine which actions are possible and which are not as an event unfolds (Turvey, 1992). The perception of an affordance will therefore depend on the player's ability to tune into the dynamics of relevant visual information that defines the affordance. For the visual domain, affordances may be directly specified by the changing pattern of light that is detected by the observer (e.g. the speed of the approaching line of defensive players in rugby (Correia et al., 2011), or in the auditory domain from the patterning of event-related sounds that specify a particular action (e.g. deceptive movement in basketball, Camponogara et al., 2017).

An important feature of the information that specifies affordances, especially in sport, is that it allows for the prospective control of action. That is to say, actions are adapted in anticipation of what the environment affords, based on current information that specifies the future course of events, i.e. if current conditions persist. Being able to directly perceive or 'tune into' relevant information that specifies the 'current future' plays a critical role in maintaining the online control of action as it unfolds. A series of recent studies carried out from this perspective have been able to identify the information that influences decisions and judgements in soccer (Craig et al., 2009; Valkinidis et al., 2020), handball (Vignais et al., 2010) and rugby (Watson et al., 2011; Brault et al., 2012; Correia et al., 2011). This approach is popular as it can account for performance under tight spatial-temporal constraints and variability in sporting situations.

Having discussed the main theoretical perspectives on decision-making in sport, and the methodologies used to research decision-making, we now raise the question – can research findings feed back into practice by offering potential methods to train decision-making skills? Outside of research, from a practitioner's point of view, it is beneficial to provide feedback for all facets of a player's performance. Typical performance analysis will involve video sessions where athletes review and discuss their own decision-making performance, usually with a coach or member of support staff. However, for the reasons previously discussed, it may be difficult for players to take this feedback and apply it to a game situation in the future because the video capture of the game simply does not match the information that is available *to that player* for making decisions during the game. In fact, seeing an event unfold from a different perspective may make it unrecognisable in terms of what the player actually remembers. While these types of sessions may be useful for a coach to illustrate a point about team dynamics, it is difficult to extrapolate to individual performance.

In **6.33** (Expertise) reference was made to studies that used video simulations in order to train perceptual skills such as anticipation, and mixed results were reported in terms of effectiveness. The methodological shortcomings that may limit the effectiveness of this type of training are the same ones that limit the realism of displays used in research protocols: a viewpoint that does not update or change over time according to the performer's movement, a loss of space-time pressure and also limited dimensionality in terms of depth-based information. Immersive, interactive Virtual Reality (VR) technology has proved to be an interesting methodological tool that allows for more realistic presentation of visual information in laboratory settings and is starting to be used as a measurement and training tool for players in soccer (see BeYourBest that measures and trains scanning behaviours in soccer players and INCISIV's CleanSheet that has been designed to improve decision-making in goalkeepers). The power of immersive, interactive VR allows a user to be totally immersed (360 degrees) in a virtual environment. By wearing a head-mounted display (HMD) that contains an integrated head tracker, movements in the real world can be tracked and translated into parallel movements in the virtual world. In other words, a movement to the left in the real world is detected by the tracker and is represented visually in the virtual environment as simultaneous movement to the left in the virtual environment. This technology not only allows for an egocentric perspective of an event, it also allows the experimenters to control the information presented to the participants (perception) and measure how they respond to that information (action). In other words, it is an ideal tool to study the perception/action cycle and how information influences decisions about when and how to act.

Craig (2014) highlights not only the advantages that VR offers over video playback in decision-making research but also the importance of this technology in terms of the emerging results. For example, in a perception-only rugby-based task, where a real defender is confronted with a virtual attacker performing a deceptive stepping movement, results showed that there was a clear expert advantage over novices, with experts (professional rugby players) being better able to judge the correct final running direction much sooner than novices. Most interestingly, the professional players judged by the coach to play the best 'heads-up' rugby were significantly better than the other professional players tested. These results suggest that certain expert players can tune into the right information that specifies the correct final running direction and not the deceptive body-based information that is specifying the incorrect final running direction (Brault et al., 2012). Other studies have also shown how this technology can allow us to study how information picked up from a ball trajectory (e.g. a curved free kick in soccer) influences decisions about how and when to act. Again, a clear expert advantage has been shown, with experienced international goalkeepers waiting longer before responding, leading to less movement errors in the wrong direction (Dessing and Craig, 2010). These cases present examples where VR has been shown to be an effective means of presenting sport scenarios in a realistic yet controllable way. Furthermore, with significant technological advances, there are now promising possibilities of using this technology for practitioners through the development of off-field, virtual decision-making training environments. This may be especially beneficial for injured players in that they could still benefit from the perceptual experience without having to carry out the physical practice.

The aim of this chapter was not only to describe theoretical and methodological approaches to studying decision-making but also to discuss recent work using new techniques. The use of such new and exciting technology as VR will continue to expand our understanding of the mechanisms underlying decision-making and judgement by allowing the creation of more realistic environments through which to observe athletic performance.

KEY READINGS

Brault, S., Bideau, B., Kulpa, R. and Craig, C. (2012) 'Detecting deception in movement: The case of the sidestep in rugby', *PloS ONE*. Doi: 10.1371/journal.pone.0037494.

Fajen, B.R., Riley, M.A. and Turvey, M.T. (2008) 'Information, affordances and the control of action in sport', *International Journal of Sport Psychology*, 40 (1), 79–107.

Gibson, J.J. (1979) *An Ecological Approach to Visual Perception*. Boston, MA: Houghton-Mifflin.

Valkanidis, T., Craig, C.M., Cummins, A. and Dessing, J. (2020) 'Effects of visual occlusion by the wall on goalkeeper performance during free kicks in football', *PloS ONE*, 15 (12), e0243287.

PRACTICAL QUESTIONS

- A 1.74m, 75kg rugby player has the ball. She sees space on her right for the winger to run into but she knows her long pass is weak. The defensive line is moving up fast. She decides to keep the ball and go to contact. Use the theory of affordances to explain her decision-making process.
- Outline three main advantages of using immersive, interactive virtual reality over video to study decision-making in sport.

REFERENCES

Brault, S., Bideau, B., Kulpa, R. and Craig, C. (2012) 'Detecting deception in movement: The case of the sidestep in rugby', *PloS ONE*, Doi: 10.1371/journal.pone.0037494.

Camponogara, I., Rodger, M., Craig, C. and Cesari, P. (2017) 'Hearing the game: Basketball players outperform non-players by accurately detecting an opponent's movement intentions through sound alone', *Journal of Experimental Psychology: Human Perception and Performance*, 43 (2), 348–59.

Correia, V., Araujo, D., Craig, C. and Passos P. (2011) 'Prospective information for pass decisional behaviour in rugby union', *Human Movement Science* 30 (5), 984–97.

Craig C.M. (2014) 'Understanding perception and action in sport: How can virtual reality technology help?', *Sports Technology*, 6, 161–9.

Craig, C.M., Goulon, C., Berton, E., Rao, G., Fernandez, L. and Bootsma, R.J. (2009) 'Optic variables used to judge future ball arrival position in expert and novice soccer players', *Attention, Perception and Psychophysics*, 71, 515–22.

Dessing, J.C. and Craig, C.M. (2010) 'Bending it like Beckham: How to visually fool the goalkeeper', *PloS One*, 5 (10), e13161. doi:10.1371/journal.pone.0013161.

Fajen, B.R., Riley, M.A. and Turvey, M.T. (2008) 'Information, affordances and the control of action in sport', *International Journal of Sport Psychology*, 40 (1), 79–107.

Gibson, J.J. (1979) *An Ecological Approach to Visual Perception*. Boston, MA: Houghton-Mifflin.

Helsen, W. and Pauwels, J.M. (1988) 'The use of a simulator in evaluation and training of tactical skills in soccer', in T. Reilly, A. Lees, K. Davids and W. Murphy (eds), *Science and Football. London: Spon*. pp. 493–7.

Pepping, G.J. and Li, F.X. (2000) 'Changing action capabilities and the perception of affordances', *Journal of Human Movement Studies*. 39 (2), 115–40.

Tenenbaum, G. (2003) 'Expert athletes: An integrated approach to decision-making', in J.L. Starkes and K.A. Ericsson (eds), *Expert Performance in Sports: Advances in Research on Sport Expertise*. Champaign, IL: Human Kinetics. pp. 191–219.

Tenenbaum, G. and Bar-Eli, M. (1993) 'Decision-making in sport: A cognitive perspective', in R.N. Singer, M. Murphy and L.K. Tennant (eds), *Handbook of Research on Sport Psychology*. New York: Macmillan. pp. 171–92.

Turvey, M.T. (1992) 'Ecological foundations of cognition: Invariants of perception and action', in H.L. Pick, Jr., P. van den Broek and D.C. Knill (eds), *Cognition: Conceptual and Methodological Issues*. Washington, DC: American Psychological Association. pp. 85–117.

Valkanidis, T., Craig, C.M., Cummins, A. and Dessing, J. (2020) 'Effects of visual occlusion by the wall on goalkeeper performance during free kicks in football'. *PloS ONE*, 15 (12), e0243287.

Vignais, N., Kulpa, R., Craig, C. and Bideau, B. (2010) 'Virtual Thrower vs. real goalkeeper: influence of different visual conditions on performance', *Presence: Teleoperators and virtual environments*, 19, 281–90.

Watson, G., Brault, S., Kulpa, R., Bideau, B., Butterfield, J. and Craig, C.M. (2011) 'Judging the "passability" of dynamic gaps in a virtual rugby environment', *Human Movement Science*, 30 (5), 942–56.

Wickens, C.D. (1992) *Engineering Psychology and Human Performance* (2nd ed.). London: Harper Collins.

6.35 PRACTISING MOTOR SKILLS

Definition: Practice is the deliberate, effortful and repetitive rehearsal of transferable skills, both physical and mental, that are relevant to performance during competition itself.

Whether it be once a week for the local pub team or a daily occurrence as a professional athlete, practice is an integral part of sports performance. While practice schedules can include tactical and strategic planning, rehearsal of the sport specific motor skills tends to be the key component. Several famous sports personalities are renowned for their almost obsessive practice routines, but none more so than Jonny Wilkinson, an English rugby out-half who famously dropped a goal to win England the World Cup in 2003. When writing for *The Times* newspaper in 2008, he reported that each week leading up to a big game:

> I hit about 250 to 300 practice place kicks alone. I average 200 to 250 punts using my left foot and exactly the same number using my right. A daily total of 20 dropped goals with each foot and 15 to 20 restarts, six to seven times a week, would pretty much constitute a solid preparational build-up. … That makes a total of about 1,000 kicks to prepare for just 20 (typical kicks per match). … That's near enough 50 rehearsals for each single defining event. To me that has been a totally acceptable ratio.

Cristiano Ronaldo, LeBron James and the Williams sisters have also been known to put in some gruelling practice routines, but is it the case that repetitive rehearsal of the same skills yields better performance, and how should practice be designed and carried out so as to facilitate the learning process?

When discussing expertise (see **6.33**), the amount of deliberate practice was said to be related to the level of attainment. Repeatedly practising specific actions helps develop those abilities. That being said, it is crucial that practice itself has a structure that is adapted to the learner's current skill level in order to help them improve. Deliberate practice is more than mechanical repetition, it involves slight adjustments to the execution over time, so the player moves ever closer to their goal. For it to be most effective, deliberate practice is often guided by an expert, skilled coach, or mentor, someone who has an expert or trained eye to identify the weaknesses and give feedback. The quality and quantity of feedback allows athletes to understand how to improve as an individual.

In an attempt to understand the relationship between deliberate practice and expertise, Ericsson and his colleagues studied a group of violin students at an elite music academy in Berlin (Ericsson et al., 1993). The study showed that the most accomplished musicians had put in at least 10,000 hours by the time they turned 20 years old and so the rule of around 10,000 hours of practice to become an expert in any given field was born.

The relationship between deliberate practice and performance in sports is a complex one. In an attempt to unpack the relationship and make sense of the many studies on expertise and practice, Macnamara and colleagues carried out a meta-analysis (Macnamara et al., 2016). Surprisingly, their analysis showed that deliberate practice could only account for 18 per cent of the variance found in sports performance. They also noted that this contribution differed depending on the skill level of the athlete, with deliberate practice only explaining one per cent of the variance in performance for experts. This study suggests that deliberate practice cannot account for performance differences even among elite performers. Almost 30 years later, most scientists would now agree, including Ericsson himself, that 10,000 hours is an over-simplification of expertise. There is a general acceptance that it is not strictly the *number* of hours of practice that are important for the development of expertise but rather the actual *structure* and *content* of those practice hours.

Interestingly, the research studies did *not* show a relationship between high performance and the age the athletes started playing their sport. This finding challenges the notion that higher skilled performers tend to start in a sport and specialise at a younger age than lower skilled performers. Data even suggest that early specialisation may do more harm than good, with children who specialise at a young age accounting for over 50 per cent of overuse injuries observed in later life. What does appear to be clear is that coaches acknowledge that a young athlete who played many different sports will have a broader repertoire of motor skills that allows them to perform to a higher level. This along with the contributions of a broad range of other psychological factors, such as motivation and personality, will contribute to success.

Although there is debate around the amount of practice required to improve performance in a competitive context, there is universal agreement that the skills mastered in practice need to transfer to the game or performance setting. This is often hard to ensure, especially for open skills (i.e. skills that are performed in an environment that is unpredictable or in motion and that requires performers to adapt their movements in response to dynamic properties of the environment). How can coaches design a practice session to increase the likelihood that the skills practised will transfer to the game itself?

Coaches often incorporate drills and mini-games into team game practice with a two-fold aim: (a) to practise *how* to perform the skill and (b) *when* to perform the skill, i.e. the assumption that, if a similar situation arises in a game, the appropriate action will be carried out at the appropriate time. There are, however, some observable products of practising motor skills. For example, in terms of control and coordination, research has shown that performers' movements become less stiff and rigid with increased practice (e.g. for racquetball forehand backswings, Southard and Higgins, 1987). Changes in the patterns of muscle activity also occur over time with practice, as shown by EMG studies, such as Moore and Martiniuk (1986) who showed that, with practice, 'co-contraction' (the simultaneous contraction of agonistic and antagonistic muscles) diminishes and the movement pattern shifts to sequential contraction (where agonists and antagonists contract only at the appropriate and necessary times). Such mechanisms result in more efficient movement whereby the energy costs of the movement diminish with practice (Sparrow and Irizarry-Lopez, 1987).

The old adage 'practice makes perfect' is often rephrased by researchers as 'effectively designed practice makes perfect' (Schmidt and Wrisberg, 2004). So, what constitutes effectively designed practice? What rehearsal techniques might be used in order to facilitate the learning experience and how might practice sessions be structured so as to get the best from them? In terms of motor learning, the most important contributor is the act of proper physical rehearsal.

Part practice refers to 'a procedure involving the practice of a complex skill in a more simplified form' (Schmidt and Wrisberg, 2004) whereby complex skills can be: fractioned (e.g. practising only the leg kick in swimming); simplified (e.g. use of an oversized ball in tennis, or performing slow motion movements); or segmented (progressive part practice, e.g. practising the toss, followed by the toss and the racquet swing in the tennis serve). Part practice works best for serial tasks where the actions involved in one part do not influence the actions involved in the next (e.g. passing the baton in a relay race) and is least effective for rapid, discrete actions such as hitting a golf ball.

As well as physical rehearsal techniques, practice can be in the form of mental rehearsal whereby people think through or imagine performing a motor skill in the absence of overt movement (see **4.17** and **4.18**). While evidence suggests that physical rehearsal alone is superior to mental rehearsal when learning movement skills (e.g. Hird et al., 1991), it also suggests that mental rehearsal is always superior to no rehearsal and so may prove useful when supplementing physical practice or when the opportunity to practise physically is unavailable. Furthermore, it is a combination of both mental and physical practice that appears to yield the best results of all.

Newell's Model of Constraints, developed in 1986 (Newell, 1986), provides an excellent theoretical basis from which to design practice sessions. This elegant model suggests that all movements are influenced by the interaction of three main factors: the individual, the environment and the task being performed (Haywood and Getchell, 2009). The theory proposes that if one of these factors changes, the overall movement pattern of the action changes as well (Haywood and Getchell, 2009). In recent years, researchers working in ecological dynamics have taken this theory further to show how a more learner-centred approach to practice will allow new behaviours to emerge as a result of the complex interaction between organism, task and environment. This model is not only important for understanding human motor behaviour but is key to ensuring transfer between practice and the game.

To fully understand the benefits of such an approach it is important to draw the distinction between practice involving isolated activities and practice following a constraints-led approach. When practising an isolated activity, the environment is predictable and the solution is usually prescribed by the coach. Let's take the example of a ball mastery activity in soccer. Isolated practice would involve the players dribbling the ball around a set of cones, while avoiding poles that are supposed to represent opposition players. In this type of activity, the player does have to demonstrate skill to control the movement of the ball to go around the cones – but the poles (representing defending players) do not move. This means the environment is static and predictable so the player does not have to adapt their dribbling technique to accommodate the dynamic changes that may be happening around them. In the game of soccer, the player has to continuously perceive and act according to these changes (e.g. movement of other players, position on the pitch, weather conditions, etc.). A constraints-led approach attempts to address this deficit by designing practice sessions that manipulate the task constraints in a dynamic fashion. In this case the solution emerges implicitly from the player's interaction with the constraints imposed. So, a constraints-led approach to the ball mastery practice session would involve the use of an opposition player as the point of reference for the dribbling activity instead of static poles and cones. Players could assume two different roles, one a tagger and the other a runner. The aim of the runner is to avoid being tagged for 15 seconds and the aim of the tagger is to tag the runner. Both players must be in possession of a football at all times. In this example, the environmental and individual constraints stay the same, but the task constraints have been manipulated. By manipulating the constraints of the task, such as the size of the pitch, the number of defenders, the rules of the game, the opportunities for action or affordances will also change. In addition to the motor act of dribbling a ball, the players have also to tune into, and actively perceive, the dynamics of the constantly changing environment.

Small-sided games represent another example where the constraints of the task can be manipulated, but what about environmental or individual constraints? Prior to the England versus Ireland game in the Six Nations Tournament in 2019, the media were amused to see that the English team were practising throwing and catching soapy balls at their training camp in Portugal. However, on deeper analysis it could be seen that there was method in the supposed madness, with Eddie Jones adopting a constraints-led approach to preparing his players for possible inclement Irish weather. By using slippery balls, he was manipulating the environment and giving his players the opportunity to practise and hone their technique so they would be able to confidently catch and pass a slippery ball if the match was played on a wet day. Other examples include practising passing with a weighted ball. In these cases, the environment is changed, and the player has to learn to adapt the force they use to pass the ball successfully to different targets. Again, the player implicitly adapts their motor behaviour to perform the goal of the movement (i.e. hit the target).

Practice sessions can be structured in many different ways, each of which can influence the learning process. It is important to understand the pros and cons of the main features of a practice session. Should practice be blocked or random? Should it be constant or varied? And finally, how should it be balanced with rest? Imagine a practice schedule for a badminton player that devotes one session to serving, one session to forehand drives, one session to smashes and so on. This is an example of blocked practice – a sequence in which individuals repeatedly rehearse the same task. Compare this to a practice sequence where the badminton player would perform a number of different tasks in no particular order, thus avoiding consecutive repetitions of the same task. This is known as random practice. Research has shown superior learning in random practice as opposed to blocked practice (e.g. Tsutsui et al., 1998). Practically speaking, blocked practice has been shown to be more effective during initial rehearsal but does not promote lasting learning. It is thought that, in blocked practice, athletes fail to practise the target skill within the target context. This is because the practice context does not approximate closely the movement and environmental conditions of the target context, i.e. the specificity of learning.

In sum, repetitions are important in practice, but repetitiveness is ineffective (Schmidt and Wrisberg, 2004). Similar to the notion of blocked practice is that of constant practice. This describes a practice sequence which involves an athlete rehearsing only one variation of a class of tasks in one session. For example, a cricket fielder only practising short throws for run outs. An alternative to this would be the cricket fielder practising not only short throws but long throws from the boundary, thereby rehearsing a number of variations of the given class of task during one session. This is referred to as varied practice. Again, according to the notion of specificity of learning, which advocates learning of specific actions to accomplish specific goals, varied practice would seem logical. It would allow the cricket fielder to use the same generalised motor programme (see **6.32**) and to parameterise dimensions of the action, e.g. select the velocity and force required for a particular throw. This facilitates the development of more effective schemata, namely the sets of rules relating the various outcomes of a person's actions to the parameter values the person chooses to produce those outcomes (Schmidt, 1975). In terms synonymous with a constraints-led approach to motor behaviour, random and varied practice would represent the variability present in the real world, where movement emerges as a result of constantly changing task constraints.

Finally, with the physical and mental demands of rehearsal taking its toll, it is vitally important to balance practice and rest in any training schedule. Researchers have classified practice as being either massed (where the amount of rest between practice attempts or sessions is relatively shorter than the amount of time spent practising) or distributed (rest time is relatively longer than practice time). The effectiveness of each approach depends on the nature of the task in question. For discrete tasks (e.g. shooting a netball), reducing rest time between performances has little or no influence on learning (Lee and Genovese, 1988). Therefore, fatigue during practice sessions is not a problem and repetitions can be increased. For continuous skills (e.g. cycling), reduced periods of rest between performances degrades performances and has a negative and relatively permanent effect on learning. Therefore, ample rest should be taken so as not to generate sloppy performances or, worse still, cause an injury. Energy requirements of the task, or the physical load, should be carefully analysed and practice conditions tailored accordingly. The role of the coach or support staff in an athlete's career is therefore pivotal. Careful thought needs to be given to design an effective practice schedule that helps the athlete achieve peak performance while protecting him or her from potential injury or burnout.

KEY READINGS

Lee, T.D. and Genovese, E.D. (1988) 'Distribution of practice is motor skill acquisition: Learning and performance effects reconsidered', *Research Quarterly for Exercise and Sport*, 59, 277–87.

Macnamara, B.N., Moreau, D. and Hambrick D.Z. (2016) 'The relationship between deliberate practice and performance in sports: A meta-analysis', *Perspective in Psychological Science*, 11, 333–50.

Renshaw, I., Davids, K. and Savelsbergh G.J.P. (2010) *Motor Learning in Practice: A Constraints-Led Approach*. London: Routledge.

Starkes, J.L. and Ericsson, K.A. (eds) (2003) *Expert Performance in Sports: Advances in Research on Sport Expertise*. Champaign, IL: Human Kinetics.

PRACTICAL QUESTIONS

- What are the main differences between a blocked and random practice session? When should you use blocked and when should you use random practice sessions?
- How can the constraints-led approach to practice help explain why small-sided games could help improve team performance?

REFERENCES

Ericsson, K.A., Krampe, R.T. and Tesch-Römer, C. (1993) 'The role of deliberate practice in the acquisition of expert performance', *Psychological Review*, 100 (3), 363–406.

Haywood, K.M. and Getchell, N. (2009) *Life Span Motor Development* (5th ed.). Champaign, IL: Human Kinetics.

Hird, J.S., Landers, D.M., Thomas, J.R. and Horan, J.J. (1991) 'Physical practice is superior to mental practice in enhancing cognitive and motor task performance', *Journal of Sport and Exercise Psychology*, 8, 281–93.

Lee, T.D. and Genovese, E.D. (1988) 'Distribution of practice is motor skill acquisition: Learning and performance effects reconsidered', *Research Quarterly for Exercise and Sport*, 59, 277–87.

Macnamara, B.N., Moreau, D. and Hambrick D.Z. (2016) 'The relationship between deliberate practice and performance in sports: A meta-analysis', *Perspective in Psychological Science*, 11, 333–50.

Moore, S.P. and Martiniuk, R.G. (1986) 'Kinematic and electromyographic changes that occur as a function of learning a time-constrained aiming task', *Journal of Motor Behaviour*, 18, 397–426.

Schmidt, R.A. (1975) 'A schema theory of discrete motor skill learning', *Psychological Review*, 82, 225–60.

Schmidt, R.A. and Wrisberg, C.A. (2004) *Motor Learning and Performance: A Problem Based Learning Approach* (3rd ed.). Champaign, IL: Human Kinetics.

Southard, D. and Higgins, T. (1987) 'Changing movement patterns: Effects of demonstration and practice', *Research Quarterly for Exercise and Sport*, 58, 77–80.

Sparrow, W.A. and Irizarry-Lopez, V.M. (1987) 'Mechanical efficiency and metabolic cost as measures of learning a novel gross motor task', *Journal of Motor Behaviour*, 19, 240–64.

Tsutsui, S., Lee, T.D. and Hodges, N.J. (1998) 'Contextual interference in learning new patterns of bimanual coordination', *Journal of Motor Behavior*, 30, 151–7.

6.36 ANALYSIS AND MEASUREMENT OF MOTOR PERFORMANCE

Definition: Procedures for measuring human movement that are objective, reliable and valid, and that yield results that are transferable from the laboratory to competition.

Peter Drucker famously once said, 'If you can't measure it, you can't improve it'. Although the business guru was talking primarily about the world of commerce, the same quote very much applies to sport. The analysis and measurement of motor performance is an important aspect in both motor behaviour research and sport practice and understandably involves the use of many different technologies. In research, the performance of motor skills is studied scientifically in order to enhance our understanding of the skill and the control of movement. In practice, motor performance is analysed for different reasons, namely performance enhancement, injury prevention or to examine the effects of athletic devices (e.g. protective equipment). Although the aims and objectives outlined are different, the methods and measurements used in both cases are the same. Before describing such methods and measurements it is necessary to address the following questions. What exactly is meant by motor performance and how does it differ from motor learning? What are the criteria for good motor performance measurement systems? And finally, how is the analysis and measurement of motor performance approached?

Schmidt and Wrisberg (2004) defined motor performance as the observable attempt of a person to produce a voluntary action. They also explained how the level of a person's performance is susceptible to fluctuations in temporary factors such as motivation, arousal, fatigue and physical condition. This differs from the definition of motor learning (see **6.32**), put forward by the same authors, which is described as 'Changes in internal processes that determine a person's capability for producing a motor task'. The key difference is that motor performance is observable and motor learning is not. Therefore, anytime you observe an athlete running, kicking a football, swinging a golf club, you are observing motor skills being performed (i.e. motor performance). The fact that motor performance is observable leaves it open to subjective appraisal – we often admire a 'fluid' golf swing or a 'natural' cricket bowling action without being able to describe exactly what it is that makes it so pleasing to watch. One may then ask if everyone finds it pleasing to watch? For scientific study and for detailed analysis, objective, reliable and valid scientific means of measurement are required. These are the criteria which must be considered for any good measurement system, and measuring motor behaviour is no different. Objectivity refers to the extent that two observers evaluating the same performance arrive at the same (or very similar) measurements. For example, in sports such as gymnastics, diving and figure skating, judges often report similar scores due to the strict criteria and scoring systems that they adhere to, even though judgement of the performance appears subjective. On the other hand, measuring the club head speed during a golf swing using a highly accurate electronic measurement system will yield the same measurement regardless of who takes the reading. The measurement of motor performance must be as objective as possible. Reliability, the second consideration, refers to the repeatability of the measurement under similar conditions. In order for measurements to be reliable, sources of variability must be minimised. Using quality recording apparatus and careful procedures will limit variability due to technological error; however, intra-subject variability (variability in the same person performing the same skill repeatedly) is much more difficult to control. Maintaining experimental control in a laboratory setting minimises this variability as researchers can account for variables that may be difficult to control if analysing the same motor performance in a natural setting (e.g. during a golf competition). The final consideration is validity. Validity refers to the extent to which a test or measuring device measures what it is intended to measure and whether or not these measures reflect the underlying construct of interest (Schmidt and Lee, 2005). For example, we would not use a racquet head velocity measurement as a function of ball velocity if we wanted to measure the efficiency of a tennis serve. This relates to the different levels of analysis when considering motor performance, which we will now move on to discuss.

Consider the analysis of a tennis serve once more. For a researcher there are three ways of approaching this analysis. First, they may be interested in describing outcome measures (e.g. the accuracy of the serve in terms of number of serves 'in'). Second, they may be interested in describing the characteristics of the serving action itself (e.g. location of body parts throughout the serving action, the joint angles or the relative timing of body parts to one another). Finally, they may be interested in the role of the central nervous system in movement production (e.g. electromyography (EMG) traces which indicate the electrical activity in a muscle, or electroencephalogram (EEG) traces for brain activity). The remainder of this chapter will deal with describing outcome measures and then focus on methods of capturing and characterising movement itself as this is widely used in the analysis of sports performance. Analysis of sports performance at a neural level is less common due to the intolerance of such techniques when performing large-scale movements.

Research shows that coaches and players, like any other humans, recall fewer than half the important actions and movements that happen during a game. Emotions may run high, with positive and/or negative events overshadowing other tactically relevant actions players may have made. Analysing video recordings of a game can help remove these types of biases and provide a more objective view of what really happened. Many sports, even at amateur level, now record videos of a game and analyse the performance of individual players. They then code the different events that happened during competition (e.g. tackles, passes, shots) and create relevant metrics that describe the frequency of these events. These types of performance analysis tools are usually complemented by Global Positioning System (GPS) technology that provides information on distance covered by players and their top speeds.

The problem with these measures is that they capture individual actions in isolation and fail to account for the dynamics of the competition that influences the action choices the players make. In other words, there is a strong focus on the frequency of certain actions (such as number of tackles) or distances covered but no information on the quality and accuracy of these actions or the context within which those actions took place (e.g. placement of other players, movement of the ball, etc.).

Describing performance outcome measures quantifies the extent to which a movement achieved the goal that was intended. The achievement of such goals is often assessed through measures of accuracy or measures of time and speed. Taking measures of accuracy first, an accurate performance of a skill is one that is performed with minimum error. If a performer's target is taken to mean a particular force, distance, speed or time (e.g. an archer hitting a bulls-eye, a baseball batter connecting with the ball or a weightlifter exerting a certain force) then it is possible to measure deviations from this target (error) throughout a number of movement attempts. Scores can be combined in a number of ways in order to measure and analyse performance. For example, constant error, variable error, total variability, absolute error and absolute constant error can be calculated (for details on how to calculate and interpret these error measurements see Schmidt and Lee, 1999). The most common measures in terms of time and speed that are used in research are Reaction Time (RT) and Movement Time (MT). RT is 'a measure of the time from the arrival of a suddenly presented and unanticipated signal to the beginning of the response to it'. MT is defined as 'the interval from the initiation of the response (end of RT) to the completion of the movement' (Schmidt and Lee, 2005). As discussed in the expertise chapter (see **6.33**), experts are often shown to react faster and to complete movements faster than novices and the basic assumption when looking at such measures is that the performer who can complete a movement in less time or accomplish more in a given amount of time is the more skilful. This tends to apply to sports behaviours where maximising the speed of movement is directly correlated to performance excellence. For example, a 100m sprinter has to react as fast as possible once they hear the gun (i.e. reduce RT to a minimum) and move fastest (i.e. cover 100m in the shortest time (lowest MT). In these cases, RT and MT are direct measures of motor performance and have high validity. In some instances, both measures of accuracy and measures of speed can negatively interact to produce the troublesome 'speed-accuracy trade-off' which describes a common observed phenomenon where precision is sacrificed when attempting to perform a skill more quickly (e.g. kick a penalty in soccer too hard).

When analysing the characteristics of motor performance rather than the outcome measures associated with it, it is first necessary to capture the movement in some way. Following this, motor performance can be observed at different speeds and biomechanical analyses can be performed using kinematic measures (studying the 'pure' movement without taking into account the forces that produced it) and/or kinetic measures (studying motion with respect to the forces that produced it). Such analyses allow researchers to further understand the mechanisms which translate muscular contractions about articulating joints into functional movement such as dancing, performing a triple jump or pitching a baseball. These techniques also allow practitioners to assess technique and performance by acquiring performance markers and feeding back to the athlete.

Human motion analysis and the desire to understand and depict human motion can be traced back through history and has shaped the types of techniques still used today. For instance, Aristotle (384–322 BC) described animals' bodies as mechanical systems in his book *De Motu Animalium* (On the Movement of Animals), Da Vinci's (1452–1519) anatomical drawings depicted the mechanics of jumping while Galileo provided some of the earliest examples of attempts to analyse physiological function mathematically. Borelli (1608–1679) studied the equilibrium of forces in the joints, determined the position of the human centre of gravity and was able to show that inspiration was muscle driven. This work was followed by that of Newton (1642–1727) with his laws of physics and others of equal fame. Two leading figures in terms of depicting motion then emerged in E.J. Marey (1830–1904) and Eadweard Muybridge (1830–1904). Through chronophotography and the use of his 'photographic gun', Marey was able to capture 12 frames of motion per second and used this to depict animal motion. At the same time, Muybridge was using multiple cameras to capture animal locomotion and could display animations through a device called the zoopraxiscope. His techniques were able to prove that during galloping all four of the horse's hooves are airborne. These figures are thought to strongly influence modern-day imaging techniques used to capture motion.

Today, motion capture techniques fall into two categories, direct methods and imaging methods. Direct methods include the use of accelerometers and goniometers – hinged devices which are fitted at the joints and measure the changes in angle between limb segments during movement. However, by far the most widely used methods for measuring and analysing motor performance are imaging techniques, such as video imaging and optoelectronic imaging (Barris and Button, 2008). As mentioned above, video capture, a relatively inexpensive method, is widely used by sport practitioners to analyse performance. Coaches can video individual or team performances and use software to codify relevant aspects of the performance from the video footage. High-speed video capture (more frames per second) and analysis allows a more in-depth (frame by frame) analysis of a particular technique and provides an opportunity for player and coach to analyse performance together, particularly for high-speed actions such as a golf swing or swinging a bat to hit a ball in cricket or baseball. Optoelectronic methods are used widely in both research and practice due to the level of analysis that can be performed. This technique involves fitting markers to limbs and joints in the body. These markers are either reflective (passive) or light emitting (active). Passive marker systems use infrared cameras and reflective markers. Full body motion capture for one person will usually involve somewhere in the region of 40 markers and 12 cameras. Rich data relating to the change of position over time for each individual marker are fed to a computer. From there, detailed analysis of the movement can be performed and outputs produced, such as displacement plots for the elbow during throwing. For kinetic analysis of a movement, this system is often integrated with force plates which can measure the ground reaction force, the centre of pressure and the vertical moment of force generated by standing on or moving across them. The data collected from this motion capture technique can then be used to analyse the kinematics of movement performance or reconstruct human movement to produce realistic motion for computer simulations. This technique is used extensively in animated films and computer game development.

The problem with many of these systems is that they focus on capturing and analysing the actions performed by the athlete without considering the *context* within which these actions were performed. For example, GPS manufacturers often claim to have different metrics that correlate with performance, such as the number of dives to the right or left a goalkeeper makes during a game. The problem with this metric is that it cannot be viewed in isolation (i.e. a dive to the left or right – the action performed) but needs to be considered as a function of how the ball was moving towards the goalkeeper (i.e. the perceptual input). Although still in its infancy, vision-based technology is starting to emerge that captures the complexity of the movement of both players and the ball. More work is still required to extract useful performance metrics that capture how the informational landscape (perception) influences the decisions made by the individual players (action) (Stein et al., 2018). Some metrics such as expected goals (XG – StatsPerform) are starting to emerge, where the performance metric reflects the opportunity a particular action afforded an individual player (i.e. a metric based on the probability that they should have scored that takes into account shot angle, distance from goal, previous performance and an individual player's skill set).

In conclusion, it is evident that the measurement and analysis of motor performance draws on a wide range of techniques that can be applied in an equally wide range of disciplines. As technology and measurement systems advance, the future will only bring more exciting ways of analysing motor performance, all of which will provide more insight and understanding of complex motor performance.

KEY READINGS

Barris, S. and Button, C.A. (2008) 'Review of vision-based motion analysis in sport', *Sports Medicine*, 38, 1025–43.

Bush, M., Barnes, C., Archer, D.T., Hogg, B. and Bradley, P.S. (2015) 'Evolution of match performance parameters for various playing positions in the English Premier League', *Human Movement Science*, 39, 1–11.

Hughes, M., Franks, I.M. and Dancs, H. (eds) (2019) *Essentials of Performance Analysis in Sport*. London: Routledge.

Schmidt, R.A. and Wrisberg, C.A. (2004). *Motor Learning and Performance: A Problem Based Learning Approach* (3rd ed.). Champaign, IL: Human Kinetics.

PRACTICAL QUESTIONS

- Use your mobile phone to video record yourself throwing a ball of paper into a wastepaper basket set at two different distances from you (2m and 5m). Come up with relevant performance metrics that allow you to quantify your performance.
- What are the advantages and disadvantanges of using motion capture technology to understand motor performance?

REFERENCES

Barris, S. and Button, C.A. (2008) 'Review of vision-based motion analysis in sport', *Sports Medicine*, 38, 1025–43.

Schmidt, R., and Lee, T. (1999). *Motor Control and Learning: A Behavioural Emphasis* (3rd ed.). Champaign, IL: Human Kinetics.

Schmidt, R.A. and Wrisberg, C.A. (2004) *Motor Learning and Performance: A Problem Based Learning Approach* (3rd ed.). Champaign, IL: Human Kinetics.

Stein, M., Janetzko, H., Lamprecht, A., Breitkreutz, T. and Zimmermann, P. (2018) 'Bring it to the pitch: Combining video and movement data to enhance team sport analysis', *IEEE Transactions on Visualization and Computer Graphics*, 24, 13–22.

Sport, Mental Health and Wellbeing

Chapter Summary: The positive benefits of sport to mental and physical health have long been recognised and promoted. However, it must also be acknowledged that under certain circumstances sport can be detrimental to mental health and wellbeing, especially if it is taken too far, or if engagement with sport and/or exercise is for the wrong reasons. In this chapter we consider the broader topics of gender, identity and inclusion, before focusing on areas where athletes may need advice or support with their psychological safety and self-care. Key areas include: overtraining and exercise addiction; supporting athletes through injury and retirement; mental health awareness; mental disorder prevalence; resilience; mindfulness; and wellbeing.

7.37 Gender, Diversity and Inclusion 226
7.38 Overtraining and Exercise Addiction 234
7.39 Injury and Retirement 243
7.40 Mental Health Awareness in Sport 251
7.41 Mental Health Disorder in Sport 256
7.42 Resilience 260
7.43 Mindfulness and Wellbeing in Sport 264

7.37 GENDER, DIVERSITY AND INCLUSION

Definitions: The impact of sex (biological and physiological characteristics), gender (socially constructed roles, behaviours and attributes), and minority identity on motivation towards, and engagement with, sport.

For those from minority communities generally, and for many sportswomen in particular, the much heralded 'level playing field' of sport is often more fiction than fact, with a growing number of commentators acknowledging the forces which, over time, have placed obstacles in the path of those with minority status who sought no more than to try to realise their sporting potential, or help others realise that goal. While the literature on gender in sport is extensive, that relating to black and minority ethnic (BAME) community members historically is less well established but equally deserving of attention, and this section aspires to cover both.

It is now widely accepted that androcentrism (i.e. a worldview centred on men) has often tried to airbrush the role played by women out of sport's history (see **1.1**). This is despite the reality that both sexes have played an active role in competition from the time of the ancient Greeks (Miller, 2004). In fact, it was only during the mid to late Victorian era (i.e. from the 1850s onwards) that today's gendered world of sport first truly emerged (Anderson, 2010). At that time women's so-called 'fragility' and femininity were 'protected' by ensuring that women and girls were only permitted to engage in 'lady-like' activities that did not involve undue exertion (i.e. perspiring) or challenge. In this way, it was argued, their reproductive capacity could be safeguarded.

Alongside this undoubted gender bias there also existed a world of sport that, while populated by those from many diverse ethnic backgrounds, has been run predominantly by white men for the benefit of white men. To this day, the under-representation of those from BAME communities in leadership roles in sport, whether as captains, officials, managers, coaches or administrators, remains unacceptably low and, in particular, when set against the playing numbers from these ethnic groups (Bradbury et al., 2018).

Social and cultural identity is multifaceted and while there has been evidence of positive change in sport over the decades, progress in relation to different aspects of identity has been far from uniform. For example, the most recent TIDE Report in relation to gender and racism issues in US sport has moved US Major League Soccer (MLS) to an 'A' for racial hiring practices (the highest grade among all US male professional leagues), but still only a 'C–' for gender hiring practices (Lapchick, 2020), and the profile across all sports remains at best patchy.

SEX AND GENDER IDENTITY

While BAME issues tend to be characterised by under-representation and structural/institutional racism inherent within sporting bodies (e.g. Onuora, 2015), historically gender issues have not only included these types of bias but also the development of gender-specific activities, and the gendered world of sport in which we now live (Allender et al., 2006). For example, while many sports were simply off limits for Victorian girls and women, many other sports were 'adapted' or made safe by limiting either space, speed or contact (e.g. men's basketball/women's netball), or physical contact through use of an implement (field hockey/lacrosse) (Hargreaves, 1994).

Set against this unhealthy historical backcloth, it is encouraging to see that today's participation rates in sport are undoubtedly changing, with many sports now embracing both sexes (e.g. boxing, rugby, cricket, soccer). Soccer in particular has seen increased participation rates and cultural appeal amongst women and girls both in Europe and in the United States, where many view female soccer as culturally (if not more) significant than male football. However, across sport as a whole there continue to be significant differences between the sexes, and there is still some way to travel before genuine gender equality is achieved. In the context of physical activity and exercise generally, the largest increases in participation among women have tended to be in aerobics and fitness/circuit classes, but not necessarily in organised competitive sport. In addition, women remain under-represented in sports' infrastructure, including positions such as coaches, referees, administrators, journalists and leisure managers, and women's sport continues to receive less sponsorship and less media coverage. Coleman and Brooks (2009) found that adolescent boys are still more likely to engage in organised sport and physical activity than girls, and the gap in participation between the sexes continues to grow over the teenage years (Wetton et al., 2013).

As to why, research still shows that young women are likely to encounter more barriers to participation than young men (Sport England, 2006; Wetton et al., 2013), with embarrassment regarding body shape and evaluation of appearance by peers (and especially boys) of particular concern during adolescence (Cockburn and Clarke, 2002; Biddle et al., 2005; Sport England, 2006). Hence, while traditional gender stereotypes may be increasingly challenged there is still evidence to suggest that subtle stereotypical gender roles operate to discourage many girls from entering the world of competitive sport. Sex differences *per se* are unable to account for these trends; instead there is a need to consider the roles that gender roles and gender identity continue to play in determining our sporting attitudes and behaviours.

Looking back, early academic reviews of sex/gender in sport and exercise tended to attribute differences to innate biological distinctions between men and women. 'Sex' is defined by genetically predetermined physiological characteristics, while 'gender' or gender identity refers to cultural customs, roles and expectations associated with being male or female. Although a significant link with biological sex and masculinity/femininity exists, gender identity comprises many elements of personality, including the extent to which the person displays both masculinity and femininity as independent psychological characteristics, or self-identifies as male or female.

In recent years, among young people in particular, there has been growing disquiet regarding the value of a simple and traditional binary distinction between genders, and a call for a more fluid or non-binary acceptance of opportunities for transition between different gender identities across the life cycle. Given the role that biological attributes and physicality in particular play in sport, these debates raise many philosophical, ethical and indeed practical concerns regarding individual rights and choice, along with principles of fair competition and equity. This is most especially true in sports that incorporate tests of physicality and/or strength. Regarding trans issues in particular, the rights of those who are at different stages of transition from transgendered to transsexual continue to raise significant issues for many sports, and these remain far from being resolved satisfactorily (Jones et al., 2017).

In some respects, a related concern is how sport has accommodated the issue of sexual orientation, and including engagement with those from the lesbian, gay and bisexual (LGB) communities. While transgender issues are often conflated with those relating to sexual orientation (i.e. LGB&T), this can serve to cause confusion where priorities may not coincide, and including within sport. For example, while many transgender/transsexual issues relate to participation rights for transgendered and transexual people in men's and women's sports, LGB concerns are more often related to the barriers and prejudices faced by members of these communities across *all* sports (Sartore and Cunningham, 2009), and in particular those that have been characterised by a traditionally 'macho' and anti-gay culture.

At the very least, recent research would argue that definitions of sex, gender identity and sexual orientation must be sufficiently flexible to accommodate considerable variation within and between each category, with categorical discriminations often quite arbitrary. For this reason it seems prudent to accept a more tolerant notion of both sex and gender categorisation, where each individual is seen as comprising a mosaic of male and female biological and socio-cultural components.

Equally, by constantly focusing attention on innate *sex differences*, there is also a danger that *gender similarities* will be disregarded. As Diane Gill (2020: 828) remarks, 'Today, most psychologists look beyond the male-female and masculine-feminine dichotomies to developmental and social cognitive models. That is, how people think males and females differ is more important than how they actually differ.'

While the search for sex/gender differences in sport may persist, the study of gender issues within sport and exercise psychology has shifted considerably over recent years (Knoppers and McDonald, 2010; Gill, 2020). Birrell (2000) argues that the history of sport science, and including sport psychology, can be represented in three stages. Up until the late 1970s, the field is best described as atheoretical. Sport was a man's world and where gender was researched it tended to be directed towards understanding sex or gender roles in sport, differences in traits and motives between men and women, and the role conflict experienced by women who took part in competitive sport. In particular, it was believed that men almost literally ran towards or embraced their sex role stereotype (based on masculinity) through sport while women ran away from their stereotype (based on femininity).

In the late 1970s and 1980s, and influenced by the liberal feminist movement, there was a move away from considering gender as a variable or category and towards understanding gender relations and how personal agency and culture impact on these relations. This was a time when first and second wave liberal feminism led the way in opening new dialogues as to how sport perpetuated masculine values and excluded women, and a time when real change was achieved through civil action. For example, in the US, Title IX of the Education Amendments legislation of 1972 established that no person should be denied access to sports within state-funded schools on grounds of sex, a statute that continues to attract controversy and debate to this day (Dulac, 2008).

From this period emerged the third stage, characterised by more theoretically critical approaches and more diverse methodologies. According to Birrell (2000), four key agenda issues dominate the literature in this final phase: (a) the production of an ideology of male power or hegemony through sport; (b) the media practices through which dominant images of women in sport are reproduced; (c) physicality and sexuality as the 'body sites' for defining gender relations; and (d) the resistance of women to dominant male practices in sport.

While sport studies may have witnessed this sea change over the last 30–40 years, within sport psychology the agenda has moved more slowly (Knoppers and McDonald, 2010). However, the emphasis on studying biological differences between men and women has given way to a broader consideration of gender roles and relationships, with greater prominence afforded to social psychological perspectives that emphasise social constructionist and feminist analyses of gender and sport.

For example, one of the leading proponents in this field, Diane Gill (1994, 2020) has suggested that attention should focus on gender-schematic processing by significant others and how this comes to influence young people's views of sport and exercise (Giuliano et al., 2000). Parents and PE teachers, in particular, will often reinforce stereotypes of boys as being more dominant and as possessing greater physical prowess in comparison with girls, who tend to be described in terms of their appearance and presentation and not their sporting abilities. Over time, such influences will inevitably shape perceptions of the appropriateness of particular activities for boys and girls.

The gendered nature of physical activity throughout life is revealed in many ways, not least in psychological responses to sport participation. Scully et al. (1998) describe a tendency for women to have greater concern with their body as an aesthetic statement while men traditionally have focused more on kinaesthetics (coordination, strength and speed) and physicality. At the same time, evidence grows that body dysmorphic disorder

(BDD), or obsessive preoccupation with bodily defects, is a problem now common among both men and women (see **7.38**), with women often showing greater concern for reducing their size while men seek to increase their bulk.

Among women, it has been argued that a greater emphasis on the female form may go on to foster feelings of social-physique anxiety (SPA), often exacerbated by the proliferation of revealing sportswear (Frederick and Shaw, 1995). Among young men, there is growing evidence of similar concerns (Pope et al., 2002), typified by gym cultures that can promote unhealthy (and sometimes unlawful) techniques for increasing musculature. Previous research has suggested that body image in general has tended to be less positive among women, and is more closely linked to women's overall self-esteem. More recently it has been shown that, for both men and women, significant investment and concern with the *gender ideal* body often reflects in poorer health and wellbeing (Sanchez and Crocker, 2005).

Equally, earlier work considered differences in masculinity or androgyny between those who took part in sport, both men and women, and those who did not. Unsurprisingly it was found that masculinity and sport often go hand in hand, but the superordinate construct that appears to overlap both is *competitiveness*. While men do tend to score higher than women on measures of competitiveness, the gender effect is strongest and most consistent specifically for competitive sport behaviour rather than general achievement. Also, gender differences are less pronounced than differences between athletes and non-athletes of either gender (Gill, 2020).

A second psychological variable which reveals gender differences is self-confidence. In general terms, women tend to have lower expectations of success and to make fewer achievement-oriented attributions than men but a meta-analysis has suggested that gender differences in self-confidence may be in decline, with a key mediating variable being the sex-linked nature of the task (Lirgg, 1991).

Finally, looking to gender-specific issues, and in some respects echoing much earlier Victorian concerns, there continues to be research dealing with how exercise may impact on women's wellbeing, and including the stability of the menstrual cycle. Menstrual irregularities including amenorrhoea (i.e. fewer than one period in the previous six months) and oligomenorrhoea (i.e. a menstrual cycle lasting longer than 35 days) have been associated with sports that combine low body fat with rigorous training regimens, including long-distance running, gymnastics and dance. In a more positive vein, other research has shown the potential benefits of physical exercise for alleviating menstrual cycle disorders (see Daley, 2009), with moderate physical exercise in particular having been shown to be effective in the reduction of various physical and psychological symptoms commonly associated with pre-menstrual syndrome (PMS).

Since the 1970s there has been a plethora of work linking exercise with eating disorders including anorexia and bulimia in both women and men (Petrie and Greenleaf, 2007; Thompson and Trattner Sherman, 2010). This work suggests that athletes may be more likely to develop eating disorders than non-athletes due to an emphasis in certain sports on low body fat and the drive for perfection, especially in 'thinness-demand sports' such as running, gymnastics, ice-skating, dance and diving. Taken together, the evidence suggests that many women, and men, in these sports present with pathological weight control behaviours, display attitudes towards food and dieting which are similar to clinically diagnosed eating disorders, and have coaches who may unwittingly encourage pathogenic weight loss due to their own relatively negative attitudes toward, and limited knowledge about, weight and weight control. The need to raise awareness of these issues remains critical as available evidence, and recent media coverage of several elite sports, including gymnastics, would suggest that, in the absence of professional interventions, the risk remains high and is unacceptable.

MINORITY IDENTITY

While gender has long attracted attention across a number of sport science subdisciplines, it is only much more recently that a similar focus has fallen on longstanding under-representation among other minority groups and including those often characterised as BAME, whether in relation to competitive sport or physical activity more generally. A recent report by Sport England (Sport England, 2020), based on a sample size of 49,000 adults and 57,700 children, revealed that members of the BAME community were far more likely to be physically inactive than those who were classified as white, and were also far less likely to volunteer for coaching, officiating or administrative roles in sport, and enjoy the benefits associated with this engagement.

This confirms findings from other studies highlighting the invisibility of many ethnic groups in mainstream sports such as soccer, and the historical lack of motivation to remedy these deficits (Bradbury et al., 2018; Onuora, 2015).

Partly in response to movements such as Black Lives Matter, it is noticeable how rapidly so many sport organisations and governing bodies are now moving to put in place policies and procedures in relation to equity, inclusion and diversity. However, the acid test will be whether these fine words and principles go on to be reflected in greater opportunities for those from minority communities, and eventually higher levels of engagement and participation.

While a fledgling literature is starting to emerge in sport psychology describing the impact of racism in sport (e.g. Burdsey, 2004), in contrast with gender research, overarching theoretical frameworks are less conspicuous. One potential candidate is Critical Race Theory (CRT), which has already been applied to help understand fan behaviour (see **5.30**). Based originally on Critical Theory, CRT examines society and culture at both a micro and macro level, and how structures and institutions relate to race, law and power, and ultimately the perpetuation of white supremacy. Work based on CRT has been useful in challenging existing hegemonies, and could usefully be applied to the world of sport, where resistance to change so often continues to operate at both a conscious and non-conscious level (e.g. Ratna, 2011).

KEY READINGS

Gill, D. (2020) 'Gender and culture', in G. Tenenbaum and R.C. Eklund (eds), *Handbook of Sport Psychology* (4th ed.). Hoboken, NJ: John Wiley & Sons. pp. 1131–51.

Jones, B.A., Arcelus, J., Bouman, W.P. and Haycraft, A. (2017) 'Sport and transgender people: A systematic review of the literature relating to sport participation and competitive sport policies', *Sports Medicine*, 47, 701–16. https://doi.org/10.1007/s40279-016-0621-y.

Onuora, E. (2015) *Pitch Black: The Story of Black British Footballers*. London: Biteback Publishing.

Sport England (2020) *Sport for All? Why Ethnicity and Culture Matters in Sport and Physical Activity*. London: Sport England.

PRACTICAL QUESTIONS

- What policies and procedures should a governing body have in place to ensure fair participation, and what positive actions should be taken to support these measures?
- To what extent are the playing fields of sport now level for those from minority communities, and what can be done to increase levels of participation among all sections of society?

REFERENCES

Allender, S., Cowburn, G. and Foster, C. (2006) 'Understanding participation in sport and physical activity among children and adults: A review of qualitative studies', *Health Education Research*, 21 (6), 826–35.

Anderson, N.F. (2010) *The Sporting Life: Victorian Sports and Games*. Westport, CT: Praeger.

Biddle, S.J.H., Whitehead, S.H., O'Donovan, T.M. and Nevill M.E. (2005) 'Correlates of participation in physical activity for adolescent girls: A systematic review of recent literature', *Journal of Physical Activity and Health*, 2, 423–34.

Birrell, S. (2000) 'Feminist theories for sport', in J. Coakley and E. Dunning (eds), *Handbook of Sports Studies*. Sage, London. pp. 61–76.

Bradbury, S., Van Sterkenburg, J. and Mignon, P. (2018) 'The under-representation and experiences of elite level minority coaches in professional football in England, France and the Netherlands', *International Review for the Sociology of Sport*, 53 (3), 313–34.

Burdsey, D. (2004) 'Obstacle race? "Race", racism and the recruitment of British Asian professional footballers', *Patterns of Prejudice*, 38 (3), 279–99. doi:10.1080/0031322042000250466.

Cockburn, C. and Clarke, G. (2002) '"Everybody's looking at you!": Girls negotiating the "femininity deficit" they incur in physical education', *Women's Studies International Forum*, 25, 651–65.

Coleman, J. and Brooks, F. (2009) *Key Data on Adolescence 2009* (7th ed.). Brighton: Young People in Focus.

Daley, A. (2009) 'The role of exercise in the treatment of menstrual disorders: The evidence'. *British Journal of General Practice*, 59 (561), 241–242.

Dulac, C. (2008) *A Bibliography of Title IX of the Education Amendments of 1972 and its Impact on Intercollegiate Athletics*. Available at SSRN: https://ssrn.com/abstract=1116692 or http://dx.doi.org/10.2139/ssrn.1116692.

Frederick, C. and Shaw, S. (1995) 'Body image as a leisure constraint: Examining the experience of aerobic exercise classes for young women', *Leisure Science*, 17, 57–73

Gill, D. (1994) 'Psychological perspectives on women in sport and exercise', in D.M. Costa and S.R. Guthrie (eds), *Women and Sport: Interdisciplinary Perspectives*. Champaign, IL: Human Kinetics. pp. 253–84.

Gill, D. (2020) 'Gender and culture', in G. Tenenbaum and R.C. Eklund (eds), *Handbook of Sport Psychology* (4th ed.). Hoboken, NJ: John Wiley & Sons. pp. 1131–51.

Giuliano, T., Popp, K. and Knight, J. (2000) 'Football versus Barbies: Childhood play activities as predictors of sport participation by women', *Sex Roles*, 42, 159–81.

Hargreaves, J.A. (1994) *Sporting Females: Critical Issues in the History and the Sociology of Women's Sport*. London: Routledge.

Jones, B.A., Arcelus, J., Bouman, W.P. and Haycraft, A. (2017) 'Sport and transgender people: A systematic review of the literature relating to sport participation and competitive sport policies', *Sports Medicine*, 47, 701–16. https://doi.org/10.1007/s40279-016-0621-y.

Knoppers, A. and McDonald, M. (2010) 'Scholarship on gender and sport in *Sex Roles* and beyond', *Sex Roles*, 63, 311–23.

Lapchick, R.E. (2020) *The 2020 Racial and Gender Report Card: Major League Soccer*. Orlando, FL: University of Central Florida, TIDES. https://43530132-36e9-4f52-811a-182c7a91933b.filesusr.com/ugd/326b62_b206eccbe5a7467da6b05fcbddda16ea.pdf.

Lirgg, C. D. (1991) 'Gender differences in self-confidence in physical activity: A meta-analysis of recent studies', *Journal of Sport and Exercise Psychology*, 13 (3), 294–310.

Miller, S.G. (2004) *Ancient Greek Athletics*. New Haven, CT: Yale University Press.

Onuora, E. (2015) *Pitch Black: The Story of Black British Footballers*. London: Biteback Publishing.

Petrie, T.A. and Greenleaf, C.A. (2007) 'Eating disorders in sport: From theory to research to intervention', in G. Tenenbaum and R.C. Eklund (eds), *Handbook of Sport Psychology*. London: John Wiley & Sons. pp. 352–78.

Pope, H.G., Phillips, K.A. and Olivardia, R. (2002) The Adonis Complex: How to Identify, *Treat, and Prevent Body Obsession in Men and Boys*. New York: Free Press

Ratna, A. (2011) '"Who wants to make aloo gobi when you can bend it like Beckham?" British

Asian females and their racialised experiences of gender and identity in women's football', *Soccer and Society*, 12 (3), 382–401. doi:10.1080/14660970.2011.568105.

Sanchez, D.T. and Crocker, J. (2005) 'How investment in gender ideals affects well-being: The role of external contingencies of self-worth', *Psychology of Women Quarterly*, 29, 63–77.

Sartore, M.L. and Cunningham, G.B. (2009) 'Gender, sexual prejudice and sport participation: Implications for sexual minorities', *Sex Roles*, 60, 100–13. https://doi.org/10.1007/s11199-008-9502-7.

Scully, D., Reilly, J., and Clarke, J. (1998) 'Perspectives on gender in sport and exercise'. *Irish Journal of Psychology*, 19 (4), 424-438.

Sport England (2006) *Understanding Participation in Sport: What Determines Sports Participation among 15–19 Year Old Women?* London: Sport England.

Sport England (2020) *Sport for All? Why Ethnicity and Culture Matters in Sport and Physical Activity*. London: Sport England.

Thompson, R.A. and Trattner Sherman, R. (2010) *Eating Disorders in Sport*. New York: Routledge.

Wetton, A.R., Radley, R., Jones, A.R. and Pearce, M.S. (2013) 'What are the barriers which discourage 15–16 year-old girls from participating in team sports and how can we overcome them?', *BioMed Research International*. https://doi.org/10.1155/2013/738705.

7.38 OVERTRAINING AND EXERCISE ADDICTION

Definitions: Overtraining involves progressively increasing training to a level that is inappropriate for performance management. Exercise addiction is an excessive and unhealthy dependence on an exercise regime characterised by increasing amounts of exercise, withdrawal symptoms, tolerance and loss of control that may lead to physical, psychological and emotional damage.

Typically, sport is presented as a 'good news story', promoting healthy competition along with a healthy lifestyle. In other words, *mens sana in corpore sano*, or a healthy mind in a healthy body. While this may be true in the majority of cases, there can be a downside to competitive sport and exercise which should not be ignored. This may happen where the reasons for taking part have become unhealthy, and the individual begins to show symptoms that the line has been crossed. For some, what was once a recreation or pastime increasingly resembles an obsession, compulsion or lack of control, and often with dangerous consequences (Adams and Kirkby, 2001, 2002; Jones and Tenenbaum, 2009). Within mainstream psychology, these impulse-control characteristics (often described as cravings, disrupted emotional responses, lack of control and an inability to recognise potential harmful consequences) are interpreted as a sign of addiction (Aiken et al., 2018; Huang and Leung, 2009; Hirschman, 1992).

As one example, the syndrome of overtraining can easily lead to a situation where the body is unable to replenish itself before the next bout of exercise, and the result can be catastrophic, both physically and psychologically. Along with overtraining, related phenomena have been identified including *overreaching*. Overreaching is generally defined as a temporary condition that occurs in response to heavy or intense training loads. While overreaching may lead to short-term but usually recoverable decrements in performance, overtraining is more serious and may have significant long-term consequences. Symptoms of overtraining syndrome include the following: accumulated fatigue; a deterioration in performance; difficulties in training and an absence of motivation; behavioural disorders (irritability, melancholy); sleeping disorders; difficulty in recovery; symptoms of depression; increased occurrence of muscular accidents; and higher sensitivity to infections (Lac and Maso, 2004). Some researchers suggest overtraining syndrome should be regarded as a consequence of non-functional overreaching (Halson and Jeukendrup, 2004; Kenttä and Hassmén, 1998; Urhausen and Kindermann, 2002), with a sense of behavioural control reducing as the syndrome takes hold.

With increasing pressures on top-level athletes to continue to peak for a number of consecutive competitions, and with shorter breaks between competitions and with longer playing seasons, it is likely that the incidence of overtraining will continue to increase over coming years. Halson and Jeukendrup (2004) suggest that this is the case, although they also report that further investigation is necessary to truly understand the nature of the phenomenon. Despite a relative lack of research, studies have reported that one of the most revealing symptoms of overtraining is psychological staleness, accompanied by mood disturbance. Staleness can be reflected in a raft of symptoms that together conspire to detract from optimal performance and which can have long-term consequences on commitment and motivation unless appropriate action is taken.

Overtraining is routinely reported by both elite and non-elite athletes, with figures as high as 64 per cent reported among elite athletes, along with evidence that a history of staleness may increase susceptibility to future risk. Excessive overtraining, when combined with inadequate recovery, injury and even career termination, can make athletes vulnerable to certain mental disorders (Gulliver et al., 2015; Rice et al., 2016). As to the remedy, according to Berger and Tobar (2007: 608), the answer is simple: 'The only proven treatment for staleness is rest.' In reality, this solution may be rather simplistic as for many athletes the core of the problem may lie deeper, for example, where the 'pure' motive for taking part in the sport may have become lost over time as extrinsic factors come to dominate over intrinsic factors, and especially fun and enjoyment (Kremer et al., 2019). In a joint statement from the European College of Sport Science (ECSS) and the American College of Sports Medicine (ACSM) on the prevention, diagnosis and treatment of overtraining syndrome (Meeusen et al, 2013), the psychological symptoms are duly acknowledged, as are the effects of nutrition, biochemistry and physiology on the athlete's continued wellbeing. The statement was welcomed in providing guidance, albeit the authors acknowledged the need for even further research on the topic. A list of 15 considerations for coaches and physicians are provided to manage overtraining, with two psychological suggestions being especially worthy of note:

- 'Communication with the athletes (maybe through an online training diary) about their physical, mental, and emotional concerns is important; and
- Include regular psychological questionnaires to evaluate the emotional and psychological state of the athlete.' (Meeusen et al., 2013)

Beyond overtraining, a wider literature has focused on 'too much' exercise as a problem area in sport. There has been debate about the best term to use: exercise 'addiction', 'adherence' or 'dependence' (Kremer et al., 2011). Berczik et al. (2012) advocate that 'exercise addiction' is used as it incorporates elements of both compulsion and dependence. Elaborating on this definition further, exercise addiction is characterised by increasing amounts of exercise, withdrawal symptoms, tolerance and loss of control (Lichtenstein and Hinze, 2020). Not surprisingly, it is also often linked to related clinical conditions including eating disorders and mood disorders. For many dedicated exercisers a good number of these boxes would easily be ticked, and so the term 'addiction' may not be a misnomer. Also, it is important to recognise that the addiction may be either primary (an end in itself) or secondary (a means to an end, e.g. weight loss, health improvement), and categorising the addiction as either one or the other may be useful in terms of its subsequent treatment.

It is probably no surprise that the first ever study on exercise addiction was conducted with long-distance runners. Interestingly, the author argued that running behaviour was generally positive, and could produce feelings of joy and pleasure (Glasser, 1976). However, it was not long before the negative effects of excessive training also began to be reported (Morgan, 1979). Today, a substantial literature on both the positive and negative facets of exercise addiction is available (e.g. Demetrovics and Kurimay, 2008; Nogueira et al., 2018), involving not only endurance athletes but also triathletes, college athletes and football players.

A measurement scale to assess running addiction has also been developed (Sancho and Ruiz-Juan, 2011). In keeping with later research, Bamber et al. (2000: 131) found that, among both men and women who exercised to excess, those whose exercise was best characterised as *primary* (i.e. exercise for its own sake) did not show greater signs of morbidity in comparison with a control group, while those whose exercise was seen as motivated by *secondary* factors reported higher levels of 'psychological morbidity, neuroticism, dispositional addictiveness, and impulsiveness, lower self-esteem, greater concern with body shape and weight, as well as with the social, psychological, and aesthetic costs of not exercising'. In many ways the psychological profile of these individuals mirrored that which would be characteristic of those with eating disorders (Lichtenstein and Hinze, 2020).

According to several authors, the prevalence of exercise addiction among both men and women ranges from three to 42 per cent depending on the measurement tool and sport type (Lichtenstein and Hinze, 2020). Originally, the literature would have paid greatest attention to those who obviously appear to have suffered through loss of weight, and in particular young women. However, evidence for similar effects in men has emerged, mainly in anaerobic exercise activities, including weightlifting, and these conditions tend to be placed under the more general label of body dysmorphia or body dysmorphic disorder (BDD) (e.g. Corazza et al., 2019), in other words, a mental health condition where a person spends a lot of time worrying about flaws in their appearance, often when flaws are not obvious to others (see **7.37**).

Since the 1970s there has been accumulating evidence to support the existence of a connection between exercise addiction and conditions linked to BDD, including bulimia nervosa and anorexia nervosa (Demetrovics and Kurimey, 2008). For example, Caroline Davis has found a significant relationship between exercise dependence, weight preoccupation and obsessive-compulsive personality traits among eating-disordered women (Davis et al., 1998). Furthermore, the same author revealed a significant relationship between the extent of physical activity and obsessive-compulsiveness in high-exercising women without eating disorders. It is often reported that exercise can act as an analogue for disordered eating where there is a preoccupation with body weight, and when, for example, an athlete is injured or not training for some reason, then eating disorders can quickly appear.

Certain sports that value leanness or low body weight have been linked with disordered eating, including gymnastics, middle/long-distance running, ice skating and dance (Scully et al., 1998). Further, these have also been associated with what was referred to as the Female Athlete Triad (FAT), a syndrome in which eating disorders, amenorrhoea/oligomenorrhoea (i.e. delay or interruption of the menstrual cycle for at least three months) and decreased bone mineral density (osteoporosis and osteopenia) are often linked through the combination of too much exercise and too little weight (see **7.37**).

In 2014, the International Olympic Committee (IOC) published a consensus statement moving beyond the FAT to discuss the dangers of Relative Energy Deficiency in Sport (RED-S). RED-S refers to 'impaired physiological functioning caused by relative energy deficiency, and includes but is not limited to impairments of metabolic rate, menstrual function, bone health, immunity, protein synthesis, and cardiovascular health'. The statement has attracted considerable research and conceptual attention, leading to the consensus statement being further updated in 2018 (De Souza et al., 2014; Mountjoy et al., 2018: 316). The updated version highlights the health consequences of RED-S, including an expanded conceptualisation of the FAT to acknowledge a wider range of outcomes, and how some of these can read across to male athletes. The outcomes include: impaired judgement; decreased concentration; irritability; depression; decreased endurance performance; increased risk of injury; decreased training response; decreased coordination; decreased glycogen stores and decreased muscle strength.

The updated model also recognises that psychological consequences can either precede RED-S or be the result of RED-S (Mountjoy et al., 2018). Among young men there is a growing evidence of a type of BDD which is distinct from that found among women (Phillips and Diaz, 1997). Whereas women may use aerobic exercise to limit their body size and weight, men use anaerobic exercise, including gym work and weightlifting, to increase the size of their bodies, otherwise known as 'reverse anorexia', 'bigorexia' or 'muscle dysmorphia' (Pope et al., 2000; Tod and Lavallee, 2010; Petrie et al., 2014) (see **7.37**).

It is now widely acknowledged that competitive sport at all levels is often associated with the use of illegal Performance and Appearance Enhancing Substances (PAEDs), including Anabolic Androgenic Steroids (AAS) (Henning and Dimeo, 2018; Sjöqvist et al., 2008). Indeed, based on blood and urine testing by the World Anti-Doping Agency (WADA), it has been estimated that around one and two per cent of competitive elite athletes may be using prohibited PAEDs at any one time. Disturbingly, self-report measures portray an even darker picture with 14–39 per cent of elite athletes reporting having used doping substances (de Hon et al., 2015), while data from across five European countries showed that 20 per cent of athletes aged 16–25 years reported having used PAEDs at least once.

These figures are deeply concerning and suggest that there is a lot to be done in terms of advising and supporting athletes, whether in relation to awareness raising, promoting avoidance techniques, or indeed providing psychological support and care after substance misuse (Gilmore et al., 2020). On a more positive note, there is emerging research data to suggest that evidence-based intervention programmes can help and are effective in reducing illegal substance misuse (Ntoumanis et al., 2020; Elbe and Barkousis, 2017).

Over recent years, the term *super-adherer* has begun to appear more frequently in the sport and exercise psychology literature (Clingman and Hilliard, 1987). The term refers to those people who simply cannot give up exercise, who seek out ever more demanding challenges or exertions, and whose lives can become dominated by their quest for the next physical endeavour. Clingman and Hilliard (1987) found that certain personality types were more prevalent among these super-adherers where the motivation to achieve and succeed often bordered on the obsessive.

While super-adherers may be at the end of the exercise spectrum, the reasons why any type of exercise dependence may develop are still not fully understood. In the 1980s and 1990s, the phenomenon of *runner's high* first attracted considerable attention as a potential explanation (Battista, 2004). The mood-enhancing and analgesic properties associated with exercise were found to be linked to naturally occurring chemicals in the brain (endorphins) which exerted an effect similar to opiates. Hence it was suggested that the craving for this endogenous drug drove athletes to continue to *work out*. Evidence supporting this association was however weak, and instead it is now generally accepted that a combination of perspectives based on social (e.g. lifestyle, social identity), psychological (e.g. personality type, personal identity) and physiological (e.g. endorphins, thermogenics) mechanisms may act in combination to make a dependence on exercise less than wholesome (Scully et al., 1998).

Where the individual has developed a dependence on exercise that is unhealthy, it is not surprising that, when the person is deprived of that stimulation for some reason (e.g. through illness, injury, retirement or lockdown due to a viral pandemic), the effects can be traumatic. Research has confirmed this fact, although typically studies are based on short-term deprivation experiments and not longitudinal natural fieldwork. Those who run competitively, for example, have been shown to exhibit disturbed mood states (e.g. increased anxiety, depression, restlessness, guilt) and withdrawal symptoms after no more than one day without exercise (Aidman and Woollard, 2003), and that complete cessation can be linked to even more serious disturbances. This is likely to be especially true where the person's sense of identity is closely linked to their activity and where the removal of that significant aspect of their being requires a major re-evaluation and cognitive reframing.

During the COVID-19 pandemic, the government lockdown in the United Kingdom, as in other countries, forced either a reduction or cessation of competitive sport. Studies have begun to look at the effects of this disruption on the health and wellbeing of sportspeople. For instance, in one survey conducted during lockdown, athletes reported greater anxiety for not being able to exercise than non-athletes, with the higher anxiety levels attributed to their strong sense of having an identity defined by their engagement with sport (Knowles et al., in press). Other unpublished research on the Parkrun Community in the UK during COVID-19 showed that runners across all levels of ability experienced reduced wellbeing and happiness, while also perceiving that their general mental health was adversely affected and that their perceptions of community connectedness were lower during the time that they were unable to participate. At the time of writing, it remains to be seen whether these effects are short or long term – hopefully the former.

KEY READINGS

Gilmore, H., Shannon, S., Leavey, G., Dempster, M., Gallagher, S. and Breslin, G. (2020) 'Help-seeking beliefs among anabolic androgenic steroid users experiencing side effects: An interpretive phenomenological analysis', *Journal of Clinical Sport Psychology*, 1(aop), 1–17.

Meeusen, R., Duclos, M., Foster, C., Fry, A., Gleeson, M., Nieman, D., ... and Urhausen, A. (2013) 'Prevention, diagnosis and treatment of the overtraining syndrome: Joint consensus statement of the European College of Sport Science (ECSS) and the American College of Sports Medicine (ACSM)', *European Journal of Sport Science*, 13 (1), 1–24.

Mountjoy, M., Sundgot-Borgen, J., Burke, L., Ackerman, K.E., Blauwet, C., Constantini, N. and Sherman, R. (2018) 'International Olympic Committee (IOC) consensus statement on relative energy deficiency in sport (RED-S): 2018 update', *International Journal of Sport Nutrition and Exercise Metabolism*, 28 (4), 316–31.

Tod, D. and Lavallee, D. (2010) 'Towards a conceptual understanding of muscle dysmorphia development and sustainment', *International Review of Sport Psychology*, 3 (2), 111–31.

PRACTICAL QUESTIONS

- Participation in sport has many health benefits; however for some athletes knowing when to stop is a challenge. What would you advise a governing body of sport to do if asked about avoiding the dangers of exercise addiction?
- Describe some of the factors that play a part in Relative Energy Deficiency in Sport (RED-S). How important are the psychological factors in determining the onset and persistence of RED-S?

REFERENCES

Adams, J. and Kirkby, R. (2001) 'Exercise dependence and overtraining: The physiological and psychological consequences of excessive exercise', *Research in Sports Medicine*, 10, 199–222.

Adams, J. and Kirkby, R. (2002) 'Excessive exercise as an addiction: A review', *Addiction Research and Theory*, 10, 415–37.

Aidman, E. and Woollard, S. (2003) 'The influence of self-reported exercise addiction on acute emotional and physiological responses to brief exercise deprivation', *Psychology of Sport and Exercise*, 4 (3), 225–36.

Aiken, K.D., Bee, C. and Walker, N. (2018) 'From passion to obsession: Development and validation of a scale to measure compulsive sport consumption', *Journal of Business Research*, 87, 69–79.

Bamber, D., Cockerill, I. and Carroll, D. (2000) 'The pathological status of exercise dependence', *British Journal of Sports Medicine*, 34, 125–32.

Battista, G. (ed.) (2004) *The Runner's High: Illuminations and Ecstasy in Motion*. Halcottsville, NY: Breakaway Books.

Berczik, K., Szabó, A., Griffiths, M.D., Kurimay, T., Kun, B., Urbán, R. and Demetrovics, Z. (2012) 'Exercise addiction: Symptoms, diagnosis, epidemiology, and etiology', *Substance Use & Misuse*, 47 (4), 403–17.

Berger, B.G. and Tobar, D.A. (2007) 'Physical activity and quality of life', in G. Tenenbaum and R.C. Eklund (eds), *Handbook of Sport Psychology* (3rd ed.). Hoboken, NJ: Wiley. pp. 598–620.

Clingman, G.R. and Hilliard, D.V. (1987) 'Some personality characteristics of the super-adherer: Following those who go beyond fitness', *Journal of Sport Behavior*, 10 (3), 123–36.

Corazza, O., Simonato, P., Demetrovics, Z., Mooney, R., van de Ven, K., Roman-Urrestarazu, A., Rácmolnár, L., De Luca, I., Cinosi, E., Santacroce, R., Marini, M., Wellsted, D., Sullivan, K., Bersani, G. and Martinotti, G. (2019) 'The emergence of exercise addiction, body dysmorphic disorder, and other image-related psychopathological correlates in fitness settings: A cross sectional study', *PloS ONE*, 14 (4), e0213060. https://doi.org/10.1371/journal.pone.0213060.

Davis, C., Kaptein, S., Kaplan, A.S., Olmsted, M.P. and Woodside, D.B. (1998) 'Obsessionality in anorexia nervosa: The moderating influence of exercise', *Psychosomatic Medicine*, 60 (2), 192–7.

de Hon, O., Kuipers, H. and van Bottenburg, M. (2015) 'Prevalence of doping use in elite sports: a review of numbers and methods', *Sports Medicine*, 45 (1), 57–69. doi: 10.1007/s40279-014-0247-x. PMID: 25169441.

Demetrovics, Z. and Kurimay, T. (2008) 'Exercise addiction: A literature review', *Psychiatria Hungarica*, 23 (2), 129.

De Souza, M.J., Nattiv, A., Joy, E., Misra, M., Williams, N.I., Mallinson, R.J., … and Matheson, G. (2014) 'Female Athlete Triad Coalition Consensus Statement on treatment and return to play of the female athlete triad: 1st International Conference held in San Francisco, California, May 2012 and 2nd International Conference held in Indianapolis, Indiana, May 2013', *British Journal of Sports Medicine*, 48 (4), 289.

Elbe, A.M. and Barkoukis, V. (2017) 'The psychology of doping', *Current Opinion in Psychology*, 16, 67–71, https://doi.org/10.1016/j.copsyc.2017.04.017.

Gilmore, H., Shannon, S., Leavey, G., Dempster, M., Gallagher, S. and Breslin, G. (2020) 'Help-seeking beliefs among anabolic androgenic steroid users experiencing side effects: An interpretive phenomenological analysis', *Journal of Clinical Sport Psychology*, 1, 1–17.

Glasser, W. (1976) *Positive Addiction*. Oxford: Harper & Row.

Gulliver, A., Griffiths, K.M., Mackinnon, A., Batterham, P.J. and Stanimirovic, R. (2015) 'The mental health of Australian elite athletes', *Journal of Science and Medicine in Sport*, 18 (3), 255–61.

Halson, S.L. and Jeukendrup, A.E. (2004) 'Does overtraining exist? An analysis of overreaching and overtraining research', *Sports Medicine*, 34 (14), 967–81.

Henning, A.D. and Dimeo, P. (2018) 'The new front in the war on doping: Amateur athletes', *International Journal of Drug Policy*, 51, 128–36.

Hirschman, E.C. (1992) 'The consciousness of addiction: Toward a general theory of compulsive consumption', *Journal of Consumer Research*, 19 (2), 155–79.

Huang, H., and Leung, L. (2009) 'Instant messaging addiction among teenagers in China: Shyness, alienation, and academic performance decrement', *CyberPsychology and Behavior*, 12 (6), 675–9.

Knowles, C., Shannon, S., Prentice, G. and Breslin, G. (in press) 'Comparing mental health of athletes and non-athletes as they emerge from the COVID-19 pandemic lockdown', *Frontiers in Psychology*.

Jones, C.M. and Tenenbaum, G. (2009) 'Adjustment disorder: A new way of conceptualising the overtraining syndrome', *International Review of Sport Psychology*, 2 (2), 181–97.

Kenttä, G. and Hassmén, P. (1998) 'Overtraining and recovery', *Sports Medicine*, 26 (1), 1–16.

Kremer, J., Moran, A.P. and Kearney, C. J. (2019) *Pure Sport: Sport Psychology in Action*. London: Routledge.

Kremer, J.M., Moran, A., Walker, G. and Craig, C. (2011) *Key Concepts in Sport Psychology*. London: SAGE.

Lac, G. and Maso, F. (2004) 'Biological markers for the follow-up of athletes throughout the training season', *Pathologie-Biologie*, 52 (1), 43–9.

Lichtenstein, M.B. and Hinze, C.J. (2020) 'Exercise addiction', in C.A. Essau and P. Delfabbro (eds), *Adolescent Addiction: Epidemiology, Assessment and Treatment*. Amsterdam: Academic Press. pp. 265–88.

Meeusen, R., Duclos, M., Foster, C., Fry, A., Gleeson, M., Nieman, D., … and Urhausen, A. (2013) 'Prevention, diagnosis and treatment of the overtraining syndrome: Joint consensus statement of the European College of Sport Science (ECSS) and the American College of Sports Medicine (ACSM)', *European Journal of Sport Science*, 13 (1), 1–24.

Mountjoy, M., Sundgot-Borgen, J., Burke, L., Ackerman, K.E., Blauwet, C., Constantini, N., … and Sherman, R. (2018) 'International Olympic Committee (IOC) consensus statement on relative energy deficiency in sport (RED-S): 2018 update', *International Journal of Sport Nutrition and Exercise Metabolism*, 28 (4), 316–31.

Morgan, W. P. (1979) 'Negative addiction in runners', *The Physician and Sports Medicine*, 7 (2), 55–77.

Nogueira, A., Molinero, O., Salguero, A. and Márquez, S. (2018) 'Exercise addiction in practitioners of endurance sports: A literature review', *Frontiers in Psychology*, 9, 1484. https://doi.org/10.3389/fpsyg.2018.01484.

Ntoumanis, N., Quested, E., Patterson, L., Kaffe, S., Backhouse, S.H., Pavlidis, G., … and Gucciardi, D.F. (2020) 'An intervention to optimise coach-created motivational climates and reduce athlete willingness to dope (CoachMADE): A three-country cluster randomised controlled trial', *British Journal of Sports Medicine*.

Phillips, K.A. and Diaz, S.F. (1997) 'Gender differences in body dysmorphic disorder', *Journal of Nervous and Mental Disease*, 185 (9), 570–7.

Pope, H.G., Phillips, K.A. and Olivardia, R. (2000) *The Adonis Complex: The Secret Crisis of Male Body Obsession*. New York: Free Press.

Rice, S.M., Purcell, R., De Silva, S., Mawren, D., McGorry, P.D., and Parker, A.G. (2016) 'The mental health of elite athletes: A narrative systematic review', *Sports Medicine*, 46 (9), 1333–53.

Petrie, T., Galli, N., Greenleaf, C., et al. (2014) 'Psychosocial correlates of bulimic symptomatology among male athletes', *Psychology of Sport and Exercise*, 15, 680–7.

Sancho, A.Z. and Ruiz-Juan, F. (2011) 'Psychometric properties of the Spanish version of the Running Addiction Scale (RAS)', *Spanish Journal of Psychology*, 14 (2), 967.

Scully, D., Kremer, J., Meade, M.M., Graham, R. and Dudgeon, K. (1998) 'Physical exercise and psychological well-being: A critical review', *British Journal of Sports Medicine*, 32, 111–20.

Sjöqvist, F., Garle, M. and Rane, A. (2008) 'Use of doping agents, particularly anabolic steroids, in sports and society', *The Lancet*, 371 (9627), 1872–82.

Tod, D. and Lavallee, D. (2010) 'Towards a conceptual understanding of muscle dysmorphia development and sustainment', *International Review of Sport Psychology*, 3 (2), 111–31.

Urhausen, A. and Kindermann, W. (2002) 'Diagnosis of overtraining: What tools do we have?', *Sports Medicine*, 32 (2), 95–102.

7.39 INJURY AND RETIREMENT

Definition: Those occasions where an athlete is either compelled to give up sport through physical injury on a permanent or temporary basis, or chooses to disengage from sport through voluntary retirement.

Recent years have seen a rapid acceleration in the globalised marketing of sport, and increasingly where sport has come to be viewed and treated as a multinational business. It was reported that David Beckham's departure from Real Madrid cost the Spanish soccer giants between £24 and £30 million in shirt and ticket sales alone. Increasingly, it would appear that sports stars are now brands, but when one considers the apparent increase in the incidence of serious injury in elite level sport (Orchard and Seward, 2002), it becomes obvious just how fragile and transitory these brands can be. It is a truism that any athlete is only ever one misstep away from a career-threatening or career-ending injury.

In the modern and commercial world of professional sport, monitoring of injury is important for many reasons, not only to guard valuable business assets but also to protect the welfare of athletes from exploitation and abuse. In this environment it is not surprising that a number of National and Organisational Monitoring Systems (NOMS) have been established to ensure standards are maintained in relation to safe equipment, environments, training procedures and policies to protect the athlete (Appaneal and Habif, 2013).

What is noteworthy in the majority of these established monitoring systems is not the presence of technical policies and procedures regarding safety in training/playing, but the *absence* of concern for psychological factors (Ljungqvist et al., 2009), although there are hopeful signs that this is beginning to change.

Why should we bother? The answer is straightforward – research on psychological factors such as the relationship between stress-illness and injury provides valuable insight as to how injury occurs, what factors may precipitate an injury and, in turn, how injuries can be prevented (e.g. Bramwell et al., 1975; Holmes, 1970; Mathema et al., 2016). As the evidence builds, so opportunities for interventions can also be developed. How then do athletes cope with the spectre of injury, and what can psychologists do to overcome the difficulties associated with it? In light of these questions it is important to consider the psychological effects of failing to return from injury, that is, those injuries that ultimately lead to athlete retirement.

The first issue to be addressed is the psychological effects of experiencing an injury. Initially, this area was influenced by one of the seminal psychological theories, Kubler-Ross's Stage Theory of Grief (1969). This theory describes the five stages associated with the grieving process. In particular, Kubler-Ross examined responses to the diagnosis of terminal illness. The five proposed stages of grief are: denial; anger; bargaining; depression; and acceptance.

Although primarily concerned with bereavement, the theory grew in popularity throughout the 1980s and 1990s as a way of understanding the psychological effects of injury as a response to a traumatic loss of functioning. Initial enthusiasm has now dampened as emerging empirical evidence has cast doubt on the notion of a universal and sequential psychological response to sport injury. Indeed, some have questioned the presence of either *denial* or *bargaining* in typical athlete responses to injury. With the benefit of hindsight, it certainly would appear quite a leap of faith to uniformly apply a theory associated with terminal illness to every possible injury an athlete may experience, no matter the severity.

Offering an alternative, Cognitive Appraisal Models have been shown to be more effective in considering the role of injury severity – specifically, they outline the process by which an individual assesses their ability to cope with a situation, in this instance, injury. The first step, *primary appraisal*, involves the individual coming to an understanding of the possible implications of the situation they find themselves in. It is reasonable at this point to suggest that an athlete experiencing a groin strain will experience different emotions from one with a serious knee ligament injury. What follows, *secondary appraisal*, is the process by which the individual assesses the viability of the coping strategies available. The net result of these appraisals will inform how the individual feels about the situation and, ultimately, the behaviours exhibited.

By way of compromise, Wiese-Bjornstal et al. (1998) have outlined a sport-specific model that seeks to accommodate elements of both the Grief Stages and the Cognitive Appraisal Models. In their Integrated Stress Process Model, they suggest that, while cognitive appraisal may influence emotional response, which in turn may influence behaviour, these relationships are better characterised as bi-directional and circular, for example, behaviour may influence cognition just as much as cognitions may influence behaviour. The role of grief in this model is related to the loss of identity that may accompany a negative appraisal, leading to the emotions associated with grief.

Additional to this, the suggestion is also made that personal and situational factors must be taken into account when understanding cognitive appraisals. This model has helped facilitate research into the responses associated with injury (e.g. Walker et al., 2007). In their comprehensive review of the literature, Wiese-Bjornstal et al. (1998) cite numerous studies pointing to emotional responses including tension, anger, depression, frustration and boredom. They also point to the importance of behavioural responses, including adherence to rehabilitation programmes and their subsequent impact on recovery. However, as Walker et al. (2007) report, exact processes still remain unclear: for example, outlining which emotions lead to which behaviours. In truth this is unsurprising when the myriad of factors that may influence an athlete's reaction to injury are taken into account.

The undoubted strength of the models proposed thus far lies in the structure they provide for practitioners assessing and treating athletes experiencing injury. In a similar vein, Anderson's (2001) biopsychosocial model provides a comprehensive framework within which five sets of factors are seen to affect *intermediate biological outcomes*, which in turn impact on rehabilitation outcomes. The five categories are: injury type; socio-demographic factors (including age and experience); biological factors (including sleep, tissue repair, etc.); psychological factors (including affect and behaviour); and social factors (including social support and rehabilitation support). The relationships between these factors are complex and interactive; that is, no factor stands alone, each affects the other and the net result of these interactions will affect rehabilitation outcomes. The strength of this model for practitioners is that it provides a comprehensive framework for assessing various life domains, their relationships and, ultimately, particular responses to injury by the athlete that may require specific types of tailored intervention.

This leads naturally to the question, 'What actually can be done to help athletes experiencing injury?' The answer very much depends on which factors are of primary concern. In terms of managing the social factors associated with injury, Podlog and Eklund (2007) highlight the danger of athletes losing the sense of relatedness or identity that they may have previously derived from their sport. This may come in terms of isolation from others involved in their sport, a perceived lack of attention from managers and feelings of isolation associated with missing familiar routines. The implications of these findings are clear for those in a position to offer support. Coaches, physiotherapists and psychologists are all well placed to provide the injured athlete with social support. Additionally, it has been suggested that isolation may lead to a premature return, which may ultimately lead to reinjury. In such cases, social support as well as appropriate goal-setting and realistic expectations appear important.

These findings relate to another important area of injury management as highlighted by Podlog and Eklund (2007) – the *pressure* to return from injury. It is the case that athletes may not always feel psychologically prepared to return from injury at the time of their physical recovery. However, it has been reported that often athletes experience feeling under pressure to return before they are ready, either physically or mentally. One reason that athletes may succumb to the temptation to return early is that they have invested heavily in their athletic identity, to the point that they view a prompt return from injury as a duty. Podlog and Eklund document numerous counterproductive outcomes from a premature return from injury, including poor motivation, tentative play, lowered confidence and reinjury. Again, powerful implications for the design of interventions may be drawn. More recently, the significant effect of the athlete's own personality, and specifically *perfectionism*, can play in returning to sport prematurely after injury. Perfectionism has been one of the most widely studied personality characteristics in sport psychology, consisting of various components including: setting high standards; feeling concern over mistakes; and being highly organised. On the face of it, perfectionism can be seen as a positive characteristic, but unfortunately it is probably better described as double edged. *Self-oriented perfectionism* is the degree to which a person sets high personal standards and stringently self-evaluates relative to those standards, while *socially prescribed perfectionism* is the degree to which the person perceives that significant others hold high standards for him/herself and bases approval on meeting those standards. Depending on the specific components characterising a perfectionistic personality, perfectionism can lead to highly positive adaptive behaviours or extremely negative maladaptive behaviours, often with drastic consequences. In many cases, reminding athletes that it is okay not to be perfect or to be too hard on themselves can reduce distress or high expectations on return to sport. Furthermore, structured goal-setting programmes (see **3.12**), incorporating techniques such as successive approximation, should assist the athlete in gradually building confidence while at the same time ensuring that the return to sport is not rushed (Cox, 2002).

A common theme in much of the intervention literature highlights the danger of athletes developing negative cognitions associated with their injuries, particularly in terms of a fear of reinjury or a loss of confidence. Again, there are now interventions available to practitioners for dealing with such difficulties. These include systematic desensitisation along with the use of visualisation techniques. Such approaches would appear to sit well within cognitive behavioural therapy approaches to managing negative cognitions, and also represent an area ripe for future research.

A further suggestion concerns the accumulation and promulgation of this knowledge in order to lead to a more preventative rather than reactive approach to injury management. Coach and athlete education regarding the common pitfalls associated with injury will hopefully lead to proactive injury management strategies designed to ensure that negative outcomes are avoided (Evans, 2016). One major shortcoming of the literature as it stands is the relative reliance on anecdotal and case-study evidence. The development of large-scale longitudinal empirical studies that incorporate psychological factors and profiling is a challenge that still faces the field.

In keeping with this work, recent years have seen an increasing focus on the management of the return to competition. It would appear that there is much overlap between successful management of the rehabilitation process and the psychological readiness to return to competition. However, there are specific concerns that should be addressed post-rehabilitation. Taylor and Taylor (1997) suggest a *stage-based approach* to return to competition. The five stages they suggest are: initial return; recovery confirmation; return of physical and technical abilities; high intensity training; and the return to competition. Although this model does provide a structure for the athlete returning from injury, as well as a vehicle for exploring fears surrounding the return, it is perhaps too linear and sequential to allow for the accommodation of individual differences. Instead, Podlog and Eklund (2007) suggest a checklist that could be used to ensure athletes are ready to return. This checklist consists of discussion of prospective return dates; approval from sports medicine specialists; assessment of injury related cognitions; and deciding who will make the final decision that the athlete is ready to return to competition.

While the return to sport may be a difficult transition, it is perhaps not surprising that the failure to ever return can be even more traumatic. It is reported that an involuntary retirement can lead to feelings of depression, as well as anger and anxiety. These difficulties may be further compounded by a lack of preparedness for retirement (Wylleman et al., 2004). This is not to say that all retirements are traumatic – research suggests that only around 13–15 per cent fall into this category (Alfermann, 1995) but it is worth noting the particular difficulties that retirement due to injury may bring. While early research tended to highlight the negative outcomes that may be associated with retirement, it is now viewed as a transitional process that, if well managed, can in fact be a positive experience (Lavallee et al., 2012). According to the guidelines laid down by the European Commission, the Lifespan Model of Athletes' Career Transitions (Wylleman and Lavallee, 2004), more recently referred to as the Holistic Athlete Career Model (Wylleman and Rosier, 2016), provides an appropriate framework to interpret an athlete's psychosocial development.

The Holistic Athlete Career Model argues that an athlete develops in multiple life domains concurrently. The emphasis of this model is not solely on athletic development; it is much broader in scope, incorporating vocational, psychological, psychosocial and financial factors. While this model is to be commended, there are nevertheless gaps, including a consideration of the critical role played by the organisation and environment within which the athlete is supported (Breslin et al., 2019).

In recent years, it has been shown that athletes involved in dual career programmes tend to fare better than those who do not in terms of their health, development, social identity and future employment prospects (see Table **7.1**). A 'dual career' is defined as being successful on the national or international stage in sport while maintaining or completing compulsory education with necessary grades to facilitate further study or higher education. The European Commission (2012) has provided guidelines on supporting athlete dual career development that include the model described below. Within ten years there has been a significant increase in dual career research, thereby establishing an evidence base as to how best to protect and support athletes pre- and post-retirement, but there still remains plenty of work to do, in particular looking at how the guidelines have been implemented in practice.

Table 7.1 Athlete Benefits of Having a Dual Career (adapted from Breslin et al., 2019)

Health-related benefits	Balanced lifestyle, reduced stress levels, increased wellbeing
Developmental benefits	Better conditions to develop life skills applicable in sport, education and other spheres of life, development of personal identity, positive effects on athletes' self-regulation abilities
Social benefits	Positive socialisation experiences such as expanded social networks and social support systems with better peer relationships
Benefits related to athletic retirement and adaptation in life after sport	Better career/retirement planning, shorter adaptation period, prevention of identity crisis
Enhanced future employment prospects	Higher employability and access to paid employment.

The adoption of dual careers for athletes implicitly supports a 'whole person' or holistic approach to athlete development and wellbeing (Stambulova and Wylleman, 2019). Indeed, without an emphasis on life outside sport then, almost by definition, a narrow or unidimensional social identity will result, an identity that is unlikely to protect an athlete's mental health and wellbeing in the longer term (Breslin et al., 2017).

One practical way of successfully transitioning in sport is revealed in the recent trend for elite-level athletes to *relocate* in their sport, whether this is through playing a role in coaching, youth development or work in the media (Torregrosa et al., 2004). This trend may reflect the growth of retirement preparation programmes (see Wylleman et al., 2004 for a review), and the recognition that athletic retirement should not be viewed in isolation but instead placed in the context of a realignment of other life domains (Wylleman et al., 2004). An example of this is the recent initiative by UEFA to fund dual career football academies for national youth players, where academic achievement as well as sporting performance is supported.

Murphy (1995) highlights the key areas of self-identity, social and emotional support, coping skills and a sense of control as the main concerns facing the retiring athlete. Similar to the injured athlete, a retiring athlete with a unidimensional athletic identity appears more likely to experience difficulties (Cecic Erpic et al., 2004). Perhaps unsurprisingly, it is also reported that athletes who feel they have achieved their career goals are more likely to adapt successfully to retirement (Cecic Erpic et al., 2004). The implications for athletes experiencing a career-ending injury appear clear. They may lack a sense of control, they may not have achieved their career goals, they may have not made the decision of their own volition, and they may be totally unprepared for a life beyond sport. When set alongside the difficulties that may be associated with the initial injury as previously discussed, it becomes apparent that this set of circumstances brings serious challenges to the athlete. In these situations, there is likely to be a need for psychological intervention, for example through cognitive restructuring, or for the sport itself to take responsibility for long-term career planning of its retired athletes (Wylleman et al., 2004; Breslin et al., 2019).

While elite-level sport may be increasingly viewed as big business, the potentially negative reactions to injury and retirement suggest that sport continues to provide a strong sense of identity and purpose for athletes who are fit, healthy and still performing. At the same time, this commitment means that inappropriately managed injuries and retirements may bring with them negative psychological effects. Fortunately, much progress has been made in understanding these difficulties, and in highlighting the positive management steps that can be taken to assist athletes in developing a life beyond.

KEY READINGS

European Commission (2012) *EU Guidelines on Dual Careers of Athletes Recommended Policy Actions in Support of Dual Careers in High Performance Sport*. Brussels: European Commission.

Ljungqvist, A., Jenoure, P., Engebretsen, L., Alonso, J.M., Bahr, R., Clough, A., ... and Meeuwisse, W. (2009) 'The International Olympic Committee (IOC) Consensus Statement on periodic health evaluation of elite athletes', *British Journal of Sports Medicine*, 43 (9), 631–43.

Mathema, P., Evans, D., Moore, I.S., Ranson, C. and Martin, R. (2016) 'Concussed or not? An assessment of concussion experience and knowledge within elite and semi-professional rugby union', *Clinical Journal of Sport Medicine*, 26 (4), 320–5.

Stambulova, N.B. and Wylleman, P. (2019) 'Psychology of athletes' dual careers: A state-of-the-art critical review of the European discourse', *Psychology of Sport and Exercise*, 42, 74–88.

PRACTICAL QUESTIONS

- Injury and transition can be stressful for athletes. Applying one of the models described above, what support can you provide for an athlete, and who would provide that support?
- What are the benefits of supporting an athlete's dual career, and what could be some of the challenges in convincing athletes and coaches of these benefits?

REFERENCES

Alfermann, D. (1995) 'Career transitions of elite athletes: Drop-out and retirement', in R. Vanfraechem-Raway and Y. Vanden Auweele (eds), *Proceedings of the Ninth European Congress of Sport Psychology. Brussels: European Federation of Sports Psychology FEPSAC*. pp. 828–33.

Anderson, M.B. (2001) 'Returning to action and the prevention of future injury', in J. Crossman (ed.), *Coping with Sports Injuries: Psychological Strategies for Rehabilitation*. Oxford: Oxford University Press. pp. 162–73.

Appaneal, R.N. and Habif, S. (2013) 'Psychological antecedents to sport injury', in M. Arvinen-Barrow and N.C. Walker (eds), *The Psychology of Sport Injury and Rehabilitation. London: Routledge*. pp. 6–22.

Bramwell, S.T., Masuda, M., Wagner, N.N., and Holmes, T.H. (1975) 'Psychosocial factors in athletic injuries: Development and application of the social and athletic readjustment rating scale (SARRS)', *Journal of Human Stress*, 1 (2), 6–20.

Breslin, G., Ferguson, K., Shannon, S., Haughey, M.T. and Connor, M.S. (2019) *Player Transition Out of Football to Protect Wellbeing: A Dual Career Identity Study*. Nyon, Switzerland: UEFA.

Cecic Erpic, S., Wylleman, P. and Zupancic, M. (2004) 'The effect of athletic and non-athletic factors on the sports career termination process', *Psychology of Sport and Exercise*, 5, 45–59.

Cox, R. (2002) 'The psychological rehabilitation of a severely injured rugby player', in I. Cockerill (ed.), *Solutions in Sport Psychology. London: Thomson*. pp. 159–72.

European Commission (2012) *EU Guidelines on Dual Careers of Athletes Recommended Policy Actions in Support of Dual Careers in High Performance Sport*. Brussels: European Commission.

Evans, L. (2016) 'Returning to sport after serious injury: A case study of a professional rugby union player', in S. Cotterill, N. Weston and G. Breslin (eds), *Sport and Exercise Psychology: Practitioner Case Studies*. John Wiley & Sons. pp. 93–110.

Holmes, T.H. (1970) *Psychological Screening in Football Injuries*. Washington, DC: National Academy of Sciences. pp. 211–14.

Kubler-Ross, E. (1969) *On Death and Dying*, London: Tavistock.

Ljungqvist, A., Jenoure, P., Engebretsen, L., Alonso, J.M., Bahr, R., Clough, A., ... and Meeuwisse, W. (2009) 'The International Olympic Committee (IOC) Consensus Statement on periodic health evaluation of elite athletes March 2009', *British Journal of Sports Medicine,* 43 (9), 631–43.

Lavallee, D., Kremer, J., Moran, A.P. and Williams, M. (2012) *Sport Psychology: Contemporary Themes*. London: Palgrave Macmillan. pp. 209–32.

Mathema, P., Evans, D., Moore, I. S., Ranson, C., and Martin, R. (2016) 'Concussed or not? An assessment of concussion experience and knowledge within elite and semiprofessional rugby union', *Clinical Journal of Sport Medicine*, 26 (4), 320–5.

Murphy, S.M. (ed.) (1995) *Sport Psychology Interventions*. Champaign, IL: Human Kinetics.

Orchard, J. and Seward, H. (2002) 'Epidemiology of injuries in the Australian Football League, seasons 1997–2000', *British Journal of Sports Medicine*, 36, 39–44.

Podlog, L. and Eklund, R.C. (2007) 'The psychosocial aspects of a return to sport following serious injury: A review of the literature from a self-determination perspective', *Psychology of Sport and Exercise*, 8, 535–66.

Taylor, J. and Taylor, S. (1997) *Psychological Approaches to Sports Injury Rehabilitation.* Gaithenburg, MD: Aspen Publications.

Stambulova, N.B. and Wylleman, P. (2019) 'Psychology of athletes' dual careers: A state-of-the-art critical review of the European discourse', *Psychology of Sport and Exercise*, 42, 74–88.

Torregrosa, M., Boixados, M., Valiente, L. and Cruz, J. (2004) 'Elite athletes' image of retirement: The way to relocation in sport', *Psychology of Sport and Exercise*, 5, 35–43.

Walker, N., Thatcher, J. and Lavallee, D. (2007) 'Psychological responses to injury in competitive sport: A critical review', *Royal Society for the Promotion of Health*, 127 (4), 174–80.

Wiese-Bjornstal, D.M., Smith, A.M., Shaffer, S.M. and Morrey, M.A. (1998) 'An integrated model of response to sport injury: Psychological and sociological dynamics', *Journal of Applied Sport Psychology*, 10, 46–69.

Wylleman, P. and Lavallee, D. (2004) 'A developmental perspective on transitions faced by athletes', in M. Weiss (ed.), *Developmental Sport Psychology: A Lifespan Perspective.* Morgantown, WV: Fitness Information Technology. pp. 503–23.

Wylleman, P. and Rosier, N. (2016) 'Holistic perspective on the development of elite athletes', in *Sport and Exercise Psychology Research.* Cambridge, MA: Academic Press. pp. 269–88.

Wylleman, P., Alfermann, D. and Lavallee, D. (2004) 'Career transitions in sport: European perspectives', *Psychology of Sport and Exercise*, 5, 7–20.

Wylleman, P., Reints, A., and De Knop, P. (2013) 'A developmental and holistic perspective on the athletic career', in L. Wei (ed.), *Abstracts of the ISSP 13th World Congress of Sport Psychology. Beijing: ISSP – Beijing Sport University*. p. 2.

7.40 MENTAL HEALTH AWARENESS IN SPORT

Definition: 'Mental health is not merely the absence of illness, but a state of well-being in which those involved in competitive sport realise their purpose and potential, can cope with competitive sport demands and normal life stressors, can work productively and fruitfully, can act autonomously according to their personal values, are able to make a contribution to their community and feel they can seek support when required' (Breslin et al., 2019: 4).

Sport participation can bring a lot of pleasure, enjoyment and personal happiness to many people, along with a sense of identity, community connectedness and long-enduring friendships. It is these positive experiences and opportunities that may help explain why we continue to participate and invest so much time and energy in sport (Breslin and Leavey, 2019). The health and wellbeing benefits of sport participation, and particularly those associated with physical activity, are scientifically well-established (Biddle et al., 2015), and the promotion of exercise and its benefits are increasingly part of the public health message for all age groups in many countries (Hallal et al., 2012; Piercy et al., 2018). However, can there ever be *too much*?

Recent high-profile early retirements in sports, including rugby, cricket, athletics, basketball, boxing, horse racing and football, suggest that the demands of elite-level sport can become too much for some, and particularly when performance expectations and the pursuit of success begin to overshadow personal wellbeing or enjoyment (Bauman, 2016; Breslin and Leavey, 2019). In a recent interview, Sir Tony McCoy, the most successful jump jockey of all time, summed this up well. 'You look at the elite sportspeople, they've all got a madness inside them. They've all got a psychopathic switch that means you'd die for it rather than fail' (*Racing Post*, 31 January 2021, p. 13).

Recent evidence suggests that competitive elite sport can at times overwhelm athletes and especially when additional stressors are present, such as relentlessly striving to achieve success; long periods of separation from friends and family; negative psychological sequelae during and following injury; alcohol and substance misuse; fear of failure, social media intrusion; relationship difficulties; financial issues; and the challenges of securing steady employment and income across a career (Breslin and Leavey, 2019).

As far back in time as the ancient Greeks and Roman cultures (see **1.1**), historical accounts show the emergence of an idealised view of athletes as paragons of health, strength and physique, with attendant virtues of discipline, morality and beauty. Unfortunately, a more realistic appraisal of athletes and athleticism reveals a picture that is far from this 'ideal', and one which has seldom been examined, until recently. Perhaps as a reflection of this adulation, athletes have traditionally been poorly supported in the management of their mental health needs, and indeed mental health promotion within sport has often been considered as superfluous and/or irrelevant. Instead, like the ancient Greek gymnasia, sport club cultures have fostered the celebration of mental toughness, a concomitant disapproval of weakness and/or disclosure, and the enforcement of a stigma attaching to disclosure of mental health issues (Bauman, 2016). In some cases, the environment and culture of sport has bred a *win at all costs* ethos, where indeed the costs for some athletes have been massive (Breslin and Leavey, 2019). As a consequence of traditional sport cultures where a social norm not to show weakness has prevailed, psychological, emotional and social problems can remain hidden from view. This can lead to significant problems going undetected, problems which need to be addressed at a systemic level as a matter of urgency (Breslin et al., 2019).

Furthermore, it is not only athletes who need support and protection. Coaches and managers can also experience stressors and hence require assistance themselves for managing their own mental health as well as the health of others (Ferguson et al., 2019). Discussions with coaches suggests that all too often they strive to exude a steely image of confidence and composure, while inwardly feeling fragile and vulnerable within a culture that demands consistent peak performance and rewards winning at all costs (Carson et al., 2018).

In promoting wellbeing among coaching and support staff, Carson and colleagues (2018) outline the six dimensions (workload, control, reward, fairness, community and values) of their Work Life Model and go on to describe how the model provides a framework for promoting mental health and reducing coach stress and burnout. They describe coaches as performers, and offer ideas as to how their mental health and wellbeing can be supported.

A further example of support for coaches has involved a mental health confidence and help-seeking awareness programme (Sebbens et al., 2016). The programme emphasised the role of psycho-educational training and modelling as important in transitioning or modifying norms around help-seeking behaviours. For example, a coach portraying or modelling characteristics of invulnerability can exacerbate existing problems among athletes and, unfortunately, athletes and their coaches can then become trapped in a culture of denial in which the mental health costs are high. Alternatively, if a coach demonstrates vulnerability, and promotes a culture where asking for support is encouraged, then athletes are likely to adopt a similar approach.

There remains much work to be done in terms of encouraging the propensity to speak out about mental health, among both coaches and athletes, but some promising advances have been made. For instance, in the last five years there has been a surge of interest in supporting the mental health and wellbeing of those taking part in sport and their supporters (e.g. athletes, coaches, officials, parents, fans and the local community). In some cases, mental health awareness programmes have been delivered. Programmes have included content that aimed to increase mental health literacy, that is to (a) raise awareness of mental health symptoms and causes; (b) reduce stigma towards mental health; (c) use cognitive-behavioural techniques to enhance coping (i.e. mindfulness, resilience, family behavioural therapy, rational–emotive behaviour therapy); and (d) engage club members in the promotion of mental health discussions.

Despite the recent surge in the number of intervention programmes available, important variations in content, design and measurement have been noted (Breslin et al., 2017). A systematic review of such programmes revealed ten studies that met sufficient methodological criteria for inclusion, and within these a range of outcomes were found to assess indices of mental health awareness. Mental health referral efficacy was improved in six studies, while three reported an increase in knowledge about mental health disorders. Seven studies demonstrated a high risk of bias when allocating participants to groups, thus limiting the reliability of emerging results. The conclusion from the review was that further, well-designed controlled intervention studies are required before definitive conclusions can be reached, and that mental health awareness in sport is lagging behind other areas (e.g. schools, workplaces, etc.) (Breslin et al., 2017).

This review was instrumental in prompting the development of an 'International consensus statement on the psychosocial and policy-related approaches to mental health awareness programmes in sport' (Breslin et al., 2019). The statement serves to assist programme designers, policy makers and commissioners with regard to (a) definitions of mental health awareness; (b) key design principles, including target populations, and the importance of partnership working; (c) implementation programme outcomes; and (d) methods for conducting and reporting interventions with sporting population groups (i.e. coaches, athletes, officials).

It is encouraging to note that policy position and consensus statements have now been launched to support athlete mental health by a number of high profile bodies, including the International Olympic Committee (Reardon, 2019), the International Society of Sport Psychology (Schinke et al., 2018) and the European Federation of Sport Psychology and Physical Activity (FEPSAC; Moesch et al., 2018). Time will tell as to whether these initiatives will eventually be reflected in a systemic shift in culture and attitudes towards mental health within sport, but for the sake of all those involved in sport, it is to be hoped so.

KEY READINGS

Bauman, N.J. (2016) 'The stigma of mental health in athletes: Are mental toughness and mental health seen as contradictory in elite sport?', *British Journal of Sports Medicine*, 50 (3), 135–6.

Breslin, G., Shannon, S., Haughey, T., Donnelly, P. and Leavey, G. (2017) 'A systematic review of interventions to increase awareness of mental health and well-being in athletes, coaches and officials', *Systematic Reviews*, 6 (177), 1–15.

Breslin, G., Smith, A., Donohue, B., Donnelly, P., Shannon, S., Haughey, T. J., ... and Rogers, T. (2019) 'International consensus statement on the psychosocial and policy-related approaches to mental health awareness programmes in sport', *BMJ Open: Sport and Exercise Medicine*, 5 (1), e000585.

Reardon, C.L., Hainline, B., Aron, C.M., Baron, D., Baum, A.L., Bindra, A. and Derevensky, J.L. (2019) 'Mental health in elite athletes: International Olympic Committee consensus statement (2019)', *British Journal of Sports Medicine*, 53 (11), 667–99.

PRACTICAL QUESTIONS

- Outline the reasons why it is important for sport clubs to introduce mental health awareness training for coaches and athletes?
- What is the role of a coach when considering athlete mental health?

REFERENCES

Bauman, N.J. (2016) 'The stigma of mental health in athletes: Are mental toughness and mental health seen as contradictory in elite sport?', *British Journal of Sports Medicine*, 50 (3), 135–6.

Biddle, S.J.H., Mutrie, N. and Gorely, T. (2015) *Psychology of Physical Activity*. Florence: Taylor & Francis.

Breslin, G. and Leavey, G. (eds) (2019) *Mental Health and Well-Being Interventions in Sport: Research, Theory and Practice*. London: Routledge.

Breslin, G., Shannon, S., Haughey, T., Donnelly, P. and Leavey, G. (2017) 'A systematic review of interventions to increase awareness of mental health and well-being in athletes, coaches and officials', *Systematic Reviews*, 6 (177), 1–15.

Breslin, G., Smith, A., Donohue, B., Donnelly, P., Shannon, S., Haughey, T.J., … and Rogers, T. (2019) 'International consensus statement on the psychosocial and policy-related approaches to mental health awareness programmes in sport', *BMJ Open Sport and Exercise Medicine*, 5 (1), e000585.

Carson, F., Walsh, J., Main, L.C., and Kremer, P. (2018) 'High performance coaches' mental health and wellbeing: Applying the areas of work life model', *International Sport Coaching Journal*, 5 (3), 293–300.

Ferguson, H.L., Swann, C., Liddle, S.K., and Vella, S.A. (2019) 'Investigating youth sports coaches' perceptions of their role in adolescent mental health', *Journal of Applied Sport Psychology*, 31 (2), 235–52.

Hallal, P.C., Andersen, L.B., Bull, F.C., Guthold, R., Haskell, W., Ekelund, U. and Lancet Physical Activity Series Working Group (2012) 'Global physical activity levels: Surveillance progress, pitfalls, and prospects', *The Lancet*, 380 (9838), 247–57.

Moesch, K., Kenttä, G., Kleinert, J., Quignon-Fleuret, C., Cecil, S. and Bertollo, M. (2018) 'FEPSAC position statement: Mental health disorders in elite athletes and models of service provision', *Psychology of Sport and Exercise*, 38, 61–71.

Piercy, K.L., Troiano, R.P., Ballard, R.M., Carlson, S.A., Fulton, J.E., Galuska, D.A., … and Olson, R.D. (2018) 'The physical activity guidelines for Americans', *Jama*, 320 (19), 2020–8.

Reardon, C.L., Hainline, B., Aron, C.M., Baron, D., Baum, A.L., Bindra, A… . and Derevensky, J.L. (2019) 'Mental health in elite athletes: International Olympic Committee consensus statement (2019)', *British Journal of Sports Medicine*, 53 (11), 667–99.

Sebbens, J., Hassmén, P., Crisp, D. and Wensley, K. (2016) 'Mental health in sport (MHS): Improving the early intervention knowledge and confidence of elite sport staff', *Frontiers in Psychology*, 7, 911.

Schinke, R.J., Stambulova, N.B., Si, G. and Moore, Z. (2018) 'International society of sport psychology position stand: Athletes' mental health, performance, and development', *International Journal of Sport and Exercise Psychology*, 16 (6), 622–39.

7.41 MENTAL HEALTH DISORDER IN SPORT

Definition: Mental Health Disorder is characterised by abnormal thoughts, perceptions, emotions and behaviours. Diagnosis can include depression, bipolar disorder, schizophrenia, psychoses, dementia and developmental disorders (e.g., autism).

Mental Health Disorders (MHDs) such as depression and anxiety are among the most common causes of disease burden worldwide. Other conditions include personality disorders, post-traumatic stress disorder (PTSD) and a range of psychotic disorders which together combine to present significant challenges to the health community across the globe. The World Health Organisation (2014) estimates that one in four of the population will experience a mental illness at some point in their lives. It is therefore of public health concern that effective mental health interventions are developed and are widely available to support the population (Huppert, 2009), including within the world of sport.

MHDs among elite athletes have received increased attention over recent years (Moesch et al., 2018). In 2015, the UK Government launched a 'Mental Health in Sport' initiative in which several sport associations, including the Rugby Football Union, UK Athletics and the Football Association committed to reducing stigma towards mental illness. A number of high-profile athletes likewise pledged their support through public disclosure of their struggles with mental illness, in an effort to normalise disclosure and help-seeking behaviour. These public acts of self-disclosure have prompted various sporting organisations to openly acknowledge that athletes can be prone to mental health issues, and that some stressors inherent in sport have been normalised or accepted, thereby contributing to ongoing poor mental health and MHD (Rice et al., 2016) (see **7.38**).

Several reports have revealed that athletes with MHD are at greater risk of injury and delayed recovery from injury (Mistry et al., 2020). Furthermore, elite athletes have been shown to display the same level of symptom severity associated with depression, anxiety, eating and substance use disorders as the general population (Rice et al., 2016). However, such severity rates need to be treated with some caution. For example, recorded rates of symptoms associated with disorders in adult athletes have varied from 17 per cent (Schaal et al., 2011) to 68 per cent (Hammond et al., 2013). The disparity in prevalence rates between studies would suggest the need for greater consistency and consensus in measurement of MHD across studies. Also, data on prevalence rates within younger, mainly adolescent age groups are not yet widely available. Beyond prevalence rates, a promising endeavour has involved the integration of mental health awareness initiatives in sport (see **7.40**).

Theoretical frameworks that conceptualise MHDs in sport and are presented in a way that genuinely engages with athletes have also been considered (Uphill et al., 2016). According to a review by Uphill et al. (2016), care should be taken not to blind with science, nor to 'over-medicalise' and thereby further stigmatise the subject. In their review they propose the adoption of Keyes's (2002) two continuum model, where mental illness and mental health are considered as two distinct but related dimensions. This is different from the more common lay assumption that mental health and mental illness reside at opposite ends of a single continuum. The first continuum relates to the absence or presence of *mental illness* while the second pertains to the absence or presence of *mental health*. Using the two continua in combination, a number of conceptual possibilities emerge. For example, an athlete could have high levels of mental health and yet experience mental illness and hence be 'struggling'. Alternatively, an athlete could be free from mental illness yet be 'languishing' (i.e. experiencing low levels of mental health). By presenting health and illness in this orthogonal way within mental health awareness programmes, perhaps some of the stigma surrounding MHDs may be reduced, and help-seeking thereby encouraged. Already, empirical studies which have evaluated the effectiveness of programmes using these concepts have shown promise (Shannon et al., 2020).

The provision of clinical services for MHDs varies considerably within elite sport, while even less is known about provision within amateur sports. A recent position statement that included a review of service delivery in elite sport across European national sport institutes highlighted the extent of variation (Moesch et al., 2018). At the same time, it is also clear that sport psychologists can play an important role in identifying the early onset of mental illness, and then supporting and referring athletes to appropriate clinical professionals, whether they be counsellors, clinical psychologists or sport psychiatrists.

Sport psychiatry has received increasing attention in recent years. In contrast with sport and exercise psychologists who, coming from a background in psychology and sport science, have always operated in various roles (e.g. research, educational, clinical; see **1.2**), sport psychiatrists (with a medical training) in the past tended to focus exclusively on the diagnosis and treatment of psychiatric illness in athletes. However, it would appear that their role is continuing to evolve and expand, now extending to sport psychology approaches to performance enhancement, as well as the promotion of wellbeing generally among elite athletes.

There was considerable scepticism as to what sport psychiatry may have to offer over and above sport psychology (other than having the authority to prescribe psychotropic medication), but scepticism appears to have waned with national sporting associations being ever more accepting. For example, in recent years sport psychiatrists have contributed to national institutes of sport service delivery (e.g. English Institute of Sport); the International Olympic Committee's consensus statement on mental health in sport; special issues on psychiatry and sport in peer-reviewed journals (e.g. *British Journal of Sports Medicine*, June 2019); textbooks (Mistry et al., 2020); webinars; and a sport psychiatry curriculum developed by the International Society for Sports Psychiatry. Taking a medical, diagnostic and treatment approach, combined with a consideration of emotional, social and environmental factors, they continue principally to provide individual medical psychiatric services for athletes, but with the addition of inputs derived from the field of sport psychology.

Alcohol anxiety and sleep
Depression
Psychosis
Concussion and mental illness symptoms
Trauma and touring
Low mood and gambling
Self-harm and suicideation
Exercise addiction
Disordered eating
Mental health emergencies

Figure 7.1 Sport Psychiatry Case Study Example Topics

As sport psychiatry is in its infancy, with no solid foundation or experimental evidence base with regard to sport-specific treatments, clinicians at this point still tend to rely on extrapolation from psychiatric studies with the general population, although evidence from case studies in sport (see Figure **7.1**) has been used increasingly to support thoughtful and safe individualised prescription regimens (Mistry et al., 2020). Clearly, the overlap between sport psychiatry and applied sport psychology, in terms of both theory and practice, is considerable, and is likely to grow not shrink. It is to be hoped that the future relationship between the two subdisciplines is one which can be best characterised as collaborative rather than competitive.

KEY READINGS

Keyes, C.L.M. (2002) 'The mental health continuum: From languishing to flourishing in life', *Journal of Health and Social Behavior*, 43, 207–22. DOI: 10.2307/3090197.

Mistry, A.D., McCabe, T. and Currie, A. (eds) (2020) *Case Studies in Sports Psychiatry*. Cambridge: Cambridge University Press.

Reardon, C.L., Hainline, B., Aron, C.M., Baron, D., Baum, A.L., Bindra, A.... and Derevensky, J.L. (2019) 'Mental health in elite athletes: International Olympic Committee consensus statement (2019)', *British Journal of Sports Medicine*, 53 (11), 667–99.

Rice, S.M., Purcell, R., De Silva, S., Mawren, D., McGorry, P.D. and Parker, A.G. (2016) 'The mental health of elite athletes: A narrative systematic review', *Sports Medicine*, 46 (9), 1333–53.

PRACTICAL QUESTIONS

- Compare and contrast mental illness and mental health. Describe Keyes's (2002) two continuum model of mental health and mental illness, and discuss how it could be useful for reducing stigma towards those with mental illness.
- What is the role of the sport psychiatrist and how does this differ from a sport psychologist when supporting elite athletes?

REFERENCES

Hammond, T., Gialloreto, C., Kubas, H. and Davis IV, H.H. (2013) 'The prevalence of failure-based depression among elite athletes', *Clinical Journal of Sport Medicine*, 23 (4), 273–7.

Huppert, F.A. (2009) 'Psychological well-being: Evidence regarding its causes and consequences', *Applied Psychology*, 1, 137–64.

Keyes, C.L.M. (2002) 'The mental health continuum: From languishing to flourishing in life', *Journal of Health and Social Behavior*, 43, 207–22. DOI: 10.2307/3090197.

Mistry, A.D., McCabe, T. and Currie, A. (eds) (2020) *Case Studies in Sports Psychiatry*. Cambridge: Cambridge University Press.

Moesch, K., Kenttä, G., Kleinert, J., Quignon-Fleuret, C., Cecil, S. and Bertollo, M. (2018) 'FEPSAC position statement: Mental health disorders in elite athletes and models of service provision', *Psychology of Sport and Exercise*, 38, 61–71.

Reardon, C.L., Hainline, B., Aron, C.M., Baron, D., Baum, A.L., Bindra, A.… and Derevensky, J.L. (2019) 'Mental health in elite athletes: International Olympic Committee consensus statement (2019)', *British Journal of Sports Medicine*, 53 (11), 667–99.

Rice, S.M., Purcell, R., De Silva, S., Mawren, D., McGorry, P.D. and Parker, A.G. (2016) 'The mental health of elite athletes: A narrative systematic review', *Sports Medicine*, 46 (9), 1333–53.

Schaal, K., Tafflet, M., Nassif, H., Thibault, V., Pichard, C., Alcotte, M., … and Toussaint, J.F. (2011) 'Psychological balance in high level athletes: Gender-based differences and sport-specific patterns', *PloS one*, 6 (5), e19007.

Shannon, S., Hanna, D., Leavey, G., Haughey, T., Neill, D. and Breslin, G. (2020) 'The association between mindfulness and mental health outcomes in athletes: Testing the mediating role of autonomy satisfaction as a core psychological need', *International Journal of Sport and Exercise Psychology*, 1–16.

Uphill, M., Sly, D. and Swain, J. (2016) 'From mental health to mental wealth in athletes: Looking back and moving forward', *Frontiers in Psychology*, 7, 935.

World Health Organization (WHO). (2014) Mental health: A state of well-being (2014). Accessed 09/08/2021 from: http://www.who.int/mediacentre/factsheets/fs220/en/.

7.42 RESILIENCE

Definition: Resilience refers to the process and capability to endure, and bounce back, after overcoming extreme adversity.

There are times in an athlete's career when he or she feels under intense pressure to succeed, has failed, but has persevered through adversity to achieve set goals. The term resilience has been used to describe the capacity to overcome adversity, as have other terms such as mental toughness (see **4.21**), hardiness and grit. Research in the area of resilience, especially around conceptual clarity and measurement, has grown substantially over the past two decades. In common with work on mental toughness, a plethora of working definitions of resilience have now been proposed (mainly within the subdiscipline of child development), but applied research in sport with elite athletes has also been invaluable in providing greater conceptual clarity. With a clearer definition of the resilience concept, we are getting closer to a more effective approach to athlete intervention and assessment.

Once more in keeping with work on mental toughness, early research described resilience as a personality trait (i.e. ego resilience), characterising a person who can think and emotionally react differently to adversity in comparison with the average person on the street, or pitch (Block and Block, 1980). In addition to trait approaches the importance of the interplay of the environment and social interactions was also seen to have a contributing role in determining resilience (Bonanno and Diminich, 2013). Best et al. (1990: 426) describe resilience as 'the process of, capacity for, or outcome of successful adaptation despite challenging or threatening circumstances'. Best et al.'s three-part definition describes resilience not at a point in time but as a characteristic developed across time, and as part of a dynamic personality. Furthermore, Best et al.'s definition has an interesting experiential element insofar as they argue that an individual must *overcome* adversity in order to be resilient. What seems contradictory within this definition is that, if resilience is primarily regarded as a trait (i.e. something relatively permanent and pre-existing from birth), how then can characteristics of resilience be acquired through the process of experiential learning? Instead perhaps, the dynamic interplay between traits and environmental factors, nature and nurture, must play a part. Furthermore, the role played by cognitive skills in resilience formation must also require consideration, as is often apparent in sport.

As sport environments have their own nuances (e.g. unique performance environment; drive for success; long-term performance goals; threat of injury; team or individual selection, etc.), a separate working definition of resilience for use in the context of sport may seem sensible. As one example, and returning to an earlier point, resilience in sport must take into consideration the cognitive skills needed to reframe negative situations, and indeed has been defined as, 'The role of mental processes and behaviour in promoting personal assets and protecting an individual from the potential negative effect of stressors'

(Fletcher and Sarkar, 2012: 675). This definition highlights cognitive processes or skills, and arguably suggests that resilience can be learned through engaging in skills training. Not surprisingly, it is Fletcher and Sarkar's definition that has been used most frequently in sport to date.

In a review of sport and resilience research (Galli and Gonzalez, 2015), based largely on qualitative investigations, two broad approaches to the study of resilience were identifiable: (a) the assessment of psychosocial factors that characterise athletes who have not succeeded but then go on to succeed, through the use of pre- and post- follow-up prospective research designs or retrospective case study reports; and (b) an assessment of affect, behaviours and cognitions (ABCs) of athletes who have overcome adversity, mainly through qualitative interviews. Studies cited in the review include the following as types of sport adversity: stress of training and competition; physical injury; team adversity; and under par performance.

Undoubtedly these adversities vary in intensity, and when compared to the child development literature on trauma experience, it could be argued that many sport adversities would be on the low end of any relative scale. Taking these issues into consideration, the psychological resilience factors perceived as crucial for overcoming adversity for athletes have included: achievement motivation; social support; metacognition; focus; confidence; high perceptions of ability; and optimistic versus pessimistic explanatory style.

The review also highlighted the need to operationalise what constitutes adversity for athletes. Adversity in child development research is often linked to trauma and deprivation, but the links to major, life-changing threats within sport can be less obvious. That said, if an individual has a very restricted and unidimensional identity that is linked to their sport alone, with few other interests, the sporting failure or adverse event can be truly traumatic (see **7.39** and **7.41**).

Regarding the measurement of resilience, there are a number of measures already available in mainstream psychology and some that have been put to use within sporting contexts. Gucciardi et al. (2011) recommended that, at the very least, a standardised measure is required for the assessment of resilience in athletes, and one that has taken on board the methodological issues raised in previous studies, a view echoed by Sarker and Fletcher (2013) when recommending what should characterise any sport-specific measure of resilience.

Measures that are readily available to assess resilience include the Connor–Davidson Resilience Scale (CD-RISC; Connor and Davidson, 2003), a trait-based ten-item measure, deemed valid for use with athletes (Extremera et al., 2017). A further example is the Resilience Scale for Athletes (RSA; Subhan and Ijaz, 2012), a 27-item questionnaire consisting of three factors: self-determination; physical toughness; and emotional control and maturity. The RSA has been shown to have high internal consistency and validity when used with student athletes. So far, and despite several reviews and critiques, a more recent measure of resilience in sport has yet to appear. If, or when, one is produced, then the contents of that measurement tool (or a collection of measurement tools according to Sarker and Fletcher, 2013), should perhaps aim to assess three primary elements: (a) adversity; (b) positive adaptation; and (c) protective athlete factors.

To date, few resilience intervention programmes have included an evaluation component, and very few seem to adhere to the definitions as described by either Best et al. (1990), or Sarker and Fletcher (2013). This may reflect the timing of the publications but it is more likely that there is a divergence between theory and practice, with the conceptual nature of resilience not always closely aligned with programme development, content and evaluation. For example, one resilience programme that has been implemented with athletes focused primarily on *optimism raising* – and yet this is a construct that has attracted little attention, if any, in the resilience literature in sport.

The programme that was developed aspired to enhance athletes' cognitive skills, with three specific aims: (a) to evaluate personal assumptions or thoughts regarding a situation; (b) to become aware of negative thoughts and to replace these with positive thoughts; and (c) to encourage finding optimism and to avoid catastrophising (Schinke and Jerome, 2002). How this programme maps on to the resilience constructs as described above is not immediately obvious, but instead it would appear to be linked to Seligman's work on learned helplessness (Seligman et al., 1990; Seligman, 1991). Looking to the future, outside of sport other domains that may be helpful in shaping the design of resilience-based programmes include the military and educational settings. More recently, moving beyond the individual to the collective, there has been interesting research on developing team (Morgan et al., 2019) and organisational resilience in sport (Fasey et al., 2020), and these represent enterprises are worthy of further consideration.

KEY READINGS

Fasey, K.J., Sarkar, M., Wagstaff, C.R. and Johnston, J. (2020) 'Defining and characterizing organizational resilience in elite sport', *Psychology of Sport and Exercise*, 52, 1–36. DOI: 10.1016/j.psychsport.2020.101834.

Galli, N. and Gonzalez, S.P. (2015) 'Psychological resilience in sport: A review of the literature and implications for research and practice', *International Journal of Sport and Exercise Psychology*, 13 (3), 243–57.

Morgan, P.B., Fletcher, D. and Sarkar, M. (2019) 'Developing team resilience: A season-long study of psychosocial enablers and strategies in a high-level sports team', *Psychology of Sport and Exercise*, 45, 101543.

Sarkar, M. and Fletcher, D. (2013) 'How should we measure psychological resilience in sport performers?', *Measurement in Physical Education and Exercise Science*, 17 (4), 264–80. DOI: 10.1080/1091367X.2013.805141.

PRACTICAL QUESTIONS

- Critically discuss how Best et al's definition of resilience can be applied to the development of a resilience programme for use in a high-performance sport of your choice.
- In practical ways, illustrate how a sport psychologist can enhance an athlete's resilience across his or her career.

REFERENCES

Best, K., Garmezy, N. and Masten, A.S. (1990) 'Resilience and development: Contributions from the study of children who overcome adversity', *Development and Psychopathology*, 2, 425–44. doi:10.1017/s0954579400005812.

Block, J.H. and Block, J. (1980) 'The role of ego-control and ego-resiliency in the organization of behavior', in W.A. Collins (ed.), *The Minnesota Symposia on Child Psychology: Development of Cognition, Affect, and Social Relations*, vol. 13. Hillsdale, NJ: Erlbaum. pp. 39–101.

Bonanno, G.A. and Diminich, E.D. (2013) 'Annual research review: Positive adjustment to adversity – trajectories of minimal-impact resilience and emergent resilience', *Journal of Child Psychology and Psychiatry*, 54, 378–401. doi:10.1111/jcpp.12021.

Connor, K.M. and Davidson, J.R.T. (2003) 'Development of a new resilience scale: The Connor-Davidson resilience scale (CD-RISC)', *Depression and Anxiety*, 18, 76–82. doi:10.1002/da.10113.

Extremera, M.O., Moreno, E.O., González, M.C., Ortega, F.Z. and Ruz, R.P. (2017) 'Validation of Resilience Scale (CD-RISC) in elite athletes through a structural equation model', *RETOS. Nuevas Tendencias en Educación Física, Deporte y Recreación*, (32), 96–100.

Fasey, K.J., Sarkar, M., Wagstaff, C.R. and Johnston, J. (2020) 'Defining and characterizing organizational resilience in elite sport', *Psychology of Sport and Exercise*, 52, 1–36. DOI: 10.1016/j.psychsport.2020.101834.

Fletcher, D. and Sarkar, M. (2012) 'A grounded theory of psychological resilience in Olympic champions', *Psychology of Sport and Exercise*, 13, 669–78. doi:10.1016/j.psychsport.2012.04.007.

Galli, N. and Gonzalez, S.P. (2015) 'Psychological resilience in sport: A review of the literature and implications for research and practice', *International Journal of Sport and Exercise Psychology*, 13 (3), 243–57.

Gucciardi, D.F., Jackson, B., Coulter, T.J. and Mallett, C.J. (2011) 'The Connor-Davidson Resilience Scale (CD-RISC): Dimensionality and age-related measurement invariance with Australian cricketers', *Psychology of Sport and Exercise*, 12 (4), 423–33.

Morgan, P.B., Fletcher, D. and Sarkar, M. (2019) 'Developing team resilience: A season-long study of psychosocial enablers and strategies in a high-level sports team', *Psychology of Sport and Exercise*, 45, 101543.

Sarkar, M. and Fletcher, D. (2013) 'How should we measure psychological resilience in sport performers? *Measurement in Physical*

Education and Exercise Science, 17 (4), 264–80, DOI: 10.1080/1091367X.2013.805141.

Schinke, R.J., and Jerome, W.C. (2002) 'Understanding and refining the resilience of elite athletes: An intervention strategy', *Athletic Insight*, 4, 1–13.

Seligman, M.E.P. (1991) *Learned Optimism*. New York: Knopf.

Seligman, M.E., Nolen-Hoeksema, S., Thornton, N. and Thornton, K.M. (1990) 'Explanatory style as a mechanism of disappointing athletic performance', *Psychological Science*, 1, 143–6. doi:10.1111/j. 1467-9280.1990.tb00084.x.

Subhan, S. and Ijaz, T. (2012) 'Resilience scale for athletes', *FWU Journal of Social Sciences*, 6 (2), 171.

7.43 MINDFULNESS AND WELLBEING IN SPORT

Definition: Mindfulness is paying attention on purpose, in the present moment, being aware and non-judgmental. It involves an openness to experience with characteristics of kindness and acceptance of oneself.

Mindfulness interventions aim to increase a person's non-judgmental awareness of internal cognitions, emotions, and physiological sensations (Pickert, 2014; Gardner, 2016; Gardner and Moore, 2017), not in a way to challenge or change those thoughts but rather to experience and accept them. Immediately it is obvious that these types of intervention differ from the traditional Psychological Skills Training (PST) approaches, as adopted by psychologists in the past, and they not only challenge but also seek to provide individuals with the tools to control their thoughts and so aid performance.

In the last two decades there has been an increased interest in mindfulness-based interventions in sport. One important interest for sport psychologists is having the opportunity to enhance performance while supporting the athlete's self-regulation, thereby aiding performance and wellbeing. Indeed, mindfulness has been shown to improve attention, working memory and emotion regulation in sport (Gardner and Moore, 2020), with supporting evidence from neuroscience that mindfulness is associated with changes in brain function and structure (Davidson, 2002). This section will focus on the effects of mindfulness on wellbeing and describe empirical studies that support this approach.

The Mindfulness–Acceptance–Commitment (MAC) model was first introduced in sport psychology by Gardner and Moore (2007) at a time when traditional Psychological Skills Training Theory was the main 'go to' for sport psychologists. Gardner and Moore proposed the MAC protocol as an alternative for use with clinical and non-clinical populations in order to improve wellbeing. For instance, meditative approaches like mindfulness and acceptance therapy have been shown to reduce anxiety and stress (Chiesa and Serretti, 2010; Chen et al., 2013). Also, in a recent meta-analysis, mindfulness programmes were shown to reduce depression when compared with non-specific treatment controls. Furthermore, Goldberg et al. (2018) examined the efficacy of mindfulness-based interventions for clinical populations with disorder-specific symptoms, involving 12,005 participants in total. At post-treatment and follow-up, mindfulness interventions were found to be significantly superior to no treatment conditions ($d = 0.55$; $d = 0.50$ respectively).

Beyond clinical populations, mindfulness-based protocols have demonstrated improved mood, wellbeing (Remmers et al., 2016) and immune function in the general population (Black and Slavich, 2016). Although there are fewer studies on the effectiveness of mindfulness in sport, as compared to clinical populations, the evidence of effectiveness is increasingly being presented in sports such as football, rowing, cycling, swimming, diving, running, archery and golf (see Gardner and Moore, 2017; 2020; Gross, 2020). Those who have received mindfulness training include student athletes, elite youth athletes (Gustafsson et al., 2015), Olympic athletes (Haberl, 2016) and coaches (Pawsey, 2019). These groups have been supported to tackle burnout (Gustafsson et al., 2015), emotion regulation (Moore, 2016), stress (Goodman et al., 2014), mental health (Gross et al., 2015), distress tolerance (Baltzell, 2016), and injury rehabilitation (Ivarsson et al., 2015).

Looking more closely at the strength of the evidence for the effectiveness of mindfulness interventions, case-study evidence of the benefits that mindfulness brings for improving wellbeing is plentiful, while even more convincing are the results of studies using both randomised controlled trials (RCTs) and non-randomised controlled trials (non-RCTs). In a non-RCT study, NCAA Division 1 male college athletes were recruited to take part in eight MAC programme sessions. On completion of the sessions, the MAC group reported lower levels of stress compared to a control group (Goodman et al., 2014). In an RCT, again with NCAA athletes, a group receiving the MAC programme was compared to those on a traditional PST programme, pre, post intervention, then one month later. As well as performance improvements at one-month follow-up, the MAC group reported reductions in substance use, hostility, anxiety, dysfunctional eating and psychological distress (Gross et al., 2015). In a further RCT study, where PST and mindfulness training were compared, both forms of mental training led to improvements in performance-related psychological factors, especially concerning the handling of emotions and attention control (Gross et al., 2018). In combination, these findings may suggest that different psychological mechanisms play a part in each form of intervention but both lead to positive and desired outcomes; accordingly, both forms of mental training seem to be efficacious (Röthlin et al., 2020).

The mechanisms which account for the positive effect of mindfulness on performance and wellbeing continue to be explored. Several studies have been carried out, with authors providing various explanations for the positive effects. According to Hölzel et al's (2011) review of neuroscientific processes, mindfulness practice is associated with neuroplasticity changes in the anterior cingulate cortex, insula, temporal-parietal junction, frontal-limbic network and default mode network structures, with each of these neural mechanisms working in synergy to establish a process of enhanced self-regulation.

An alternative, psychosocial explanation proposes that mindfulness may improve wellbeing as a result of the moderating influence of *autonomy*. A recent study showed mindfulness directly predicted autonomy, satisfaction, wellbeing and stress (Shannon et al., 2020). The authors concluded that mindfulness may improve wellbeing and reduce stress through increasing the athletes' capacity to self-regulate, satisfying the basic psychological need for autonomy and personal choice.

To measure mindfulness in sport, several self-report inventories are now available, some of which are more convincing than others in their validity and reliability. These include the 15-item Mindfulness Inventory for Sport (MIS; Thienot et al, 2014); the Athlete Mindfulness Questionnaire (AMQ; Zhang et al., 2017); and the Decentering Scale for Sport (DSS; Zhang et al., 2016). General mindfulness measures have also been recommended for use in sport, on the basis that athletes are people too, a view that embraces the holistic approach to enhancing wellbeing among athletes (see **7.39**), encouraging the development of an identity that is not too narrowly focused on sport alone (see Gardner and Moore, 2020).

While there has been a great deal of research on the theory and practice of mindfulness in sport, some questions remain unanswered. Future research is required to determine what frequency of mindfulness sessions is required to gain improvements in wellbeing outcomes. More RCTs, with larger sample sizes, are also required to determine specific outcomes associated with specific types of intervention. Studies could also include individual and team sports at different performance levels (e.g. novice, amateur and elite). Further exploration of the neural mechanisms and psychosocial factors underlying mindfulness-based interventions is warranted, especially to explore the finding that mindfulness alters cognitive neuroplasticity along with basic brain structures and associated functions (Gardner and Moore, 2019).

KEY READINGS

Gardner, F.L. (2016) 'Scientific advancement of mindfulness and acceptance-based models in sport psychology: A decade in time, a seismic shift in philosophy and practice', in A. Baltzell (ed.), *Mindfulness and Performance*. Cambridge: Cambridge University Press. pp. 127–52.

Gardner, F.L. and Moore, Z.E. (2019) 'Mindfulness in sport: Neuroscience and practical applications', in M.H. Ansel, T.A. Petrie and J.A. Steinfeldt (eds), *APA Handbooks in Psychology Series: APA Handbook of Sport and Exercise Psychology*, vol. 1. *Sport Psychology*. Washington, DC: American Psychological Association. pp. 325–42. https://doi.org/10.1037/0000123-017.

Gustafsson, H., Skoog, T., Davis, P., Kentta, G. and Haberl, P. (2015) 'Mindfulness and its relationship with perceived stress, affect, and burnout in elite junior athletes', *Journal of Clinical Sport Psychology*, 9, 263–81. http://dx.doi.org/10.1123/jcsp.2014-0051.

Shannon, S., Hanna, D., Leavey, G., Haughey, T., Neill, D. and Breslin, G. (2020) 'The association between mindfulness and mental health outcomes in athletes: Testing the mediating role of autonomy satisfaction as a core psychological need', *International Journal of Sport and Exercise Psychology*, 1–16.

PRACTICAL QUESTIONS

- What are the likely challenges in integrating a mindfulness programme with athletes to enhance wellbeing, and how can these challenges be overcome?
- Discuss how psychological skills training (PST) based approaches differ from mindfulness-based approaches in supporting athletes, illustrating your answer with examples of each type of intervention.

REFERENCES

Baltzell, A. (2016) 'Self-compassion, distress tolerance, and mindfulness in performance', in A. Baltzell (ed.), *Mindfulness and Performance*. Cambridge: Cambridge University Press. pp. 53–77.

Black, D.S. and Slavich, G.M. (2016) 'Mindfulness meditation and the immune system: A systematic review of randomized controlled trials', *Annals NY Academy of Science*, 1373, 13–24. http://dx.doi.org/10.1111/nyas.12998.

Chen, Y., Yang, X., Wang, L. and Zhang, X. (2013) 'A randomized controlled trial of the effects of brief mindfulness meditation on anxiety symptoms and systolic blood pressure in Chinese nursing students', *Nurse Education Today*, 33 (10), 1166–72.

Chiesa, A. and Serretti, A. (2010) 'A systematic review of neurobiological and clinical features of mindfulness meditations', *Psychological Medicine*, 40 (8), 1239.

Davidson, R.J. (2002) 'Toward a biology of positive affect and compassion', in R.J. Davidson and A. Harrington (eds), *Visions of Compassion: Western Scientists and Tibetan Buddhists Examine Human Nature*. New York: Oxford University Press. pp. 107–30.

Gardner, F.L. (2016) 'Scientific advancement of mindfulness and acceptance-based models in sport psychology: A decade in time, a seismic shift in philosophy and practice', in A. Baltzell (ed.), *Mindfulness and Performance*. Cambridge: Cambridge University Press. pp. 127–52.

Gardner, F.L. and Moore, Z.E. (2007) *The Psychology of Enhancing Human Performance: The Mindfulness-Acceptance-Commitment (MAC) Approach*. Springer Publishing Company.

Gardner, F.L. and Moore, Z.E. (2017) 'Mindfulness-based and acceptance-based interventions in sport and performance contexts', *Current Opinion in Psychology*, 16, 180–4.

Gardner, F.L. and Moore, Z.E. (2019) 'Mindfulness in sport: Neuroscience and practical applications', in M.H. Ansel, T.A. Petrie and J.A. Steinfeldt (eds), *APA Handbooks in Psychology Series: APA Handbook of Sport and Exercise Psychology*, vol. 1. *Sport Psychology*. Washington, DC: American Psychological Association. pp. 325–42. https://doi.org/10.1037/0000123-017.

Gardner, F.L. and Moore, Z.E. (2020) 'Mindfulness in sport contexts', in G. Tenenbaum and R.C. Eklund (eds), *Handbook of Sport Psychology*, vol. 4. London: John Wiley & Sons. pp. 738–50.

Goldberg, S.B., Tucker, R.P., Greene, P.A., Davidson, R.J., Wampold, B.E., Kearney, D.J. and Simpson, T.L. (2018) 'Mindfulness-based interventions for psychiatric disorders: A systematic review and meta-analysis', *Clinical Psychology Review*, 59, 52–60.

Goodman, F.R., Kashdan, T.B., Mallard, T.T. and Schumann, M. (2014) 'A brief mindfulness and yoga intervention with an entire NCAA Division I athletic team: An initial investigation', *Psychology of Consciousness: Theory, Research and Practice*, 1 (4), 339–51. doi:http://dx.doi.org/10.1037/cns0000022.

Gross, M. (2020) 'Mindfulness approaches to athlete well-being', in E. Hong and A. Rao (eds), *Mental Health in the Athlete*. New York: Springer. pp. 231–44.

Gross, M., Moore, Z.E., Gardner, F.L., Wolanin, A.T., Pess, R. and Marks, D.R. (2015) 'The Mindfulness Acceptance-Commitment (MAC) approach: An intervention for the mental health and sport performance of student athletes', unpublished doctoral dissertation, Kean University, Union, NJ, in preparation for submission.

Gross, M., Moore, Z.E., Gardner, F.L., Wolanin, A.T., Pess, R. and Marks, D.R. (2018) 'An empirical examination comparing the mindfulness-acceptance-commitment approach and psychological skills training for the mental health and sport performance of female student athletes', *International Journal of Sport and Exercise Psychology*, 16 (4), 431–51.

Gustafsson, H., Skoog, T., Davis, P., Kentta, G. and Haberl, P. (2015) 'Mindfulness and its relationship with perceived stress, affect, and burnout in elite junior athletes', *Journal of Clinical Sport Psychology*, 9, 263–81. http://dx.doi.org/10.1123/jcsp.2014-0051.

Haberl, P. (2016) 'Mindfulness and the Olympic athlete – A personal journey', in A. Baltzell (ed.), *Mindfulness and Performance: Current Perspectives in Social and Behavioral Sciences*. Cambridge: Cambridge University Press. pp. 211–34.

Hölzel, B.K., Lazar, S.W., Gard, T., Schuman-Olivier, Z., Vago, D.R. and Ott, U. (2011) 'How does mindfulness meditation work? Proposing mechanisms of action from a conceptual and neural perspective', *Perspectives on Psychological Science,* 6 (6), 537–59.

Ivarsson, A., Johnson, U., Andersen, M.B., Fallby, J. and Altemyr, M. (2015) 'It pays to pay attention: A mindfulness-based program for injury prevention with soccer players', *Journal of Applied Sport Psychology*, 27 (3), 319–34.

Moore, Z.E. (2016) 'Mindfulness, emotion regulation, and performance', in A. Baltzell (ed.), *Mindfulness and Performance: Current Perspectives in Social and Behavioral Sciences*. Cambridge: Cambridge University Press. pp. 29–52.

Pawsey, F. (2019) 'Sport coaches, mindfulness, and daily life: The role of mindfulness in promoting wellbeing', unpublished doctoral dissertation, University of Canterbury, New Zealand.

Pickert, K. (2014) 'The mindfulness revolution', *Time Magazine*, 183 (4), 3 February.

Remmers, C., Topolinski, S. and Koole, S.L. (2016) 'Why being mindful may have more benefits than you realize: Mindfulness improves both explicit and implicit mood regulation', *Mindfulness*, 829–37. http://dx.doi.org/10.1007/s12671-016-0520-1.

Röthlin, P., Horvath, S., Trösch, S., Grosse Holtforth, M. and Birrer, D. (2020) 'Differential and shared effects of psychological skills training and mindfulness training on performance-relevant psychological factors in sport: A randomized controlled trial', *BMC Psychology*, 8 (1), 1–13.

Shannon, S., Hanna, D., Leavey, G., Haughey, T., Neill, D. and Breslin, G. (2020) 'The association between mindfulness and mental health outcomes in athletes: Testing the mediating role of autonomy satisfaction as a core psychological need', *International Journal of Sport and Exercise Psychology*, 1–16.

Thienot, E., Jackson, B., Dimmock, J., Grove, J.R., Bernier, M. and Fournier, J.F. (2014) 'Development and preliminary validation of the mindfulness inventory for sport', *Psychology of Sport and Exercise*, 15, 72–80. doi: 0.1016/j.psychsport.2013.10.003.

Zhang, C.Q., Chung, P.K. and Si, G. (2017) 'Assessing acceptance in mindfulness with direct-worded items: The development and initial validation of the Athlete Mindfulness Questionnaire', *Journal of Sport and Health Science*, 6, 311–20.

Zhang, C.Q., Chung, P.K., Si, G. and Gucciardi, D.F. (2016) 'Measuring decentering as a unidimensional construct: The development and initial validation of the Decentering Scale for Sport', *Psychology of Sport and Exercise*, 24, 147–58.

Index

Page numbers in *italics* refer to figures; page numbers in **bold** refer to tables.

2×2 Achievement Goal framework, 95–96

Abernethy, B., 203
abuse, 18
accreditation, 5, 7–8
Achievement Goal Theory (AGT), 78, 92–96, 101
activity choice, 67
Adlington, Rebecca (swimming), 37–38
adversity. *See* resilience
affordances, 199, 204, 208–209
aggression, 177–180
Aiello, J.R., 157
Allender, S., 67
Allport, F., 155
American College of Sports Medicine (ACSM), 236
American Psychological Association (APA), 5, 14–15, *15*, 16–17, 19, 22
Ames, C., 92
amotivation, 65
Anabolic Androgenic Steroids (AAS), 238
Andersen, M.B., 18
Anderson, J.R., 203
Anderson, M.B., 245
androcentrism, 226
anorexia, 230–231, 237
Anshel, M.H., 56, 57–58
anticipatory shame, 83
Antonelli, F., 5
anxiety. *See* stress and anxiety
Apter, M.J., **32**
Aristotle, 222
arousal, 30–35, **32**, 38–39. *See also* stress and anxiety
Arthur, C.A., 160, 161, *161*
Asher-Smith, Dina (athletics), 54–55
Association for Applied Sport Psychology (AASP), 22–23
Association for the Advancement of Applied Sport Psychology (AAASP), 5, 15–16, 17
associative cognitive strategies, 123
Atherton, Mike (cricket), 120
Athlete Burnout Questionnaire (ABQ), 71, 72
Athlete Mindfulness Questionnaire (AMQ), 266
Atkinson, J.W., 64, 82–85
attachment, 18
attention, 117–120
Attentional Control Theory (ACT), **32**, 34
attribution retraining, 151
attribution theory, 148–152, *149*
Australian Psychological Society (APS), 14, 23
Automatic Self-Talk Questionnaire for Sports (ASTQS), 124
autonomy, 266
avoidance, 56

Baggio, Roberto (soccer), 50
Baker, J.S., 44–45
Bamber, D., 237
Bandura, A., 98, 99, 100–101, 102, 173, 179
Baron, R.A., 177
Barsky, S.F., 173
Basic Psychological Needs Theory (BPNT), 90
Bastardoz, N., 160, 161, *161*
Baumeister, R.F., 157
Beauchamp, M.R., 100, 101
Beckham, David (soccer), 243
behavioural anxiety, 39
Beilock, S.L., 51–52
beneficence, 14
Berczik, K., 236
Berger, B.G., 235–236
Best, K., 260, 262
Biddle, S.J.H., 150
bio-informational theory, 113, 114
biopsychosocial model, 245
Birrell, S., 228–229
black and minority ethnic (BAME) communities, 168, 226–227, 231
Black Lives Matter, 231
body dysmorphic disorder (BDD), 229–230, 237
Bond, C.F., 156
Borelli, G.A., 222
Boutcher, S.H., 44
Bowman, B., 120
Breslin, G., 251
British Association of Sport and Exercise Sciences (BASES), 5, 7–8, 16, 17, 23
British Association of Sports Science (BASS), 23
British Market Research Bureau (BMRB), 183
British Psychological Society (BPS), 5, 7–8, 14, 16, 17, 23–24
Brooks, F., 227
Brunel, P.C., 156
Bruner, M.W., 191
bulimia, 230–231, 237
burnout, 70–74, *73*
Burton, D., 77, 78–79
Butt, J., 78

Caljouw, S. R., 199
Calmels, C., 109
Calvo, M.G., **32**, 50–51
Cannon, W., 82
Canter, D., 186
Carr, T.H., 51
Carron, A.V., 137, 138, 139, 172–173
Carson, F., 253
Carvalhaes, J., 4–5
Carver, C.S., 56
Catastrophe Theory, 31, **32**, 33
catharsis, 63
Cattell, R.B., 128–129
causal attribution, 64, 148–152, *149*, 184
cheating, 19
Chelladurai, P., 160–161
choking under pressure, 49–53
chronometric paradigm, 106, 109, 113
Cink, Stewart (golf), 49–50
Clancy, R.B., 64
Clingman, G.R., 239
clinical sport psychologists, 9
Clough, B., 169
Clough, P., 129
Coach Behaviour Assessment System (CBAS), 166–167
coaching, 165–169, *167*, 191
Coakley, J., 72
Code of Ethics (APS, 2007), 14
Code of Ethics and Conduct (BPS, 2018), 14
cognitive anxiety, 31–32, 33–34, 38, 40
Cognitive Appraisal Models, 244
cognitive approach (symbolic approach), 113–114
cognitive centrality, 190–191
Cognitive Evaluation Theory (CET), 88–89
cognitive expertise, 202

cognitive processes in sport
  attention and concentration, 117–120, 131
  mental imagery, 106–109, 120
  mental practice (MP), 111–115, 120
  mental toughness, 127–132, 156, 260
  self-talk, 122–125
Coleman, J., 227
Collective Effort Model, 157
Collective Self-Esteem Scale (CSES), 192
collectivism, 136
Collet, C., 109
Collins, D., 113, 114
commitment, 71–72
competency, 17–18
Competitive Goal Setting Model (CGS-3), 79
Competitive State Anxiety Inventory-2 (CSAI-2), 39, 40
Competitive State Anxiety Inventory-2D (CSAI-2D), 40
competitiveness, 230
concentration, 117–120, 131
Conceptual Model of Athletic Performance Anxiety, **32**, 33
confidentiality, 17
Connor–Davidson Resilience Scale (CD-RISC), 261
Connor, K.M., 261
Conroy, D.E., 84
Conscious Processing Hypothesis (CPH), **32**, 33–34, 51
Constraints Model, 198–199, 215–216
Contingency Model of Situational Control, 160
control, 180
COPE inventory, 56
coping strategies, 54–58
Coping Strategies Inventory, 56
Copper, C., 138, 139
Cotterill, S., 44, 46–47, 119
Cottrell, N.B., 155
Courneya, K.S., 172–173
covert rehearsal. *See* mental practice (MP)
COVID-19 pandemic, 118–119, 171, 173, 182, 239
Cox, R.H., 40
Craig C.M., 210
Cresswell, S.L., 73–74
Crews, D.J., 44
Critical Race Theory (CRT), 187, 231
Crocker, J., 192
Curry, Stephen (basketball), 206–207
Czyż, S.H., 156

Damisch, L., 46
Davidson, J.R.T., 261
Davis, C., 187, 237
Davis, K.E., 148
Davis, P.A., 119
Decentering Scale for Sport (DSS), 266
Deci, E.L., 72, 87–88, 89, 102
decision-making, 206–210
deliberate practice, 204, 212–213
dependency, 18
depression, 256
Diagnostic and Statistical Manual of Mental Disorders, 30
Diem, C., 3
Dimmock, J.A., 49, 51
dissociative cognitive strategies, 123
distraction theories, 50–52
divided attention, 117–118
Dodson, J.D., **32**
doping, 238
Douthill, E.A., 157
Driskell, J., 112
Drive Theory, **32**
drop-out, 70–74, *73*
Drucker, P., 219
drugs, 19
dual career programmes, 10, 247–248, **248**
Duda, J.L., 58
Dunning, E., 186, 187
Dweck, C., 92
dynamogism, 2

eating disorders, 230–231
Eccles, J.S., 102

ecological approach, 197–199, 204, 208–209
educational sport psychologists, 9
Eklund, R.C., 245–246, 247
Ellemers, N., 192
Elliot, A.J., 78, 95–96
emotion-focused coping strategies, 55–58
emotional expertise, 202
Endler, N., 56
enjoyment, 66
Ericsson, K.A., 204, 212
Espenschade, A., 198
Ethical Priniciples and Code of Conduct (APA, 2002, 2017), 14–15, *15*, 16–17
ethics and ethical issues, 14–19, *15*
European College of Sport Science (ECSS), 236
European Commission (EC), 247
European Federation of Sport Psychology and Physical Activity (FEPSAC), 254
European Network of Young Specialists in Sport Psychology (ENYSSP), 24
exercise addiction, 234–235, 236–239
Expectancy-Value Theory, 102
expertise, 201–205, 221
Explicit Monitoring Hypothesis (EMH), 51
extrinsic motivation, 72
Eys, M.A., 162
Eysenck, M.W., **32**, 50–51

Fajen, B.R., 208
fans, 182–187, *185*. *See also* causal attribution; home advantage; social facilitation
Farrell, Owen (rugby), 206
Faulkner, G., 152
fear of failure, 82–85
Fédération Européenne de Psychologie des Sports et des Activités Corporelles (FEPSAC; European Federation of Sport Psychology), 5, 24
Federer, Roger (tennis), 130
Female Athlete Triad (FAT), 237–238
feminist movement, 229
Ferrand, C., 38
fidelity, 14
Fiedler, F., 160
fight–flight response, 64, 82
Finlay, S.J., 152
fitness, 67
Fletcher, D., 260–262
Fletcher, R.B., 138
Folkman, S., 55, 57
followership, 162
football, 227
Football Association, 256
Foster, C., 66
Foster, D.J., 46
Fransen, K., 162–163
Fraser-Thomas, J., 65
Freud, S., 179
Frustration Aggression Hypothesis, 179
Frustration Aggression (Revised) Theory, 179
Fun Integration Theory (FIT), 66
functional equivalence hypothesis, 109, 113
Fundamental Goal Concept, 78–79
Funk, D.C., 185–186, *185*

Galilei, G., 222
Gardner, F.L., 264–265
gender
 activity choice and, 67
 inclusion and, 226–231
 structural barriers and, 68
 See also women
General Coping Questionnaire, 56
Gerber, M., 72
Geron, E., 4
Gesell, A., 198
Getchell, N., 197
Gibson, J., 199, 204, 208–209
Gill, D., 4, 228, 229
Glasgow, R., 198
Goal Contents Theory (GCT), 89–90
goal setting, 76–81, 131, 246
goal-setting theory (GST), 77–78

Golby, J., 131
Goldberg, S.B., 265
Gould, D., 30
Graf, Steffi (tennis), 50
Gretzky, W., 202
grieving process, 244–245
Griffith, C., 3–4, 159
Grimm, C., 3–4
Gröpel, P., 52
Group Environment Questionnaire (GEQ), 138
Group Mental Rotations Test (GMRT), 108
Gucciardi, D.F., 49, 51, 261
Guillot, A., 109
Gustafsson, H., 72

Hall, C.R., 107–108
Halson, S.L., 235
Hamilton, Lewis (Formula One), 30
Hamilton, R.A., 124
Hanin, Y.L., **32**, 34
Hanrahan, S.J., 150
Hardy, J., 123, 124
Hardy, L., 31, **32**, 33
Harkins, S.G., 157
Harris, D., 4
Harter, S., 98, 101–102
Harwood, C.G., 95
Haugen, T., 156
Haywood, K.M., 197
health, 67. *See also* mental health
Health and Care Professions Council (HCPC), 8, 17
Healy, L.C., 78
Heider, F., 148
Hellstedt, J.C., 66
Heuze, J.-P., 156
Heyman, S.R., 18
Hill, D.M., 49
Hilliard, D.V., 239
Hillman, C.H., 202
Hinkle, S., 192
Hoch, Scott (golf), 49–50
Holder, R., 171
Holistic Athlete Career Model, 247
Holmes, P., 113, 114
Hölzel, B.K., 266
home advantage, 171–175, *172*, 184
hooliganism, 186–187
Howard, G., 183
Huff, G., 3
Hull, C., **32**, 63

identity theory, 184
Ijaz, T., 261
illegality, 19
imaginary practice. *See* mental practice (MP)
Immelman, Trevor (golf), 117
in-depth interviews, 108–109
in-group affect, 190–191
in-group ties, 190–191
inclusion, 226–231
Individual Zone of Optimal Functioning (IZOF) Hypothesis, **32**, 34
individualism, 136
information-processing perspective, 197–199
institutional racism, 227
instructional self-talk, 123
instrumental aggression, 178
Integrated Stress Process Model, 244–245
integrity, 14
International Journal of Sport Psychology (journal), 5
International Olympic Committee (IOC), 238, 254, 257
International Society for Sports Psychiatry (ISSP), 25, 257
International Society of Sport Psychology (ISSP), 4, 5, 25, 177, 254
intrinsic motivation, 63, 64–65, 82
Inverted-U Hypothesis, **32**
Isaac, A., 107

Jackson, R.C., 44–45
Jacobson, B., 184

James, J., 185–186, *185*
James, LeBron (basketball), 212
James, W., 112
Janelle, C.M., 202
Jenkins, Neil (rugby), 44–45
Jeukendrup, A.E., 235
Johnson, U., 56
Jones, Eddie (rugby), 216
Jones, E.E., 148
Jones, G., 31
Jones, J.G., 40
Jones, M.B., 172, 173
Jordet, G., 50
Jowett, S., 167–168
justice, 14–15

Karau, S.J., 157
Kelley, H.H., 148–149
Kelso, S., 199
Kerr, J.H., **32**, 187
Keyes, C.L.M., 257
Kim, K.A., 58
Kim, S., 66
kinaesthetic imagery (motor imagery), 106, 107
Kobasa, S.C., 129
Kocher, M.G., 174
Kolovelonis, A., 125
Kremer, J., 10
Kubler-Ross, E., 244
Kugler, P., 199
Kuse, A.R., 108

Lamme, A., 4
Lane, A.M., 40
Langan, E., 73
Latham, G.P., 77–78
Lavallee, D., 247
Lawrence, S., 187
Lazarus, R.S., 55
leadership, 159–163, *161*, 166, *167*
Leadership Scale for Sports (LSS), 161
Lee, T., 196
Lemyre, P., 73
Leonardo da Vinci, 222
lesbian, gay and bisexual (LGB) communities, 228
Lewin, K., 160
Li, C., 72
Li, F.-X., 208
Lifespan Model of Athletes' Career Transitions, 247
Locke, E.A., 77–78, 79
Loeher, J.E., 129
Lonsdale, C., 45
Lubans, D.R., 66, 67
Luhtanen, R., 192

MacIntyre, T., 108–109, 113
Macnamara, B.N., 212
Maehr, M., 92
Mageean, Ciara (running), 76
Mahony, D., 185
management. *See* leadership
MAPS (Mission; Assessment; Plan; Systematic evaluation), 143–144, **143**
Maranise, A. M., 45
Marcotti, G., 160
Marey, E.J., 222
Martens, R., 9, **32**, 33, 39
Martin, K.A., 107
Martin, L.J., 145
Martinent, G., 38
Martiniuk, R.G., 214
Masters, K.S., 123
Masters, R.S.W., **32**, 33–34, 51
maturational perspective, 197–199
Maxwell, J.P., **32**, 33–34, 51
May, J.R., 143
McClelland, D., 64, 82–85
McCoy, Tony (horse racing), 130, 252
McGraw, M., 198
McIlroy, Rory (golf), 49
McPherson, B.D., 184

mediational model of leadership, 166, *167*
menstrual cycle, 230
mental health
  exercise addiction and, 234–235, 236–239
  inclusion and, 226–231
  mindfulness and, 264–266
  overtraining and, 234–236
  physical injury and, 243–249, **248**, 256
  resilience and, 128, 131, 260–262
  Social Identity Theory (SIT) and, 191
  See also stress and anxiety
mental health awareness, 251–254
Mental Health Disorders (MHDs), 256–258, *258*. *See also* stress and anxiety
mental imagery (visualisation), 106–109, 120, 131
mental practice (MP), 111–115, 120
mental toughness, 127–132, 156, 260. *See also* resilience
Mental Toughness Questionnaire-18 (MTQ-18), 129–130
Mental Toughness Questionnaire-48 (MTQ-48), 129–130
Mesagno, C., 44, 52–53
Methany, E., 4
mindfulness, 264–266
Mindfulness–Acceptance–Commitment (MAC) model, 264–265
Mindfulness Inventory for Sport (MIS), 266
minority identity, 168, 226–227, 231
Modrić, Luka (soccer), 204
mood state, 65
Moore, S.P., 214
Moore, Z.E., 264–265
Moran, A., 108–109, 113, 131
Morgan, W.P., 123
Morris, T., 10–12
motion capture techniques, 222–223
motivation
  Achievement Goal Theory and, 78, 92–96, 101
  attribution theory and, 151
  burnout and drop-out and, 70–74, *73*
  fear of failure and need to achieve and, 82–85, *83*
  goal setting and, 76–81, 131, 246
  models and theories of, 62–68, *63–64*
  perceived competence and, 98, 101–102
  Self-Determination Theory and, 64, 72, 73, 87–90, *88*, 102
  self-efficacy and, 98–101, *99*
motivational self-talk, 123
motor development, 196–200
motor imagery (kinaesthetic imagery), 106, 107
motor learning, 196, 219
motor performance, 219–223
motor skills
  analysis and measurement, 219–223
  decision-making, 206–210
  expertise, 201–205, 221
  motor development, 196–200
  practice, 212–217
Movement Imagery Questionnaire (MIQ-R), 107
Movement Time (MT), 221
Mullane-Grant, T., 52–53
Mullen, B., 138, 139, 157
Multidimensional Anxiety Theory, **32**, 33
Multidimensional Model of Leadership (MML), 160–162, *161*
Murphy, S.M., 248
Muybridge, E., 222

Nadal, Rafael (tennis), 30, 45
National and Organisational Monitoring Systems (NOMS), 243
Need Achievement Theory (NAT), 82–85, *83*
need to achieve, 82–85, *83*
Neuer, Manuel (soccer), 206–207
neuromuscular model, 113
Nevill, A.M., 171, 174
Newell, K.M., 198–199, 215–216
Newton, I., 222

Nicholls, A.R., 55, 56, 57
Nicholls, J.G., 92, 93
Nicklaus, Jack (golf), 56
Niemiec, C.P., 89–90
non-randomised controlled trials (non-RCTs), 265
nonmaleficence, 14
Norman, Greg (golf), 49–50
Normative Theory, 160
North American Society for the Psychology of Sport and Physical Activity (NASPSPA), 4, 5, 17, 25–26
notational analysis, 3–4
Novotna, Jana (tennis), 50

objectivity, 219–220
obsessive passion, 180
occupational psychology, 160
Ogles, B.M., 123
Olusoga, P., 57
Olympic Games, 3, 5. *See also* International Olympic Committee (IOC)
optimism raising, 262
organisational psychology, 160
Organismic Integration Theory (OIT), 89
Orwell, G., 177, 180
Oudejans, R.R.D., 52
overreaching, 235
overtraining, 234–236

Paivio, A., 107–108
Panza, M.J., 65
Parker, J., 56
passion, 180
passion theories, 90
Path-Goal Theory, 160
Patrick, G.T.W., 183
Pelé, 5
Pensgaard, A.M., 56
Pepper, Dottie (golf), 106
Pepping, G.-J., 208
perceived competence, 98, 101–102
perception-action approach, 199
Perception of Sport Questionnaire (POSQ), 95
perfectionism, 246
performance, 30–35, **32**
Performance and Appearance Enhancing Substances (PAEDs), 238
Perry, Ellyse (cricket and soccer), 198
personality disorders, 256
personality theory, 128–129, 260
Pété, E., 56, 58
Petitpas, A.J., 15–16
PETTLEP approach, 113, 114
Phelps, Michael (swimming), 106, 120
physical injury, 243–249, **248**, 256
physiological expertise, 202
Pijpers, J.R., 52
Poczwardowski, A., 167–168
Podlog, L., 245–246, 247
Pollock, M.L., 123
Polman, R.C., 56, 57
Popplewell Inquiry into Crowd Safety and Control at Sports Grounds (1986), 186
post-mistake routines, 44
post-traumatic stress disorder (PTSD), 256
practice, 212–217
practice philosophy, 9–10
pre-event routines, 44
pre-performance routines (PPRs), 43–47, 52–53, 119
problem-focused coping strategies, 55, 56–58
problem-solving skills, 168–169
Processing Efficiency Theory (PET), **32**, 34, 50–51
Profile of Mood States Questionnaire (POMS), 65
psychiatry, 9, 22
psychodynamic theories, 179
Psychological Continuum Model (PCM), 185–186, *185*
Psychological Performance Inventory, 131
Psychological Skills Training (PST), 264
Psychological Society of Ireland (PSI), 17

psychometric tests, 18–19, 39–41, 106–108
psychophysiological indices, 39
psychotic disorders, 256
Puni, A.C., 3, 5

Qualification in Sport and Exercise Psychology (QSEP), 8
qualitative research, 106, 108–109

racism, 187, 227, 231
Radcliffe, Paula (athletics), 119–120
Rae, Jonathan (motorcycle racing), 117, 130
Raedeke, T.D., 70–71, 72
randomised controlled trials (RCTs), 265
Rarick, L., 198
Reaction Time (RT), 221
reactive aggression, 178
Reeve, J., 98
Reeves, C.W., 57
relational coaching, 168
Relative Energy Deficiency in Sport (RED-S), 238
relaxation exercises, 55–56, 131
reliability, 220
resilience, 128, 131, 260–262
Resilience Scale for Athletes (RSA), 261
respect for people's rights and dignity, 15
responsibility, 14
retirement, 248–249, 252
Reversal Theory, **32**, 187
Revised Competitive State Anxiety Inventory (CSAI-2R), 40
Richards, H., 56
Richardson, D.R., 177
Ringelmann, M., 154, 156
rituals, 45–47
Roberts, G.C., 56
Roberts, R., 107
Ronaldinho (soccer), 106
Ronaldo, Cristiano (soccer), 212
Rosier, N., 247
Roudik, P., 3
Rowe, K., 68
Rubin, Chanda (tennis), 50
Rugby Football Union, 256
runner's high, 239
Ruth, B., 136
Rutter, M., 129
Ryan, R.M., 72, 87–88, 89, 90, 102

Saleh, S.D., 161
sanctioned aggression, 178–179
Sanders, Doug (golf), 119
Sanna, L.J., 157
Sarkar, M., 260–262
Schein, E.H., 143
Schema Theory, 198
Schippers, M.C., 46
Schmidt, G.W., 72
Schmidt, R.A., 196, 198, 214–215, 219
Schumacher, Michael (Formula One racing), 130
Schwartz, B., 173
Scully, D., 10, 229
selective attention, 117–118
self-concept, 157
Self Concordance Model, 78
self-confidence, 230
Self-Determination Theory (SDT), 64, 72, 73, 87–90, *88*, 102
self-efficacy
  attribution theory and, 150, 151
  home advantage and, 173
  motivation and, 98–101, *99*
  pre-performance routines and, 46
  social facilitation and, 157
  social loafing and, 157
self-esteem, 150
self-focus theories, 50, 51–52
self-oriented perfectionism, 246
self-regulation. *See* self-talk
self-talk, 122–125
self-worth, 150

seven-phase model (Morris and Thomas), 10–12
sex, 227–228. *See also* gender
sexual orientation, 228
Sheard, M., 127–128, 130, 131–132
Sheldon, K.M., 78
significant others, 66
Simons, Y., 187
Singer, R.N., 43
Situational Leadership Theory, 160
Skubic, V., 4
SMART Goal Setting, 77–78
Smith, A.L., 72
Smith, R.E., **32**, 33, 39, 71, 166–167
Smoll, F.L., **32**, 33
social categorisation, 190–192, *191*
Social-Cognitive Theory, 100–101, 102
social cohesion, 137–138, **137**
social comparison, 190–192, *191*
social facilitation, 2, 154–156, 157, 184
social identification, 190–192, *191*
Social Identification Measure, 192
Social Identity Measure, 192
Social Identity Theory (SIT), 184, 190–192, *191*
social learning theory, 98, 179
social loafing, 154, 156–157
social-physique anxiety (SPA), 230
social psychology of sport
  aggression, 177–180
  causal attribution, 148–152, *149*, 184
  coaching, 165–169, *167*, 191
  fans and spectators, 182–187, *185*
  home advantage, 171–175, *172*, 184
  leadership, 159–163, *161*, 166, *167*
  social facilitation, 154–156, 157, 184
  Social Identity Theory (SIT), 184, 190–192, *191*
  social loafing, 154, 156–157
  team building, 142–146, **143**
  team cohesion, 136–140, **137**
socially prescribed perfectionism, 246
somatic anxiety, 31, 38–39
spectators, 182–187, *185*. *See also* causal attribution; home advantage; social facilitation
Spence, K., 63
Spielberger, C.S., 38
Spink, K.S., 162
sport and exercise psychologists, 5, 7–9, 257. *See also* sport psychology
Sport and Exercise Psychology Accreditation Route (SEPAR), 8
Sport Anxiety Scale (SAS), 39
Sport Anxiety Scale-2 (SAS-2), 39
Sport Competition Anxiety Test (SCAT), 39
Sport England, 231
Sport Fan Motivation Scale (SFMS), 184
Sport Imagery Questionnaire (SIQ), 107–108
sport psychiatry, 9, 257–258, *258*
sport psychology
  ethical issues in, 14–19, *15*
  history of, 2–5
  organisations, sources and resources on, 21–26
  practice of, 7–12
  See also sport and exercise psychologists
sport sciences, 4–5, 21–22. *See also* sport psychology
Sport Team Personality Scale (STPS), 186
SPORTPSY (electronic bulletin board), 26
Sports Mental Toughness Questionnaire, 131
The Sportswoman (magazine), 4
'spotlight' approach, 118–119
Stadley Blank, A., 186
stage-based approach, 247
Stage Theory of Grief, 244
star player effect, 174
Starkes, J.L., 202
Stein, G.L., 72
Strahler, K., 38–39
stress and anxiety
  burnout and drop-out and, 71
  choking under pressure and, 49–53

stress and anxiety *cont.*
coping strategies, 54–58
definitions and concepts of, 30–31, 38–39
measurement of, 37–41
mental health and, 30
mental toughness and, 130
performance and, 30–35, **32**
pre-performance routines and, 43–47, 52–53, 119
structural barriers, 67–68
Subhan, S., 261
super-adherers, 238–239
superstitions, 45–47, 151–152
Supportive, Active, Autonomous, Fair, Enjoyable (SAAFE) principles, 66, 67
Sutter, M., 174
Swain, A.B.J., 31, 40
symbolic approach (cognitive approach), 113–114
symbolic rehearsal. *See* mental practice (MP)
sympathetic nervous system, 30–31
Szymanski, K., 157

Tam, J.T.M., 45
Task and Ego Orientation Sports Questionnaire (TEOSQ), 95
task cohesion, 137–138, **137**
Taylor, J., 187, 247
Taylor, Katie (boxing), 62–63
Taylor, M.K., 122
Taylor, Phil (darts), 130
Taylor Report (1989), 186
Taylor, S., 247
team, definition of, 137
team building, 142–146, **143**
team cohesion, 136–140, **137**
Team Environment AssessMent (TEAM) procedure, 145
team identification, 184
team spirit, 136
technical expertise, 202
Tenenbaum, G., 207
Theory of Sport Confidence, 101
Thienot, E., 266
Thomas, O., 31
Thomas, P., 10–12
thought control, 122–125
thought stopping, 124–125, 131
Titus, L.J., 156
Tobar, D.A., 235–236
Toner, J., 131
transformational leadership, 161–162
transgender issues, 228
Triplett, N., 2–3, 154, 155
Turvey, M., 199
Tyson, Mike (boxing), 178

UK Athletics, 256
United States Olympic Committee (USOC), 5
unsanctioned aggression, 178–179
Uphill, M., 40, 256–257

validity, 220
Vallerand, R.J., 88, 90
van de Velde, Jean (golf), 49–50
Van Lange, P.A., 46
Van Raalte, J.L., 123
Vandenberg, S., 108
Vanek, M., 5
Veach, T.L., 143
Vealey, R., 10
Vealey, R.S., 100, 101
Vella, S.A., 191
verbal persusasion, 173
Verner-Filion, J., 90
Vickers, J.N., 33
video simulation methods, 204–205, 209–210
virtual engagement, 19
Virtual Reality (VR) technology, 205, 209–210
Visek, A.J., 66
visualisation (mental imagery), 106–109, 120, 131
Vividness of Movement Imagery Questionnaire (VMIQ), 107

Vividness of Movement Imagery Questionnaire-2 (VMIQ-2), 107

Walker, N., 245
Wann, D., 184
Warren, W.H., 199
Watson, Tom (golf), 49
Wegner, D.M., 119, 124–125
Weinberg, R., 78
Weiner, B., 149, *149*
Weiss, C., 78–79
Weston, N.J.V., 57
White, G.F., 187
Whitton, S.M., 138
Wickens, C.D., 207
Widmeyer, W.N., 138
Wie, Michelle (golf), 206
Wiese-Bjornstal, D.M., 244–245
Wigfield, A., 102
Wilkinson, Jonny (rugby), 212–213
Williams, A.M., 33, 202
Williams, K.D., 157
Williams, Serena (tennis), 45, 122, 204, 212
Williams, Sonny "Bill" (rugby and boxing), 198
Williams, Venus (tennis), 122, 204, 212
Wilson, M.R, 34
Wilson, M.R., 34
Withagen, R., 199
women
  coaching and, 168
  exercise addiction and, 237–238
  sport psychology and, 4
  See also gender
Wood, G., 34
Woodman, T., 119
Woods, Tiger (golf), 31, 45
Woosnam, I., 51
Work Life Model, 253
World Anti-Doping Agency (WADA), 238
World Health Organization (WHO), 256
Wright, F.L., 201–202
Wrigley, P., 3
Wrisberg, C.A., 214–215, 219
Wulf, G., 117
Wylleman, P., 247

Yerkes, R.M.D., **32**

Zajonc, R.B., 155
Zhang, C.Q., 266
Zhang, J., 161
Zourbanos, N., 124
Zuppke, R., 3